Women and the Family in Chinese History

This is a collection of essays by one of the leading scholars of Chinese history, Patricia Buckley Ebrey. In the essays she has selected for this fascinating volume, Professor Ebrey explores the Chinese family, gender, and kinship systems as practices and ideas intimately connected to history and therefore subject to change over time. The essays cover topics ranging from dowries and the sale of women as concubines to the huge size of the imperial harem, misunderstandings of foot binding, surnames as ethnic markers, and changes in ways of dealing with the dead.

Patricia Ebrey places these studies of kinship and gender practices in historical context; her work shows the impact of historical change on the ways people lived. Her work ranges over the late imperial period, with a specific focus on the Song period (920–1276), a time of marked social and cultural change that is widely viewed as the beginning of the modern period in Chinese history.

With its wide-ranging examination of issues relating to women and the family, this book will be essential reading for scholars of Chinese history and gender studies

Patricia Buckley Ebrey is Professor of History and Chinese Studies at the University of Washington. She has published widely on Chinese history, including *The Cambridge Illustrated History of China* (Cambridge University Press: 1999) and *Inner Quarters: Marriage and the Lives of Chinese Women in the Sung Period* (University of California Press: 1993).

Critical Asian Scholarship
Edited by Mark Selden
Binghamton and Cornell Universities

The series is intended to showcase the most important individual contributions to scholarship in Asian Studies. Each of the volumes presents a leading Asian scholar addressing themes that are central to his or her most significant and lasting contribution to Asian studies. The series is committed to the rich variety of research and writing on Asia, and is not restricted to any particular discipline, theoretical approach or geographical expertise.

Women and the Family in Chinese History

Patricia Buckley Ebrey

Routledge
Taylor & Francis Group

LONDON AND NEW YORK

First published 2003 by Routledge
11 New Fetter Lane, London EC4P 4EE

Simultaneously published in the USA and Canada
by Routledge
29 West 35th Street, New York, NY 10001

Routledge is an imprint of the Taylor & Francis Group

© 2002 Patricia Buckley Ebrey

Typeset in 10/12pt Times New Roman
by Graphicraft Limited, Hong Kong
Printed and bound in Great Britain by The Cromwell Press,
Trowbridge, Wiltshire

British Library Cataloguing in Publication Data
A catalogue record for this book is available from the
British Library

Library of Congress Cataloging in Publication Data
A catalog record for this book has been requested

ISBN 0-415-28822-3 (hbk)
ISBN 0-415-28823-1 (pbk)

Contents

List of illustrations

FIGURES

TABLES

Acknowledgments

When Mark Selden approached me about putting together a collection of my articles for this series, I had some trepidation. Which of my articles did I want people to read today? Which ones would work best together? I was forced to take a hard look at the various directions my research has taken over the past quarter century, to look for links among articles written for disparate purposes and decide which ones held up the best. Mark and I went back and forth by email numerous times discussing various possibilities, given Routledge's page limits. Mark naturally wanted a book that would have a wide appeal and tended to favor the broadest essays; I usually found the ones based on the most thorough research the most suitable for republishing. At least three possible foci suggested themselves: Chinese social history, which would have allowed me to include a couple of my articles on the Han to Tang period; the social and cultural history of the Song period, which would have allowed me to include some of my more recent work on Chinese visual culture; and family-gender-kinship in Chinese history, which had been the major thrust of at least half my work. In the end we settled on this last alternative, as it allowed a balance between short and long articles, ones that cover a long time span and ones focused on the Song period, ones that dealt with women and gender as well as ones that ranged further into questions of kinship organization, rituals central to family life, and even the connection between kinship and ethnic identity. It also represents a more-or-less complete body of research, as my research interests have turned in other directions over the last few years.

From my perspective, there were a couple of other incentives to putting together this volume. I was happy to get the chance to convert the romanization style of older articles from Wade-Giles to pinyin, as fewer and fewer undergraduates today are comfortable with Wade-Giles. I also appreciated the possibility of adding illustrations. The only article that had any illustrations in its original publication is the last one on "Gender and Sinology," and even in that case several additional illustrations have been added. Six of the other illustrations come from a single source, an illustrated elaboration of the Kangxi emperor's Sacred Edict, first published in 1681 and reprinted in 1903. This work had illustrations not only of general phenomena discussed in my articles, but also sometimes the same stories, such as the story of Zhu Shouchang giving up his office to go in search of his mother, a concubine whom his father had left behind many years earlier. Generally, in my text I use these stories to make rather different points than the author and illustrator of this book intended. Still, I think the illustrations add more than simple visual pleasure to the issues and arguments presented in this book, and I hope readers will pause to consider what the Chinese illustrators chose to convey in their pictures.

Because the work presented here was done over a period of nearly twenty years, it would be impossible to identify all the people or organizations who aided it in some way. I would like to acknowledge, however, how much my work owes to those who provided opportunities for me to collaborate with other scholars through conferences and symposia. Not only have I benefited from the response of other scholars when I presented papers at these meetings, but these occasions helped create communities of scholars whose ongoing conversations I wished to join. Almost all of the papers in this volume have some connection to collaborative work of this sort, though in some cases they were inspired by participation in a conference rather than written to present at a conference. In my view, the flowering of American scholarship on China over the last several decades owes a great deal to the willingness of funders such as the American Council of Learned Societies, the Social Science Research Council, the National Endowment for the Humanities, and the Chiang Ching-Kuo Foundation, as well as university East Asia centers and China programs to provide opportunities for scholars to engage each other face-to-face. The hardest work, of course, continues to be done alone in the study, but it gains meaning from knowing there is an audience of students and scholars who find the issues intellectually significant.

Finally, let me thank the two graduate students at the University of Washington, Barbara Grub and Elif Akçetin, who helped me scan the older articles, convert romanization to pinyin, prepare the unified bibliography, and standardize citations. I have not tried to edit or improve the articles as originally published, but have corrected typos and other errors, imposed some uniformity of style, and changed the editions of some of the primary sources when the original articles had cited more than one edition.

Introduction

Westerners have long been fascinated by the Chinese family and Chinese women, though the approaches they have brought to these topics have naturally changed over time. In the nineteenth and early twentieth centuries, missionaries emphasized the features of the Chinese family that stood in contrast to Western practices, such as ancestor worship, legally recognized concubinage, and large multigenerational families with several married brothers living together. Many were reformers at heart and took up the cause of the subjection of women. They wrote with feeling of the plight of girls who might be killed at birth by parents who did not need another daughter, who could be sold at 5 or 6 as indentured servants, whose feet were bound so small that they could hardly walk, who were denied education, who had to marry whomever their fathers chose, who had few legal rights to property, who could be divorced easily and denied custody of their children, and who might be pressured not to remarry after their husbands' deaths.

By the mid-twentieth century social scientists occupied a similar position of authority in writing about Chinese women and the family for Western audiences. They not surprisingly framed their work in very different ways, trying to avoid both ethnocentrism and condescension. They placed China in a comparative framework that classified family systems according to their method of reckoning descent, their forms of marriage, their ways of transmitting property, and the like, leading to our common understandings of the Chinese family as patrilineal, patrilocal, and patriarchal. Long-term change was not a part of this analysis, and historians impressed by the anthropological model usually discussed the Chinese family as part of the background to Chinese history, much like its geography or language, rather than treating its development as integral to their main historical narrative. Anthropologists themselves commonly treated the household as relatively well understood and devoted much of their fieldwork to analyses of kinship organization beyond the household. One reason for this was that the Chinese lineage corresponded in interesting ways to the segmentary lineages found in Africa, and by studying Chinese lineages they could contribute to anthropological debates on lineage structure. Women were rarely key players in lineages, and thus a view of Chinese kinship that makes lineages central shifted emphasis away from women.

After 1980, historians of premodern China began taking more and more of an interest in the subject of women and the family. One stimulus was certainly the growth within the larger historical profession first of family history and then of women's history. Another was the outpouring of books re-evaluating China's modern gender system, made possible by the opening of China to Western researchers. These books decried the failures of the Chinese revolution to meet its oft-stated goal of liberating Chinese women from positions of inferiority. But the authors generally prefaced their discussion of the original goals of the revolution by repeating stereotypes of women's lot in traditional times as exceptionally bleak. To historians of earlier periods, myself among them, it was time to re-examine these undifferentiated pictures of women's situations in earlier times. There was no reason why the Chinese family should be seen as somehow outside history, unaffected by developments in the state, economy, religion, or culture.

The nine essays collected in this volume represent some of my efforts to historicize the Chinese family, gender, and kinship systems. They analyze features of these systems as historical phenomena, as practices and ideas intimately connected to other historical phenomena and thus subject to change over time. Some cover long periods, but over half focus on the Song period (960–1276), a time of marked social and cultural change, often considered the beginnings of the modern period in Chinese history, and without doubt better documented than any earlier period because of the introduction of printing. The essays were written for different audiences, but share some common concerns. Implicit in most of them are basic comparative questions: How would one compare earlier periods of Chinese history to what we know of more recent times? How would we compare forms of social organization in China of the past to forms found in other societies, past or present? Many of them also tackle the difficult question of identifying the stages of change and the processes and agents that brought it about.

The essays collected here can be read in any order, but there is a rationale for the order I have adopted. "Women, money, and class: Sima Guang and Song Neo-Confucian views on women" was placed first because it brings together several of the central strands in my work: the interconnections between social and intellectual phenomena, the competing logics of property and the descent line, and the articulation of gender distinctions. For anyone with time to read only one of my essays, I would recommend this one. Its starting-point is the commonly heard charge that the revival of Confucianism in the Song period led to a decline in the status of women. I shift attention from Cheng Yi (1033–1107), famous for his remarks on widow remarriage, to Sima Guang (1019–1086), a much more prolific writer on women whose texts strongly influenced Zhu Xi (1130–1200), in the long run the most influential thinker of the age. Evaluating the charge against Neo-Confucianism requires me to unpack the variety of ways that the ideas of leading thinkers could influence social practices as well as the ways their ideas were shaped by their circumstances and experiences. I argue that to understand Sima Guang's writings we must consider how his contemporaries talked about the interconnections between women and money, money and sexuality, and money and social standing. Because of the dangers he saw in the nexus of women and money, Sima Guang worked hard to bolster the stable, hierarchical, side of the family. In particular, he disapproved of wives having any control over their dowries or families taking dowries into account in selecting brides, both of which he saw as undermining family hierarchy. Zhu Xi adopted most of Sima Guang's ideas, but during the Song these ideas had not yet had much noticeable effect on the behavior of the educated class, where daughters were still commonly given large dowries and young widows frequently remarried. The story I tell, thus, is neither a simple one of orthodox ideas directly limiting women nor one in which ideas are of little import. Rather it is a complex one in which economic change, such as the increased use of money, and social change, such as the expansion of the educated class, encouraged re-assertion of certain old ideas, but these ideas did not have much impact on behavior for centuries to come, when other social and political conditions fostered new attitudes.

Those who come to this volume because of comparative interests may prefer to start with Chapter 2, "Concubines in Song China," since this essay was originally written for a comparative audience and makes no assumptions about knowledge of Chinese history or culture. Its starting-point is the distinction between concubines and co-wives as analyzed by the anthropologist Jack Goody. In true polygamous societies co-wives have largely the same rights, with only minor differentiation by seniority. Co-wives are generally found in relatively egalitarian societies, as class inequalities are maintained and reproduced best by monogamous marriage systems, whether or not concubinage is also practiced. In this essay I show how well these insights fit the Chinese case and argue that the women called *qie* in premodern China should not be classed as secondary wives, as they commonly have been, but as concubines. Looking specifically at Song evidence, I show that the differences in law, ritual, and ordinary social life between wives and concubines were substantial. Wives were acquired though a betrothal process that entailed exchange of gifts and ceremonies; concubines were purchased through a market in female labor much as maids were. A wife's relatives became kin of her husband and his family; a concubine's did not. A man could take as many concubines as he could afford; he could marry only one wife. The sons of a concubine had the same rights of inheritance as the sons of a wife, but they had to treat their father's wife as their legal mother, honoring their "birth mother" to a lesser degree. A concubine had to treat the wife as her mistress, and she might well by used by the wife as a personal maid. The wife could rear the concubine's children herself if she chose to and would be their legal guardian if the father died. Adult stepsons would inherit in full and could turn her out of the house. Class inequalities were reproduced by this system because poverty was the main reason a woman would become a concubine rather than a wife.

Both Chapters 1 and 2 highlight the significance of buying and selling women. Chapter 3, "Shifts in marriage finance from the sixth to the thirteenth century," deals with another side of the connection between wealth and women's standing: the dowries that wives brought with them into marriage. Much of the essay is devoted to marshalling the evidence to show that China's system of marriage finance changed substantially from the Tang to the Song in line with changes in the elite from an aristocracy of super-elite families that largely married exclusively within its own circle to an expanding elite that incorporated new members through the civil service examination system. The principal change in marriage finance was an escalation in the value of dowries, a phenomenon that has happened in other places as well during periods of social and economic change, such as Renaissance Italy. In China's case, because daughters did not normally inherit family property, large dowries also marked a shift toward the transmission of property through both daughters and sons rather than exclusively through sons. When the families of brides devoted substantial resources, including land, to supplementing whatever they got from the groom's family by way of betrothal gifts, they were transferring property permanently to another patriline because the woman's dowry would eventually pass to her children, members of her husband's patriline. At the same time a generous dowry enhanced the status of a bride entering a new family and enlarged the range of actions she could take.

The first three essays cite many examples of particular women who lived during the Song period, but not many women or families are examined in depth. To make up for this deficiency, these essays are followed by Chapter 4, "The women in Liu Kezhuang's family." Although Chinese historical records are poor in the diaries, letters, and memoirs that European historians have used to reconstruct the emotional texture of family life, in this essay I show that there is much that can be done with the thousands of epitaphs that have been preserved in educated men's collected works. Liu Kezhuang (1187–1269), a late-Song official and poet, wrote forty-three epitaphs for close relatives who died before him, many of them women. Among the women he sketches are his mother, who presided over the home of her sons and grandchildren for more than thirty years after her husband's death; his sister, who often left her husband's family to come back to keep her mother company; his wife, who traveled with him and died young; his concubine, who took over the duties of this wife; and his sister-in-law, who poured her efforts into her husband's sons by other women. The vital data included in the epitaphs Liu Kezhuang wrote allow us to see the high proportion of children born to concubines and maids rather than wives in this family and also the impact of early deaths on family life. Most of these women's lives were shaped in profound ways by the chance mortality of those around them, especially their parents, husbands, and sons.

The next three chapters shift the focus from women to other features of the family and kinship systems. Chapter 5, "The early stages in the development of descent group organization," is similar to Chapter 3 in that it attempts to identify and explain change, in this case the appearance of a repertoire of practices that characterize the modern Chinese lineage. The practices examined run the gamut from labeling people as kinsmen, to extending aid to them on an ad hoc basis, to forming giant households with them, to assembling at graves of common patrilineal ancestors for joint worship, to setting aside property to pay for such rituals, to building halls so that rites could also be performed in town, to compiling genealogies in order to encourage kinsmen to identify with each other, and so on. In examining the appearance of these practices, I pay particular attention to the question of elite leadership. I show that some of these practices, such as worshipping ancestors at their graves, began as commoners' local practices, while others, such as the modern-style genealogy and the charitable estate, were innovations purposely instituted by educated men. By reinterpreting classical injunctions Neo-Confucian writers played a part as well, making it easier for educated men to take leadership roles in their local descent groups.

In my analysis of the origins of descent groups, I see participation in rituals, most notably rites to early ancestors, as fostering group formation, a view that places me at odds with much of the anthropological literature, which sees groups forming for political or economic reasons, then adopting rituals to enhance solidarity. In Chapter 6, "Cremation in Song China," I extend this interest in the rituals of family life through a detailed study of two major changes in Chinese ritual behavior, first the spread of cremation and later its decline. The spread of cremation marked a fundamental change in the treatment of the dead because until then the dominant Chinese preference had been to dispose of the dead in ways that would delay decay, such as burial in thick heavily lacquered coffins placed within vaults of stone or brick. Although Buddhism certainly played a part in the spread of cremation, and often ran the crematory used by city residents, in this essay I try to show that the history of cremation is much more complex than a simple story of the rise and decline of Buddhism. Neo-Confucian scholars wrote against the practice and the government issued laws against it, but they cannot be given full credit for suppressing the practice either. Archaeological and literary evidence shows that other mortuary customs were changing as well, such as a decline in the use of grave goods and an increase in attention to geomancy, and in this essay I try to show that part of the context of the history of cremation is folk beliefs about bodies, ghosts, and graves. In popular belief, the dead suffered more from their bones being left to rest in the wrong place than from the method through which they were reduced to bones.

Although I have taken considerable pains to demonstrate that the Chinese family, kinship, and gender systems were not unchanging, I do not deny that there are some remarkable continuities in Chinese social practices.

Chapters 7 and 8, in rather different ways, deal with practices that had very long histories in China. Chapter 7, "Surnames and Han Chinese identity," goes beyond kinship *per se* to look at the power of habits of thinking about patrilineal kinship to a realm outside kinship, ethnic identity. In it I argue that Confucian relativism notwithstanding, there was a genuinely ethnic dimension to Chinese identity rooted in the habit of imagining the Hua, Xia, or Han, metaphorically at least, as a giant patrilineal descent group made up of intermarrying surname groups. Especially in south China adopting a Chinese surname may have been nothing more than an expedient act, facilitating communication with Han Chinese, but over time those with Chinese surnames tended to acquire Han Chinese genealogies as well, forgetting or dismissing earlier identities. Even if becoming Han Chinese through assimilation was approved in Confucian theory, people in south China preferred to see themselves as descendants of migrants from the north, not descendants of indigenous peoples who had assimilated. Imagining the linkage among Chinese as a matter of patrilineal kinship differs in interesting ways from other ways of imagining group identities, such as associating the group with biological substance, with a language community, or with a state. In particular, it does not lend itself as well to racialist thinking, as surname inheritance does not map to genetic inheritance. That is, a person inherits genes from all his or her sixteen great-great grandparents, but the surname from only one. In cases of intermarriage, when a Han Chinese man married a local woman, the children of course got genes from both sides and probably even learned ideas and cultural practices from both sides, but identity was tied up in the name.

The last two chapters in this volume take me away from the study of the family system of ordinary Chinese, though they grow from my earlier work on those subjects and my interest in the workings of the Chinese gender system. Chapter 8, "Rethinking the imperial harem: Why where there so many palace women?" is the only essay not to have been published before. Reflecting its origins as a talk rather than an article, it concentrates on a single question: why did so many emperors surround themselves with thousands of palace ladies? I refer to these women as the emperor's harem because they formed a pool of potential consorts. Most of the essay is devoted to eliminating the functional explanation of their numbers in terms of the need for successors. By taking the case of the Northern Song, I show that neither the emperors who had difficulty begetting heirs nor the emperors who had dozens of sons had any need for more than a few dozen women in their harem, as they were usually producing children by no more than half a dozen women at a time. I go on to suggest several alternative explanations for the persistent tendency for the palace establishment to grow huge, ranging from the interests of the widowed consorts of previous emperors, who stood to see their world enlarged as more women entered the palace, to the notion that women were needed to furnish palaces in elegant style, to conceptions of imperial majesty that drew from the myth of the Yellow

Emperor as the ultimate male, his potency reinforced by his access to unlimited supplies of young virgins.

The last chapter, "Gender and sinology: shifting Western interpretations of footbinding, 1300–1890" approaches the historiography of Chinese women's history from a different direction. Even working on the Song period, a period before writings by Western visitors provide much evidence, I have undoubtedly been influenced in subtle ways by the habits of generations of Western scholars and writers who before the end of the nineteenth century had already made footbinding, concubinage, infanticide, and arranged marriages topics that had to be discussed in any treatment of Chinese women. To place these ways of framing the topic of Chinese women in historical context, I take the case of Western writing on the highly charged subject of footbinding. I show both the difficulties Western observers had in describing and making sense of the practice and how their approaches changed over time as their views on Chinese culture more generally changed. I stress the ways gender proprieties complicated inquiry because most of the Western authors were men who turned to other men, Western or Chinese, to learn about Chinese women. Although over time Western comprehension of footbinding certainly improved, this was not due to advances of sinology in the sense of mastery of Chinese texts. The greatest sinologists were rarely insightful on the topic of footbinding, probably because books were not central to how the practice was reproduced and the Chinese scholars they studied with did not consider footbinding a topic worth talking about.

These chapters are all separate studies, each with its own set of questions, even if overlapping concerns run through them. There are also questions that emerge from placing these essays side by side that none of them alone addresses. Let me conclude by taking up one of them here: How separate are the histories of family, women, gender, and kinship in China?

Certainly the history of women is related to the history of the family, and my studies here of concubines and marriage finance were conceived as much as contributions to women's history as family history. The relationship between women's history and the history of the family is double-edged. How women lived their lives was shaped by elements of family and marriage practice, such as the age at which they married, how their spouses were selected, where they lived after marriage, their access to property, the choices open to them if widowed, and the like. But one can also highlight women's participation in creating and maintaining the family and marriage systems, not only as mothers and mothers-in-law, but also as wives, concubines, maids, and daughters. Even when men were the primary actors, as, for instance, they were in writing about both women's virtues and family ethics, they were responding to situations in which women were important actors.

On the other hand, the more I have studied China's gender system, the more convinced I am that there are elements in it that are deeper than the family system, that reflect very basic ways of thinking about natural phenomena. The essay here that brings that out most clearly is Chapter 9 on the imperial harem. Notions such as decorating the palace with elegantly dressed palace ladies and the association of large numbers of palace ladies with the Yellow Emperor and immortality do not seem to derive from the family system, even the imperial family system. They would seem to be sustained and reproduced more through popular culture and popular religion than the logic of either family property or the ancestral cult.

A good case can also be made for the autonomy of the history of kinship organization in China, though perhaps not to the same degree as gender. Although I show some links in these essays – in Chapter 1 I speculate that the interest shown by leading Song Neo-Confucian thinkers in reviving the *zong* system played a role in undermining women's property rights and in Chapter 5 suggest that the same phenomena aided the legitimation of the descent group – on the whole the history of descent groups and the history of the household do not seem either to be closely linked or to follow the same trajectory. Although Chapters 3, 5, and 6 cover pretty much the same period, mid-Tang through Yuan, changes in forms of marriage finance, descent group organization, and disposal of the dead show no signs of being closely tied to each other. It is not the case that one central change – the famed "Tang–Song transition" – brought about changes in all these realms.

True, the agents and processes of change were often similar in these different realms, in the sense that economic development and social dislocation affected them all, and in many cases we can also see some role for the state, elite leadership, and popular ideas. Yet when one looks more closely, differences in the ways these common elements were implicated are at least as interesting as similarities.

To give just one possible example, the role of Buddhism was much more marked in some domains than others. At the level of the household, Buddhism did not have anywhere near the sort of impact on China that Christianity had in the West. In Europe, Christianity led to the end of the Roman ancestral cult; in China Buddhism co-existed with the ancestral cult. In Europe, concubinage became illegal with Christianity; in China, marriage law was unaffected by Buddhism. In Europe, Christianity elevated celibacy, even for those who did not become clerics; in China Buddhism did not make it easier for women to reject marriage unless they became nuns.

On the other hand, Buddhism had a major impact on the performance of family rituals, especially those related to the dead. Families often let Buddhist temples perform ancestral rites for them, which was one of the reasons Neo-Confucian scholars like Cheng Yi and Zhang Zai wanted to revive ancient forms of ancestral rites. Buddhist clergy also, as discussed in Chapter 6, offered a range of support for those faced with a death in the family, from prayer services, to storage of coffins, to crematoriums where bodies could be burnt and ponds where ashes could be disposed. Although I see no reason to think that these services changed in any major way household, kinship, or gender relations, they certainly did draw protest from the Confucian elite, who thought they threatened traditional family ethics and the central value of filial piety. Thus any impact they had on the family was probably mediated through their impact on leading Confucian thinkers, who in reaction to their success made new efforts to define the core of Confucian family rituals.

The impact of Buddhism on kinship organization was of a different sort. As discussed in Chapter 5, setting aside land to be used for charitable purposes indefinitely to support kinsmen seems to be based on the earlier success of Buddhist endowments. Similarly, entrusting care of graves to Buddhist temples seems to have come before setting aside land in the name of a descent group for the same purpose. Elsewhere I have also proposed that use of portraits in ancestral rites may have been inspired by the huge role images played in Buddhist devotions. None of these changes were advocated or in any other way encouraged by Buddhist clergy; they were indirect effects of the way Buddhism enlarged China's repertoire of forms of social organization and practice.

If we considered the case of increased circulation of money, migration to the south, the expansion of the examination system, changes in state activism, the Neo-Confucian movement, or the like, we would see similar variability in how these more general historical changes were connected to changes in the family, gender, and kinship systems. There are processes we discern only when we look at these domains together; but there are others we see only when we take each case separately.

1 Women, money, and class

Sima Guang and Song
Neo-Confucian views on women*

Most historians of China have heard the charge that the revival of Confucianism in the Song period initiated a decline in the status of women. The principal accusations are that Neo-Confucianism fostered the seclusion of women, footbinding, and the cult of widow chastity. It is widely recognized that these constraints on women had become more oppressive by the Qing dynasty, but their roots are traced back to the Song period.[1] Cheng Yi's (1033–1107) statement that "To starve to death is a small matter, but to lose one's chastity is a great matter" is commonly blamed for much of the misery of women in late imperial China.

The evidence offered to support these charges is of several sorts. In his *Zhongguo funü shenghuo shi* (History of Chinese Women's Lives), written in 1928, Chen Dongyuan argued that women's lives started to deteriorate after Cheng Yi and Zhu Xi (1130–1200) promoted "the idea that women must value chastity." Thus "the Song really was the turning point in women's lives."[2] More recently, Zhu Ruixi, after examining a wide range of evidence concerning views on women and marriage in the Song, concluded that these attitudes gradually hardened during the Song, bringing in divorce as well as remarriage.

> Especially from the time of Song Lizong [r.1225–1264], because of the honor granted Neo-Confucianism in the intellectual sphere, the right of women to seek divorces was almost completely eliminated, and their right to remarry after the death of their husbands decreased every day.[3]

Popularizers and polemicists have been quicker to assert the influence of Neo-Confucianism on female seclusion, footbinding, and even female infanticide. Lin Yutang in *My Country and My People* and Howard Levy in *Chinese Footbinding* report that Zhu Xi, while prefect of Zhangzhou in southern Fujian, promoted footbinding as a way to foster the separation of

---

* This article originally was published in *Papers on Society and Culture of Early Modern China*, ed. by Institute of History and Philology, Academia Sinica, Taipei, 1992, pp. 613–69. Reproduced with permission.

men and women and encourage chastity by making it difficult for women to move about.[4] Feminists have picked up these charges. Elisabeth Croll writes that "the Neo-Confucian philosophers of the Song dynasty (960–1267) further elaborated the code of feminine ethics by re-emphasizing the practices of segregation and seclusion, and introducing the practice of bound feet."[5] Esther Yao states that "Infanticide was extremely prevalent in the Song Dynasty – being greatly influenced by the philosophy of Neo-Confucianism which denied women basic human rights, including the right to live."[6] Authors of textbooks have also incorporated these charges against Neo-Confucianism. Dun J. Li, in his textbook for American students, *The Ageless Chinese: A History*, argues that stricter sexual segregation from Song on was a result of the acceptance of Neo-Confucianism.

> Zhu Xi, for instance, not only advocated strict sexual segregation but glorified widowhood as well; he thought he did society a great service by encouraging widows to join their dead husbands at the earliest possible moment. As his philosophy dominated the intellectual and ethical scene for the next seven hundred years, his bleak, puritanical ideas began to be accepted as the lofty goal which every gentry family strove to achieve. With the popularity of his ideas, the status of women declined.[7]

For an historian, these charges against Neo-Confucianism are problematic on several grounds.[8] From the historically well-grounded evidence that Zhu Xi agreed with Cheng Yi that remarriage was morally wrong for widows, the bolder of these authors go on to charge them with attempts to constrain and control women in other ways, without providing any evidence from Song sources. The logic seems to be that anyone so misogynist as to oppose the remarriage of young widows must take misogynist stands on all other issues. Second, these charges attribute enormous power to ideas articulated by male philosophers. Did the structure of the society and economy have nothing to do with the position of women in society? Are general mentalities shaped solely by philosophers? Did women themselves have nothing to do with the creation of the social and cultural system in which they participated? Third, it is anachronistic to look to the Song to explain Ming and Qing situations. Surely no one today believes that Ming and Qing Confucianism was simply the automatic working out of the ideas proposed in the Song. There must have been something about the social and cultural situation in the Ming and Qing that led people to give emphasis to these particular points among the very large body of statements made by Song Confucians.

At the same time, at a much more general level, these charges against Neo-Confucianism may capture a certain truth. Confucianism, including classical and Han Confucianism, provided a view of the cosmos and social order that legitimated the Chinese patrilineal, patrilocal, and patriarchal family system. Confucian emphasis on obligations to patrilineal ancestors and Confucian exaltation of filial piety contributed to a moral order in which families were central to human identity and to a family system organized hierarchically so that men and older generations had considerable power over women and younger generations. Neither Buddhism nor Taoism made the family so central, though in practice their clergy did not challenge Confucian family ethics. At this rather general level, then, the revival of Confucianism in the Song, and the particular form this revival took, could plausibly have strengthened patrilineal and patriarchal ideology, and in the process buttressed a family system in which women were disadvantaged.[9]

In this essay I do not have the space to demonstrate the more obvious flaws in the most extreme of the charges against Neo-Confucianism. I will not give the evidence that Song Neo-Confucian scholars treated widow chastity as an ideal that those of great virtue should strive to achieve, not a standard by which everyone should be judged, or that they did not advocate either female infanticide or footbinding.[10] Rather I will focus on the more plausible hypothesis that the Song revival of Confucianism subtly altered old understandings of women in the family system in ways that imposed greater constraints on women.

My overall argument is as follows. The attention given Cheng Yi has been misplaced. The "orthodox" Cheng-Zhu view of the family and women articulated by Zhu Xi in such widely circulated works such as his *Elementary Learning* (*Xiaoxue*) and *Family Rituals* (*Jiali*) owed at least as much to the ideas of Sima Guang (1019–1086) as it did to ideas more particular to Cheng Yi. Moreover, Cheng Yi's surviving writings say relatively little on women, and therefore the one famous passage has been viewed out of context, whereas the writings of Sima Guang include several lengthy works dealing with family management, family ethics, and family rituals which allow us to see particular ideas in context.[11] From this context, it seems that the focus on the sexual dimensions of widow remarriage has been overdone. Women's sexuality was not the only thing about them that was troubling to men and their families. Other problems were the tenuous nature of their ties to their husband's families; the potential threats created by their claims to property; the confusion of patterns of solidarity and authority created by concubines and multiple mothers; and the ways women's insecurity reflected on the insecurity of the *shidafu* as a class.

I further will argue that in taking the stands that he did, Sima Guang was responding to social, political, and economic changes that brought to the fore the ambiguous and dangerous relationships between women and money, money and sexuality, money and interpersonal relationships, and money and social standing. There were, of course, courtesans and concubines, dowries and heiresses, in earlier dynasties. Yet the problem of the relationship of women to money was more acute in the mid-eleventh century than it had been earlier. Without doubt the amount of money needed for a respectable dowry had risen. Commercialization of the economy and changes in the nature of the political and social elite both seem to have contributed to the increased transmission of family property through daughters' dowries. Men competed for desirable sons-in-law, attempting to attract them by the size of the dowries they would give their daughters. Affines could be of great value in political careers, and men with wealth were willing to use some of it to build up useful networks.[12] At the same time, the increase in the circulation of money, the growing prosperity of merchants, and the growth in the size of the *shidafu* stratum all seem to have led to an increase in the demand for luxury items, prominent among which were the sorts of women who could be bought (courtesans, concubines, maids). Whether these women entered *shidafu* homes or stayed in entertainment quarters, they impinged on the lives of *shidafu* men and their wives and daughters. The relationships between maids and concubines and the members of the families that they entered had an undeniable commercial cast, and were sometimes subject to renegotiation as financial conditions changed. The boundaries between the world of *shidafu* families and the world of courtesans were permeable, in no small part because some men brought ex-courtesans home as concubines and had them entertain their guests. The permeability of these boundaries contributed, I suspect, to the slow but steady spread of footbinding. It also fostered more rigid notions of modesty, for "respectable" women now had to conceal themselves in an increasing range of situations. Veiling their faces marked them off more clearly from the sorts of women who showed their faces to men to entertain them.

Women were not merely passive agents in this system; many played active roles in keeping the system going. Mothers trained their daughters to occupy certain statuses in this system, fostering in them the modesty expected of upper-class wives, the charm expected in courtesans, the obedience expected in maids. Women purchased most of the maids and many of the concubines. A wife whose husband took a concubine could to some degree limit or shape her husband's behavior by arousing fears of what she might do to the other woman if sufficiently provoked. And women were of course also actors as concubines, maids, and courtesans. Not only did some women choose an economically secure position as a concubine over a life of poverty as a poor man's wife, but even those who had been sold quite against their will were not entirely powerless. So long as there were chances to improve their situations, they could strive to gain the favor of their master or mistress, working within the system and thereby also helping to validate it and reproduce it.

I do not have space to substantiate all the links in my chain of arguments. I will say no more about the commercialization of the economy, the growth in the market in women, or women's role in confirming and creating this social system. Rather I will confine myself more narrowly to the antecedents of Zhu Xi's views on women. I will start by showing that the relationships of class, money, sexuality, and interpersonal relationships was troubling to men at the center of the mid-eleventh century scholarly world, then show that the conservative approach to these troublesome issues adopted by Sima

Guang involved an attempt to reconcile the need to protect both daughters and the patrilineal family, and finally argue that Zhu Xi accepted much of this approach while placing it in a slightly altered context.

THE INTRUSIONS OF THE MARKET IN WOMEN

To illustrate the mixed perceptions, feelings, and judgments that eleventh-century *shidafu* men had about the relationships between women, money, and class, I shall briefly recount a dozen incidents they talked about. I have selected ones that involved or came to the attention of men whom Sima Guang knew: these are his brother Sima Dan (1006–1087), Du Yan (978–1057), Chen Zhizhong (991–1059), Zhang Fangping (1007–1091) and his son Zhang Shu, Su Shi (1036–1101), his brother Su Zhe (1039–1112), two unrelated Sus, Su Shunqin (1008–1048) and Su Song (1020–1101), Wang Anshi (1021–1086), and his brother Wang Anguo (1028–1074).

These stories were recorded because *shidafu* of the Song thought that they revealed character or insight. A man who would use his personal funds to provide a dowry for the orphaned daughter of an official was a man of generosity. A man who used state funds for courtesans was lacking in probity or good sense. A man who could not control his concubines was a bad manager. A man who could successfully re-establish a filial relationship to a concubine mother ousted by his father was a heroic figure, much more admirable than one who preferred to pretend his mother did not exist. Neither Sima Guang nor other Song *shidafu* explicitly inferred from these anecdotes the point I think they also conveyed: the nexus of women, money, and class created many problems.

Wives and daughters of good families sold into concubinage

The first three incidents are known only in the sketchiest of terms. Sima Guang's elder brother Sima Dan once gave part of his monthly salary to a cashiered official left with no means of support. The former official, having no other way to repay Sima Dan, offered him his daughter as a concubine. Startled, Dan declined the offer, and instead quickly assembled enough goods from his wife's dowry to marry the girl out.[13] Much the same thing is said to have once happened to Wang Anshi. His wife purchased a woman to be his concubine. When Wang Anshi questioned her, he discovered that she was the wife of a military officer whose family property had been confiscated to compensate for the loss of a boat loaded with tax rice. By selling her, the officer had raised 900,000 cash. Wang Anshi summoned the husband, returned his wife to him, and let him keep the money.[14] The same motif recurs in Zhang Fangping's epitaph for Fu Qiu (1003–1073). Noticing that the girl he had bought as a concubine had unusual abilities and demeanor, Fu questioned her and learned that she was the daughter of an

official he had once known and had been married to a gentleman (*shi*). Fu
Qiu made inquiries and learned that her mother had already remarried. He
therefore took care of everything to arrange a suitable marriage for her
rather than keep her as his concubine.[15]

One reason a man willing to buy a concubine would be uncomfortable
with one from an official family was that the fate of the concubine was
considered an extremely unfortunate one: it was pitiful to see someone fall
from the greatest heights to the lowest depths. This side of the issue is
brought out in a poem written by Wang Anguo and a tale written by Liu Fu
(ca. 1040–1113+). Wang Qiongnu was the daughter of an official, used to a
life of luxury and able to embroider and compose poetry. When she was 13,
her father was posted as a judicial official in the Huainan area. In the late
1050s, her father was dismissed for being too harsh. On the road home,
both he and his wife died. Qiongnu's elder brother and his wife then left
with most of the property. Her fiancé no longer wished to marry her now
that she was poor, and Qiongnu had little to live on. A neighboring woman
offered to arrange a marriage for her, but Qiongnu declined any match with
a merchant or craftsman. Finally, when she had reached 18 *sui* and had
nothing to eat, the old wife of a servant suggested that she become the
concubine of a rich official. "Although it is not marrying, it is still marrying." Qiongnu agreed, and the next day she was decked out in finery and
brought to her new home. The official was immediately attracted to her,
which made the other concubines jealous. They slandered her to the wife,
who became angry, cursed her, and beat her. When the beatings continued,
Qiongnu appealed to the official, who, however, was unwilling to do anything to protect her. Qiongnu, thus, had to put up with regular humiliation
and beatings. Once while traveling with the official, she inscribed her story
and her suicidal thoughts on the wall of an inn, which occasioned Wang
Anguo's poem. The poem castigated all involved, but particularly the official. In his house the wife oppresses her husband. "If he knew that Qiongnu
came from an official family, how could he bear to let her receive whippings
for no reason?" Wang Anguo then, rhetorically, offered to redeem her.[16]

In these anecdotes, men who did not disapprove of concubinage in general were deeply disturbed by the thought that women of their own social
class might fall into it. They realized that marrying a daughter properly into
her own social class required a suitable dowry, and knew that it sometimes
happened that the daughters or wives of officials were sold into concubinage
when the family was financially ruined. They considered this not merely
among the more unfortunate facts of life, to be lamented, but something so
wrong that efforts should be made to remedy it, even at considerable personal expense. Undoubtedly, part of their anguish derived from their own
insecurity. Many officials did not have the wherewithal to protect their
families' social and economic standing if they were to die suddenly or lose
their posts. They were too dependent on money, a fickle medium that could
disturb and transmute all of the foundations of order.

Complications caused by women's property

Du Yan was one of the most eminent men of the generation senior to Sima Guang. In his epitaph for Du Yan, Ouyang Xiu (1007–1072) stressed the family's illustrious history back to eminent officials of the Tang dynasty. He reported that the Du family had been very rich, but when the property was divided, Du Yan had let his brothers take all of his share as they were poor.[17] Zhang Fangping, in his epitaph for Du Yan's wife, mentioned that Du Yan's father died when he was a small child and that his mother returned home, leaving him with few relatives on whom to depend.[18] In his *Sushui jiwen*, Sima Guang gave what appears to be the less varnished version of Du Yan's family background. In his account, Du Yan's experiences were complexly shaped by struggles over women's property. Du's father died before he was born and he was raised by his grandfather. Du Yan's two half brothers by his father's previous wife were disrespectful to his mother, so she left to marry into another family. When Du Yan was 15 or 16, his grandfather died. His two older half-brothers then demanded his mother's "private property" (*sicai*), meaning her dowry. When he refused to turn it over, they turned to force. One drew a sword and wounded Du Yan on the head. Bleeding profusely, he fled to his aunt, who hid him from his half-brothers, saving his life. With no paternal home to go to, he turned to his mother, but her new husband would not let him stay. He then traveled around, very poor, supporting himself by working as a scribe. (So much for the way Du Yan selflessly renounced his share of the family property!) On his travels, Du Yan encountered a rich man surnamed Xiangli. Impressed by Du Yan, Mr. Xiangli not only gave him his daughter to be his wife, but also provided enough for him to live rather comfortably. Du Yan was then able to take the examinations, coming in fourth in the *jinshi* examinations.[19] Later, another source tells us, after he reached high rank, he repaid his debt to the Xiangli family by using his "protection" privilege to get his wife's brother an official post.[20]

The implications of a story like this are several-fold. A man of good family without resources, like Du Yan, could become established by marrying the daughter of a wealthy family through the dowry provided for her. Yet such "women's property" could be the cause of enmity between brothers: it was because of his mother's property that Du Yan was stabbed by his half-brother, making it necessary to run away from home, breaking the ties of the patrilineal family. Moreover, this property had not even assured his mother a comfortable widowhood, as his half-brothers were able to harass her into leaving the family.

Political trouble incurred through relations with courtesans or concubines

It was not uncommon in Song times for prominent officials to suffer from accusations concerning their relationships with women.[21] In 1043, factional

struggles at court led to the expulsion of Su Shunqin from the ranks of offi-
cialdom. Su was a target because he was a son-in-law of Du Yan and had
been recommended by Fan Zhongyan (989–1052). The charge, however,
concerned women. He was accused of using funds from the sale of government waste paper to hire two government courtesans for a party he had
arranged for his colleagues. According to some reports, even after using
government funds, Su still had to charge each of the guests ten strings of
cash to pay for the party. After the guests had been drinking awhile, he dismissed the actors and summoned the two government courtesans. Someone
angry that he had not been admitted to the party is said to have spread the
story of Su Shunqin's misconduct. In the end all those who attended the party,
even the courtesans, were punished.[22] Money is very much at the center of
this story: to entertain well, Su Shunqin needed money to hire expensive
courtesans, but the way he acquired the money – like the way much money
is acquired – cast his activities into even greater moral ambiguity.

At just about this time Zhang Fangping took up a post in Chengdu,
where he met Su Shi and Su Zhe, then young men ready to go to the capital
for the examinations. He also met and became enamored of a registered
courtesan named Chen Fengyi. Perhaps because of the trouble Su Shunqin
had gotten into, Zhang Fangping became worried. When a relative through
marriage, Wang Su (1007–1073), went to Chengdu, Zhang wrote to him for
help. Wang Su then called on Chen Fengyi to see if she had kept any of
Zhang's letters. When she produced them, he stuffed them in a bag. He told
her that Zhang had many enemies at court, and he would not let her use the
letters to harm his reputation. He then burned the bag full of letters, earning
Zhang Fangping's gratitude.[23]

Some ten years later, in 1054, Chen Zhizhong lost his post as chief councilor
because of something his favorite concubine did. When it was found that
she had beat one of their female slaves to death, he was charged with failure
to manage his household properly. In the end, after some clamor from officials, including Ouyang Xiu, he was relieved of his post.[24] His reputation
had clearly suffered; when Han Wei (1017–1098) discussed his posthumous
name he noted that "Within his inner quarters, the distinctions of ceremony
were not clear. His wife was treated poorly; the concubine was cruel and un-
governable. His management of his family was unspeakable."[25] As it turned
out, some years later the murderous concubine was herself killed by the wife
and maids of her son, with the son's complicity. Chen Zhizhong's son and
these women were all executed, compounding the damage inflicted on his
family directly and indirectly by his favorite concubine.[26] Running through
this story and many ones like it going back centuries is the perception that
lower-class women of the sort likely to be bought as concubines are particularly prone to malice and violence. And men, because they have selected
such women on the basis of sexual attraction, cannot properly control them.

A little over ten years later, Li Ding (1028–1087) ran into a different sort
of problem relating to concubinage. His father had had a concubine Qiu,

who bore his older brother and perhaps Ding as well. She, at any rate, had nursed him.[27] Later, according to one source, she left and married into the Gao family.[28] Li Ding himself was a protégé of Wang Anshi. When the woman Qiu died, Li Ding did not retire to mourn her, but he did ask to be relieved of his post to care for his father, then 89.[29] Later, when he returned to court, his failure to mourn Qiu as a mother was labeled a major breach of the rules of filial piety. Starting in 1070 officials wrote memorials asking for him to be dismissed. An official inquiry was ordered, and when it cleared Li Ding of intentional wrong-doing on the grounds that his father denied that Qiu was his mother, officials continued protesting. Wang Anshi came to Li Ding's defense, saying that he had mourned her in the fifth degree as the concubine mother of his brother and as his wet nurse, and should not be expected to quit his post to mourn her as a full parent now, especially since the facts of his parentage could not be definitively established.[30] Two officials were demoted to posts out of the capital when they submitted six or seven memorials asking for Li Ding's dismissal.[31] Li Ding did manage to remain in office but he never freed himself of the taint of the label "unfilial."[32]

Each of these cases shows a different facet of the political vulnerability of men linked in one way or another to women who were bought. The connections created by these links were ambiguous, carrying overtones of indecent pleasures, lower-class violence, and impermanence. They thus created ample potential for accusations motivated primarily by factional struggles. Su Shunqin gave his critics grounds for portraying him as frivolous and corrupt by hiring courtesans for a party. Chen Zhizhong lost his contemporaries' respect by failing to control the violence of his favorite concubine. Li Ding ran into a quandary when it was widely reputed that he was the son of a concubine whom his father had sent away and would not recognize. What runs through these cases is the danger of the ambiguous relationships created when women come and go like goods in the market.

Legal trouble brought on by concubines

Su Song and Su Zhe each recorded cases of educated men who ran foul of the law through their connections with concubines. Su Zhe reported that Zhou Gao, a wealthy, arrogant, and undisciplined official, once took several tens of courtesan-concubines (*jiqie*) with him on a trip to Hangzhou.[33] One, because of "the harm caused by jealousy," drowned herself. When her parents took the case to court, it happened that the magistrate had a maid who had once served in Zhou's house. She took a peek at those in the courtroom and recognized that one of Zhou Gao's concubines had been his father's concubine and had borne a son by him. Thus the magistrate was able to charge Zhou with the more serious offense of incest, and he was exiled.[34]

The case reported by Su Song concerned a man and his father's maid/concubine. When the man passed the examinations and was assigned a post, he wished to take his widowed father with him, but his father declined. The official then purchased a local woman to take care of his father, and gradually his father came to treat this maid "like a mate." When the official returned, sensing his father's feelings, he treated the woman politely and once used the term *niang,* "mom," to refer to her in a letter to his father. Some time later, after the man had gone on to hold other posts, his father died. When the man returned he found the woman acting like a "genuine mother." She cursed and beat his wife, and when he could stand it no longer, he beat her back. She then went to the magistrate, charging him with unfiliality. She brought the letter he had written to prove that she was his "mother." The case dragged on until a clever official found a way out.[35]

The ambiguity of the relationships created by purchasing women, thus, did not endanger only high officials subject to slander in factional disputes. Concubines as young or younger than sons created suspicions of incest; concubines of widowers might claim to be wives with all the authority of mothers over their master's children.

Embarrassment and grief due to the impermanence of connections based on concubinage

Scholars may have clamored to condemn Li Ding's neglect of his concubine/ mother, but they recognized that he faced a real problem. Men, perhaps especially officials and merchants, might take a concubine to keep them company while they resided away from home, then abandon her when they left. The children of such concubines might loose all contact with their biological mothers. In the late 1060s, condemnation of Li Ding's solution – ignoring his mother – was coupled with praise for Su Shi's friend, Zhu Shouchang, who had responded in a different fashion. Zhu's father took a concubine while serving as prefect of Jingzhao. She bore Shouchang, and when he was 2 *sui* she was sent away to be married into a commoner's family.[36] Zhu Shouchang then saw nothing of his biological mother for fifty years. As he served in office around the country, he sought her out. Finally, in about 1068 or 1069, he gave up his office and left his family, declaring "I will not return until I see my mother." He found her in Tongzhou, over 70 years of age, married into the Dang family and the mother of several sons. Zhu Shouchang took the whole family home with him. His story was first publicized by Qian Mingyi (1015–1071), "then the *shidafu,* from Wang Anshi, Su Song, and Su Shi on down, competed to praise his actions in poems."[37] Su Shi's poem praising Zhu Shouchang was taken by Li Ding as a criticism of him, and became part of the dossier Li Ding put together against Su Shi some years later.[38]

It was not solely the children of concubines who could suffer from the fragility of the kinship ties of concubines. Their masters could also be embarrassed by it. It was reported, for instance, that Su Shi, while prefect of Huangzhou, got to know Xu Dezhi, the son-in-law of Han Jiang (1012–1088). Xu kept several concubines and Su Shi often saw them when music

Figure 1.1 Zhu Shouchang finally finding his concubine mother, left behind by his father.
Source: After SYXJ 1.26a.

was played as entertainment for guests. After Xu died and Su Shi was on his way back north, he stopped to visit Zhang Shu, the son of Zhang Fangping. At the banquet, Su Shi recognized Xu's favorite concubine. "Unconsciously he covered his face and wailed. The concubine then turned to her peers and gave a big laugh. Dongpo would always mention this to people as a warning against keeping maids."[39]

Su Shi's embarrassment at women changing men so easily may have been a premonition of what would happen to him. Some of Su Dongpo's concubines did not wait until after he died to leave. According to the preface he wrote to a poem, his concubines left him one after the other over a four-to-five year period, so that only Zhaoyun accompanied him into exile.[40]

Fragility, impermanence, ambiguity – these are all words with negative connotations, and all seem to have more to do with women than men. In a patrilineal, patrilocal society like China's, women will always be more associated with discontinuity than men. Men remain tied to the family into which they are born. A woman, in the best of circumstances, moves once to be married. In less fortunate circumstances, she can be sold and resold as a maid or concubine; she can be divorced; she can be sent away when widowed. Money similarly has a tendency to come and go. Land and rank could be counted on to endure for some time; money, by contrast, can be quickly earned or quickly squandered. As these anecdotes attest, when women and money are crossed, the potential for discontinuity is multiplied.

THE VIEWS OF SIMA GUANG ON WOMEN AND THE FAMILY

Sima Guang had a reputation as a man of austere and upright character, one of the least likely of any of the great men of his age to succumb to the attractions of women. The only stories told about him in which women played a part concerned his indifference to them. Because he had no sons, we are told, his wife and her sister once acquired a concubine for him. When he paid no attention to her, the sister arranged for the wife to be absent, then had the concubine get dressed up and bring him tea. Sima Guang got angry at the girl's presumption: "You lowly person, what are you doing here when your mistress is out of the house?" suggesting that he looked on her as his wife's maid, not his concubine.[41] In another account, the new concubine tried to make conversation with Sima Guang by picking up a book and asking him what it was. He raised his hands in a salute and with a solemn expression said, "This is the *Book of Documents*," at which she retreated.[42]

Whatever the historical accuracy of these anecdotes, there is ample evidence in Sima Guang's own writings that his sense of decorum required avoiding any mixed-sex frivolity. In 1062, while serving in a censorial post, he wrote a memorial to the emperor complaining that it was unseemly for the emperor to reward female wrestlers along with other entertainers performing at the gate during the lantern festival. "Above there is the exalted emperor; below there are the multitudinous people; the empress and consorts are on the side, the ladies looking on. And yet women are allowed to compete as a game before them all. This, I fear, is not the way to demonstrate to the realm the importance of rituals and laws." He further asked that an edict be issued prohibiting women from gathering on the streets for amusements.[43]

Sima Guang was, moreover, against the sort of lavish entertainment that seems to have become common among his peers. He reported that his contemporaries were afraid they would be called stingy unless their parties lasted several days and involved rare foods and drink. He did not explicitly mention the extravagance of female entertainers at parties, but did point to the cautionary example of Kou Zhun (961–1023), known for extravagant all night parties, for dancing and making music with female entertainers, and for a concubine who composed poetry at his parties.[44] By his own time, Sima Guang pointed out, Kou's descendants were impoverished.[45]

Whatever his own experiences, Sima Guang was acquainted with the men mentioned above, and undoubtedly had heard stories about them like the ones above. What I should like to argue is that his views on women's education, women's property, and the permanent, fixed, moral basis for the relations between wives and their husbands' families are all best understood in the light of the ways his contemporaries talked about such incidents. It is true, of course, that he drew on traditional materials, especially the classics and the accumulated stories of self-effacing sons, wise mothers, deferential daughters-in-law, and other such heroic figures. But the way he organized this material reflected his own values and concerns.[46] On the surface, the model men and women he described in such writings as his ten-chapter *Precepts for Family Life* (*Jiafan*) had nothing in common with the men and women discussed above, but that is precisely the point. It was because the market intruded into kinship relationships that he wished to banish it. He not only wanted men to avoid these embarrassing circumstances, he also wanted to protect both the daughters of *shidafu* families who might become victims of the market, and the families themselves, as wives with property could pose threats. He wished to demarcate a sphere into which money would not intrude.

Sima Guang's views on the family are largely congruent with his views on social and political organization more generally.[47] He had a well-developed sense of hierarchy. He believed that in all social groups there should be a clear division of tasks and clear lines of authority. Discipline and ritual were the means to create and maintain this hierarchy. Those in charge should work for the good of the unit, preserve their dignity, give clear instructions, enforce them impartially, and avoid being carried away by emotion. Those in subordinate positions should cultivate deference, loyalty, diligence, and endurance. They should put up with unreasonable superiors, trying to win them over through their patience, devotion, and good humor.[48] In the case of the family, the unit for which superiors and subordinates alike had to work was the family as a corporate unit, the *jia*. This family was not merely the collection of individuals then living together, but the family that persists through time: the ancestors and descendants, the house and property, the traditions and honor. Like many other Confucian scholars before and after him, Sima Guang saw the ideal family as the large, complex family, undivided for several generations, with uncles and nephews, first and second cousins all living together and sharing the same property.[49] Because property was essential to the survival and identity of the family, Sima Guang was against extravagance, frivolity, or willfulness as they might lead to its loss.

This family was primarily a group of men bound to each other by patrilineal links and common ties to property. But women were attached to these men as mothers, sisters, daughters, and wives. As he made clear in his *Precepts for Family Life,* these women could advance or thwart the pursuit of family goals through their own actions and their influence on men. Gender distinctions were, moreover, an essential feature of the hierarchy in the family. The family was not composed simply of superiors and subordinates; it was composed of male superiors and male subordinates, female superiors and female subordinates.

From the examples Sima Guang provides, it would seem that what he most admired in women was total devotion to the *jia* of their husbands. The following exemplary story quoted in his *Precepts for Family Life* is typical of the many he cites.

> Han Ji's wife was Miss Yu. (Her father, Shi, was a grand deputy for the [Northern] Zhou). At 14 she married Ji. Although she was born and grew up in a wealthy house of great eminence, she observed ritual decorum and was personally frugal and restrained. The entire clan respected her. When she was 18 [her husband] Ji died in battle. Miss Yu became emaciated through grief, moving those who passed her by. Every morning and evening, she offered the funerary oblations with her own hands. At the end of the mourning period, her parents wished to marry her to someone else as she was still young and had no children. She swore she would not consent, then made Shilong, her husband's son by a concubine, the heir and raised him herself, loving him as much as if she had actually borne him. Her training was systematic, and in the end he succeeded in establishing himself.
>
> From the time she began to live as a widow, she never went anywhere other than occasional visits home or to relatives. When senior relatives called on her, she never went out of her house to greet or bid farewell to them. To the end of her life she ate only vegetarian food, dressed in plain cloth, and did not listen to music.[50]

This story touched on many of the themes important to Sima Guang: for a woman, her husband's family must become her focus of identity and attention. She must forget the wealth and comfort of her parents' family, must show restraint and frugality, and think of heirs from a patrilineal point of view, as heirs to her husband, unconcerned with whether or not they were her own children. She must in no way act like a courtesan: frugality and duty were needed, not beauty and entertainment. Her husband's death should in no way weaken her commitment to his patriline. The role of wife was a highly respectable one, and a woman should devote herself to fulfilling it well.[51]

To analyze Sima Guang's attitudes in more depth, I shall consider here his views on gender differentiation, women's property, women's virtues, women's education, and the nature of marriage.

Gender distinctions

Sima Guang, like Confucians since at least the Han, saw the distinctions between men and women as part of the natural order of *yin* and *yang*, not the social order of institutions artificially created by men. In his *Precepts for Family Life*, Sima Guang explained the underlying distinctions between men and women in this way:

> The husband is Heaven; the wife is earth. The husband is the sun; the wife is the moon. The husband is yang; the wife is yin. Heaven is honored and occupies the space above. Earth is lowly and occupies the space below. The sun does not have any deficiencies in its fullness; the moon is sometimes round and sometimes incomplete. Yang sings out and gives life to things; yin joins in and completes things. Therefore wives take as their virtues gentleness and compliance and do not excel through strength or intellectual discrimination.[52]

Yin and yang complement each other but not in equal ways. Sima Guang took for granted that action and initiation are more valued than endurance and completion. Like others who used yin–yang ideas to discuss male-female differentiation, Sima Guang drew the inference that the proper social role of men was to lead and women to follow.[53]

The complementarity of yin and yang did not require them both to be present at the same time. To the contrary, yin–yang thinking was generally coupled with the classical phrase, "the distinction of male and female" (*nannü zhi bie*). The term "distinction" when applied to men and women could range in meaning from physical segregation to conceptual distinction in the roles that they performed. Sima Guang wanted both. Men belonged on the outside, women on the inside. Outer was not merely the outer quarter of the house but the outer world of work and social life. He quoted a passage from the *Record of Ritual's* (*Li ji*) "Domestic Regulations" (*Neize*) to the effect that men should not discuss the affairs of the inner sphere nor women discuss the affairs of the outer sphere. But to attain the separation of functions, physical separation was of great value. In his *Precepts for Family Life*,

es not go out, which means
hat a father should not enter
and a brother should not sit
me.[55] In his "Miscellaneous
Etiquette for Family Life" (Jujia zayi), Sima Guang paraphrased and elaborated on the rules for sexual segregation in the "Domestic Regulations."

> In housing there should be a strict demarcation between the inner and outer parts, with a door separating them. The two parts should share neither a well, a wash room, or a privy. The men are in charge of all affairs on the outside; the women manage the inside affairs. During the day, without good reason the men do not stay in their private rooms nor the women go beyond the inner door. A woman who has to leave the inner quarters must cover her face (for example, with a veil). Men who walk around at night must hold a candle. Menservants do not enter the inner quarters unless to make house repairs or in cases of calamity (such as floods, fires, or robberies). If they must enter, the women should avoid them. If they cannot help being seen (as in floods, fires, and robberies), they must cover their faces with their sleeves. Maids should never cross the inner gate without good reason (young slave-girls also); if they must do so they too should cover their faces. The doorman and old servants serve to pass messages and objects between the inner and outer quarters of the house, but must not be allowed to enter rooms or kitchens at will.[56]

The need for respectable women to conceal their faces when they might be seen by unrelated men is reiterated many times in Sima Guang's writings.[57] Although the historical sources are scanty, it does seem that the practice of wearing veils was growing in this period.[58] Sima Guang, if aware that anything had changed, found this change quite acceptable.

Sima Guang may have thought of physical segregation of males and females as important because it promoted clear separation of functions, but we can see that it was also based on fears of the consequences of unregulated sexuality. Men and women might be sexually attracted to each other if allowed to see each other and such attractions could lead to all sorts of unwanted behavior. Sima Guang never seems to point to women as evil temptresses – it is men who should see to the physical separation of men and women. Sima Guang does not discuss unregulated sexual relations enough for us to know exactly how he thought of them, but I would suspect that he saw them more as imprudent than as sinful.

Women's property

Sima Guang, like his contemporaries, took it as normal that men would send out their daughters with dowries. It was proper for men to help prepare dowries for orphaned relatives, but speed in getting the marriage arranged while the girls were still young was more important than the size of the dowry.[59] But Sima Guang was repelled by any suggestion that daughters had rights to property or that marriage was a financial transaction. He pointed to the tragedy of a contemporary who had built up his family's property but had neglected the moral education of his children and grandchildren. After he died, not only did his sons fight over the property, but also "his unmarried daughters veiled their heads, grasped the documents, and personally laid charges before the government in a struggle for their dowries," making a laughing stock of the family.[60]

Sima Guang saw greed for dowries as rampant among prospective parents-in-law:

> Nowadays, it is the custom for covetous and vulgar people first to ask about the value of the dowry when selecting a bride and the amount of the wedding present when marrying a daughter. Some even draw up a contract saying "such goods, in such numbers, such goods, in such numbers," thereby treating their daughters as an item in a sales transaction. There are also cases where people go back on their agreements after the wedding is over. These are the methods used by brokers dealing in male and female bondservants. How can such a transaction be called a gentleman-official [*shidafu*] marriage?[61]

Treating marriage like a transaction was bad for both the bride and for her family. The bride would not be protected by her property; rather she (like Du Yan's mother) would be endangered by it:

> When the parents-in-law have been deceived [about the size of the dowry], they will maltreat the daughter-in-law as a way to vent their fury. Fearing this, those who love their daughter put together generous dowries in the hope of pleasing her parents-in-law, not realizing that such covetous, vulgar people are insatiable. When the dowry is depleted, what use will the bride be to these parents-in-law? They will then "pawn" her to get further payment from her family. Her family's wealth has a limit, but their demands will never stop. Therefore, families linked by marriage often end up enemies.[62]

The husband's family also suffers when a wife looks on her property as a source of power or independence.

> Whether a family thrives or declines depends on the wife. A bride chosen because of greediness for transient wealth and rank will seldom fail to presume upon them and treat her husband with contempt and her parents-in-law with disdain. High-handed and jealous streaks of her personality will be fostered, leading one day to disaster. Where will it

end? How could a man of spirit retain his pride if he got rich by using his wife's assets or gained high station by relying on her influence?[63]

Sima Guang's views of women's property were shaped by his perception that private property is the major threat to family solidarity. In complex, undivided families with several generations' depth, women's dowries, if kept separate, continually threatened the survival of the family.[64] Sima Guang argued that wives should have no private property, citing with approval a passage from the *Li ji* which said a daughter-in-law should "have nothing of her own, neither personal savings, nor private belongings." Even gifts she received had to be turned over to her parents-in-law, and she could make no gifts herself, not even of the things she had once received as gifts.[65]

Although the basic Confucian objection to women's private property had old roots, Song circumstances – especially escalation of dowry – probably led to even stronger articulation of these views. The trend toward sending daughters off with large dowries undoubtedly contributed to the great elaboration of women's property rights that can be seen in Song legal texts.[66] Since wives' natal families were supplying the bulk of the dowry from their own funds, they had a strong interest in seeing that it served to benefit their daughter and her heirs. But the growth in dowry also accounts for opposition to women's property rights on the part of those like Sima Guang thinking in terms of threats to the authority of family heads.

Women's virtues

Sima Guang's statements about women in general commonly assigned them goals more modest than those assigned to men. Living on the inside as they did, the virtues they needed were compliance, purity, lack of jealousy, frugality, attentiveness, and diligence.[67] Elsewhere he stated that no virtue was more important to a woman than lack of jealousy. Concubines were sanctioned in the classics, so it was up to wives to live harmoniously with them.[68] Frugality and diligence were obviously related to Sima Guang's concerns with preserving the family's property and preventing its division. He included the exemplary case of a widow who continued to weave until midnight each night long after her son had gained office and salary.[69] Sima Guang praised his own wife for never showing anger, arguing with others, or harboring resentment. She was generous to the maids and concubines, sympathizing with them and never showing jealousy. She was frugal in her daily expenses, but never complained if he gave assistance to his relatives.[70]

In his *Precepts for Family Life*, Sima Guang cited for emulation many cases of widows who refused to remarry. He wrote, "'Wife' means an equal match. Once she is matched with him, she does not change for the rest of her life. Therefore loyal subjects do not serve two masters, and chaste women do not serve two husbands."[71] There is no sign that Sima Guang found female self-sacrifice to be emotionally or morally more satisfying than male self-sacrifice. He did not offer as models any widows who committed suicide rather than remarry. Rather his heroes resisted their parents' efforts to re-marry them so that they could care for their husbands' parents or children.[72] They might mutilate themselves to discourage suitors, but did not throw their lives away.[73] Both men and women might give up their lives, but for other purposes, such as to save a parent or to escape from an unreconcili-able conflict of duty.[74] Some women did show strong determination to protect their chastity: girls, wives, or widows would commit suicide to avoid being raped.[75] But remarriage was not equated with rape.

In a certain sense Sima Guang judged men and women by the same standards: they were both to be admired for selfless behavior, for identifying completely with the higher cause of loyalty to the family. A widow who with-stood every test was like the heroic man who overcame all odds to preserve an undivided family for six, eight, or ten generations' depth, or the filial son who would put up with a cruel stepmother and eventually win her over. In each case the hero put the norms of filial piety and loyalty to the larger family before personal goals.

Widowhood, moreover, did not provide the only test for women. Before marriage a woman could demonstrate loyalty to her father's family. Sima Guang retold the story of three sisters without brothers who refused to marry so they could care for their aged grandparents, in the end managing their funerals and residing by their graves; the story of a daughter who offered to become a palace slave to redeem her imprisoned father; the story of three sisters who killed two relatives to avenge their father's death.[76] In these cases the women were extolled for virtues much like those admired in filial sons.[77] Wives might also demonstrate loyalty to their husbands' fam-ilies without being widowed. He told of women who humored oppressive mothers-in-law, who saved the children of their husbands' brothers rather than their own, who used the wealth their fathers gave them for the sake of their husbands' families, and a great many who had good influence on the character of their husbands or sons.

In the biographical accounts Sima Guang wrote for the wives and mothers of his contemporaries, he attributed to them the same virtues he extolled in his *Precepts for Family Life.* Su Shi's mother, for instance, was praised for forgetting the wealth of her natal family and diligently serving her superiors in the much poorer family into which she was married. Her literacy was a cause for praise, especially since it enabled her to educate her sons.[78] The mother of Han Duo was praised for treating all six sons of her husband equ-ally, so that even close relatives could not tell which had different mothers.[79] Sima Guang lavished his highest praise on a woman of more obscure social standing who met the highest standards of self-abnegation. Surrepti-tiously sold by her step-mother at age 7, she accidentally rediscovered her father twenty-one years later. She not only persuaded her father to forgive her step-mother, but when he died, she patiently delayed marrying herself to care for her step-mother, carrying her on her back when she lost the ability to walk.[80]

Women's education

A married woman who stays within the house, avoiding contact even with her father and brothers, has no need for the same sort of education as her husband. Still Sima Guang approved of girls' learning to read. In his *Precepts* he quoted Ban Zhao's arguments that women would make better wives if they had learned to read.[81] He added his own conclusion,

> People who do not study do not know ritual and morality, and those who do not know ritual and morality cannot distinguish good and bad, right and wrong . . . Thus everyone must study. How are males and females different in this regard?[82]

In his "Miscellaneous Etiquette" he wrote a brief schedule for learning for both boys and girls. It was based on the *Li ji*'s "Domestic Regulations" but modified to add book learning for girls. Even though they did not follow the same schedule as their brothers, they would learn to read as well as how to deport themselves as wives.

> At the age of 6, a child is taught the words for numbers (1, 10, 100, 1,000, 10,000) and directions (east, west, south, north). Boys should begin learning how to write and girls should be taught simple women's work. At the age of 7, boys and girls no longer sit together or eat together. At this age boys recite the *Classic of Filial Piety* [*Xiaojing*] and the *Analects* [*Lunyu*]. It is a good idea for girls to recite them too. . . .
>
> [At the age of 8 children] begin to learn modesty and yielding. Boys recite the *Book of Documents* [*Shangshu*] and young girls no longer go past the door of the inner quarters. At 9 years boys read the *Spring and Autumn Annals* [*Chunqiu*] and other histories. The texts are now explained to them, so that they can understand moral principle. At this age girls have explained to them the *Analects*, the *Classic of Filial Piety*, and such books as *Biographies of Admirable Women* [*Lienü zhuan*] and *Admonitions for Women* [*Nujie*] so that they comprehend the main ideas.[83]
>
> [Note:] In ancient times all virtuous women read illustrated histories to educate themselves; some such as Cao Dagu [Ban Zhao] became quite conversant in the classics and could discuss issues intelligently. Nowadays some people teach their daughters to write songs and poems and play popular music; these are entirely inappropriate activities.[84]

Sima Guang did not want girls to become too accomplished in music and singing, perhaps because such accomplishments might make them seem too much like courtesans. Instead they should learn "women's work."

At the age of 10, boys ought to go out to study under a school master and should stay in the outer quarters or away from home . . . For girls, at this age instruction in compliance and obedience and the principal household tasks should begin.

[Note:] Household tasks such as breeding silkworms, weaving, sewing, and cooking are the proper duties of a woman. In addition, instruction in them lets a girl learn the hardships through which food and clothing are obtained so that she will not dare to be extravagant. Concerning delicate crafts, however, no instruction is needed.[85]

Sima Guang knew that most of the wives of his peers had maids who did the physical labor involved in cooking, cleaning, and sewing. But he thought training in these tasks would make women more responsible.[86] Besides domestic chores, Sima Guang had both women and girls participate in family rituals. These rituals would both teach and reproduce the hierarchy of the family. In his "Miscellaneous Etiquette," he urged others to copy the example of his family:

In our family there are so many relatives living together that we have a mass ceremony in the hall for the winter solstice, New Year, and the new and full moons. (Here I assume that the hall faces south; if it does not, make appropriate adjustments.) The men ascend the main hall from the western steps and stand on the left; the women ascend from the eastern steps and stand on the right (left and right of the family head). Everyone faces north in line, in order of age (wives are ordered in accordance with their husbands' ages, not their own). Then all members of the family salute the head of the family together. Afterwards, the eldest son goes to the left of the door, and the eldest daughter to the right of the door, both facing south, and all their brothers and sisters bow to them successively. Then each returns to where he or she was. All the husbands go up the western steps and wives go up the eastern steps, where they receive the bows of all the children. (This is because there are too many family members. If each couple were to be bowed to separately, it would become impossibly tiring.) When this salutation is completed, the elders leave the room and the children step up to the east and west sides of the door and receive bows from their younger brothers and sisters, just as their parents had done.[87]

These formalized greetings, performed twice a month, would reinforce all of the hierarchical distinctions in the family: men and women were kept apart; men preceded women; women themselves are also differentiated by generation and rank; but wives' rankings were based on their husbands'.

In Sima Guang's manual for family rituals, his *Letters and Etiquette* [*Sima shi shuyi*], women played active roles in other rituals as well. They attended all of the more major ancestral rites, lined up on one side of the hall by age and generation. The wife of the family head stood opposite him, handled the tablets for female ancestors, and personally put out many of the offerings of food and drink. Women were just as involved as men in wailing for the dead, and would be lined up on one side of the coffin while men were on the other.[88]

Nature of marriage

Sima Guang admired women who sacrificed themselves for their husbands and children, but he did not take an entirely one-sided view of the bonds of marriage. Men as well could demonstrate loyalty to the family by not remarrying. For men the issue often was the future of their sons – stepmothers were bad. He quoted the case of Zhu Hui in the Later Han who lost his wife at 50. His brothers wished to get a new wife for him, but he demurred: "In current custom it is rare for a second wife not to ruin the family." Sima Guang commented, "Men today of advanced years with sons and grandsons should compare themselves against this example of a past worthy."[89]

Sima Guang also expressed admiration for men who expressed grief at the death of their wives.

Formerly Zhuang Zhou [i.e., Zhuang Zi] drummed on a plate and sang when his wife died. Xue Qin, the grand administrator of Shanyang in the Han dynasty, did not wail when his wife died. Rather when he approached her body he said, "I was lucky she did not die young. What regrets should I have?" When the Grand Commandant Wang Gong's wife died, he wore mourning and walked with a staff along with his sons, for which his contemporaries made fun of him. When Liu Shi, the great commandant during the Jin dynasty, lost his wife, for the whole mourning period he used the hut and staff and abstained from carriages and meat. Although others belittled and ridiculed him for this, he paid no attention. Zhuang and Xue discarded morality; Wang and Liu accorded with principles – they could hardly be further apart. How could one criticize them![90]

Sima Guang's admiration for faithful husbands should not be taken as a sign that he saw marriage as a lifetime commitment for a man. He reiterated several times that a man's obligations to his parents and to his family could make it imperative that he divorce a wife who was disrupting family harmony. It could be an act of loyalty to the family to divorce a wife who was disrespectful to one's mother.[91] Indeed, Sima Guang saw a general responsibility to divorce a wife who in any way violated the duties of her role.[92] Sima Guang did not merely urge husbands to accept the necessity of divorcing their wives; he also urged wives' parents to look on their daughters as the guilty parties and work to reform them. He cited the case of a woman who had married out her daughter three times, only to have her sent back three times. When she asked her daughter what had happened, the daughter spoke contemptuously of her husband. The mother then beat her on the grounds that wives were supposed to be submissive, not haughty. She then kept her home for three years, and on the fourth try she made an ideal wife. By contrast, in his day, Sima Guang observed, parents were more likely to sue the families of their sons-in-law than to blame their daughters.[93]

Much of the misogyny modern readers see in Neo-Confucian writings on women stems, I believe, from fundamentally different notions of marriage. In Western ways of thinking, marriage is about acquiring a spouse, and both men and women get married. The marriage lasts until divorce or the death of one of the spouses. To impose on a widow faithfulness to her dead husband without imposing similar faithfulness on widowers hardly seems equal treatment.

To Sima Guang and probably most of his contemporaries, marriage was only in part about the joining of two spouses. It was primarily about how families perpetuate themselves through the incorporation of new members. A man was incorporated at birth or through adoption. His loyalty to the family into which he had been incorporated could be tested in many ways: he might have to endure a vicious step-mother, a high-handed half-brother, or deal with a wife who told tales about his brothers or otherwise disrupted the family. Overcoming these circumstances allowed the family to survive. A woman's loyalty to the family into which she had been incorporated by marriage could also be tested: by a nasty mother-in-law, by a husband who kept concubines, by a concubine's bearing sons while she did not, by her husband's dying before her children were grown, by brothers-in-law or step-sons who made her unwelcome after her husband died or made off with her children's property. Her heroism in meeting these tests could have just as much to do with the survival of the family as anything a man might do. Remarriage was thus simply not the same thing for a man and a woman. If a man had no children or his children were very young, he should remarry for the sake of the family. If he had half-grown or grown children, remarrying would be an act of indulgence more likely to harm the family than help it. For a woman, remarriage meant renouncing the family which she had joined. It was comparable to an adopted son abandoning his adoptive parents, not a man taking a new wife.

Sima Guang never directly addressed how to deal with the ambiguities created by concubinage. He knew that concubines caused problems. In his *Precepts* he wrote that

> when brothers do not get along, it is often because they have different mothers. When they are the wife and a concubine, the hatred and jealousy are even worse than when they are the first and a successor wife. Since the mothers have strong feelings, the sons become separate factions.[94]

Yet he did not give much guidance to the sons of concubines or the sons of the legal wife who had half-brothers by concubines. His examples of filial sons do not include any known primarily for their loyalty to concubine mothers mistreated by their fathers or legal mothers. His only solution to the problems of concubinage was more ritual and hierarchy. He endorsed the idea that the wife of the household head ran the women's quarters much like the household head ran the family as a whole, giving her authority over his concubines, their sons' wives and concubines, and all the maids.[95] He held up as a model a concubine who remained deferential to the wife long after their master/husband died, even though she had borne sons and the wife had not.[96]

To sum up, running through Sima Guang's views on women and marriage is a strong distaste for blurred, ambiguous, or negotiable interpersonal relationships, a distaste undoubtedly developed by the prevalence of such relationships in his society. Marriage could not be treated as a commercial transaction, with all the implications that it was a matter of temporary convenience. When a woman married into a family she had to acquire a tie to it as enduring as the one a son acquired when he was born there. Reforming the entire world would be the best course, but in the meantime, to protect their sisters and daughters from the market in women, men had to see that they were kept secluded, given educations untainted by any suggestion that they were entertainers or playthings, given dowries so that they could marry respectably, and helped if misfortune struck them. At the same time, the patrilineal family had to be protected from the disruptive effects of incoming wives with property or interfering relatives. It also had to be protected from the ambiguity of concubinage by insisting that concubines submit to wives in all matters, and the sons of both treat each other as equals while showing appropriately graded respect for each others' mothers.

The influence of Sima Guang's views on Zhu Xi and Huang Gan

Zhu Xi had great respect for Sima Guang's integrity and his writings on family virtues, rituals, and management. He cited Sima Guang's family as one to be emulated for its sound management. Sima Guang himself was held up as a model brother, exceptionally loving and polite to his elder brother, treating him almost like a father even when his brother was 80 and he was over 60.[97] In 1194 when Zhu Xi set up a shrine to "former worthies" at Blue Waterside Academy, it included statues for four ancient worthies (Confucius and his disciples) and seven Song scholars, Zhou Dunyi, Cheng Yi, Cheng Hao (1032–1085), Zhang Zai (1020–1077), Shao Yong (1011–1077), Sima Guang, and Zhu Xi's own teacher Li Tong (1093–1163).[98] Zhu Xi once asked Fu Zide (1116–1183) to publish together three moral tracts, Ban Zhao's *Admonitions for Women*, Sima Guang's "Miscellaneous Etiquette," and the "Duties for Children," a section from the *Guan Zi*.

Figure 1.2 Exemplary widowed concubine who remains deferential to the wife even
though she is the mother of the only son.
Source: After SYXJ 4.29a.

Zhu Xi later sent this book to many of his friends.[99] Zhu Xi also frequently recommended Sima Guang's *Letters and Etiquette* as a guide to family rituals in conversations or letters to friends and disciples.[100] He once recommended Sima Guang's *Precepts for Family Life* as a suitable text for teaching to girls.[101]

Zhu Xi most convincingly demonstrated his respect for Sima Guang's writings by paraphrasing them in his own writings. His *Family Rituals* (*Jiali*) relies very heavily on Sima Guang's *Letters and Etiquette* and incorporates verbatim Sima Guang's "Miscellaneous Etiquette."[102] Zhu Xi's *Elementary Learning*, published in 1187, makes considerable use of Sima Guang's *Precepts for Family Life* for its treatment of parent–child and husband–wife relationships. Often exemplary stories in the *Elementary Learning* seem to have been drawn from the *Precepts for Family Life* rather than from the original source.[103]

On such issues as the separation of the sexes, women's education, women's virtues, and the need for women to identify with their husbands' families, there is little sign that Zhu Xi found anything in Sima Guang to quarrel with, even when his language was not directly borrowed from Sima Guang.[104] Zhu Xi's emphasis is perhaps not quite as sexually balanced as Sima Guang's – he did not cite any cases of girls refusing to marry to care for their parents or grandparents, or any cases of men refusing to remarry because of their worries about the disruptions of stepmothers – but his thrust is the same.

Nevertheless, Zhu Xi subtly altered the significance of some of Sima Guang's views on women's property, education, and virtues by placing them in a different context. As I have discussed elsewhere, Sima Guang thought in terms of the family defined by common residence and common purse and managed by the oldest brother in the oldest generation. This family could be large and complex, but it was organized on the same hierarchical principles as a small family of parents and children. Zhang Zai and Cheng Yi, by contrast, had urged the revival of the patrilineal descent line (*zong*) principles, which elevated birth order over age and generation. They wished to see the principles specified in the classics for succession to responsibility for sacrifices extended to other family matters. Thus the eldest son of the eldest son of the eldest son would take priority over his grandfather's younger brother if his father and grandfather were not living, even if he were 20, his uncle 30, and his granduncle 50. Property would not be divided equally among brothers but be under the control of the eldest son (primary heir) who would also continue the family sacrifices.[105] Zhu Xi accepted Zhang Zai and Cheng Yi on the *zong*, and in fact in his *Family Rituals* extended these ideas further than they had.[106]

Thus even though on such issues as women's virtues and women's education, Zhu Xi largely copied Sima Guang, there are subtle differences in what the advice meant in context. Sima Guang decried the insidious effects of women's treating their dowries like their private property, but his view of the family, focused as it was on the group that lived together with common property, undermined his own stance. If property were so important to the family, family heads would prefer daughters-in-law with substantial dowries, and those who brought them would have an edge over their sisters-in-law without them. Sima Guang wished to overcome this structural problem by moral education and moral effort: parents-in-law should not be greedy; brides should not be haughty.

The basis for a structural solution to this problem was provided by advocates of the revival of *zong* principles. Cheng Yi had argued for redirecting attention away from the *jia* to the *zong*. In the *zong* women are minor actors. Wives are needed to bear heirs and assist in rites, but the family they came from and the property they bring do not directly effect the *zong*. Indeed, as Zhu Xi pointed out in the *Elementary Learning* (quoting Hu Yuan, 993–1059), it was better for wives to come from families of less standing and wealth so that they would more easily adjust to subordinate positions.[107]

Zhu Xi did not go much beyond Sima Guang with regard to women's property. In his *Family Rituals* he cited several passages from Sima Guang against looking on marriage as a transaction or letting a wife gain undue power because of her private property. He also, like many of his contemporaries, praised women who used their dowries for the sake of their husbands' families. In epitaphs he wrote for wives, Zhu Xi sounds much like Sima Guang in the praise he gave to women who thought in terms of their husbands' patrilineal families and freely handed over their dowries for larger family purposes.[108]

Zhu Xi's disciple Huang Gan (1152–1221), however, did bring out the full implications of combining descent line ideology with Sima Guang's fears of the consequences of allowing women to treat their dowries like private property. Huang Gan was a major disciple of Zhu Xi, author of his biography, and husband of his daughter. While serving as an official, he wrote two legal case decisions that argue that women have weaker claims to their dowries than their husbands or sons do.

The first case concerned a widow née Chen who had married a Xu. After her husband's death she returned to her natal family, leaving the three daughters and one son born of this marriage, but taking the 200 *mu* of dowry fields. Previously her son had taken her to court to try to get the fields back, but the judge had ruled that a son could not sue his mother. On an appeal, Huang Gan reversed the ruling by refocusing the case as a dispute between a son and his mother's brother. He wrote:

> Her father gave the fields to her family [of marriage], thus they are Xu family fields. Even though the property is called dowry, it is Xu family property. How can the Chen family get it? If the Xu family had been without children, then it would be all right for Miss Chen to take the fields, but she has four children and the land should be divided among them.[109]

In this case, Huang Gan recognized the claim of a widow without children to take her dowry when she returns home. However, he insists that land that accompanies a woman on marriage is not the same as a trousseau and the woman is not free to dispose of it as she wishes when she has children.

Huang Gan went even further in circumscribing women's property rights in the other case, which concerned a man who had one son by his wife and two by a concubine. His original family property was assessed a tax of six strings of cash and the fields his wife had brought as dowry also had a tax assessment of six strings, so was presumably of similar size. After the man and his wife died, the original family property was divided among the three sons, but the son of the wife kept his mother's dowry fields. At the time, the younger sons did not dispute it. Sixty years later when their elder brother died, however, they brought their claims to court. They took the case to the county, then three times to the judicial intendant, and then twice to the military commissioner. Most of these officials ruled that the concubine's sons had no claim to the legal mother's dowry, but two thought it should be divided in thirds, and one thought the wife's son should get half and the other two each a quarter. Huang Gan, arguing that dowry becomes husband's property, sided with those who favored dividing it equally.[110] Most of those asked to judge this case apparently recognized that the woman would only have wanted the property to go to her own son and distributed the property the way she would have. Huang Gan challenged the whole idea that a wife's land is something other than her husband's property. In Ming times, the basic premise of Huang Gan's argument was given legal recognition. In the Ming code, widows and most divorcées were explicitly denied any right to take their dowries with them if they returned home or married again.[111]

Although Huang Gan did not develop this line of thinking, one might also note that denying wives any ownership of their dowries could have two further benefits for those influenced by Neo-Confucian writings on women and the family. First, it could dampen the escalation of dowries, as families gave dowries in part to help their daughters; this would be beneficial because the less property diverted into dowries, the more there would be under full control of the family head, and also because it would reduce the tendency to think of marriage as a commercial transaction. Second, weaker claims to their dowries would make it more difficult for widows to remarry.

CONCLUSIONS

In this essay I have only begun to probe the connections between social and intellectual phenomena. I have suggested that Sima Guang's views about women and marriage are best understood as the response of someone vaguely aware that the nexus of women and money confused class and kinship solidarities and created ambiguous and sometimes fragile kinship links. To gain a sense of surety and security in a fluid world, Sima Guang wanted to place people firmly in well-defined roles. Women in the *shidafu* class should be kept far away from the outside world of buying and selling, of entertainment and commercialized sexuality. They should have to throw in their lot with the patriline of their husbands, giving up any economic or social independence, but gaining in return the equally deep loyalty of their sons. Men and women alike should exert moral effort to keep distinctions of rank, function, and role in place. In this essay, I have also tried to show that Sima Guang's views were largely endorsed by Zhu Xi, who also endorsed *zong* principles. With Huang Gan, one sees how this combination of views could further undermine the independence of women by weakening their legal claims to property.

In this essay I have not moved at all to the next set of issues: the social and cultural conditions under which more and more men and women would come to agree with and act on these Song Neo-Confucian views of women, and the social and cultural consequences of such changed understandings. I would like to end, however, by noting that Sima Guang's and Zhu Xi's views were not widely acted on during the Song. Through the end of the Song officials and other educated men, especially perhaps in Hangzhou, were as caught up as ever with courtesans and concubines.[112] Indeed, in this period it was not rare for men to "rent" a concubine for a specified period of years, returning her at the expiration of the contract.[113] Sima Guang's solution to the ambiguities of concubinage – more hierarchy – may have made sense to some, but others, like Yuan Cai (fl. 1140–1195), saw the problems of concubinage as unsolvable.[114] Even in late Song some educated men approved of girls from good families learning poetry,[115] and more and more such girls were getting their feet bound, something still confined to courtesans in Sima Guang's time.[116] Educated men did not necessarily view remarriage of widows as particularly reprehensible. Not only did men like Yuan Cai, largely outside the Cheng-Zhu stream of Neo-Confucianism, take remarriage as normal,[117] but others much closer to Zhu Xi did as well. The daughter of Wei Liaoweng (1178–1237), one of Zhu Xi's best known disciples, apparently remarried.[118] From the late Song judicial case book, *Qingming ji,* it is clear that Huang Gan's approach to women's claims to their dowries was not common in his day. Other judges, even ones with ties to the Neo-Confucian movement, such as Weng Fu and Liu Kezhuang (1187–1269), generally defended the claims of wives and widows to the use and management of their dowries.[119]

Changes in conventional wisdom on these issues probably owe something to the establishment of a Neo-Confucian orthodoxy in the Yuan and early Ming. But they must also owe something to changing social, economic, and political conditions in those centuries.[120]

2   Concubines in Song China*

In a patrilineal and patrilocal Chinese household, women belonged to one of two categories: those born there – daughters – or those brought in from outside – wives, concubines, and maids. This essay concerns the latter category of women, especially concubines, during the Song dynasty (960–1279). The standard Chinese term here translated as concubine was *qie*, a term used since ancient times.[1] Concubines resembled wives (*qi*) in that they were recognized sexual partners of a male family member, expected to bear children by him. They resembled maids (*bi*) in the way they were acquired and the marginality of their kinship status. In traditional China it was illegal and socially disreputable for a man to have more than one wife at a time, but he could have as many concubines as he could afford.[2] In English the term *concubine* also is used for the secondary consorts of emperors, some of very high rank; in Chinese such consorts seldom were called *qie* and they did not share the attributes of *qie* to be discussed in this essay.[3]

The aim of this essay is to make one argument: concubines in Song China should not be thought of as wives, even *secondary wives*. Among the women brought in from outside, concubines fell more to the side of the maids than to that of wives. Observers have overestimated the status of concubines largely because their sons were equal to those of the wife in matters of inheritance. But in China the status of a son did not depend on that of his mother or on the classification of the tie between her and his father.

The view that I am arguing draws on the distinctions made by the anthropologist Jack Goody. In *Production and Reproduction* Goody distinguishes between co-wives, common in African polygynous societies, and concubines, found in many parts of Asia. These concubines were not wives or married with the same ceremonies as wives. He describes such concubinage as institutionalized polycoity to distinguish it from polygyny.[4] In societies with concubinage, wives were married with dowries but concubines were not. Concubines could even be slaves:

* This article was originally published in *Journal of Family History* 11.1 (1986): 1–24. Copyright ©1986 by JAI Press, Inc. Reproduced by permission of Sage Publications.

A free man could acquire a slave girl for the purpose of sexual gratification, just as he could purchase a male or female slave to do all kinds of work inside the home. Such a slave girl retained her servile status but her master was not supposed to sell her, and especially not if she had borne him children. The children of a concubine had the same status as the children of full wives.[5]

Although the fit between Goody's model and the Chinese case is remarkably good, it does not seem to have been picked up (or explicitly rejected) by writers on the Chinese family who still speak of secondary wives and plural marriages.[6] I would therefore like to lend support to Goody's argument by examining concubinage during the Song dynasty.

Concubines, like servants, were more common the richer the family. They were a normal feature of well-to-do Song families, especially families of *shidafu* ("gentlemen and officials"), where perhaps a third had a concubine at some time.[7] The presence of these concubines helps to account for the appearance of large sets of siblings in *shidafu* families.[8] Admittedly *shidafu* constituted only a few percent of the total population in the Song, but almost all those of political or cultural importance at the time were *shidafu*, making their family organization a subject of considerable historical importance. In the literature that touches on Chinese concubines, little has been made of the institutionalized superiority of wives over concubines. Most of the traditional literature relating to concubinage could be classed as romantic, focusing on the love a man could feel toward an attractive young girl.[9] To some modern authorities, the function of concubinage in the Chinese family system was to provide an outlet for romantic impulses, often impossible in marriages arranged by parents.[10] Even the literature critical of concubinage most often concentrates on the plight of the wife who must somehow live with a young concubine her husband has brought home, suppressing any feelings of jealousy or distaste. Yet the jealousy a wife may have felt toward a concubine was never a jealousy for her status. As will be seen below, a concubine had little to fall back on without her master's affection, especially the significant portion who never bore sons, or whose sons were largely taken over by the wife. To be loved may be gratifying, but total dependence on another's affection has obvious drawbacks.

RITUAL STATUS OF CONCUBINES

In the Confucian tradition there was a large literature on the rituals (*li*) of family and kinship. Ritual was taken to include ancestral rites, mourning obligations, patterns of deference and authority, daily courtesies, and life-cycle ceremonies (coming of age, marriage, and funerals). Rules for all of these ritual matters could be found in classical texts, especially the *Li ji* (Record of Ritual) and *Yi li* (Etiquette and Ritual). Both of these texts

進詩寓諷

Figure 2.1 Kou Zhun's concubine singing a song she composed to admonish him.
Source: After SYXJ 8.26a.

reached final form by the first century BC, but their meaning was regularly reinterpreted in commentaries.

Concubinage was assumed in the classics; indeed, the number and ranks of secondary women a noble should have was prescribed in much the same way as carriages or clothing. For Song families, the major problem in using the ritual classics to decide on the correct way to treat concubines was that most of the relevant passages in the classics referred to the concubines of feudal lords and kings. Even passages referring to ordinary gentlemen (*shi*) were difficult to apply because they were phrased in terms of a long-abandoned system of birth-order distinctions among sons.

In the classics concubines were considered sufficiently married to their master so that surname exogamy applied, as it did for wives. From ancient times on, ritual texts repeated the rule that if one were uncertain of the surname of a purchased *qie*, a divination should be made to assure that it was not the same as the master's.[11] Nevertheless, the classics describe no wedding ceremonies to mark the incorporation of a concubine into a home (except in the ancient royal form in which the wife brings the concubines with her, including when possible her own younger sisters or nieces). In line with this lack of a wedding ceremony is the injunction that concubines were not to call their mate "husband" (*fu*) but, rather "master" (*jun*), as would a servant. According to one commentary, this was to reinforce the distinction between concubines and wives.[12] The wives they called "mistress" (*nüjun*). Given that Song manuals for family rites also provide almost no guidelines for ritualizing the introduction of a concubine, it is possible that concubines took up their duties with no more ceremonies than maids. In Sima Guang's (1019–1086) ritual manual, the *Shuyi*, references to concubines mainly concern subservience to their masters and mistresses, such as the rule that they obey their master's or mistress's orders promptly.[13]

Chinese theories of kinship were most elaborate with regard to ancestral rites and mourning obligations. Concubines are hardly mentioned in discussions of ancestral rites, and the references that do exist are conflicting. In one place the *Li ji* states that if a concubine had children, after her death her own sons would make offerings to her, but these offerings were not continued by her grandsons, who only made offerings to their grandfather's wife.[14] According to this passage, then, concubines could not become ancestresses. Yet another passage implies that tablets for concubines were retained, as they were to be put next to the tablet for the grandfather's concubine.[15] The Neo-Confucian philosopher Cheng Yi (1033–1107), who in general favored expanding the ancestral cult to include ancestors earlier prohibited,[16] nevertheless came out strongly against including concubines who were mothers in ancestral rites. He stated that tablets for concubine-mothers are never to be placed in ancestral shrines; such a woman's sons should make offerings to her in a private room.[17]

The Chinese classification of mourning obligations specifies a range of kin each person must mourn and also the circle of those who mourn him or her.

Women who became wives had reduced obligations to their natal kin but mourned nearly all the relatives their husbands did (such as his brothers, uncles, cousins, and their wives and children). These relatives all reciprocated and mourned the wife. The wife's shift in mourning obligations symbolized her transfer of loyalties from one family to another. By contrast, concubines retained their obligations to their natal kin,[18] though in practice they seldom could have fulfilled them all. Their obligations to their master's family were much more circumscribed than were a wife's: concubines mourned their master, their mistress, and the master's children. Only if the concubine bore children did the master and his children reciprocate and also mourn her (though not to the same degree). The mistress did not mourn her under any circumstances. In the case of the master, the difference in degree was extreme: the concubine mourned her master to the highest degree (grade 1a; that is, "three years," actually twenty-five months); he mourned her at the lowest (grade 5; i.e., three months).

A more complicated issue was the mourning a son of a concubine wore for her. In the classics, a father's wife is the "legal mother" and must be honored at a level higher than that of any other woman attached to the father or son, including concubine-mothers, mothers who had been divorced, wet nurses, and foster mothers/governesses. These other women were mourned at relatively low levels out of respect for the legal mother. This is not because a man could mourn only one woman as a mother: if his mother died and his father took another wife, who also died, the son mourned each of them as legal mothers.[19]

The *Yi li* had four passages that Song scholars could use in deciding on a son's mourning for a concubine-mother. One gives mourning for one's mother as grade 1b if one's father was already dead. Another gives it as grade 2 if the father was still alive. A third says "a secondary son (*shuzi*) who is to be his father's successor (*hou*)" mourns the woman who bore him at the lowest (fifth) grade. The fourth gives mourning for a *shumu* (normally defined as a concubine of one's father who has had children) as grade 5.[20] Knowing which sons of concubines were their fathers' successors was complicated; the classics assumed only one son succeeded, but in Song times equal division of property was the rule. Were they all successors, or only the eldest? To handle the problem of sons of concubines who were their father's successors, one Song writer suggested that they follow fifth-grade mourning but also practice "mourning in the heart" (*xinsang*) for three years,[21] as an adopted son did for his natural parents.

A more serious problem was that the classics do not provide enough evidence to be certain whether the son of a concubine should look on her as a *shumu*, therefore wearing only three months of mourning for her, or whether that is a term only his stepbrothers would use. The commentator Zheng Xuan (127–200) took the latter view and offered a compromise grade for the son of a concubine for his own mother.[22] Song legal rulings allowed that if the father commanded a son of a concubine to treat a particular concubine (not necessarily his own birth mother) as a mother, he would mourn her at the same level as a legal mother.[23] However, some Song writers continued to assume that one's mother, if a concubine, was a *shumu*, to be mourned at the lowest grade. For instance, the mourning tables in the late Song reference work *Shilin guangji* gloss *shumu* as follows: "A concubine of the father who has children. The children she bears call her *shumu*. They wear grade 5 duty (*yi*) mourning for her; she wears regular (*zheng*) mourning of grade 2 for them."[24] The eminent philosopher Zhu Xi (1130–1200) disagreed. He argued in a letter that the correspondent was mistaken in thinking his mother was a *shumu* just because she was his father's concubine; she was his mother and he should mourn her for three years.[25]

Part of the problem in these ambiguous cases is the term *mother* in prescriptive texts. Does it always imply "legal mother," or "birth mother," or both? Even though Zhu Xi thought that "birth mother" was implied, there was ample legal precedent for assuming only "legal mother." In cases of honorary titles that officials could petition to have granted to their wives, mothers, grandmothers, and great-grandmothers, the law explicitly stated that these honors were not for concubines. Indeed, it was a punishable offense to ask for a title for a woman who was "not ritually married as a proper wife" (*fei li hun zheng shi*).[26] In 1017, however, it was granted that titles could be given to birth mothers when the father was dead and there was no living legal mother or legal stepmother.[27] In other words, once those a concubine served as master or mistress were dead, her status as mother could gain ritual priority over her status as a servitor.

Did the ritual marginality of concubines matter in actual social life? I have seen no evidence that men were troubled by the inability of their concubines to play a larger role in family rituals. Sons, however, did at times object to the limitations placed on the ways they could honor their concubine-mothers, and the Song trend seems to have been to allow them greater leeway in this regard. What concubines themselves thought is a matter solely for conjecture.

LEGAL STATUS OF CONCUBINES

In the legal code of the Tang (618–906), much of which was copied verbatim into its Song successor, the *Song xingtong*, many of the ritual distinctions drawn in the classics were given force of law. As in the classics, rules of exogamy and incest were largely the same for wives and concubines.[28] Moreover, a concubine was considered sufficiently married to her master so that if anyone else had sexual relations with her, the crime was classed as adultery, not fornication.[29] In most other matters, however, wives and concubines were treated differently. Above all, it was a major offense to make a concubine into a wife, or vice versa.[30] This law, although probably not enforced, does seem to reflect social attitudes. In the Song it was treated as a serious breach of social ethics to promote a concubine to a wife.[31]

Part of the desire to keep a strict separation between wives and concubines probably derives from feelings of class and status hierarchy. Confusing wife and concubine was like confusing lord and servitor. In numerous anecdotes men are shocked to find a daughter or wife of an official reduced to the status of concubine. To rectify the situation they collect a dowry so that woman can be married in a more appropriate fashion. For instance, when one man discovered that the girl he had bought as a concubine to accompany his daughter on her marriage was the child of an official, he declared, "How can I bear to place her among the ranks of those who take orders," and he arranged a marriage for her before his own daughter was married.[32]

In assessing penalties in criminal law, concubines stood between wives and maids. It was less serious for a family head to kill a maid than to kill a concubine; it was more serious for a concubine to injure a relative of her master than for a wife to do so, and so on.[33] In the Tang there had been a real gap in status between concubines and maids (*bi*). According to Tang code, if a maid bore a son by the master she could be "freed" (*fang*) and promoted to concubine.[34] In other words, Tang code still saw *bi* as female slaves who needed to be "freed" for their status to change.

This line between *qie* and *bi* was much blurred in practice during the Song, in part because *bi* were not really slaves, but bondservants whose parents might retain more rights over them than did the parents of "married" *qie*. As a consequence, writers often used *biqie* as a compound term meaning lower-status women in the home, and they might even use the terms *bi* and *qie* nearly interchangeably.[35] In theory, of course, *qie* were recognized sexual partners, expected to bear children, and *bi* were not. However, masters not infrequently had sexual relationships with maids without making them *qie*, so sexual intimacy did not provide a hard-and-fast dividing line.[36]

Socially, people recognized status differences among concubines that the law did not recognize. The highest level would be the "housekeeper" concubine taken after a wife had died. Men who treasured the memory of their wives and did not wish to violate it by remarrying normally took concubines to manage household affairs. Sometimes a relatively high-status concubine would be called a "side room" (*ceshi*) or "rear quarters" (*houfang*), stressing her role as a companion and sexual partner. The courts did not recognize these distinctions, however. This is brought out in a complex legal decision recorded by Liu Kezhuang (1187–1269). He mentioned that two women were not considered of equivalent status by family members, one managing household affairs even during her master's lifetime, the other (belonging to her master's son) looked down on by her as a concubine (*qieying*). However, since neither had been ritually married (*fei li hun*), neither could be considered a wife.[37]

From a concubine's point of view, probably the most important difference in legal rights between her and a wife were her rights as a "widow." On the death of the husband, a widowed wife had certain legal and ritual safeguards. No other male in the family could claim her as a mate, or keep her from using the family property to support her children, or stop her from adopting an heir for her husband. Her natal family could and often did intervene in her affairs. After all, they had not sold her, but had married her with a dowry.[38] A concubine was different. After her master's death, stepsons might drive her away or pension her off.[39] According to the law, a concubine was not to be taken over by a close relative of her former master (a somewhat narrower circle than for a wife), but it seems to have shocked people less when this happened than when a wife met a similar fate.[40] Moreover, a wife could largely take over a concubine's children, giving the latter little stake in the family. And if no wife survived and there were no male heirs, a concubine does not seem to have had the right to appoint a posthumous heir.[41]

MARKETS AND BROKERS

As striking as the ritual and legal distinctions between wives and concubines were, one could imagine that they meant little in practice. After all, the rituals and even the legal code refer to distinctions between wives' sons and concubines' sons that do not seem to have been important in social life on any regular basis. To make the case that these distinctions concerning concubines were important in social life, I will examine the differences in the ways wives and concubines entered families. The marriage ceremonies by which wives were incorporated into families involved intermediaries, formal documents, exchange of gifts, an engagement period, and feasting.[42] In most cases the families of the husband and wife were social equals. By contrast, concubines entered families through a market for female labor, one that seems to bear many similarities to the market in existence in China during the past century.[43] Reflecting the ambiguity of their social and familial position, the acquisition of concubines was referred to as "taking them in marriage" (*qu*), "taking them in" (*na*), and, most commonly, as "buying" them (*mai*). Usually these arrangements were for an indefinite term (lifetime), but sometimes only for specified periods of a few years.

Much of the evidence about the acquisition of concubines during Song times comes from literary anecdotes. There are dozens – probably hundreds – of references to concubines in anecdotes about literary men or about events that occurred in homes. If the focus of this essay were on men's erotic fantasies or their images of concubines as victims of wives, I would need to be acutely sensitive to the literary purposes of the anecdotes used as evidence. But since the incidental detail in anecdotes about brokers, contracts, and lines of authority almost certainly reflects current practice, I cite them here without much hesitation.[44]

In the Song, the most highly specialized market for concubines was in the capitals, especially in Hangzhou during the Southern Song (1127–1279).

The *Mengliang lu* (Dreams of Splendor), after discussing brokers who handled male laborers, managers, and shop assistants, discussed the female equivalent: "There are official and private female brokers (*yasao*) to assist officials or rich families who wish to buy a concubine (*chongqie*), a singer, a dancing girl, a female cook, a seamstress, or a coarse or fine maid. They bring in and line up the girls and women and one merely points to have one of them step down."[45] Thus concubines are presented as the top stratum in a market that went down to coarse maids.

Writing in the late Song, Liao Yingzhong gave a similar picture:

> Lower ranking households in the capital do not put a premium on having sons, but treasure each daughter born as though she were a jewel. As she grows up, they teach her an art in accordance with her natural talents, so that she will be ready to be chosen by some gentleman as a companion (*yushi*). A variety of names are used: attendant, helper, waitress, seamstress, front room person, entertainer, laundress, Qin player, chess player, and cook, all of which are kept separate. The cook is the lowest rank and yet only the very rich or high ranking are able to employ one.[46]

These descriptions of the availability of highly trained girls pertain to what would be called the luxury side of the market in concubines. There is adequate confirming evidence that gentlemen in the capital who sought accomplished girls could find them. Many concubines, like courtesans, could read, compose poetry, sing, and play musical instruments. In one anecdote, in late Song Hangzhou an official who sought a concubine both beautiful and accomplished in all the arts found no one to his satisfaction after days of searching. Finally he found a beautiful girl who, questioned on her accomplishments, reported her only talent as warming wine. His companions laughed, but he tested her and was so impressed with the consistency in the temperature of the wine that he took her on.[47]

This emphasis on refined accomplishments, however, should not lead one to imagine that concubines regularly came from educated families that had fallen on hard times; as mentioned above, men seem to have been able to recognize at first glance a girl from a *shidafu* family. Rather, as Liao Yingzhong mentioned in the passage above, girls from lower-class families were given special training to make them more marketable. Their training associated them with courtesans, and men do seem to have looked on talented concubines as private courtesans. They might even use them to entertain their guests. Yuan Cai, writing in 1178, warned that teaching maids and concubines to entertain guests could prove dangerous: if the women were of striking beauty or superior intelligence, "there is the danger that such a woman will arouse feelings of lust in some evil guest," leading to disastrous consequences.[48]

The lower side – and undoubtedly much larger share – of the market in female labor supplied concubines and maids who were needed to do household work and perhaps also produce heirs. Wives might well make the purchase, and the women acquired were generally under the supervision of the mistress of the house (unless they were acquired to take over the role of supervising the maids after the wife had died). This market was by no means concentrated in the capital or a few large cities. It is never described in glowing terms, probably because the practice of buying and selling people always had unappealing associations to Chinese writers. Thus, authors wrote mostly about its unsavory side, especially the practices of "enticement" and kidnapping. A twelfth-century gazetteer of Fuzhou, Fujian, records the attempt of the prefect in 1099 to suppress this practice. The prefect reported that people from neighboring prefectures often came in and with only a little capital set themselves up as "brokers in people" (*shengkou ya*). They would tell families that a girl was needed as a wife or an adopted child, enticing them to turn over a daughter or maid. The girl or woman then would be hid for a few days, after which she would be packed off to some distant place to be resold. Even if the family brought an accusation before the government when they discovered the trickery, a search would be unsuccessful, and they would never learn the whereabouts of the girl, or even whether or not she was alive.[49]

Outright kidnapping also is often mentioned.[50] It, of course, was completely illegal, as opposed to enticing, which may have involved the parents' or master's written agreement to something they did not fully understand. In one collection of didactic tales, a man who had made a living by kidnapping and enticing in the end suffered the retribution of a wasting disease.[51]

Brokers were not all kidnappers, and they served some important functions. Yuan Cai said their use was necessary in any purchase of a maid or concubine but argued none the less that the girl acquired should be closely questioned about her background. If it turned out that she had been kidnapped, the buyer should be ready to return her to her family and certainly not give her back to the broker.[52]

The existence of kidnappers and others who tried to trick people into giving up girls or women suggests a strong market demand for menial women, one that would have attracted "sellers" and had an effect on the availability of women for marriage or employment. An economically depressed area might respond to this market and "export" women, unless it became so depressed that female infanticide led to a severe shortage of women in the area.[53] If an oversupply of girls in an area kept the price low, brokers would be attracted to move girls to areas where prices were high. At the same time, in places where demand was strong and prices high, families would be drawn into the market voluntarily, as seems to have happened in Hangzhou. Forms of male servitude varied regionally during the Song in line with economic organization.[54] It is likely that the market for females of various statuses also varied regionally, although the data are not as clear.

The consequences of this complex market for female labor are likely to have been felt at many levels. Studies of more recent Chinese society have shown how subtle changes in the preferences for disposing of daughters can affect the supply of women available for different forms of marriage or employment, and this is likely also to have happened in the Song.[55] Another consequence of the great demand for serving women was that girls and younger women never posed a welfare problem. If destitute, they, or their closest relatives, could find someone willing to buy them as maids or concubines.[56]

Why would a poor farmer or city-dweller be reluctant to sell his daughter as a concubine to a rich man who could provide her a life of physical comfort? There seem to be two main reasons: first, it was more respectable for him to marry her to someone of his own social status; and second, it was widely recognized that whatever comfort she might start with, a concubine had none of the security of a wife and could end up mistreated.[57]

Within a family, wives clearly came from a higher social stratum than did concubines. Did concubines come from higher social strata than maids? I have found no evidence to imply that they did, since there seems to have been a single market for both. Rather, whether a girl would be bought as a maid or a concubine seems to have depended on her attractiveness and her mastery of the arts of entertainment.

CONTRACTS AND LEGAL OBLIGATIONS

One of the services brokers performed was to prepare a contract specifying terms of agreement between buyer and seller and to witness the transaction. The importance of this intermediating function can be seen in the cases where an agreement was initially made between principals speaking to each other in person, yet they still called in a broker. For instance, a woman famine victim was asked if she would like to stay at an official's house as a concubine. When she agreed, saying she was too hungry to walk further, the official called in a female broker (*nü guai*) to write up a contract.[58]

Contracts specified the "body price" (*shenqian*) of a concubine. This price can be seen as a hybrid between advanced wages and a bride-price. The size of the body price depended on market factors, attractive and accomplished girls getting much more than others. Figures I have encountered range from 140 strings, to 300, 400, 900, and 1000.[59] The last one was for a 22-year-old girl good at music, calligraphy, and painting.

No complete contract for a maid or concubine dating from the Song has been found. The closest we have are two slightly different sample contracts in Yuan encyclopedias for popular reference for hiring out a daughter to work as a concubine. The shorter one is translated below:

Model Form for Pawning the Services of a Daughter

X, of such-and-such a place, has a daughter of his own named Sister ————, aged ———— years, who has never been engaged to anyone. Now, for the sake of daily food, X has asked Y to be a go-between. X voluntarily sends his daughter to work in the household of Z as a concubine (*qie*). He has received ＿＿ value of presents. The girl hired out is genuinely his own and was not enticed away from someone else. There are no obstacles to this arrangement in the law. If something of that sort should occur, X will do what needs to be done and will not involve the master. Should something happen to the girl while she is in the master's home, it is her fate, and will not provide a pretext for reopening the negotiations. This contract is prepared as evidence of our agreement.[60]

The other sample contract contains some differences: there the transaction does not involve "pawning"; specific mention is made that there is no time limit (*buli nianxian*); the mother's consent is listed; and room is given to list the presents in jewelry, cloth, and cash.[61]

In both contracts the language of marriage is employed, such as "go-between" and "presents." Although the implication is that the girl will be taken to do household work, she is not called a *bi*, probably because the master's house preferred to take her for life instead of a fixed time period and to cut off any residual control by her parents. (In the Song, contracts for *bi* were not supposed to be for more than ten years.)[62] The term *dian* ("pawn" or "mortgage") in the contract quoted would imply that the girl's parents could get her back by repaying the amount given to them when they turned her over, but no specific mention is made of when or how they would do this, and probably redemption was not anticipated.[63] Passages in the *Yuan dian zhang* report that in several areas from Song times on there had been a bad practice of "pawning services" (*dianyong* or *diangu*) of males and females for specified numbers of years; it was even reported that in some areas of south China husbands might "pawn the services" of their wives to be other men's wives or concubines, and that when the three or five years were up, the women were not always returned to their husbands.[64]

Anthropologists who have discussed bride-prices (or bride-wealth) have seen them as an exchange for certain rights over the woman, such as the right to her labor and to any children she may bear.[65] Compared to the exchanges of gifts involved in marrying, the purchase of a concubine was one-sided and explicit. Did the purchaser as a consequence gain greater rights over the woman? Phrased this way, the major difference is that a master acquired the right to expel or even resell a concubine at will, which he could not so easily do to a wife.[66] Another way to put this is that a wife, who had been married by ritual, had to be treated according to ritual, but a concubine did not.

The other side of the issue of rights is that of the obligations the master incurred in taking a concubine. We can probably assume he was expected to keep her warm and fed. A more interesting question is whether he had any obligations toward her parents concerning how he or his heirs might dispose of her if she were no longer needed. Could she be resold without informing her parents? Would the master be expected to inform her parents if they moved away or she died? There are anecdotes showing cases where a concubine maintained communication with her parents,[67] and other ones where she did not.[68] The overall impression is that the sense of obligation was weak and people selling their daughters as concubines had to anticipate the possibility of never hearing from them again.

Because contracts without time limits gave almost complete control to the master, it is difficult to think of a situation that could be called breach of contract on his part. A contract of this sort could be challenged, however, if the "selling" party did not really have full rights to dispose of her; for instance, in one case a woman allowed herself to be sold without mentioning that she had a husband. This husband took the master to court, with some limited success (the judge said that if the husband reimbursed the master, he could have his wife back, but the master ignored the ruling).[69]

So far I have been discussing concubines who, like wives, were acquired for their lifetimes (or "without a time limit"). As the passage in the *Yuan dian zhang* cited earlier described, concubines were not always acquired for their lifetimes, with the master gaining all rights over them. Not only in the muddy area of pawning wives, but also in the Hangzhou luxury market, concubines could be acquired on multiyear contracts like those of maids, with parents reserving rights to make later arrangements for them. In one story in Hong Mai's (1123–1202) *Yijian zhi*, an official in the capital awaiting assignment convinced a friend to accompany him while he went out to buy two concubines. At the broker's he found that the youngest and most talented girl had a price of only eighty strings while the other two were 400 or 500 strings. On asking the broker about the difference in price, the men were told that the term for the youngest was almost up, only half a year remaining, while the other two could be taken on full three-year contracts.[70] The use of three-year contracts for accomplished concubines is also recorded in the case of Silver Flower, to be discussed below.

Limited-term contracts did impose on the master the obligation to return the woman. Given the greater wealth and social rank of the person acquiring the concubine, it is easy to imagine that the terms of a contract would be ignored if they were inconvenient. The *Yuan dian zhang* pointed to this problem in pawning wives. In his *Precepts for Social Life* (1178), Yuan Cai urged as a moral issue returning maids when their terms were over, taking for granted that many men would not bother.[71] On the other hand, such actions were abuses and could be taken to court.[72]

The ways in which concubines and maids were bought and sold suggest that, taken together, they were the female equivalent of bondservants (*pu*). Most discussions of bondservants in Chinese history restrict themselves to males, since female service was mostly domestic service and thus has little to do with broad characterizations of labor relations in Chinese society.[73] Female service has seemed less an issue because of its family setting. As Watson pointed out, because males and females had different positions in the family system, servile women could be incorporated into families with considerably greater flexibility than could males.[74] However, Song authors often spoke of male and female bondservants as a single type of person,[75] and there were undoubted similarities between concubines and male bondservants.

First, contractual language was similar. In the Yuan encyclopedia cited earlier, the similarities in language are striking; even the assimilation to kinship roles recurs, with males being called "adopted sons" instead of "concubines." Second, the legal consequences of entering into the status were comparable. Just as a man who had the status of *pu* was inferior to his master in most legal matters, a concubine had a distinctly lower legal status not only to the master, but also to the wife. Third, in the case of both *pu* and *qie* it was possible for masters to sell them to third parties if their contracts were still in effect. This certainly was a major disability, in comparison to more fully incorporated family members such as wives and adopted sons.

Nevertheless, differences between concubines and male bondservants are also significant. First of all, there is no hereditary concubinage. The daughters of concubines do not become concubines. As Goody noted, the children of concubines seem to have suffered few disabilities compared to the children of wives, because much of the point of taking concubines was to produce heirs. Second, on the male side one could posit generally that the longer the term of required service, the greater the inferiority involved: hereditary service was lowest, lifetime was considered inferior to fixed-term, and so on. On the female side, however, this relationship does not hold: wives are committed for their lifetime and concubines also could be without any loss of status. Maids, who clearly ranked lower in status, were much more likely to be on limited-term agreements.

CONCUBINES' SUBORDINATION TO WIVES

In establishing the level at which a concubine mourned her mistress, the *Yi li* says, "A *qie's* service to her mistress (*nüjun*) is equivalent to a wife's service to her parents-in-law." The Tang (618–906) commentary adds, "A *qie* serves the mistress in the same way a minister serves a ruler.... A concubine serves the legal wife; therefore she calls the legal wife 'mistress.'"[76] This long-established tradition that a concubine was both a servant to the wife and a sexual partner of the husband persisted into the Song. It was manifested in several ways. Occasionally, at least, the concubine entered the house as the wife's maid. There are cases where fathers bought concubines for their daughters to accompany them on their marriage.[77] This was an ancient practice, and may well have appealed to Song men as a way to reduce jealousy. Presumably for the first few years the *qie* was the wife's personal maid. Should the wife bear no sons, she could offer her husband this maid, who was already tied to her as a personal subordinate. In some instances, at least, it is clear that this *qie* was not expected to be sexually intimate with the master from the start.[78]

In one case a girl had grown up largely in the family of her young mistress, then followed her mistress on marriage. After her mistress died and the master remarried, she stayed on as the master's concubine.[79] Wives could also purchase *qie*, either on the request of their husbands or on their own initiative.[80] *Qie* could even be given to wives: in one case because a wife was burdened by household chores and her husband was poor, her brother's family acquired a 12-*sui* girl to do the housework for her; this girl eventually became the husband's concubine and at 28 *sui* bore a son.[81] *Qie* who started as wives' maids are likely to have had a different relationship with their mistress than ones selected by husbands as private courtesans.

In the Song, it seems to have been a widely held assumption that wives would be jealous of concubines whom their husbands favored and that the wives might well beat them or otherwise mistreat them. There certainly is anecdotal evidence of wives' cruelty to concubines.[82] Husbands might try to protect concubines they loved by isolating them from their wives. Yuan Cai wrote that "some men with jealous wives set up maids or concubines in separate houses," but warned against this practice because of the likelihood that the concubine would establish an illicit relationship and the master would end up rearing a child who was not his own.[83] Another method husbands could use was to take the concubine with them when they traveled, leaving the wife behind.[84] A man might even be nervous about leaving his concubine at home, afraid of what his wife might do to her in his absence.[85]

From an institutional point of view, it is crucial to ask why these men did not merely command their wives to leave their concubines alone. The answer, I think, is that however much the men disliked rancor in the women's quarters, they accepted the principle of the wife's authority there. One could remove the concubine from the wife's sphere of control but could not challenge her control in that sphere. This situation is parallel to the mother–wife situation. A man might love his wife and hate to watch his mother maltreat her, but he did not challenge his mother's right to give the orders. Rather, he tried to soften his mother's attitude, or take his wife with him when he traveled, and so on.

Because the mistress had considerable authority over a concubine, whether or not there was a mistress made a big difference in the life of a concubine. A concubine with no mistress might well be treated like a wife. A concubine with a mistress not only had to be personally subservient to her, but she also could lose most of the control of her children. In epitaphs for wives, it is often said that they reared the children of concubines.[86] There is never any implication that one had to ask the concubine for permission to take over care of her children. Such acts are presented as indications of the maternal love and kindness of the wife, but it is easy to imagine that a concubine could have resented the act deeply and seen her own position as fundamentally undermined by it. And for good reason: if the master/

husband died, leaving a childless wife and a concubine who had borne a son, the wife would be in charge.

In one case mentioned in the Song history, a concubine who was the mother of the heir drove off the childless widow, who became mentally ill as a result. If the roles had been reversed, this action would have been taken as routine. However, for the wife to be expelled was not acceptable and the judge intervened, restoring her property and as a consequence her mental health.[87] In other words, being a mother to the succeeding children gave the concubine no rights in the family if there was a wife. Even if there was no wife, she could be recognized as a trustee for her young children only if she lived with them.[88] This qualification seems to have recognized that concubines' children were not always under their care.

CONCUBINES AS MOTHERS

Despite all the evidence that concubines were a common feature of gentlemen's homes, their role as mothers only rarely entered the written record. Concubines had a higher status *vis-à-vis* their sons than *vis-à-vis* their masters, yet sons seem to have been more reluctant to mention them in writing than were their fathers. Perhaps this was because as children the sons had learned to look on the concubine as much like a wet nurse, a menial woman with whom they had a special intimacy but who was not a person of any importance to outsiders.

Sons of concubines often must have found their situation confusing or stressful. A concubine's son had to show filial duty to two women who often did not get along. Moreover, his father may have looked on his birth mother as a courtesan and his legal mother may have looked on her as a maid. Analyzing the psychological consequences of all of this is, unfortunately, not possible from the available sources. Certainly the child of a concubine could grow up suffering no obvious disabilities, social or psychological. Han Qi (1008–1075), one of the most prominent officials of the Northern Song, was the son of a concubine. His father Han Guohua (957–1011) had four sons by his wife, the third of whom was born in 989. By that time he had probably already taken his concubine, née Hu (968–1030). In epitaphs for a concubine it is common to suggest that her ancestry was not as lowly as her eventual status indicated, and to explain how she was reduced to such circumstances. According to Han Qi's epitaph for his birth mother, her father died when she was young and she followed her mother on her mother's remarriage; when the family her mother married into got into political trouble, she was left with no one to depend on. In the Han household she bore two sons and a daughter. Qi's father died when he was 3, and his concubine-mother stayed on almost twenty years longer. Writing many years later in 1045, Qi said that his legal mother cared for him just as she did the children she bore. Whenever his birth mother beat him, she would run over to protect him, so angry at his birth mother she would not speak to her the rest of the day. Thus, Han Qi seems to have been reared by both women, much like someone cared for by both a mother and a grandmother.

Long after all three of his parents had died, Qi reburied them in a new family graveyard. He then took the bold step of burying his concubine-mother near the tomb of his father and legal mother as an "attending" burial. He claimed no disrespect to his parents was involved because in all matters (such as the quality of the coffin) the burial of his birth mother was on a level lower than those for his parents. He realized others would see his act as a violation of ritual, and he offered as a justification the contention that rituals are intended to express feelings and are not "descended from Heaven."[89]

Han Qi's birth mother's status was enhanced by her longevity. Yet just because a concubine-mother outlived the father and legal mother did not assure that a son's relationship with her would be uncomplicated. This is seen from Fang Hui's (1227–1307) testimony, which provides a good counter to Han Qi's. Fang Hui's father Zhuo (1174–1229) had a daughter by his wife, but even after she was grown and married he had no sons. In 1221 he adopted a neighbor's child to be his heir. Three years later Fang Zhuo was banished to Guangdong. He left his wife behind and on arriving took a concubine, who later bore Hui. Hui never met his legal mother, who died when he was 2 *sui*. His father died later that year. The next year a friend of the father sent the concubine and her son back to the Fang home, where an uncle took them in. This uncle also died within the year. Another uncle, who had taken in the adopted son, then set up the concubine, the two boys, and a single male servant on a 30-*mu* plot, where they just managed to get by.

When Hui was 10, one of his uncles went down to Guangdong to retrieve what remained of Hui's father's property and arrange for the return of his body to Anhui; the property was barely enough to pay for the reburial. Five years later Hui's concubine-mother was forced to leave and go elsewhere as either a wife or concubine (the phrase used literally means she was forced to give up her desire to remain a chaste widow). Hui, even decades later, recalled the bitterness he felt when he was unable to stand up to his uncle and uncle's wife on this matter. Although Fang Hui does not say so explicitly, it is probable his uncle received money for turning over Hui's mother. Whether related to these experiences or not, Fang Hui was unusual among Chinese men of his social class in never taking a wife; according to his own report he begat seven sons and four daughters by a succession of concubines.[90] His predilections for concubines and maids led contemporaries to criticize him for dissolute ways.[91]

Fang Hui's case could hardly have been typical, but sons of concubines did face a greater prospect of separation from their mothers than did other children, especially when the concubine was taken by an official while on a temporary assignment. For instance, Zhu Shouchang was given a biography in the *Song shi* among the "Filially Righteous" because for years he searched for his birth mother. His father had taken a concubine while in office in Jingzhao and had left her there, pregnant, when he returned home. She sent the child to him after two or three years, after which no contact was maintained. When grown up, Zhu made inquiries everywhere he went in attempts to locate her; finally he resigned his post and announced that he would not return home until he found her. When he did, she was over 70, married with several children, all of whom he invited to stay with him. His story evoked so much sympathy that several poets celebrated it in poems.[92] A similar story is told of Liu Guan who, however, attended to his legal mother until she died before setting out to search for his birth mother, who had left his home soon after his birth. When he finally found her she was the concubine of a rich man.[93]

THE CASE OF THE SILVER FLOWER

To supplement the composite view of Song concubinage given above, I will describe one case in which the arrangements are known in some detail. It is not a typical case – the concubine was taken for a limited term, and she bore no children. If anything, it was one in which the woman had many protections and advantages, so in a sense it provides an example of the best the institution had to offer from the perspective of the woman involved.

Silver Flower's career as a concubine is known entirely from a letter written by the Hanlin Academician Gao Wenhu (1134–1212). Gao Wenhu was of an established official family, a nephew of the Confucian scholar Gao Kang (1097–1153) and father of Gao Sisun (ca. 1160–ca. 1230), also a scholar and official. The letter, given to Gao Wenhu's concubine to use as evidence, was written in the eighth month of 1210 and recorded several decades later by Zhou Mi (1232–1308) in his *Guixin zazhi*.[94]

In the letter, Gao Wenhu reported that his wife had died in 1163 and that for twenty-seven years he had neither remarried nor kept a concubine (*xu qie*) for fear of the consequences such an action would have for his children (who would thereby come to be treated as stepchildren). It was only in the first month of 1200, when he was 66, that he acquired a literate and musically accomplished concubine "to wait on (him) and prepare [his] medicines." This girl, surnamed He, was taken on a three-year contract with a stipulated wage of one bushel of rice a month, which her mother regularly collected. After she arrived, Gao Wenhu named her Silver Flower, a literary term for "snowflake."

The duties of Silver Flower, Gao reported, were to prepare his medicines, tidy up, and check up on him. He said she often made his morning and evening meals, and she took care of his clothes: washing, patching, and getting them ready for each change of season. If at night he had a coughing spell or could not sleep, she would get up, stir up the fire, and decoct some medicine for him. She also could read and would help him look things up and answer letters. After she had been with him a year, Gao Wenhu retired from office and went to Huizhou, where his son was an official. He took Silver Flower with him and they spent two very agreeable years there, visiting scenic places day after day. After that they moved to his permanent home in Mingzhou (Ningbo).

Soon after this move Silver Flower's contracted term of employment was up and her mother came to negotiate a new contract. She reported to Gao Wenhu that Silver Flower wanted to stay on. The mother did not ask for an increase in the old wages, but instead of coming to collect them every month as before, she wished to let them accumulate, presumably toward a dowry. Gao Wenhu readily agreed to the new arrangement.

Another three years went by, and Gao Wenhu thought more should be done for Silver Flower. He had long before turned over daily management of the family finances to his son, and so the easiest way to reward her was to give her something valuable. He tried to get her to take his silver utensils, washpans, spittoons, and so on, weighing over 100 ounces, but she refused. When her mother again returned to negotiate a new contract, Silver Flower's wages were set at 100 strings of cash a year, an increase of about 50 percent. Gao considered this her due because of her increased age and experience. The wages for the third term also were to be allowed to accumulate.

Gao Wenhu was attached enough to Silver Flower to want to see that her money really would be available for her when she left. The problem, he reported, was that he "kept not a coin by [his] side, and for expenses made withdrawals from the family treasury. Yet [every time he asked for money] there were always excuses, complications, and refusals." To escape this he ordered the sale of 600 bushels of grain from one of the family's estates, but when fifty or sixty had been sold, the monk in charge of this estate said that Gao Wenhu's son and the latter's wife wanted to sell the grain to get capital for a granary. Later his son came to placate him, telling him that he could get whatever he wanted from the family treasury, even the 1,000 strings that Wenhu said he needed. Still, every time Gao Wenhu went to the treasury he was told that it was short of money. Finally, after another two years, Gao again ordered the sale of estate grain, bringing in a total of 1,080 strings, 800 of which was to be for Silver Flower, following the agreement of 1206.

According to Gao Wenhu, Silver Flower had expressed a wish to remain in the Gao home as a widowed concubine after her master's death. Gao Wenhu knew that the circumstances in his family would not allow such an arrangement, so in 1210 he decided that it was time for her to return home. As a conclusion to his letter, he summed up the justification for giving Silver Flower 1,000 strings of cash. First, the money was his: he had earned it himself and his son had not contributed to it. Second, she deserved it: in her eleven years of serving him, Silver Flower had never been sick or received any money from the family treasury, or interfered in any way with family finances. Even her clothes he had supplied from his own funds (*ben fang*). Thus 1,000 strings for a dowry was not excessive. Should some jealous person make a wild accusation, Silver Flower should present this letter as evidence and hope for a wise judge.

Much could be drawn from this lengthy letter about the consequences to family harmony of bringing in a concubine in old age. Here, however, I will concentrate on the contractual relationship. Silver Flower was brought in on terms quite unlike the sample contracts cited. Her first contract was for three years, and it was renegotiated twice, most of the money accumulating toward a dowry. Even if a broker was used in arranging the original contract, her mother returned in person subsequently.

What rights did Gao Wenhu acquire over Silver Flower? What ones did her mother retain? First, at the seemingly trivial level, Gao Wenhu gave Silver Flower her name. This act, it seems to me, symbolizes the personal social inferiority of maids and concubines. Men did not rename their wives, but they regularly renamed maids and concubines. The names of concubines not infrequently contained the character *nu*: "slave."[95] Like Gao Wenhu, some literary men chose literary names for their concubines, and some chose decidedly capricious names for them, such as the poet Xin Jiqi (1140–1207), who gave each of his two concubines their surnames as their personal names. They were called Tian Tian and Qian Qian.[96]

Second, and quite explicitly, Gao Wenhu gained the services of Silver Flower as a companion, nurse, and maid. These services also would be provided by a wife, and there is no indication that Silver Flower did anything that a wife would not have done in this family.

Third, Gao Wenhu probably obtained rights to sexual intimacy with Silver Flower, although he implies that he did not make use of them. There is some ambiguity here. On the one hand, Gao Wenhu says he was old and no longer interested in sensual pleasures (*shengse*), and Silver Flower bore no children in eleven years. On the other hand, the animosity of his son would seem to suggest that other members of the family thought the old man was besotted with love for her (and likely to squander the family fortune on her).

What rights did Silver Flower's mother retain? The main ones were to reclaim her, to renegotiate her wages, and to make her eventual marriage arrangements. In a sense Silver Flower was sent out to accumulate her dowry so that eventually she could be married out in a regular fashion. One might wonder whether she was actually to be married; perhaps this was a euphemism and her mother would instead pocket the 1,000 strings and sell her again. If this had been her intention, however, there is no obvious reason why she would have let Silver Flower's body price accumulate instead of asking for it in advance. Moreover, the greatest market demand for maids and concubines was for relatively young ones – after eleven years Silver Flower would not be worth as much. Finally, there is evidence that women who had been concubines were sometimes married out with substantial dowries. For instance, a petty trader whose wife and son died in an epidemic learned that a concubine of the Wang family was to be married out with a dowry of 300 strings. Greedy for the money, the trader took her as a successor wife (*jishi*).[97]

In Silver Flower's case certain aspects of her contract seem to have been treated more seriously than others. Her mother did come back after three years, and it is definitely implied that Silver Flower could have left at that time if her mother had wanted her back. On the other hand, Gao Wenhu was not at all convinced that his son would pay up if he were to die suddenly. This, it would seem from anecdotal literature, was the crucial weakness in the position of concubines, especially ones who did not bear children. They depended on the favor of their master, and if he died they could not count on generous treatment from surviving family members. Even masters who tried to provide for them in wills might find their plans upset by sons who did not believe a concubine had any right to family property.[98]

If the relationship between Gao Wenhu and Silver Flower was a chaste one of nurse and invalid, why was she called a concubine and not a maid? After all, she was not considered "married" and was to be returned after a limited period. I think the major reason Silver Flower was called a *qie* instead of a *bi* is that *qie* had a higher social rank, both within the family and without. In the family, for instance, a concubine could give orders to a *bi*, and it was a more serious offense for a *bi* to strike a concubine than vice versa. It is probably because of these status issues that the accomplished young companions to literary men are almost always called *qie*. This notion of concubines as refined maids seems to have overcome somewhat at least the conception of them as spouses. The best evidence of this lies in references to the ability of concubines to "take their leave." For instance, while in political disfavor, Su Dongpo reported that over a four- to five-year period, his concubines "took their leave" (*ciqu*) one after the other, only one accompanying him to the south.[99] Wives certainly could not leave freely like this.

CONCLUSION

All of the evidence given above concerning concubines comes from a particular historical period, the Song dynasty. Yet most of the features of Song concubinage described here were present in other periods of Chinese history as well. A few of these continuities are:

1. In fiction, the kidnapping, enticing, and sale of women appears often, as does the practice of wives or concubines offering their maids to their husbands as quasi-concubines.
2. The market in concubines was strong in many areas, a common source being girls whose terms as maid were up.[100]
3. Contracts continued to be commonly used for the purchase of concubines, often with much the same language found in Song and Yuan ones.[101] One fictional story written in the twentieth century even refers

to a contract for pawning a wife to be another man's concubine for three years.[102]

4. Concubines continued to be taken without any of the ceremonies used in marriages.[103]

5. In the rules for family behavior included in nineteenth-century genealogies, the status distinctions between wives and concubines are regularly stressed. Women taken as concubines are classed in all matters below the wives of their generation.[104] Moreover, "Some rules do not permit their members to marry off their daughters as concubines in return for a sum of money as it is a degradation of the girls and a humiliation for the clan."[105]

6. The relative undesirability of becoming a concubine remained strongly felt into the twentieth century. In the 1940s, the anthropologist Francis Hsu wrote that

> Concubinage is an accepted custom, but nobody wants to be one. So strong is the aversion, that even the poorest person will be angry if it be suggested openly that his or her daughter might be a concubine. All concubines in the community come from some far distant locality. It is generally admitted that the family of a concubine and her husband's family rarely maintain any social relationship at all.[106]

Do these continuities mean that Chinese family organization was immune to change brought on by changes in society at large? Certainly not, but it does show that the current state of research on the Chinese family does not yet allow us to identify subtle patterns of historical variation, even at the level of the upper class. As a first step toward discovering such patterns, I will consider briefly the ways concubinage may have changed after the Song in response to changes in social and economic organization.

Legally, it appears that the status of concubines had improved by the time of the Qing dynasty (1644–1911), because it became permissible to promote a concubine to wife if the wife had died and the concubine was the mother of the only surviving sons.[107] Moreover, the prohibition against forcing a widow to remarry was extended to widowed concubines.[108] Ritually there was an improvement also, as tablets for concubine-mothers seem to have been more commonly placed in family ancestral altars. Similarly, genealogies of some lineages listed concubine-mothers.

Why might the status of concubines have improved? The low status of concubines in the Song was certainly related to the low status of bondservants and to more abstract notions of social ranking. By the eighteenth century there had been a lessening in the stringency of subordination of bondservants. Moreover, the *shidafu* as a social class became less stable as examination competition became intense, increasing social mobility. These changes could have reduced the perceived gulf in social rank between masters and concubines.

A second reason could be further economic development. Alternative employment for women had increased during the centuries between the Song and the Qing.[109] Families who had other ways to dispose of their daughters besides selling them as maids or concubines had more leeway to negotiate with potential masters. If in these circumstances a great enough number of parents chose to maximize the security of their daughters rather than the size of the body price, the institution of concubinage gradually could have changed.

One might even argue that the relative status of concubines would improve when the status of wives declined. It is by now fairly common for writers to argue that the status of women in China had declined markedly by the Qing.[110] The sources or signs of this decline (footbinding and the cult of widow chastity and widow suicide) had their roots in the Song period, when footbinding first gained some popularity and the leading Neo-Confucian philosophers declared that it was better for a widow to starve to death than to remarry. Even though the effects of these long-term trends were not much felt in the Song, when the legal position of wives and daughters was relatively strong,[111] the effects were felt by the time of the Qing. Footbinding made wives and concubines more alike. Concubines readied for the luxury market would certainly have bound feet, as would their mistresses. The cult of widow chastity, however, was of no direct concern to concubines; chastity as a "widow" was rarely expected of a concubine, and the chastity cult was largely concerned with matters outside their sphere (inheritance of family property, family and personal honor).[112] Yet one could also argue that by stressing the wife's permanent incorporation into her husband's home – allowing neither remarriage nor a return to her natal home in widowhood – wives were becoming closer to concubines, who severed almost all ties to their family of origin.

3 Shifts in marriage finance from the sixth to the thirteenth century*

People in the Tang period [AD 618–907] celebrated the Cuis and Lus as top-rank families. Even when descendants of these families were poor and of low political rank, they were esteemed for their pedigree. Today people do not make much of family. If a girl of a noble family is poor and without resources, she may not be able to marry in her prime. Yet village rich families can marry into noble houses and get those who passed the examinations in the top group as their sons-in-law.

Zhao Yanwei, 1206[1]

A marriage in China, as in most places, normally involved some financial outlay by both the husband's and the wife's families and therefore some redistribution of wealth. In the classical ritual prescriptions preserved in the *Yi li* (Etiquette and Ritual), the husband's family would send a goose to the wife's family on several occasions, and midway between the first proposal and the wedding itself the groom's family sent more substantial gifts, given in the *Yi li* as ten bolts of cloth and a pair of deer skins.[2] The bride's family was not obliged to present gifts to the groom's family, but the bride herself would be sent with clothes and personal items such as jewelry packed in cases, and could be supplied with female attendants who might serve as her maids or her husband's concubines. In early texts these two types of outlays are generally treated as belonging to different realms. The gifts presented by the husband's family fell into the realm of ritual. Presenting and accepting these gifts was integral to the betrothal ceremony: one was not married ritually without some token transfer of objects from the groom's family to the bride's. The classic *Li ji* (Record of Ritual) asserts: "Without receipt of the betrothal gifts there is no contact and no affinity."[3] In later periods, at least, once betrothal gifts had been received, the girl's family could be prosecuted if they broke off the

* This essay was first published in *Marriage and Inequality in Chinese Society*, ed. Rubie S. Watson and Patricia Buckley Ebrey, copyright 1991 © The Regents of the University of California. Reprinted with the permission of the University of California Press.

Figure 3.1 Dai Liang succeeds in marrying out five daughters by making the dowries
frugal.
Source: After SYXJ 9.20a.

engagement.[4] By contrast, the validity of a marriage did not depend on the bride's bringing anything. Nor were the objects she brought termed gifts; they were simply her possessions. By the Han period (202 BC–AD 220) there is scattered evidence that how well a bride was equipped depended on how much her family wished to do for her, which in turn probably depended on how rich they were, how many sons they had, the importance they placed on the match, and probably sometimes the affection they felt for her. When either family was rich, they could make their outlays in style, giving generous gifts and supplying daughters with handsome dowries. A girl without brothers, as heiress, could receive the bulk of the family property as her dowry.[5]

In this essay my concern is not with heiresses or routine marriage exchanges of modest size, but with marriage outlays that made a substantial economic difference to the two families. Demands for lavish betrothal gifts began to be heard among aristocratic families from the late fifth century on; a few centuries later demands for substantial dowries were made by the families of the Song (960–1279) upper class. The motivations for these marriages were by no means simply economic; the marriages sealed with these transfers of property brought prestige and connections to affines. I therefore try to show how the tangible financial benefits and less tangible benefits of honor and connections worked together in these two periods. I also explain how the shift in the balance of marriage finance related to the changed political and economic environment of the ruling elite.

MARRIAGE FINANCE AMONG ARISTOCRATIC FAMILIES, SIXTH–NINTH CENTURIES

After the fall of the Han dynasty, Chinese society developed in distinctly aristocratic directions. By the late fourth century in the south and the late fifth century in the north, a relatively small number of families were preeminent in social and political life. Along with admiration for aristocratic pedigrees came an inflation in the value of the betrothal gifts the highest-ranking families could expect to receive when they sent out a daughter in marriage. In the south in about 490, Shen Yue accused Wang Yuan of highly objectionable behavior. Wang had married his daughter to a man of much lower social status who had paid a "betrothal gift" (*binli*) of 50,000 cash. Wang made enough of a profit from this transaction to buy himself a concubine.[6] A few decades later in his *Family Instructions*, Yan Zhitui (531–ca. 591) complained that such transactions were all too common:

> In the present age, when marriages are arranged, some people sell their daughters for the betrothal gift or buy a wife by making a payment of silk. They compare the ancestry [of the two parties], calculate down to the smallest sum, demand much and offer little, exactly like bargaining

in a market. As a result coarse sons-in-law may enter the family or arrogant daughters-in-law take over the house.[7]

Note that Yan's complaint resembles Shen Yue's: Those who had daughters profited, while those who needed wives would have to pay. Such conditions meant that girls from families with the most esteemed ancestry were marrying down. They seemed arrogant to their in-laws, while their husbands seemed coarse to their parents. Cross-culturally, marriage exchanges have often been compared to commercial transactions, so this does not necessarily mean that marriages were in some objective sense more like "sales" in this period.[8] What was probably new was the size of the betrothal gifts and weight assigned to ancestry, not the negotiation process itself.[9]

Yan Zhitui implied that an eminent family could expect an even higher sum if they married their daughter into a family of lesser birth. Indeed, Yang Su (d. 606), perhaps the most powerful official of the early Sui (581–618), gave "extremely generous" betrothal gifts so that his son could marry the daughter of Cui Biao, a Qinghe Cui of eminent ancestry whose "family standing" (*mendi*) he valued. Yang even put up with rude behavior on the part of Cui Biao to bring the marriage about.[10] Something of the size of an "extremely generous" betrothal gift can be imagined from the case of a Northern Qi (550–577) official who got into trouble because he embezzled 400,000 cash to pay for the betrothal gift for marriage to the daughter of a Taiyuan Wang.[11] In this period, betrothal gifts could include fields and animals. One Northern Qi official known for his stinginess was accused of sending inferior items as parts of the betrothal gift when his son married a Fanyang Lu girl. These items were lame mules, infertile fields, and secondhand brass vessels.[12]

Further evidence of the size of betrothal gifts can be found in the sumptuary rules issued to regulate them. In the late fifth and sixth centuries, the various governments tried to fight persistent tendencies for prestige to become independent of the ranks and honors emanating from the court. For instance, governments in both the north and the south tried to control the publication of genealogical gazetteers that ranked families.[13] When the ability to command large betrothal gifts became a sign of high status beyond the government's power to control, the Northern Qi government promulgated rules to make these gifts correspond to political rank. At each of the "six rites" (i.e., the steps in betrothal), everyone with rank (from the emperor down to rank-nine officials) could present a lamb, a pair of geese, and a *hu* each of wine, millet, rice, and flour. Commoners could present gifts half this large. For the betrothal gift, much more detailed specifications were given for five kinds of cloth and a variety of foodstuffs, varying in quantities according to official rank. For instance, the highest officials could give 140 pieces of plain silk (*juan*), the lowest officials 34.[14] Clearly by this time gifts of much greater monetary value than anything prescribed in the classics were commonly exchanged at weddings of aristocrats and other wealthy officials.

Even though substantial betrothal gifts received imperial approval as long as they were in line with official rank, negotiating their size was never deemed morally correct in the Confucian view of marriage. Wang Tong (ca. 584–617), a Confucian teacher, wrote: "Discussing wealth in arranging a marriage is the way of the barbarians," a saying frequently quoted by later writers.[15] He probably suspected that this practice – unattested in the classics – was the legacy of the non-Han rulers of the Northern dynasties (386–581). More likely, it reflects the growth of aristocracy.

In 632, after the founding of the Tang dynasty (618–906), Emperor Taizong (r. 626–649) reiterated Yan Zhitui's complaint about mercenary marriage arrangements. The emperor directed his remarks specifically against the leading families of the northeast (the Cuis, Lus, Lis, and Zhengs), who were arrogant in their assumption of superior birth. He charged that "every time they marry out a daughter to another family they demand a large betrothal gift (*pin cai*), taking quantity to be the important thing. They discuss numbers and settle an agreement, just like merchants in the market."[16] Six years later Taizong chastised his own officials for their lack of self-respect, evident in their vying for marriage into these families out of "admiration for their ancestry (*zu zong*)." Even when they presented valuable betrothal gifts, the officials' families accepted a position of inferiority *vis-à-vis* their affinal relatives and thus had to tolerate disrespectful behavior from their daughters-in-law.[17]

In 657 the next emperor, Gaozong (r. 649–683), complained again about the snobbish exclusiveness underlying the leading families' marriage practices. He took several measures designed to curb them. First he prohibited marriage among eleven lines of seven old families of five surnames.[18] Limits were also set on how much wealth a family could receive in the form of betrothal gifts when marrying out a daughter. These limits were 300 pieces of silk for families rank three or higher, 200 for rank four and five, 100 for rank six and seven, and fifty for anyone lower. (Because in this period silk was commonly used as a currency, the intention probably was that all the gifts given should not exceed these values, rather than that only silk should be used for the gifts.) Finally, he restricted the use of betrothal gifts: the bride's family was not to make a profit by marrying a daughter out but was to use all of the betrothal gifts to supply her dowry, and her husband's family was not to appropriate the dowry either.[19] In other words, families could expend handsome sums only so long as they were seen as outfitting the bride; neither family could then be interpreted as seeking a profit or "selling" a bride.

As several scholars have shown, the highest level of the Tang elite was very largely drawn from family lines well established in earlier dynasties.[20] In this period, pedigree did not confer automatic access to office, yet a relatively small group of old families managed to do extraordinarily well in placing their sons in office through their traditions of education, success in examinations, use of "protection" privilege, reputation for correct behavior, and so on. Endogamous marriage practices were crucial in sustaining the concept of an aristocracy of "old families." In the case of the Boling Cuis, of ninety-two marriages during the Tang, 52 percent were with others of the "seven old families," another 30 percent were with the other twenty-two old families identified by Liu Fang in the mid-eighth century as "aristocratic," and all but two of the others with the hundred-odd families listed in genealogical gazetteers of the most eminent families in the country.[21]

Among the Tang elite, it was the larger "family," or patriline, of the marriage partners that mattered most.[22] That is, men could plausibly assert that it was more prestigious to marry a daughter of one of the "seven old families" than to marry the daughter of a current chief minister or even a princess. A minister in the late seventh century who had married an imperial princess is said to have lamented that he had neither gained the *jinshi* degree nor married a daughter of one of the "five surnames."[23] In the eighth century a Taiyuan Wang woman who married a Boling Cui (both among the "seven old families," or "five surnames") was praised for selecting spouses from the northeastern families rather than from the "powerful" for her offspring. She had married one son to her brother's daughter and the other to a Fanyang Lu girl.[24] An early ninth-century emperor could complain that people paid attention only to pedigree and not to official rank in selecting marriage partners.[25] Even as late as the first half of the tenth century, a Longxi Li was praised for not being arrogant like others in his family, or the Cui, Lu, and Zheng families with whom his family intermarried. Members of these families would only agree to marry a girl into another family after receiving "generous presents of gold and silk."[26]

Exclusivity reaffirms prestige. By marrying their peers, households belonging to the highest levels of the aristocracy were confirming their status. Households of aristocratic descent that were not prospering financially or politically were making use of their best resource, pedigree, when they married peers or accepted large betrothal gifts to marry others. Families that were "buying in" by taking a bride of higher status than their own were making a long-term investment in the status of their grandchildren. This was possible because pedigree through mothers was considered in assessing family standing. A ninth-century epitaph noted that although the subject's immediate patrilineal ancestors had undistinguished careers, "their relatives through marriage were the top families in the northeast."[27] This concern for maternal pedigree may explain why the ambitious are portrayed as seeking, not aristocratic sons-in-law, but aristocratic daughters-in-law who would be the mothers of their grandchildren.

The affinal relations created by these aristocratic marriages were conceived in general terms. The statement that "our families have intermarried for generations" or "we have old marriage connections" was often used to evoke the notion of affinal relationship: the individual so addressed might not have any close current tie. For instance, Li Hua (fl. 740s), a Zhaojun Li, said he had called on a Boling Cui, as their families were from "adjoining areas in the northern prefectures and had old marriage ties."[28] The man he was calling on had never lived in the northeast himself, and the visit undoubtedly took place in one of the capitals, Changan or Luoyang. The marriage ties seem to have been just as distant.

In the Tang, thus, betrothal gifts among the aristocratic families were of great monetary value and were linked to marital exclusivity and the preservation of a tiny super-elite. By marrying so disproportionately among themselves, the aristocrats showed that they believed their own claims to superiority and did not rate wealth or government title above pedigree or refinement. Tang complaints about the size of the betrothal gifts of aristocrats almost always stressed the snobbishness involved. It was not that the old families willingly gave their daughters to whoever came up with the most money. Rather they were so reluctant to marry with anyone but their own kind that outsiders had to go to extraordinary lengths if they wished to penetrate their circle.

MARRIAGE FINANCE IN THE SONG

By the Song period (960–1279), the balance in marriage finance had changed so that wives' families, especially among the upper class, had larger net outlays than husbands' families. No survey of marriage institutions in Chinese history points out this fundamental change.[29] Yet I am convinced it occurred because of evidence of six sorts: (1) complaints about mercenary marriages put more stress on men seeking large dowries; (2) people drew up detailed lists of dowries before concluding marriages; (3) the legal code was revised to protect a daughter's claims to a dowry if her father died before she was married; (4) biographies of women much more frequently mention their possession of substantial dowries; (5) discussions of family budgeting treat provision of daughters' dowries as a major family expense; and (6) the cost of dowry came to be recognized as a major problem even among ordinary people. Before reviewing this evidence, I should acknowledge that sources of all kinds survive in greater abundance for the Song than the Tang, making arguments based on the silence of Tang sources weak. Therefore, I give greatest weight to cases where the Tang sources say something, but what they say is different from what Song sources say.

Complaints about mercenary marriages

I have already reviewed Tang complaints about mercenary marriages. Wifegiving families snobbishly demanded large betrothal gifts. In the Song there were just as many complaints about marriage being treated like a transaction, with bargaining and contracts.[30] However, the issue was no longer simply the betrothal gift and its return as dowry, but the wife's family's contribution. The value of the dowry was often much larger than that of the betrothal gifts, so that the wife's family had made a major contribution to the new couple's economic foundations. Indeed, Song dowries often included land.

One of the first signs of the escalation in the size of dowries is a reference to a tax imposed on them by one of the minor states in the tenth century, the Later Shu (934–965), which controlled the Sichuan area.[31] By the mid-eleventh century something of a dowry crisis appears to have emerged among the upper class. Cai Xiang (1012–1067), while prefect of Fuzhou (Fujian) in the 1050s, posted a notice pointing out that "the purpose of marriage is to produce heirs, not to acquire wealth." Instead of recognizing this truth, he charged, people ignored family status (*menhu*) in choosing brides, their minds entirely on the dowry. Once the dowry was delivered to the groom's home,

> they inspect the dowry cases, in the morning searching through one, in the evening another. The husband cruelly keeps making more and more demands on his wife. If he is not satisfied, it can spoil their love or even lead to divorce. This custom has persisted for so long that people accept it as normal.[32]

Note how Cai would like to return to some vaguely conceived former system where men sought family status in brides, not just wealth.

Sima Guang (1019–1086) a few years later provided a similar depiction of the pressures created by demands for dowries:

> Nowadays it is the custom for covetous and vulgar people first to ask about the value of the dowry when selecting a bride and the amount of the betrothal gift when marrying a daughter. Some even draw up a contract saying "such goods, in such numbers, such goods, in such numbers," thereby treating their daughters as an item in a sales transaction. There are also cases where people go back on their agreements after the wedding is over. These are the methods used by brokers dealing in male and female bondservants. How can such a transaction be called a gentleman-official (*shidafu*) marriage?
>
> When parents-in-law have been deceived, they will maltreat the daughter-in-law as a way to vent their fury. Fearing this, parents who love their daughter put together a generous dowry in the hope of pleasing her parents-in-law, not realizing that such covetous, vulgar people are insatiable. When the dowry is depleted, what use will the bride be to these parents-in-law? They will then "pawn" her to get further payment from her family. Her family's wealth has a limit, but their demands will never stop. Therefore, families linked by marriage often end up enemies.[33]

Sima Guang mentions both dowry and betrothal gifts as open to negotiation, but seems to see the greater problem with dowry (perhaps because betrothal gifts were returned as part of the dowry). Particularly troublesome was the problem of parents-in-law mistreating the bride if her dowry was smaller than they had been led to expect. Moreover, they might make new demands on her parents, which the latter felt obliged to meet because their daughter's welfare was at stake. The situation sounds more reminiscent of India in recent times than the world of Yan Zhitui and Tang Taizong. A century later this dowry crisis had still not abated, for Yuan Cai (ca. 1140–1195) could argue that if a family did not begin planning for their daughter's dowry when she was very young, they would have to "sell land or buildings as temporary expedients, or callously watch [their] daughter's humiliation in front of others."[34]

Other Song accusations about mercenary marriages inverted the complaints of Yan Zhitui and Tang Taizong in yet another way. It was not daughters with desirable ancestry going to the highest bidders, but men with good career potential. Ding Zhi (ca. 1060) wrote:

> Your subject has heard that in recent years after a *jinshi* passes the examination, he discusses wealth before taking a bride, in full violation of ritual and morality. Families of officials, depending on how wealthy they are, send go-betweens back and forth, sometimes almost begging. If anything is not quite to his liking, [the new *jinshi*] casts them aside and goes to another family.[35]

Apparently what these new *jinshi* wanted were daughters of officials who would bring generous dowries. Similar comments were made by Zhu Yu (ca. 1075–1119):

> In our dynasty the families of high-ranking men select their sons-in-law during the years of the metropolitan examinations, choosing from among the scholars who attend. They do not inquire into *yin* and *yang* or auspiciousness, nor into ancestry (*jiashi*). This practice is called "seizing a son-in-law from under the lists." Strings of cash called "money for tying the one seized" are given to the prospective groom for his expenses in the capital. In recent years rich merchants, the vulgar, and those who have great savings also "seize a son-in-law from under the lists" when they arrange a marriage for a daughter. They make the "seizing money" generous in order to entice scholars to condescend to come. One son-in-law can cost over a thousand strings. When the wedding takes place, his family also demands "money all around" [a kind of tipping]. Often they calculate what is in the cases and sacks and want an agreement tied up like a legal document.[36]

In this case dowry (the contents of the cases and sacks) is only a part of the transaction. The girl's family has also given money directly to the future son-in-law for his "expenses," apparently a kind of earnest given to the man himself.

The type of bidding for sons-in-law that Ding Zhi and Zhu Yu criticized is confirmed in Song biographies. For instance, the biography of Feng Jing (1021–1094) reports that when he passed the metropolitan examination in first place in 1049 he was still not married. Zhang Yaozuo (987–1058), then powerful at court because a niece was the emperor's favorite consort, wanted Feng to marry his daughter; he gave him a gold belt and on another occasion brought out a list of her dowry. Feng refused the match, conceivably because he thought he could do better: he ended up marrying the daughter of Fu Bi (1004–1083), a much more influential patron.[37] A similar case is mentioned in the epitaphs for Jiang Bao (1069–1117) and his wife. After Jiang received the *jinshi* at twenty-five or twenty-six *sui*, the high official Zeng Bu (1035–1107) proposed marriage to his daughter by a concubine along with a gift of 300,000 cash. Jiang reportedly declined the gift but accepted the marriage proposal.[38]

Let me give one final quotation. Yuan Cai, writing in 1178, referred to mercenary marriages in the context of the deceptions of matchmakers. As he noted, the classical complaint was that matchmakers fooled the girl's family by saying the boy was rich and the boy's family by saying the girl was beautiful. In his own time their chicanery focused on money matters:

> Matchmakers deceive the girl's family by saying the boy does not seek a full complement of dowry presents and in fact will help in outfitting the bride. They deceive the boy's family by promising generous transfer of goods, and they make up a figure without any basis in fact.[39]

Here the whole issue is dowry: the bride's family is told it can be small and come from indirect dowry; the boy's family is assured it will be large.

In comparing Tang and Song complaints about marriage payments, differences in the meaning assigned to these payments are striking. Snobbishness and exclusivity were regularly attributed to those who demanded large betrothal gifts in the Tang, lack of self-respect to those who consented. In the Song, social exclusivity was not associated with large dowries. Families insisting that a large dowry accompany daughters-in-law were not suspected of erecting status barriers to keep lowborn women out of their homes. Men who sought large dowries were accused of greed, not disdain for those below them. The ulterior motive of a family offering a handsome dowry was generally assumed to be a desire to attach to them a young man of promise, rather than more diffuse links to a famous family. Indeed, a concern with family pedigree was contrasted to a concern with dowries.[40]

Marriage agreements

Sima Guang's charge that people drew up contracts specifying betrothal gifts and dowries can easily be confirmed in other Song sources, though most of the time the term "contract" (*qiyue*) was avoided. Song marriage agreements were much more detailed than anything surviving from the Tang.[41] The *Mengliang lu* (Record of Dreams of Glory), which describes the Southern Song (1127–1279) capital of Hangzhou, reported that an "agreement card" (*dingtie*) sent by the man's family would list the son's birth order in the family (first, second, or third son, and so on); the year, month, day, and hour of his birth; whether his parents were living, and, if not, who was presiding over the marriage; and, in the event that the marriage was uxorilocal, the wealth he would bring in "gold and silver, fields, productive property (*caichan*), houses, rooms, hills, and gardens." The card that the girl's family returned would likewise give her seniority number and time of birth, then list what she was bringing, her "cases with jewelry, gold and silver, pearls and feathers, precious objects, items for use, and bedding, as well as the property accompanying her on her marriage, such as fields, houses, businesses, hills, or gardens."[42] In other words, dowry was specified in the first proposal, as was the man's "dowry" if he were to be an uxorilocal husband.

Song guides to letter-writing often devoted several chapters to marriage correspondence. Like the *Mengliang lu*, these books show the dowry to be specified in the first proposal. In the next round of communications, lists of betrothal gifts were often attached to the "engagement letter" (*hunshu*) sent by the groom's family.[43] The bride's family sent back comparable letters, including a list of the betrothal gifts they were refusing as well as a list of the objects in the trousseau.[44] One of these books explained the difference between the items of the dowry specified on these two occasions: the "agreement card" would list the "major numbers" of land and servants, while the "trousseau list" would give the "minor numbers" of the various items of cloth, jewelry, and other goods sent "to make up the room."[45]

A Song agreement card and trousseau list survive for the marriage of the daughter of a prominent family in Kunshan county (Jiangsu). Dated 1261, the agreement card divides her dowry into three items: five hundred *mu* of land, trousseau (*lianju*) of (or worth) 110,000 strings of cash, and "marriage ties" (*diyin*) of (or worth) five thousand strings. In the trousseau list, dated fourteen months later, there is a detailed breakdown of different types of cloth and miscellaneous objects.[46]

Revision of the law code

A third sign of the increased weight given dowry in the Song is revision of the laws for division of family property so that orphaned daughters were provided with dowries. Neither the Tang nor the Song government concerned itself with the decisions a father made about the property to assign his daughter as dowry, nor did they routinely interfere with the decisions of other family seniors in undivided families. But orphans posed special problems. Stories and anecdotes often refer to the plight of orphaned daughters without dowries, even daughters from official families. It was

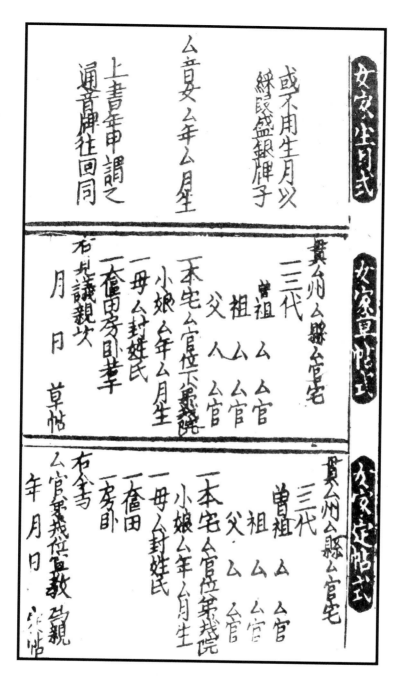

Figure 3.2 Sample of three documents the bride's family should send to the groom's. The top one gives her birth date. The second gives her father's, grandfather's and great-grandfather's names and ranks along with her date of birth, her mother's surname and her dowry in land and household items. The third is to confirm the agreement and gives the information again.

Source: From QZQQ bie 25b (p. 490).

taken for granted that their lack of a dowry would make it impossible for them to be married into an otherwise appropriate family, and might even lead to them being sold as concubines.[47] Probably because of the disastrous consequences of daughters left without dowries, Song law provided them some protection from the greed of brothers, uncles, and other potential heirs when the family property was divided.[48]

Already in the Tang, if brothers who were dividing the property included one not yet married, or if they had unmarried sisters (or aunts), marriage expenses were to be set aside before the group property was divided. Unmarried brothers were to be given the funds for a betrothal gift in addition to their share, and unmarried sisters were to get marriage funds half the size of their brothers' funds.[49] This law was probably intended to codify practice in the Tang, when the man's family gave betrothal gifts that cost more than the net outlay of the bride's family. The code said nothing about the appropriate size of betrothal gifts, but because this provision came into play only when at least one of the brothers was already married, funds similar to those used for the married brother(s) would probably be considered fair.

Later the law was revised to match Song custom more closely, for Southern Song judges cited rules that gave unmarried daughters more substantial dowries. Three particular changes in the law are noteworthy. First, at division unmarried daughters were to be assigned a share, or portion, half that of a son's share (i.e., half the size of his share of the estate, not half the size of the allotment for his marriage expenses).[50] This would mean that in families where a boy and two girls survived, none yet married, the boy would get half the property and each girl a quarter. Second, an old Tang rule was revised. When a house died out (*hujue*) for lack of an established heir, the property had gone entirely to the unmarried daughters (or, in their absence, married daughters). This law was revised to reduce the amount going to married daughters (who already had dowries)[51] and was extended to cover cases where a man in an undivided family died leaving only daughters. The revised law stipulated that his daughters could succeed to his share of the property just as though the house had died out.[52] Third, when an heir was set up posthumously, he would not be treated like a natural son or an adoptive son set up during the parents' lifetimes, whose presence would eliminate shares for married daughters and significantly reduce those for unmarried daughters (as seems to have been the case in the Tang). Instead, the property would be divided, with one-fourth to the posthumous heir and three-fourths to the unmarried daughters (if there were also married daughters, he would get one-fifth, if only married daughters, he would receive a third).[53] These changes in the law seem clearly to reflect the much greater weight dowry had come to play in the transmission of property between mid-Tang and mid-Song. Tang law left it up to the heirs to decide how to provide for their sisters, aunts, or nieces no matter what the circumstances. It made no difference if the heir was an adoptee or if the property was under the trusteeship of a widowed concubine who was not the mother of the daughters, or under the trusteeship of an uncle, and so on. Song law saw unmarried girls' need for dowries to be great enough to warrant some legal protection from unscrupulous relatives.

When judges supervised the division of an estate, they did not always follow these rules as they were codified, but they usually made substantial provisions for dowries. For instance, in the *Qingming ji*, there is an account of a man who died, leaving behind two daughters, the elder nine *sui*. A posthumous heir was appointed for him. Rather than giving a quarter to the heir and three-eighths to each daughter (as the statutes specified), the judge gave each one-third, with the daughters' property earmarked for their dowries.[54] In a case decided by Hu Ying (*jinshi* 1232), one of three brothers died before their property had been divided, leaving a single daughter (his wife was also dead). An earlier official had said the daughter should get one-third of what would normally go to her father, but Hu Ying revised this to half on the grounds that she had not been married when her father died and a girl should get half as much as a son, who would have received it all. Moreover, Hu Ying said that all of the private property of the girl's father's branch (such as her mother's dowry) was to go to her.[55] In a case decided by Liu Kezhuang (1187–1269), family property was first divided into two collateral lines. In one line, a brother got half and his two sisters each a quarter. In the other, a posthumous heir and two natural daughters each got a quarter, the remaining quarter to be used for the funeral expenses of the girls' father.[56]

One can also find cases where orphaned daughters received smaller shares. Judges took into account a variety of circumstances: fathers specifying a smaller share in the will, mothers remarrying and taking their daughters with them, or the presence of a step-mother or adopted brother.[57] But the direction of the change in the law was undoubtedly to protect orphaned girls' claims to property for dowry.

References to dowry in epitaphs and anecdotes

In Tang epitaphs for women, references to their dowries are rare.[58] By contrast, they are fairly common in Song epitaphs.[59] For instance, in the early eleventh century a woman from a rich official family married a man who passed the examinations at 17, the first in his family to have an official career that they knew of. According to her epitaph, she felt uncomfortable at having so much private property (*sicai*) when her husband's family was poor, and so contributed it all to the common pool.[60] In the early twelfth century the daughter of an official married an orphan who had just passed the examinations. It happened that one of her husband's relatives had sold the hill with the ancestral graves on it to a temple. The husband was about to borrow money to try to redeem the hill when his wife stopped him and said: "The reason my parents sent me with property was to be of aid to your family. How could I use it while your family graves are not being

preserved?" She emptied out her chests to redeem the hill and with the remain-
der bought more land and built a building on it for the protection of the
graveyard.[61] In a similar case recorded in another epitaph, some brothers
were about to sell part of the family land to pay for their father's funeral.
One of their wives insisted they should keep the ancestral property intact;
she would give them what they needed from her dowry.[62] The epitaph for a
woman who in 1160 married into a family with less than three *mu* of land
reports that she told her husband that his land might be enough for the
present but that they needed to increase it to plan for their descendants.
Consequently, when a neighbor wanted to sell his land, she quickly sold the
land she had brought as dowry in order to buy the neighbor's property and
gave the deed to her father-in-law.[63] Another epitaph records that a woman
in the mid-twelfth century sold five *mu* of her dowry land to supply the
money needed for her husband's brother to get a second wife after his first
had died.[64] Epitaphs might also praise a woman for her generosity in willing
her dowry; one reported that a woman asked that her dowry be distributed
to all the children and grandchildren in the family.[65]

These epitaphs were written by men who did not fully approve of wives'
treating dowry as private property.[66] The women are portrayed as willingly
using all or part of their dowries for larger family purposes, such as ancestral rites, funerals, or marriages of the husband's siblings, thus testifying to
their commitment to the solidarity of the family. Indeed, these epitaphs may
reasonably be used to infer that most women guarded their dowries with
vigilance and never lost sight of the difference between their own property
and the larger family's. Liu Zai (1166–1239), for instance, noted that women
by nature are tightfisted, thus making the woman he was writing about
exceptional: she not only turned over all of her ample dowry and dowry
fields to her husband, but she also never asked for an accounting of the
income or expenses.[67]

Evidence of the relative cost of dowry and betrothal gifts

Not only did dowries come to be substantial, but providing them also proved
a more onerous burden than meeting a son's wedding expenses. Yuan Cai
mentioned three expenses for which families should plan long in advance:
sons' educations, daughters' marriages, and parents' funerals. If a family
took adequate steps – such as planting 10,000 pine trees at each daughter's
birth – they would not need to worry that their daughters would "miss the
best time."[68]

Numerical estimates of the relative costs of marriages are found in some
rules for distributing income. The rules for the Fan lineage's charitable
estate, formulated in 1050, specified that when a daughter was married out,
thirty strings of cash were granted; twenty if it were her second marriage.
When a son took a first wife twenty strings were supplied, but none for a
second. These figures are on the order of the grants for funerals; the funerals

of seniors were subsidized with twenty-five strings, of juniors fifteen, and of children, from two to ten strings depending on age.[69] Lü Zuqian (1137–1181), in rules he wrote up for an undivided family, specified that 100 strings be given when a daughter was marrying and fifty when a son was marrying.[70] A charitable venture set up in 1199 in Guangdong for the dependents of officials who died there provided that five strings of cash be given to help in the marriage of daughters, but only three strings for the marriage of a son or a funeral.[71] Although each of these sets of rules stipulates different levels of funding, in each case parents of daughters were given 50 to 100 percent more than parents of sons.

Dowry in lower social levels

Substantial dowries, in Song times, were not confined to the families of officials. Memorialists sometimes complained that demands for excessively large dowries were making it impossible for girls to marry, or were forcing their families to sell land or borrow money to pay for them.[72] One official even attributed female infanticide to the high cost of dowries.[73] Hou Ke (1007–1079), while magistrate of Huacheng (Sichuan), found that many girls grew old without marrying because "When people of Ba take wives they always demand property from the girl's family." His solution was to make up a schedule for dowries according to the wealth of the family and to set punishments for anyone who exceeded it. Within a year, we are told, every spinster had been married out.[74] Sun Jue (1028–1090) found a similar situation in Fuzhou (Fujian) and simply issued an order that dowries were not to exceed 100 strings of cash, which promptly led to several hundred weddings.[75] Zhu Xi (1130–1200) found that in southern Fujian girls were sent to Buddhist cloisters in part because their parents did not have the money for their marriage expenses.[76] In these cases the clear implication is that dowry was a severe problem even among ordinary people. One Song observer, commenting on the customs in the far south, noted that there poor girls of 14 or 15 worked to earn their own dowries so that their families would not have a single cash of expense.[77] Clearly he expected his readers to understand the problem of providing dowries among the poor.

That dowries could be large among ordinary people is confirmed in cases in the *Qingming ji*. Judges never registered surprise that families neither wealthy nor well educated would give land as part of daughters' dowries. Anecdotal evidence suggests that men from families with modest means could get larger dowries if they accepted a widow, a woman who had been a concubine or courtesan, or if they entered the woman's household as the uxorilocal husband of a girl or widow. For instance, a petty trader whose wife had died in an epidemic took as his second wife a former concubine with a dowry of 300 strings.[78] Moreover, even modest dowries might be useful. In another anecdote, a dog butcher's wife brought a dowry worth several dozen strings of cash, which was used as business capital. At one point the husband sold a pair of silver hairpins from it to buy dogs to slaughter; later when he wanted to abandon the business on Buddhist grounds, his wife said that her trunks still had several bolts of cloth that they could use as capital for some new means of supporting themselves.[79]

If there were only one type of evidence indicating that the balance in marriage finance had shifted between Tang and Song, one might suspect that the change was historiographical rather than historical. References to substantial dowries could appear more often in Song epitaphs because writers wished to give more concrete examples of women's virtues, for instance. The law could have been revised to take account of customary practices that had been in existence for many centuries. Differences in the types of marriages referred to as mercenary could be accidental, the result of the chance survival of certain texts and loss of others. Yet, taking all of this evidence together, the conclusion that a major shift had occurred in marriage finance seems inescapable.[80] Moreover, in Song times dowries often included land or enough money to purchase land, something uncommon earlier.

For the rest of this paper I shall treat it as established that between the eighth and the eleventh centuries marriage finance among the elite shifted from one in which the groom's family bore the larger burden in laying the economic foundations of the marriage (through betrothal gifts used to prepare the dowry) to one in which the bride's family also made major contributions, equaling or outweighing the husband's family's. I shall now turn to examining the causes and consequences of this change in marriage finance.

SHIFTS IN MARRIAGE FINANCE AND THE TANG–SONG TRANSITION

It is by now widely recognized that Chinese society underwent major transformations between the Tang and the Song dynasties. In standard textbook presentations, these transformations include the expansion of the economy, the growth of cities, a decline in state control over the distribution of land, the replacement of the aristocracy with an examination-based elite, the growth of autocracy, the decline of Buddhism, the rise of Neo-Confucianism, the development of popular forms of culture, the shift in the center of Chinese culture to the south, the appearance of localized lineages, and so on. In this context it is not surprising that forms of marriage finance might also change. But what were the specific connections? Did certain changes in Chinese society lead to a decline in demands for expensive betrothal gifts? Did the same or other changes foster dowry escalation? Can other social or cultural changes be attributed to the increased importance of dowry?

Dowry escalation brought about not merely a change in the timing or direction of marriage payments, but a more major shift in the system of transmitting property toward "diverging devolution," to use Goody's term.[81] Dowry involves transmission of property outside the patrilineal descent group through women whose sons and daughters bear their fathers' surnames. By contrast, betrothal gifts used by the bride's family to prepare the dowry (i.e., indirect dowry) normally ended up back under the control of patrilineal descendants. That is, for one generation these funds belonged to the wife who married in, but as long as she had a son, whatever was left would go to her offspring (if it had not already been absorbed into family property). In no period of traditional China did daughters inherit like sons, though they could be residual heirs when they had no brothers.[82] In the Song, therefore, when the cost of the dowry became substantial and exceeded the value of the betrothal gifts, families began regularly transmitting a portion of their wealth outside the boundaries of their patrilineal descendants.

Questions about the shift toward larger dowries and diverging devolution can be phrased at either the individual or the societal level. That is, one can ask why men in the transition period chose to send their daughters with valuable dowries when they could probably still have married them without such expenditures. One can also ask why property holders as a class would transmit some of their property through daughters to grandsons of other surnames. The best explanation would probably make sense at both of these levels.

In modern China, dowry has generally been more lavish among the rich than the poor, and so has been attributed to the status consciousness of the members of the wife-giving family who "do not wish to demean themselves before the other family."[83] Goody's comparative analysis also links diverging devolution to stratification, particularly the kind that comes in with plow-based agriculture.[84] Linking dowry with status differentiation, however, provides no insight into the historical shift toward large dowries in China, as Tang aristocratic society was if anything more concerned with status and prestige than the Song elite. The Tang case shows that the size of betrothal gifts (largely used for indirect dowry) could just as well serve as symbols of high status as direct dowry. Moreover, social and economic inequalities seem to have been just as well reproduced by this system of transmitting property.

The presence or absence of substantial dowry (that is, dowry in excess of the betrothal gifts) has also been linked to the need for affinal connections to people in distant localities.[85] The logic here is that dowry makes marriage exchange unequal (the side that sent both the woman and the dowry clearly sent more), and as Mauss argued, unbalanced gifts keep relationships active.[86] The possibility that affinal relations became more important in Song times is discussed below.

A third explanation for the distribution of dowry payments stresses the role of commercialization.[87] Dowry is almost always displayed and its value readily interpreted by all concerned as a measure of the wealth of the bride's family. In more commercialized societies, determining status on the basis of wealth is common, as is competition for such status. Harrell and Dickey cite historical shifts where the introduction of dowry (generally in recent times) accompanied commercialization, sometimes spreading from town to country.[88]

The kinds, timing, and value of marriage prestations also changed many times over the course of European history. Early imperial Roman families gave daughters dowries, the size of which slowly escalated. Then after about AD 200 the groom or his family started making premarital gifts to the bride (indirect dowry), which also followed an inflationary course, so that by the fifth century an emperor could denounce the avarice of parents with marriageable daughters. In the sixth century Justinian ruled that each family should make equal contributions. Herlihy associates these shifts with changes in the supply of potential mates caused by such things as female infanticide, the popularity of bachelorhood, changes in the age at marriage, and religions that promoted celibacy.[89] In the Chinese case, it does not seem likely that changes in age at marriage or proportions marrying were large enough to affect the market for brides and grooms, so the Roman case is probably not a good model for comparison.

The Germanic peoples who invaded the Roman Empire in the fifth century made gifts from the husband to the bride (somewhat analogous to the indirect dowry of Chinese betrothal gifts), and these also seem to have followed an inflationary course. Gradually, the contributions of the wives' families also seem to have grown.[90] In the eleventh century, dowry from the wife's family had re-emerged in Italy, southern France, and Spain "in the wake of peace, economic and demographic growth, and the establishment of public authority" as well as land shortage and a "crisis in status."[91] By the fourteenth century, especially in northern Italy, dowries had become extremely burdensome to bride-giving families at all social levels. Hughes suggests that dowry inflation was related to its use as a mechanism for alliance in a "status-conscious yet mobile world."[92] The parallels to the Chinese case shall be explored below.

Hughes also argues that this dotal regime reflects a revision of property rights that restrengthened patrilineal principles: husbands did not want to assign rights to their property to wives, but natal families were willing to do so to daughters, on the understanding that the daughters could make no further claims on them.[93] In the Chinese case, dowry escalation may have been linked to emphasis on patrilineal principles, but my guess is that cause and effect worked the other way around: men wished to reassert patrilineal principles in part because they objected to the transfer of property through women. Goody interprets this late medieval shift from indirect to direct dowry mostly as one of timing. That is, instead of inheriting property at their parents' deaths, daughters were receiving it when they wed. As mentioned above, the Chinese case cannot be interpreted this way, for inheritance was not normally bilateral.[94]

For the Chinese case, I think that transformations in the economy laid the groundwork for the shift toward diverging devolution, but that the real growth in dowries occurred first and most crucially in the elite. Economic changes included commercialization and freer forms of land tenure. In mid-Tang the government largely gave up attempting to control the private ownership of land or its transfer from one generation to the next. The use of money also began a steady climb, with the government issuing twenty times as much money per year in the mid-eleventh century as it had at its height in the Tang. People at all social levels thus had new opportunities to use property (money, land, or the goods that could be bought with money) to offer dowries that would strengthen affinal relations. As part of their strategies for advancement, especially in the political sphere, men in the elite took to providing their daughters with substantial dowries. The prominence of the dowries of the elite brought the concept of dowry fully into the repertoire of Chinese kinship practices. The custom of channeling wealth through dowries would then have spread to lower levels largely through a trickledown effect as people regularly attempted to raise their own status by copying the mores of those a step above them. From then on, although dowry became obligatory in the highest social level, it was optional at lower levels, and in Republican times at least was found among ordinary people in some parts of the country but not in others.[95]

Because I think the escalation of dowry among the elite played a crucial role in its full admission to the repertoire of kinship practices and because there is so much more material on dowry among the elite, here I shall confine my analysis to the reasons elite men chose to send dowries with their daughters.

Social structure and dowry

Differences between Tang and Song social stratification are well known. The families that became established in the Northern Song were rarely descendants of the leading Tang families (even if some claimed such connections). Pedigree by itself was less of an asset in the Song. The growing bureaucracy offered more opportunities for members of local elite families through the expanded examination system. The notion of an educated class of families whose members occasionally held office gained general recognition, displacing the Tang notion of a super-elite of families whose members nearly all held office. Elite men were embedded in localized kinship groups, differing markedly from the dispersed kinship groups of the Tang aristocratic families.[96]

The size of the educated class grew rapidly in Song times, probably in large part because as the economy expanded, it could support more local landlords and wealthy merchants. As a consequence, the numbers of those competing for elite positions seem to have steadily outstripped the supply of valued places, at both the national and local levels. Thus the culture of the elite in Song times was if anything more competitive than in Tang. The basic rules of civil service recruitment were changed several times, and there was a persistent tendency for those with good connections to devise ways to favor people of their own kind (through "protection" privileges, "sponsorship," "facilitated," or "avoidance" examinations, and so on).[97] Song sources are full of complaints about the nepotism of those in high office. For instance, in 1041 Sun Mian charged that high officials would recommend or sponsor their affinal relatives (*qinqi*).[98] In 1165 an official protested that the advantageous "avoidance" examinations were being taken not merely by agnatic relatives but by cousins through father's sister and mother's brother (both fifth-grade mourning relatives).[99] Even more common was the complaint that "cold, solitary" (*hangu*) scholars had a hard time getting ahead. Men with high-ranking close agnatic relatives were not "cold" or "solitary," but neither were those with good affinal connections. At the same time, the dangers of nepotism were recognized and efforts made to contain them, especially by prohibiting specified relatives from serving under or examining each other.[100] These efforts to curb nepotism also served to advertise the range and depth of kin who could be of use.

Does the inflation of dowries have anything to do with the political and social changes that led to this transformation of class structure in the Song? Large betrothal gifts apparently disappeared with the social groups that practiced them. In the Tang, there is no evidence that such gifts were common outside the circle of aristocratic families. But there is no reason that the disappearance of excessive betrothal gifts would have to lead to exaggerated dowries.

The tendency for dowry to escalate in the late Five Dynasties and Song appears to be related to the ecological situation of the emerging elite. Officials and aspirants to office who needed connections in order to facilitate promotions through sponsorship, to gain allies in factional disputes, and so on had to build up networks. This could be done through nonkinship means, such as through the ties of teachers and students or officials and their subordinates. But kinship ties have advantages, for they can be extended much further, to brothers, sons, grandsons, and so on. The dislocations of the tenth century seem to have resulted in many men finding themselves cut off from both patrilineal and affinal kin. For instance, Shi Jie (1005–1045), in describing the history of his family, noted that the first ancestor to move to their current location 150 years earlier had found himself with neither brothers nor affinal kin.[101] In such cases it was easier to build up networks of affinal kin through marriages with families long settled in that place than to wait several generations for the family to grow into a sizable patrilineal descent group. This use of marriage to establish networks occurred at both the national and local levels. Robert Hartwell found that of 210 marriages involving the thirty-five most eminent "families" of the Northern Song (960–1126), just over half (115) were to others in these families originally from other parts of the country.[102] Robert Hymes found that until the end of the Northern Song when official families migrated to Fuzhou (Jiangxi), they quickly arranged marriages to the leading local families.[103]

In the Tang those with wealth could not change the key element in their social status except by fraud: their home prefecture (choronym) and family name were fixed. A family hoping to convert wealth into social status could perhaps facilitate ties to these prestigious families by offering betrothal gifts or dowries verging on bribes. But the marriages contracted could only be expected to change the general evaluation of the family's status very slowly, after at least a couple of generations. In the Song, starting with very little of an established elite, family name *per se* meant little, so there was more to be gained by "buying" marriage connections.

Granting that there may have been more men eager to convert wealth into status in the early Song, why did they use this wealth for dowries rather than betrothal gifts? Here I will argue that dowry offered three advantages over betrothal gifts: it made a better "bribe"; it provided more flexibility for family strategies; and it made affinal ties stronger.

Dowry was a superior bait because betrothal gifts were supposed to be returned as dowry. By insisting on valuable betrothal gifts when marrying out a daughter, one may have guaranteed that she would have an adequate dowry, but one was not improving the financial health of one's own patriline. Dowry, by contrast, involved transfer from one patriline to another. Although the groom's father, who arranged the marriage, was not to have any control over the dowry, and even his son was supposed to gain his wife's consent on its use, it would eventually go to his son's sons and daughters.[104] Its final destination would not be trivial to a man worried about the eventual division of the family property among several sons. Mercantile families could use handsome dowries to marry their daughters into families of officials.[105] Epitaphs for the early Song also show rich official families marrying their daughters to promising young men, giving them large dowries.[106] They did this in part to avoid marrying down or losing prestige, but also because even well-established families could benefit from connections to such men. And the groom also had much to gain. Sima Guang criticized the practice of choosing brides on the basis of transient wealth and rank. "How could a man of spirit retain his pride if he got rich by using his wife's assets or gained high station by relying on her influence?"[107] Probably many young men would forgo some pride toward those ends.

My second argument is that dowry increased the options available in advancement strategies. Transmission of property along the patrilineal line through division among sons was inflexible: all brothers' shares were to be the same. Dowry allowed, to some extent at least, a differentiation among brothers inasmuch as dowries for each incoming bride were separately negotiated. Thus, a family with several sons and daughters could make different decisions for each one. Sometimes they could concentrate on affirming their prestige by arranging the best matches, ignoring how much dowry their sons' brides would bring and using up much of their disposable income for the daughters' dowries. Alternatively, they could worry about the future estates of their sons after division and try to soften the consequences by seeking sons-in-law who would take their daughters without large dowries or daughters-in-law for their sons who would come with good dowries.

Another strategy might be to have one or more son wait until he passed the examinations before arranging his marriage in the hope of securing a better dowry for him. Of course, dowry would never be the sole consideration in marriage negotiations; a well-connected father-in-law could be worth more than an ample dowry. Moreover, a family might consider it wiser to invest more in education and less in marriages.[108]

My third argument is that the obligations inherent in an affinal relationship could be strengthened by a large dowry. In an article published in 1981, I showed that the provision of dowry to daughters was associated with continuing obligations between the families of the bride and the groom.[109] The parents of the bride could expect more from their daughter, her husband, and her sons when they had married her out with a respectable dowry. The direct evidence I cited included Yuan Cai's advice to families with ample property to give their daughters a share of it on the grounds that their sons might prove incapable and they might therefore have to depend on their daughters' families even for their funerals and ancestral sacrifices.[110] I also pointed to strong ties between daughters and their natal families, ranging from daughters who took in their widowed mothers or arranged their parents' funerals or cared for their orphaned younger brothers, to parents or brothers who took responsibility for their widowed daughters or sisters.

One can easily posit (as Yuan Cai did) that a woman who had received material assets from her parents had a greater obligation to aid them if they were ever in need than a woman who had not. One can also suppose that a widow with a dowry at her disposal (who either had no children or who was taking them with her) could more easily choose where she wished to live than one without much of a dowry. There is no obvious reason, however, for a family that had sent off a daughter with a substantial dowry to feel more obligated to take her back than one that had provided little if anything beyond recycling of the betrothal gifts. In these cases, the logic of unbalanced exchanges might be what kept these ties active. I also suspect that dowry strengthened affinal ties because it created lingering claims to common property. Just as brothers were bound to each other as coparceners of graveyards and ancestral halls even after division of the household, affinal relatives were linked through mutual interest in the disposition of the dowry and this kept their ties alive.[111]

Another way to bring out the relationship between dowry and continuing reciprocal obligations is to consider either end of the spectrum of marriage finance. Families who sold their daughter as a concubine provided no dowry but received large "betrothal gifts" of cash. It was generally understood that they were losing kinship rights over her, that they might never meet their grandchildren, that these grandchildren need not come to their funeral, and so on.[112] At the other extreme were uxorilocal arrangements whereby families took in husbands for their daughters, generally expecting little or nothing in the way of betrothal gifts but providing their daughter with a dowry of much or all of their property. Such sons-in-law had many obligations to

Table 3.1 Matrilateral and affinal relatives to be avoided by officials

Woman relative	Mourning grade[a]	Relatives to be avoided
Mother	2a	her father, grandfather (FF), great grandfather (FFF), father's brother, brother, cousin (FBS), nephew (BS and ZS), brother-in-law (ZH), and sister's daughter's husband
Wife	2b	same as mother[b]
Grandmother (FM)	2c	none
Uncle's wife (FBW)	2c	none
Daughter	2c	her husband, sons, husband's father and brother, daughter's husband
Aunt (FZ)	3	her husband
Sister	3	her husband and son
Son's wife	3	her father and brother
Nephew's wife (BSW)	3	none
Niece (BD)	3	none
Cousin (FBD)	4	none
Brother's wife	4	none
Granddaughter (SD)	4	her husband
Nephew's daughter (BSD)	5	none

Source: SHY *zhiguan* 63.4.

Notes: For simplicity's sake this table is limited to cases where the man might plausibly have lived some time in a common household with the woman who provided the link.
a The mourning grades for female agnates are those they assumed upon marriage. These grades are based on JL 4.10b–15a.
b Not given in SHY, but probably a scribal error because in all the other lists, mother's and wife's natal relatives are given together (e.g., QYTFSL 8.101).

their wives' families – to support them, bury them, and see to it that their sacrifices continued.

Among the elite, strong affinal ties could be used not merely for kinship purposes (care of widows and orphans) but also for political ones. As anecdotes attest, families of officials seem to have often thought they could recruit sons-in-law with better career prospects by offering better dowries. The goal of such efforts does not seem so much to have been prestige but connections: sons-in-law make good clients and political allies. This line of thinking is clearly reflected in Song rules on nepotism. Table 3.1 lists affinal and matrilateral relatives under whom a man could not serve according to the nepotism rules of 1070. It is organized according to the woman who served as the kinship link between the two men.

As can easily be seen, the gradation in the scope of relatives to be avoided does not correspond to mourning grades. In Chinese kinship reckoning, a man is considered closely related to his father's brother and he mourns this uncle's wife at grade 2. Yet his ties of obligation to this woman's natal family were not considered strong enough to make avoidance necessary in a bureaucratic setting. The same is true of the families of the wives of a man's brothers and nephews. Even in the case of the family into which his sister had married, only her husband and son had to be avoided, not, for instance, her husband's father or brother. A man was considered most likely to feel obligations to men in his mother's and wife's families, and then to a lesser extent, to those in the families of his daughter's husband and son's wife.

The logic here, I contend, is that of dowry and not of consanguinity. It is true that a man is related by blood to his mother's family, but he is also tied by blood to his father's mother's family, to his father's sister's family, and so on. Moreover, he is not related by blood to anyone in his wife's family. A fairly large number of people in the family that sent a girl and a dowry had to be avoided by her husband and sons, but other members of the family into which she married are generally not involved. (That is, one had to avoid serving in the same office with a first cousin of one's wife, but not with the brother or father of one's brother's wife.) The difference would seem to be that one received nothing from the dowry a brother's wife brought, but brothers, grandparents, and uncles of one's wife could all have been coparceners of the family that sent her dowry. Moreover, one was the foremost contributor to the dowry of a daughter, somewhat less to that of a sister and son's daughter, and much less to that of a brother's daughter, and so on.

Let me reorganize my argument to sort out the causal chain that includes the shift toward large dowries. I see the growth of the economy, increasing availability of money, and freer transfer of land as general preconditions for both the growth of the educated class and the greater transfer of wealth through dowry. I see the political situation of the tenth century as bringing to the fore people who had no pedigree but who had been able to build armies or staff bureaucracies through various personal connections. Whenever such connections are useful, affinal ties will gain importance. Dowry, I argue, was an especially good way for those with wealth to try to secure preferred affinal relations (because it made a better bait, allowed flexible family strategies, and strengthened the ties once they were arranged). Given the competitiveness with which Song men pursued positions in the elite, it became difficult for families to gain a useful connection through a daughter without providing a dowry. In time, through market forces, it became nearly impossible to find any sort of suitable family for her. The civil service recruitment system was, meanwhile, evolving. The usefulness of affinal connections was continually confirmed and reproduced in this arena, both through the extension of privileges of facilitated entry into office to a wide range of kin and through provisions made to cut these privileges back. By the time nepotism rules were compiled in the mid-Song, the transfer of dowry was clearly associated with the assumed flow of favors. There is no point in asking which came first: dowry as a means to transfer property; an elite that continually used affinal kinship to create and repair networks that would secure or advance one in local or national politics; or a civil service system that continuously struggled against and gave ground to the desire of those inside and outside the system to use personal connections for both entry and advancement. These three phenomena were systematically related to each other and each kept the others strong.

Conclusion

By way of conclusion, I would like to consider briefly the implications that my interpretation of the shifts in marriage finance from the Tang to the Song may have for some established ideas about marriage payments and social structure.

First I would like to consider Goody's suggestion that dowry is associated with exclusive marriage practices and tends to preserve economic inequalities, as dowered marriages are arranged predominantly among families with comparable wealth.[113] From the Chinese case, one could argue that indirect dowry serves this purpose better than direct dowry. In the Tang it was easy for the wealth of the aristocracy to stay within the aristocracy because a family's property seldom had to leave the patriline except for the journey of betrothal gifts to the homes of future brides where it was turned into dowries and then returned, to again become regular family property after a generation. If the families of the brides neither retained any of the gifts nor supplemented them (each of which happened some of the time), then all family property would eventually devolve to patrilineal descendants.

In the Song substantial dowries regularly channeled property into other patrilines. At the same time, it is much harder to identify a circle that kept property within its own boundaries. The size of the educated class steadily expanded during the Song, and new *jinshi* seem to have been able to obtain dowries and therefore wealth from either rich families with no prior official connections or the families of officials. In the Chinese case, thus, betrothal gifts (bridewealth to be returned as indirect dowry) went along with a more constricted elite that passed down its standing and probably its wealth to its patrilineal descendants, and dowry was most visibly used by an expanding elite that was absorbing new families at both the local and national levels.

The second general issue I wish to raise concerns dowry and patrilineality. Bridewealth is much more common than dowry in African societies organized into segmentary patrilineages. Dowry is much more common in societies with bilateral inheritance and other bilateral tendencies (such as Europe). The civilizations of Asia fit between these two poles, dowry often coexisting with strong patrilineal kinship organization. Is there thus any generalizable relationship between marriage finance and forms of kinship organization? Will shifts in one have anything to do with shifts in the other?

In the Chinese case, new forms of localized patrilineages began to appear in several parts of the country in late Song.[114] These local lineages brought together agnatic relatives related through a common ancestor many generations back for joint ancestral rites. Groups of agnates frequently erected halls for these rites, set aside land to pay for them, and compiled genealogies.

In many areas they became major forces in local politics. Chronologically, the shift toward substantial dowries was visible before such descent groups appeared. Could diverging devolution have somehow triggered the growth of lineages? Or could they both be manifestations of some larger change in Chinese kinship organization?

I would argue, from what evidence there is, that these began as independent developments, substantial dowries taking off first among the elite, localized lineages gaining strength among ordinary people, though in time each reached to all social levels and each shaped the other's development. Large dowries had a couple of hundred years to get well established before descent groups were significant, though later the form and distribution of dowries were shaped by a context that included descent groups. Descent groups in China developed in an environment in which the elite and often commoners transmitted some wealth through dowries.

The spread of dowry may even be thought to have had a small role in shaping the form descent groups took in China. I see a connection between the prevalence of substantial dowry and the call for a strengthening of patrilineal principles. Some Song Neo-Confucians recognized that the shift toward transmitting property through daughters was a threat to China's traditional patrilineal, patriarchal family system. Their call for a "revival of the descent line system (*zong*)" was motivated in part by their objections to the strength of affinal relations and their fears concerning the break-up of patrimonies. This descent line rhetoric, in turn, helped to shape the way Chinese descent groups and lineages were eventually conceived.[115]

Descent line rhetoric and the growth of descent groups can also be given some credit for curbing the trend toward dowry. In Yuan (1215–1368) and Ming (1368–1644) times legal restrictions were placed on married women's control of their dowries, in particular their right to take them with them if they were widowed or divorced.[116] As Jennifer Holmgren argues, these restrictions probably had much to do with problems relating to Mongol family practices, such as the levirate.[117] Yet the political success of Cheng-Zhu Neo-Confucianism also facilitated this revision of the law. Descent groups, where they existed, may also have limited the incentive for large dowries among ordinary people by providing them with an adequate set of social connections. In recent times, dowry among ordinary farmers seems to have been larger in areas without strong lineages. Where there were strong lineages, the rich gave dowries, but not the ordinary poor farmer.

By ending this essay with a discussion of how the escalation of dowries was curbed, I wish to underline the dynamic nature of the changes I have described here. The growth of dowries can be seen as an effect of economic and political changes, but it also had effects of its own. It generated not only compatible institutions (such as legal elaborations) and symbols (associations with prestige) but also opposing forces (in rhetoric, law, and descent groups). These conflicting effects also interacted through time in complex ways, obscuring simple functional relations in the flux of social life.

4   The women in Liu Kezhuang's family*

As any reader will remember well, the Jia family in the *Dream of Red Mansions* (*Honglou meng*) was centered around the elderly grandmother. To the youthful Baoyu the family's key members, other than his father, were all females; they included his grandmother, his elder cousin's wife, his elder brother's widow, and his own sisters and cousins – not to mention the senior maids and concubines. The novel informs us of the life histories of most of these women, and provides enough information on their background, experiences, and opportunities for us to find their varied fates plausible.

Despite the prominence of these women and girls in the novel, no one could assert that this family was a matrilineal or matriarchal one; the family was orthodox in almost all the formal aspects of family institutions. Descent was patrilineal, marriage was patrilocal, authority and property were vested in the senior men, and it was these men who dealt with the outer world. The women themselves did not reject the male-centered family structure in order to create an alternative world of their own. The grandmother may have felt strong affection for her brother's or daughter's children, but she never questioned that her sons' sons and their sons came first. Nevertheless, the novel shows that the constraints on women and girls created by the structure of the family did not render them unimportant in the lives of the men and boys with whom they lived. The more senior of these women had considerable authority over men; and perhaps even more importantly, the emotional dimension of life at home for men was overwhelmingly based on relations with women.

The *Dream of Red Mansions* is a unique piece of literature. There are not even many other pieces of fiction that can compare to it in the portrayal of family life. Yet the *Dream of Red Mansions* raises questions about the lives of women and their place in the emotional lives of men that historians cannot easily ignore. For most Chinese in the past, life at home could never have been as dominated by women as it was for Baoyu, given that only the wealthiest would have had so many extra female kinsmen and maids and

* This article was originally published in *Modern China* 10 (1984: 415–40). Copyright ©1984 Sage Publications. Reproduced by permission of Sage Publications.

concubines living with them. Yet modern anthropologists have described how Chinese women in small, modest families create emotional bonds to their sons and daughters that often greatly outweigh the emotional ties among men. Even if, as Margery Wolf describes it, these emotional ties were fostered by women precisely because they lacked structural resources, the feelings are no less real or powerful in people's lives.[1]

How can historians investigate the emotional life of families in the past? As most historians know, documents that reveal feelings about close relatives are relatively scarce among Chinese historical records; there are very few diaries, sets of letters, or memoirs of the sort European historians have used to reconstruct family relations.[2] When historians think of biographies of women, they usually think first of the accounts of virtuous, admirable, or chaste women included under the rubric *lienü zhuan* in many histories and gazetteers. Since the women described there were all selected as exceptional, and since the accounts of the circumstances leading up to their heroic or self-effacing acts are often very sketchy, the best historians have been able to do with this genre is study its conventions.[3] There are, however, thousands of biographies of women included within the epitaph sections of men's collected works. These women have no special characteristics other than a relationship (usually a kinship one) to someone whose writings were preserved. And because these epitaphs are included in literary collections, it is possible to see how these women fit into the larger social life of the author.

In this article I will examine the family life of Liu Kezhuang (1187–1269), the role of women in it, and the lives of these women, using as my major source the epitaphs and related items in Liu Kezhuang's 196 *juan* collected works.[4] One reason Liu Kezhuang makes a good subject is that he lived past 80 and kept writing in old age. No one wrote epitaphs for everyone important in his life, if for no other reason than that not all of them died before him – but Liu Kezhuang lived so long that most of those closest to him died before he did. Similar reconstructions of family life could be done for many other long-lived writers in the Song through Qing period, who preserved the epitaphs they wrote for relatives.

Liu Kezhuang, known primarily as a poet, was not given a biography in the *Song History* or any contemporary local history. What is known of his life is based entirely on his own writings and the epitaph and record of conduct written by his friends. Needless to say, nothing is recorded in any historical source – other than his collected works – about any of the women in his family.

About a third of Liu Kezhuang's collection deals with his political life. Zhang Yan and Sun Keguan used these documents effectively to reconstruct Liu Kezhuang's political career, which was much entangled with the factional politics of the mid-thirteenth century.[5] Altogether Kezhuang spent about five years at court, fifteen years in provincial appointments, and fifteen years at home holding temple guardianships (sinecures for literary and scholarly men).

Liu Kezhuang's social and literary life could be reconstructed in almost as much detail as his political life. His collection contains twelve *juan* of colophons he wrote on paintings, calligraphies, and manuscripts that were in his friends' collections. It also includes the prefaces he wrote for their writings, the letters he wrote to them (including a great many birthday letters), and numerous epitaphs and elegies. Forty-eight *juan* of poems (*shi*) and a few more of other forms of verse, especially songs (*ci*), are also included.[6] A large proportion of the poems had social purposes: seeing off friends; condoling at funerals; and commemorating parties, promotions, and other special occasions. Many of the poems refer to friends and male relatives (brothers, cousins, sons, nephews, brothers-in-law, and "external" cousins). If these poems are an accurate reflection, Liu Kezhuang's public social life was conducted among males, mostly local friends, but including close male relatives. By and large, the poems shared with male relatives are indistinguishable in subject matter from those shared with friends, perhaps indicating that these close relatives were seen as companions.[7]

It is quite possible that over the years Liu Kezhuang wrote many letters and poems to his mother, wife, sisters, and daughters.[8] If he did, however, they have not been preserved in his collected works (unlike ones to his uncles, brothers, male cousins, sons, and nephews). Overwhelmingly, the surviving documents that reveal aspects of his relations with women are ones he wrote after their deaths. Once his mother passed 70 it seems to have become permissible to mention her in documents that circulated publicly.[9] None of the other women, however, lived past 70. Literary pieces written after a woman's death were of several sorts. For instance, for his mother, Kezhuang wrote an epitaph (*muzhiming*), three elegies (*jiwen*), one for the encoffining, one for the sacrifice the night before the burial, and one at the

Table 4.1 Epitaphs Liu Kezhuang wrote for relatives with whom he lived

1.	Mother, 153.1a–3a
2.	Uncle Liu Mishao, 151.6a–8a
3.	Wife, 148.16a–17b
4.	Concubine, 161.10a–b
5.	Brother Liu Kesun, 153.3b–7a
6.	Kesun's wife Lady Fang, 158.3b–7a
7.	Middle Sister, 157.2b–4a
8.	Brother Liu Kegang, 156.3a–6a
9.	Brother Liu Keyong, 160.2b–4a
10.	Keyong's wife Lady Lin, 160.4a–5a
11.	First cousin Liu Cheng, 153.7a–9a
12.	Second cousin Liu Xishen, 151.5a–6a
13.	Nephew Liu Weifu, 151.4a–5a
14.	Nephew Liu Xingfu, 159.15a–16a
15.	Nephew Liu Zhifu, 165.10a–12a

Source: HCXS passim.

Table 4.2 Epitaphs Liu Kezhuang wrote for kinsmen

Wife's family
1. Father, 149.3a–7a
2. Grandfather, 148.3a–5b
3. Gather's brother, 150.8b–11a
4. Brother Lin Gongxuan, 150.11a–13a
5. Gongxuan's wife, 163.1a–2b
6. Brother Lin Gongwei, 151.2a–4a
7. Gongwei's wife, 151.8a–9a
8. Cousin, 150.15a–16a

Elder sister's family
1. Husband, 160.8a–10a

Middle sister's family
1. Husband, 157.1a–2b
2. Son, 160.15a–b
3. Daughter, 152.1a–b

Brother Keyong's wife's family
1. Father, 150.16a–17b

Son's wife's family
1. Father, 151.11a–12a
2. Mother, 158.13b–15a
3. Father's brother, 157.5a
4. Father's brother's wife, 157.5a

Daughter's family
1. Husband's grandmother, 154.3a–4b
2. Husband's mother, 154.4b–5b
3. Husband's father, 165.12a–14a
4. Daughter, 159.4a–b

Brother Kesun's daughter's first family
1. Husband, 156.13b–14b
2. Husband's father, 141.1a–7a
3. Husband's father's brother, 149.13a–14a

Brother Kesun's daughter's second family
1. Husband's father, 145.1a–7a

Son's son's wife's family
1. Grandfather, 165.16a–17a

Son's daughter's husband's family
1. Father 162.3a–6a
2. Grandfather, 149.16b–18a

Source: HCXS, passim.

closing of the tomb, and two prayers, one written a year and the other sixteen years after she died.[10] For his wife he wrote an epitaph, four elegies (a standard one, one for the funeral, one on returning home after the funeral, and one at the closing of the tomb), a poem of grief, a song, and a prayer.[11]

Similar pieces were written for his sisters and sisters-in-law, but he did not write each piece for each one.

For the historian, the main advantage of epitaphs over elegies, poems of grief, and similar pieces is that epitaphs provide more details – more names, dates, and places. Kezhuang wrote forty-three epitaphs for close relatives who died before him. (See Tables 4.1, 4.2, and Figure 4.1.) These epitaphs allow us a glimpse of a complex family from one individual's perspective, and reveal a surprising number of similarities between this family and the fictional family of Jia Baoyu.

The vital data in epitaphs includes year of birth and death for both men and women. Moreover, from wives' epitaphs it is often possible to reconstruct age at marriage of both husband and wife. Marital fertility is also often described fully. Virtually no other premodern Chinese source has anything to say about children who died young. Given that her child-bearing record was one of a woman's major claims to significance, even children who died young were often recorded in her epitaph. Moreover, in this source at least it was considered important to distinguish sons born and reared from sons merely reared. (The epitaphs for the woman's husband usually would not distinguish between these two groups of sons.)

The value of epitaphs does not depend entirely on the data in them. At least as importantly, epitaphs reveal what men thought about kinsmen and kinship. Some scholars have dismissed epitaphs as hopelessly stereotyped, classing them with the "model lives" of chaste widows and other moral heroes.[12] There were, of course, conventions for the writing of epitaphs – indeed, they had ritual purposes, associated as they were with deaths and burials. Nevertheless, their content indicates more than the ideals of their authors. Epitaphs were recognized occasions for discussing kinship matters – from the reasons why a marriage had been arranged, to little kindnesses offered relatives, to special acts of filial service to parents and parents-in-law, to advice offered to children and other relatives, to emotional responses to the death of loved ones. Moreover, the authors of epitaphs often included what they considered illuminating anecdotes, ones that to them demonstrated character or superior performance of required roles.

The major limitation of epitaphs as a source for attitudes and feelings about family life is that authors did not "speak the whole truth." In epitaphs a writer records the feelings and memories that linger after the person has died. Memories are selective; the day-to-day annoyances, disagreements, and jealousies that mar most family relations are not foremost in one's mind when recalling someone recently deceased. Beside this, epitaphs are tributes. Like letters of recommendation today, writers seek to find good things they can say about their subject and positive ways to allude to any failings. In epitaphs only positive or neutral traits are mentioned – a person might be described as sickly but not as argumentative. Thus epitaphs and other tributes are ambiguous. By failing to mention the subject's intelligence is the writer trying to indicate that the person is dull? Is a reference to someone's

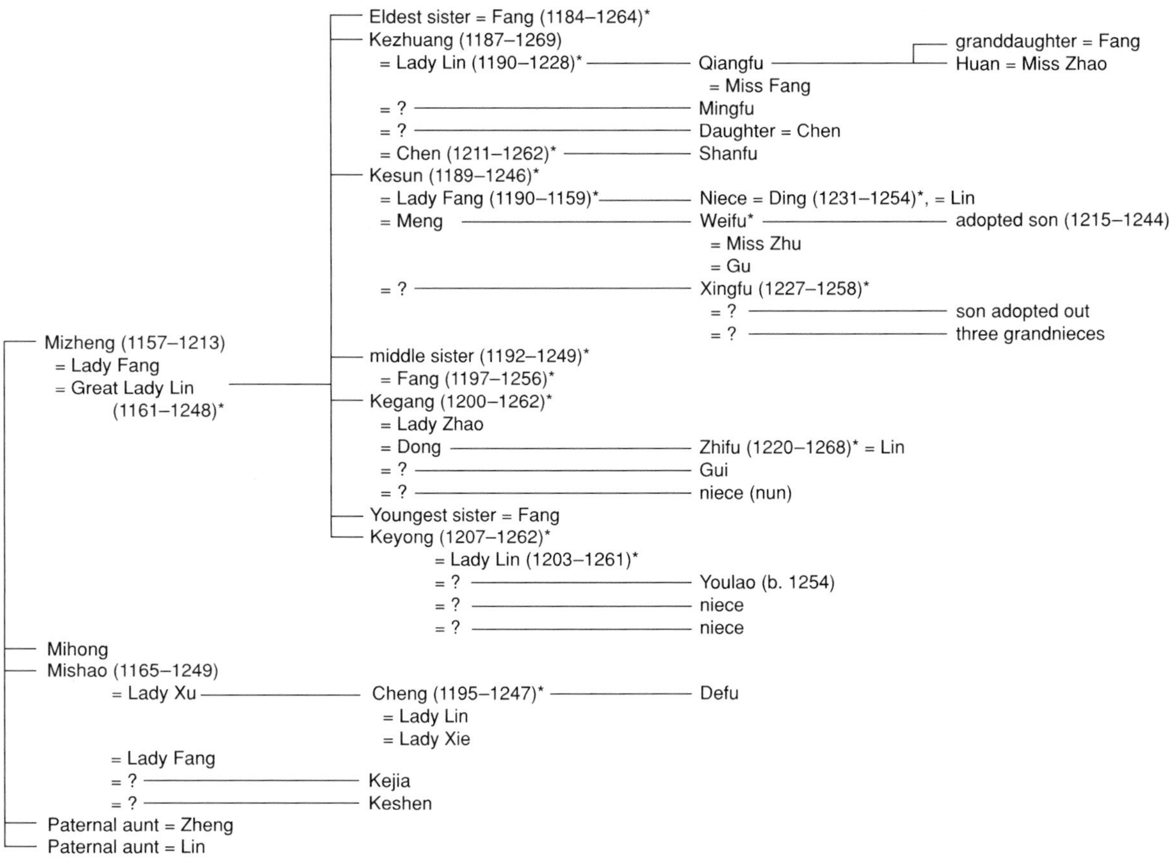

Mizheng (1157–1213)
= Lady Fang
= Great Lady Lin (1161–1248)*

Eldest sister = Fang (1184–1264)*

Kezhuang (1187–1269)
= Lady Lin (1190–1228)*
— Qiangfu
   = Miss Fang
  Mingfu
  Daughter = Chen
  Shanfu
  — granddaughter = Fang
    Huan = Miss Zhao
— = ?
— = ?

Kesun (1189–1246)*
= Lady Fang (1190–1159)*
= Chen (1211–1262)*
= Meng
= ?
— Niece = Ding (1231–1254)*, = Lin
— Weifu*
  = Miss Zhu
  = Gu
  Xingfu (1227–1258)*
  — adopted son (1215–1244)
  — son adopted out
  — three grandnieces
  = ?
  = ?

middle sister = Fang (1192–1249)*
= Fang (1197–1256)*

Kegang (1200–1262)*
= Lady Zhao
= Dong
= ?
= ?
— Zhifu (1220–1268)* = Lin
  Gui
  niece (nun)

Youngest sister = Fang

Keyong (1207–1262)*
= Lady Lin (1203–1261)*
= ?
= ?
= ?
— Youlao (b. 1254)
  niece
  niece
  niece

Mihong
Mishao (1165–1249)
= Lady Xu
= Lady Fang
= ?
= ?
— Cheng (1195–1247)*
  = Lady Lin
  = Lady Xie
  Defu
— Kejia
  Keshen

Paternal aunt = Zheng
Paternal aunt = Lin

Figure 4.1 Genealogy of Liu Kezhuang's immediate family

Source: Epitaphs as listed in Tables 4.1 and 4.2

Notes: Wives are distinguished from other mates in terms of Lady or Miss. Even when one of Liu Kezhuang's female relative's husband's name is known in full, it has been omitted for the sake of brevity, as are the names of their children.

*Subject of epitaph by Liu Kezhuang

absorption in his or her own pursuits a tactful criticism of lack of concern for others? It is only through reading many tributes that one can learn to sense the significance of an author's omissions and roundabout criticisms and recognize that he is not describing everyone in the same way, even if some of his descriptions use standard phrases and clichés.

LIU KEZHUANG'S CHILDHOOD

From the epitaphs Ye Shi (1150–1223) wrote for Liu Kezhuang's father, grandfather, and granduncle, we know that the family into which Liu Kezhuang was born was an established official family of Putian, on the coast of Fujian. His grandfather and his grandfather's brother (referred to as the Two Liu Gentlemen) had both been scholars and officials of considerable repute, but they both had died long before he was born.[13] Nevertheless, their descendants continued to live side by side with each other for nearly another century. Liu Kezhuang's grandmother was from a Lin family. Lin was a common name in coastal Fujian, borne by many eminent families.[14] The Two Liu Gentlemen each had three sons, the eldest one of whom was Kezhuang's father, Mizheng (1157–1213).[15] For a decade or two after the deaths of the Two Liu Gentlemen in 1170 and 1171 the family seems to have had a difficult time, for neither Mizheng nor any of his brothers or cousins was over 15 *sui* at the time. Still, some of them at least were able to concentrate on study, as demonstrated by the success of both Mizheng and his two cousins Qimei and Qishi in passing the *jinshi* examinations.[16]

Mizheng's first wife, Lady Fang, died early, leaving no surviving children. He took another wife, Great Lady Lin (1161–1248), who would later become the central figure in this family. She was from a prominent official family but not necessarily a relative of her husband's mother. The two surnames Fang and Lin reappear over and over in subsequent marriages, accounting for two-thirds of all known marriages of members of this family. Great Lady Lin's original family may have been richer than the one she married into because she is said later to have sold the clothes she brought as dowry to help provide for the weddings of her sisters-in-law and brothers-in-law. In her childhood home, she had also acquired an education. Under the guidance of her uncle (her father having died early), she and her elder sister had studied the *Shiji* and *Hanshu*.[17]

During the early years of her marriage, Great Lady Lin lived in a complex household headed by Grandmother Lin. Mizheng's two brothers and two sisters were not yet married and lived with them.[18] Moreover, his cousins lived in the adjoining house and treated Grandmother Lin and Mizheng as the family's seniors.[19] One of these cousins had a son born two years before Kezhuang; this boy, Xichun, would be Kezhuang's playmate and schoolmate for many years.[20]

Great Lady Lin's first surviving child was a girl, Kezhuang's elder sister. Kezhuang was born next, when Great Lady Lin was 27 *sui*. Over the next 20 years she bore five more children who survived to adulthood, and possibly some who did not. By the time Kezhuang was 6 *sui* he had a younger brother (Kesun) and a younger sister, as well as several younger cousins next door, children of his father's brother Mishao and his father's cousins Qishi, Qimei, and Qiyuan. Kezhuang's childhood thus was spent among numerous children.

During his childhood, according to Kezhuang, his middle sister, five years his junior, was his parents' favorite and the most able to please them. Great Lady Lin was a devout Buddhist, a faith that this sister also acquired.[21] When Kezhuang was in his teens, his two youngest brothers, Kegang and Keyong, were born. In his old age Kezhuang became close to his youngest brother, but he could not have known him well in their youth. In his teen years Kezhuang also met some of his "external" relatives. Two of his longterm friends, Fang Xinru and Fang Yu, were described as *biao* cousins, perhaps children of one of his father's female cousins. Kezhuang was 17 *sui* when he met Fang Yu for the first time.[22]

MARRIAGE AND EARLY ADULT YEARS

Barely had Great Lady Lin stopped bearing children herself when it was time to begin the marriages of her sons and daughters. Kezhuang's eldest sister was undoubtedly the first to be married. She married a Fang, as her two younger sisters would later do. (None of these husbands was closely related to any other.) In an epitaph Kezhuang reported that, because his father was not rich, his three sisters married men without official rank – although some of them later went on to gain it.[23] The next to marry may have been Kezhuang's first younger brother, Kesun, who had been engaged since birth to a Miss Fang. They were married in 1209, only a year after Great Lady Lin's youngest son was born.[24] Kezhuang married the same year. His wife, (senior) Lady Lin, was from a family of officials but not a relative of his mother.[25] The year they were married she was 20 *sui* and he was 23 *sui*.[26] Within two years she gave birth to a boy, Qiangfu, the first of Great Lady Lin's patrilineal grandchildren.

Soon after the marriage of his first three children, Kezhuang's father Mizheng fell ill. Kezhuang's middle sister, then about 20 *sui*, devoted herself to nursing him. She prayed to the Buddha that she be able to give her life in his stead. When he finally died in 1213, she stayed home to carry out the full mourning and attend to the needs of her mother.[27] Thus she was unable to marry until the end of the mourning period, when she was 24 or 25 *sui*, relatively old for a bride. Her husband, Mr. Fang, was five years her junior.

Despite the death of his father, Liu Kezhuang's family remained prosperous in this period, perhaps in part because Kezhuang himself now held office. The senior male, his uncle Mishao, had never served in the government, contenting himself with teaching and scholarship. Forty-nine *sui* when his elder brother Mizheng died, Mishao seems to have largely withdrawn from household affairs, for Kezhuang said that "in his late years he closed his gate and had little contact with people."[28]

Thus, although Mishao would live another thirty-odd years, his sister-in-law Great Lady Lin seems to have become the dominant personality in this home. On his death bed Mizheng had expressed great regret that he had not managed to live long enough to arrange all of his children's marriages and he asked his wife to take charge of these matters. She then, according to Kezhuang, set about seeing that the sons continued the family tradition of scholarship and that the girls married *shidafu* (gentlemen/officials).[29]

Although Great Lady Lin is described as well-educated, there is no evidence that any of her four daughters-in-law were. Nor did any of them match her in fertility. Of Great Lady Lin's four sons, only one had a surviving son by his wife. Surviving, of course, was a matter of chance. In Liu Kezhuang's case, his first wife, Senior Lady Lin, bore two boys and two girls, of which only one, the first boy, survived. During her lifetime Kezhuang also had two children of "secondary birth" (*shusheng*) who survived.[30] "Secondary birth" was the term used when the mother was either a maid or a concubine. Later Kezhuang took a more formal concubine, who bore three children, only one of whom, a son, survived.[31] None of Great Lady Lin's other three daughters-in-law had any sons who survived, and only one had a daughter. Consequently, of Great Lady Lin's twelve surviving grandchildren, ten were "of secondary birth." There is no way even to guess how many maids and concubines there were in the house, but presumably they were numerous. The daughters-in-law were all praised for their gentleness in managing them.

The two daughters-in-law who bore the major burden of serving Great Lady Lin were Kesun's wife, Lady Fang (1190–1259), and Keyong's wife, Junior Lady Lin (1203–1261). Lady Fang served Great Lady Lin, as Kezhuang reports, for over forty years, remaining filial in her manner after her own hair was white. She bore three children, but only one, a girl, survived. However, she raised her husband's two sons of secondary birth, Weifu (born in 1215) and Xinfu (born in 1227). She did not accompany her husband to his posts as did Kezhuang's wife, remaining instead in the family home.[32]

In 1223 the last daughter-in-law entered the house. She was Junior Lady Lin, four years older than her husband, Keyong, then only 17 *sui*. Keyong's marriage was most likely speeded up because Great Lady Lin was already over 60. Keyong had been only 7 *sui* when his father died, so Great Lady Lin had educated him herself, and he always stayed closely attached to her. After repeatedly failing in the examinations, he stayed at home, devoting himself to poetry writing.[33] His wife is said to have concentrated her efforts on providing Great Lady Lin a happy old age. Unfortunately, Junior Lady Lin seems to have been a sickly woman, suffering from recurrent stomach problems, perhaps ulcers. She had no children of her own, nor any to raise until much later. (The only son to survive her husband was born "of secondary birth" over thirty years after Junior Lady Lin entered the house as a bride.)[34]

After she had daughters-in-law to manage the household affairs, Great Lady Lin turned more of her attention to Buddhism, keeping to a vegetarian diet, meditating regularly, and maintaining contact with leading Buddhists at monasteries nearby. According to her son, her faith in Buddhism did not lead her to neglect her social and ritual obligations to relatives. Yet, even in such secular activities, he said, she never gave up in her efforts to convert everyone to Buddhism.[35]

Although Kezhuang and his brothers all lived with Great Lady Lin in a common residence, family finances were not pooled. In epitaphs for wives in complex families where the bulk of the assets were held as group property, it is usual to find them praised for strict fairness in any distribution of goods and devotion to the common good. By contrast, in the epitaphs for his wife and two sisters-in-law, Kezhuang stressed instead how they made do with the little available before their husbands gained office, and did not become extravagant thereafter; only their own husband's salaries seem to have had any relevance to the amount of money available for them to spend. Thus, even if there still was some common property, official salaries do not seem to have been contributed to this fund. Kezhuang said of his wife:

> During the long time I was poor she economized and took care of provisions, never once complaining that they were inadequate. Once I had a salary, she did not change anything in the way she clothed and fed the family.[36]

Kezhuang's youngest brother did not hold office; so, praise for his wife had to take a slightly different direction: "Her husband's ancestral property was very meager and he had an old mother to support. Therefore Lady Lin was particularly economical in family expenses, saving up penny by penny so that she could expand the property holdings.[37] Consequently her husband was never bothered by petty matters."[38]

In his adult years, Kezhuang maintained contact with each of his sisters. He described his elder sister's domestic life in some detail. Her husband, a Confucian scholar and teacher, devoted every bit of his energy to his studies. Meanwhile, Kezhuang's sister did all the housework, looked after the farm, and for fifty years scrimped and saved to pay for family expenses and arrange all the marriages of their children.[39]

MIDDLE AGE AND MORTALITY

Kezhuang's wife, Senior Lady Lin, was the first of his generation of brothers and their wives to die. She died in 1228, when she was 39 *sui* and he 42. In his epitaph for her he described how she accompanied him on all his travels, remaining imperturbable whatever the circumstances:

> Once the boat capsized at Songdan, and only ten people survived. When we were told that our baggage was lost in the water, I became very upset, but she remained as calm as usual. Another time when we were sailing on the Li River the boat crashed. As before she showed no sign of panic in the face of peril.[40]

On one of these journeys, on the way to take up the post of magistrate of Jianyang, Senior Lady Lin acquired a stomach ailment so serious she could not keep down any food. After a respite she became paralyzed, and neither the 100 pills Kezhuang gave her, nor the prayers to the Buddha he arranged for her, saved her life. To add to his grief, Kezhuang had to go away on an assignment and could not be with her when she died.[41]

Kezhuang seems to have been genuinely attached to his wife, promising on her death that he would remain a widower and see that he did nothing to grieve her. Her tomb would be his also, and he would devote himself to study and personal cultivation.[42] What happened next he described in the epitaph for his subsequent concubine:

> When I was 42 I was in deep grief – Lady Lin, who was so worthy, had died so young. I was not going to marry again. However, after her funeral there was no one to wait on me with towel and comb. Someone reported that there was an orphaned Miss Chen, originally of a major family, whose mother had taken her along when she remarried. The girl now had no place to go. My late mother the Great Lady Lin took her for me.[43]

Liu Kezhuang then praised the way Miss Chen, still in her teens when he took her, looked after all the little family matters for the next thirty-five years, remembering everything and managing the family finances. He referred to her neither as his wife nor as his concubine, but as his youngest son's "birth mother." He referred to himself not as her husband but as her "master."[44] Although he took Miss Chen as a concubine, Kezhuang did not forget his wife; decades after her death he wrote a prayer recalling his feelings for her.[45] Nor did he become estranged from her family. For forty years after her death, he continued to see her brothers, brothers' wives, and nephews and to write epitaphs for them.[46]

Despite the death of his wife, the 1230s seem to have been a time of great joy and prosperity for Liu Kezhuang's family. Great Lady Lin was still in good health, and three of her sons were officials so that "banners always filled the outer courtyard."[47] Moreover, at least eight grandchildren were living. In a song Kezhuang wrote on his birthday in 1242, he concluded with the comment that he had no desire to become an immortal or a Buddha or assist heaven's commands; rather he wanted his family to go on forever as they were – a fortunate family of white-haired mother and son.[48]

This joy turned to gloom in the mid-1240s as deaths of family members followed one after the other. The first to die was Kesun's eldest son Weifu. As Kezhuang showed in his epitaph for him, the family's expectations for this young man had been high:

> He was a tall young man of refined bearing, endowed with quick intelligence and articulate. Within the family, he was always readily compliant to his grandmother, parents, uncles, and elder cousins; outside he was perfectly affable in dealing with kinfolk, townsmen, and friends. His ability to handle family business was extraordinary. When he quoted the classics or discussed historical events, his comments were always worth listening to. In addition, his regulated verse was remarkably lucid.[49]

Weifu died in the capital where he was waiting to take the civil service examinations. A victim of dysentery, he was then 30 *sui*. His father and Lady Fang took his death extremely hard. Kezhuang expressed their feelings in his epitaph:

> Alas! It is common to worry about having no descendants. And once one has a son, he is afraid to hope that the son will live long enough to grow up. While the son is growing up, he dares not count on him being attractive and intelligent. Finally he grows up attractive and intelligent. Then after hoping for so long and taking so many pains, he can be lost in a moment. For [Weifu] to have no chance to carry on our family's literary tradition when he had the intelligence to do so; to have no chance to be promoted when he had the talent to give advice at court; to have this bright jade covered with external darkness – what a tragedy![50]

Weifu's father, Kesun, never got over his son's death. He died at the end of 1246, the year that he buried his son.[51] His mother also was not quick to forget him; as soon as her second stepson Xingfu (twelve years Weifu's junior) bore a son "of secondary birth," she had this child appointed Weifu's heir.[52]

When Kesun died, family members were afraid to inform Great Lady Lin, by this time in her mid-eighties and ailing. This pretense they managed to keep up for over a year.[53] Because Great Lady Lin was ill, Kezhuang's middle sister now often would "abandon the work in her husband's house" to come and tend her, staying for several months or half a year at a time. Great Lady Lin may have specially sought this daughter's company, for she was the only one of her progeny really able to discuss Buddhist philosophy with her.[54] Kezhuang himself returned home from an assignment to take charge of seeing that the younger members of the family cared for her. The following year, and the year after, he turned down official assignments to be with his mother during her last days.[55] In his memorials requesting to be excused from office he stressed that he was the eldest son and that his mother's eyes were getting worse and worse. He noted that because he was nearly 60 himself he would not have much longer to care for her and could not bear to be any distance from her.[56] Although claiming an old or ill parent was always a good excuse for avoiding undesired appointments, Kezhuang's desire to stay at home appears to have been genuine. He wrote to a friend that people suspected his motives falsely: "It is really that my old mother is 88 this year and mother and son depend on each other for their life and are inseparable."[57]

Kezhuang attributed Great Lady Lin's demise, at age 88 *sui*, to indigestion brought on by her excessive fondness for tea and rock candy.[58] Adding to the grief of losing his nephew, brother, and mother, by 1249 Kezhuang had also suffered the loss of his uncle Mishao and his elder and middle sisters. As he said in one epitaph, these deaths followed so closely one upon the other that he felt they must be punishment for some sin he had committed.[59]

OLD AGE

Kezhuang himself lived to the age of 83 *sui*, long enough to outlive his concubine and to see eight grandsons and five granddaughters born to his three sons.[60] He even lived to see two of these granddaughters marry and to arrange the marriage of his senior grandson to the daughter of one of his own friends.[61]

Despite these marriages, one senses that Kezhuang's family was never the same after the death of his mother. None of the daughters-in-law came close to attaining her stature, either by bearing many children or by living a long time. Only Lady Fang (Kesun's wife) even reached the age of 60, and she died at 70, ten years before Kezhuang's own death. Like Kezhuang's mother, Lady Fang was attended by her daughter at her death, and since she had no surviving sons it was this daughter who led the funeral.[62]

Little is known of Kezhuang's daughters-in-law or nephews' wives, the girls who married into his house. Three girls born into it survived to adulthood. One of them, Kegang's daughter, became a nun,[63] possibly in a family cloister. (Had Great Lady Lin succeeded in converting her to Buddhism?) Kesun's daughter married a Mr. Ding, who died at the age of 24.[64] Although she had a son of her own and adopted two others, she did not stay long in the Ding house, within five years of her husband's death marrying a Mr. Lin.[65] Kezhuang's own daughter married a Mr. Chen. Her only two children were daughters, both of whom died young. The elder, beloved by parents and grandparents, suffered from epilepsy. At 13 she became ill while visiting Kezhuang's house and died a few days later.[66]

In his late years Kezhuang complained often of illness and appears to have been completely blind from age 81, an affliction he described as worse than any other.[67] Nevertheless, in 1268, at the age of 82, he took the active role in arranging his grandson's marriage. The arrangements for this marriage are described in considerable detail in the epitaph and elegy Kezhuang wrote for the bride's father, Zhao Shiqi, who died before the marriage was completed.

> Alas! My friendship with you was not a fleeting one; early on we were good friends and in our late years we became especially close. In that period I once said to you, "I have already handed back my tablet of office. Gradually I have finished arranging the marriages of my sons and daughters. The only one left to worry about is Huan. He is of pure character and moreover the first son of my first son. I took advantage of the regulations to get him a court rank, and almost at once he left, without having acquired a wife. You have a grown-up, beautiful, and accomplished daughter whose virtues are talked of in the women's quarters. Wouldn't they match?" You kindly agreed, and discussed the matter very frankly with me. Among us a word was as strong as metal or stone, so the ritual steps of "Asking the Names" and "Presenting Gifts" were completed before the day was out.[68] When your carriage came to get you and we were saying good-bye at my gate, we set a date for the wedding. You seemed pleased and said sincerely, "Fu is only one day's sail from Pu.[69] I will send my daughter; you need not bother to come for her." At the end of the intercalary month in the spring, the divination was performed and I sent a servant with a letter asking you to choose a lucky day. He stayed two nights and on his return I learned the bad news [of your death].[70]

Before he had died Mr. Zhao had instructed his wife to carry on with the wedding. In the elegy Liu Kezhuang reports that he tried to get her to keep to the original schedule, arguing that the ritual rules on mourning could sometimes be adjusted to circumstances. The widow, however, requested that the marriage be postponed so that her daughter would not have to take up wifely duties while burdened with sorrow. Moreover, the widow argued, she needed her daughter's help and "loving her as much as her own life" did not want to part with her during her own grief. Therefore, the marriage did not take place until the middle of the next year, which was still a curtailment of the mourning expected of a daughter still in her father's house.[71]

CONCLUSIONS

During the 83 years of Liu Kezhuang's life, he lived in close contact with many women. There was the dowager who, for more than thirty years after her husband's death, presided over the home of her sons and grandchildren. There was a sister who often left her husband's family to come back to keep her mother company. There was a wife who traveled with him and died young and a concubine who took over the duties of this wife. There was a sister-in-law with no children to raise who tended to the dowager and another who poured her efforts into her husband's sons by other women. There was a niece who remarried and another who became a nun. There was a girl who cut short the mourning for her father so that Kezhuang could live to see a grandson married.

The lives of these women did not all fit into a standard pattern. Yet they had one thing in common: Their fates depended above all on the very chancy mortality of those around them. Statistics of high infant mortality and high mortality in youth and middle age are often read as averages or means: For instance, the average wife might bear only 1.2 sons who lived to marry. In modern life, where family sizes and number of children fall predominately within a narrow range, it is much too easy to imagine that three-quarters of the people were very close to the average. Looking at the genealogy of Liu Kezhuang's family shows how one could have a fertility rate (calculated in terms of children who survived to marry born per woman) that would not have been far from the norm, and yet have very few "typical" sibling sets. In other words, the variance around the mean was very great. Some women were highly fertile, others marginally fertile, others not at all; some lost over half their children in childhood, others, through luck, very few. Thus, assuming that Liu Kezhuang's family formally divided after his mother's death, only one of her four sons (Kezhuang himself) was able to replicate in any way the complex family in which they all had grown up.

Another reason none of Kezhuang's brothers had large complex families is that adults kept dying at all ages. Of those who lived to marry, the mean age at death for men and women was in the mid-fifties, which sounds "average," but which actually means that for each one to live into his or her seventies, another, on the average, died in their thirties, and for each to live into the eighties, another died in his or her twenties. The death of both of Kesun's sons before they had reached 33 is an example of this. The structural consequences of the wide range of ages at death were the orphans, widows, widowers, and childless that Chinese sources had always mentioned as social problems. Less-prosperous families would have suffered these consequences with at least the frequency of a wealthy family like Liu Kezhuang's.

Another striking feature of Liu Kezhuang's family must have been important mainly in prosperous families – the numbers of children born to concubines and maids. As mentioned above, ten of Great Lady Lin's surviving grandchildren were born to such women. These children of course could compensate for the shortage of sons by wives. As seen in the hopes invested in Weifu, if the wife had no children and raised the son of a concubine herself, he could be given every possible chance to carry on the family traditions. Certainly a supply of such sons must have aided greatly the social survival of the upper class.

How important were these women and girls in Liu Kezhuang's social and emotional life? No direct comparison with Jia Baoyu is possible given that we know Baoyu primarily as an adolescent and Kezhuang as an adult with many ties outside the home. Moreover, as mentioned at the beginning, epitaphs do not give "the whole truth," even on feelings and sentiments. Still, I am willing to hazard some broad generalizations. Socially, the women in his family provided Liu Kezhuang with many connections to men. Kezhuang was friendly with *biao* cousins and with men in the families connected to his by marriage, especially his wife's brothers and his sisters' husbands. For marriages among his children and nieces and nephews, the friendship may have often preceded the marriage, as was seen in the case of the marriage arranged with the daughter of Zhao Shiqi. On the whole, despite the predominance of the Lin and Fang surnames, marriages seem to have been used to extend wider circles of kinship, not reinforce a narrow one. Whereas some Song families practiced "repeat" marriages, selecting spouses from among people already quite closely related, there appears to be only one possible case of this sort among Liu Kezhuang's relatives.[72]

Women were undoubtedly even more important to Liu Kezhuang's emotional life than his social life. Yet his feelings for them are not easily summarized, given that omissions, oblique criticisms, and filial piety must all be taken into account in analyzing what he says in epitaphs. From my reading of these epitaphs, I infer that Liu Kezhuang was not involved closely with his sisters or female cousins. Sisters and married daughters were regular visitors in his home, but according to his own testimony they came more to see the women there than the men. (Kezhuang did, however, chat with his daughter's daughter on her visit to his home.) Kezhuang's attachment to his wife appears to have been strong, but because she died young she never played the focal role that his mother did. From Kezhuang's testimony, his brothers, sisters, and sisters-in-law all shaped their lives around Great Lady Lin's. To some extent this might be a polite fiction, but Liu Kezhuang provides details of the way family members gathered by her side. Keyong spent his whole life at home, in part because he did not wish to leave her. Kezhuang's own attachment to her comes out in many contexts, not least of which were his efforts to spend time with her at home. Even though the tensions that may have disrupted life in the Liu home cannot be measured, these epitaphs show some of the attachments and affection that contributed to its cohesion.

APPENDIX

To illustrate the richness of epitaphs as sources for the study of family relations, below are translations of those Liu Kezhuang wrote for his sister-in-law Lady Fang and his "external" granddaughter Miss Chen.

Lady Fang, wife of my younger brother

Lady Fang was a fourth generation descendant of the prefect of Mei named Cipeng, the great-granddaughter of the magistrate of Jinjiang named Shendao, the granddaughter of the magistrate of Haifeng named Guang, and the daughter of Rong and Miss Lin. She was the wife of my senior younger brother, the secretary of the board of works, Kesun.

Long before, my late father and her late father had been classmates. They arranged the marriages by "pointing to the bellies."[73] Therefore, Lady Fang married my brother as soon as she was of age [literally, "pinned"] and served Great Lady Lin, her mother-in-law, for over forty years. In this she was filial and attentive; even when her hair was white she would wait on Mother Lin as a daughter-in-law without any sign of remiss. My brother was untalented at making a living but loved antiques and would spend every cent to collect famous paintings and calligraphies. Lady Fang calmly made secret economies and never complained of lacking anything. Later my brother served as a prefect three times but did nothing to enrich himself. Lady Fang continued her service to those above and care for those below contentedly, spending no more than before.

Lady Fang was a widow for over ten years. During this time she arranged for her husband's tomb, completed marriage arrangements for her children, repaired the old house, and brought new fields into cultivation in order to continue the thread of our family and preserve the orphans. My brother's son Rui and daughters Shun and Rong were born of Lady Fang. Rui and Shun died young. There were two boys of secondary birth, Weifu (ranked *jiangshilang*) and Xingfu (ranked *dikonglang* and magistrate of Zhenghe in Jianning prefecture). Lady Fang tended to them in their childhood and educated them as they grew up with more thoroughness than if she had borne them herself. By nature she was considerate and she was always kind to the maids and concubines. She did not have a trace of the common female failing of jealousy. Her whole family and her whole community praised her virtue.

Weifu was the first to die. Xingfu was all there was left to represent the family, and Lady Fang invested all her hope in him. In her old age he retired from his post to care for her. Unluckily he also died young. Although Lady Fang had always been extremely philosophical, losing her two pearls wounded her spirits so much that she began to decline. She was already ill when she buried Xingfu. This illness would not get better, and in the second month, the *guimao* day, of the *siwei* year of Kaiqing [1259] she died, aged 70.

Earlier, Xingfu's son of secondary birth was made heir to Weifu. The idea was that Xingfu was in his prime and could have many more heirs himself. But he lost each one as soon as he had them. Now we will have to consult to find a close relative of the appropriate generation to be the heir.

Alas, with my brother's purity and Lady Fang's virtue, they ought to be enjoying the reward of progeny. But up in the high pavilion, behind the gauze curtain, there is only a single grandson, still being nurtured, and three granddaughters, one engaged and two still young. Anyone who hears of this laments.

Lady Fang's daughter Rong married Lin Zonghuan (ranked *dikonglang*, a preparatory agent of the pacification commission of Zhexi circuit), the oldest son of Lin Gongbin.[74] Rong was her mother's darling and did not leave her mother from the time she got sick through her death and funeral. Everyone around was moved and saddened. She was extremely earnest as she carried out the movement of the body and strictly performed the final farewell.

In the eleventh month of that year, on the day *yiyou*, Lady Fang was buried with my brother in West Mountain.[75]

My granddaughter

Miss Chen was a great-granddaughter of the Upright Lord. Her father, Yan, and mother, Miss Liu, had long had no sons; therefore, they loved their two daughters dearly. The younger one died first, and Miss Chen suffered from recurrent epilepsy.

By nature Miss Chen was so sincere and intelligent that her great-grandmother Lady Nie, grandfather Zongyuan, and grandmother Lady Zhao all were especially kind to her. By the *dingsi* year of Baoyou [1257], she was already 13 and becoming steadily more astute, not at all like the typical sickly child. When her father went to the capital to be assigned a post she would become tearful whenever she thought of him. Nothing made her happier than receiving a letter from him.

One day on a visit to our house with her mother, she and I were engaged in a lively conversation when suddenly she felt very uncomfortable. She left for home and after two nights was disoriented and unable to talk. Apparently her old ailment had acted up again and none of the doctors could do anything about it. Four days later she died on the eighth day of the ninth month. Her father returned too late to see her a final time, and could do nothing but mourn tearfully with his wife. On the 22nd of the twelfth month in the same year, she was buried together in the stone tomb by her great aunt's grave. Her maternal grandfather Houcun inscribed it.[76]

5   The early stages in the development of descent group organization*

Twenty-five years ago, Denis Twitchett wrote that "one of the most urgent tasks confronting the social historian writing on China is to provide a dynamic picture of the developments in clan organization over the past two millennia."[1] However urgent this task may have seemed, since Twitchett's own study of the Fan estate and its management, very little research has been done on the historical issues of change and development. Scholars have added a dozen or more case studies of lineages, but most of these have concentrated on analyzing how lineages operated in a static, ideal form, rather than examining how forms of organization developed or spread.[2] Moreover, scholars have often assumed that there was only one type of lineage and that features important in modern lineages, especially corporately owned landed property and genealogies, played the same roles everywhere and in all stages of lineage development.[3] Even the broad surveys of lineages done a generation ago by the Japanese legal and sociological historians Niida, Shimizu, and Makino, which drew together great quantities of information, did not altogether escape these failings.[4] This essay, therefore, will try to correct the balance by looking at the development of kinship organization in a historical context, concentrating on the period 1000–1400.

As I organized material for the overview that follows, I kept in mind three underlying questions. The first is the question of what, precisely, changed. Many of the activities of descent groups and lineages (ancestral rites, charity along kin lines, compilation of genealogies) were practiced long before there were descent groups of the type that appeared in the Song and later. What were the crucial innovations that can be linked to the appearance of this type of descent group, and when did they appear?

The second question is why these innovations appeared. Given the great continuity in kinship attitudes and practices, what social, economic, religious,

* This chapter was originally published in *Kinship Organization in Late Imperial China, 1000–1940*, ed. Patricia Buckley Ebrey and James L. Watson, copyright 1986 © The Regents of the University of California. Reproduced with the permission of the University of California Press.

or intellectual developments can account for the appearance or transformation of forms of agnatic organization? Was one change the crucial one, leading to the others, or were several independent changes in practices and attitudes involved?

The third question concerns the relationship between elite leadership and descent group formation. Historical sources largely present educated men as the catalysts of descent group or lineage organization. Acting on the basis of their own interests, values, or needs, educated men could certainly have tried to establish kinship groups. But for these groups to thrive and endure, they must also have served the needs of kinsmen who did not belong to the educated class. Sometimes it was undoubtedly the latter who formed the organization that educated men later tried to develop further. In order to detect evidence of kinship organization among uneducated commoners, I have paid special attention to cases where educated men seem to have been responding to the needs of local agnates, rather than imposing on them their own ideas.

In the survey presented here, conclusive answers are not provided for any of these questions; rather, I attempt to bring attention to the most relevant evidence and suggest plausible explanations. I have organized this overview in terms of changes in the basic repertoire of agnatic kinship practices. I adopted this framework because the notion of a cultural repertoire provides the most satisfactory way to grasp both the variability and the uniformity in people's ways of dealing with kin. This repertoire of ideas and practices related to kinship evolved over time, and its content increased significantly during the four centuries reviewed here; yet there were always a great many alternate forms, all socially acceptable and suited to different needs. Individuals and groups could actively draw from this repertoire to select appropriate courses of action, but also, often at a less conscious level, they would try to remold or reinterpret ongoing activities to fit into recognized forms.

By concentrating on the cultural repertoire, I am largely setting aside consideration of local economic conditions. There is little doubt that the development of forms of kinship organization was tied to patterns of migration, settlement, and land tenure practices. These varied considerably over the Song, both geographically and temporally.[5] A complete history of the processes by which certain forms of kinship organization came to be practiced where they did must therefore await fuller understanding of regional developments.

THE BASIC REPERTOIRE OF EXTRA-HOUSEHOLD AGNATIC KINSHIP

The primary focus of agnatic kinship from the Han period (202 BC–220 AD) on was always the family and family line, the men in the household and their patrilineal ancestors and descendants.[6] Here, however, I will only examine agnatic kinship activities outside this sphere, looking particularly at the relations among agnates whose common ancestor was further back than their grandfather. The classical prescription for these relations can be summarized in a sentence: Second and third cousins were mourning relatives and therefore had a variety of specific and diffuse obligations toward each other; fourth cousins, however, were not, and in the classics it was said that kinship ended at that point.

In practice, however, by the Han, certain forms of behavior were extended to agnates much more distant than fourth cousins. Above all, people had a concept of agnate (*zuren*) that was applied to those believed to share a common ancestor, even a distant one, but in practice mainly when the person lived in the same locality. One way agnates were treated differently from other people was by use of kinship terms.[7] Agnates would refer to each other as *zu* uncle, *zu* cousin, *zu* nephew, and call each other "uncle," "nephew," and so on. More significant, the category of agnate was used in regulating marriage and adoption. One did not marry agnates, that is, people of the same surname known to share a patrilineal ancestor.[8] Agnates were, however, the preferred source of adopted male heirs, though this preference does not seem to have been especially strong.[9]

By the Han, if not much earlier, agnates often lived near each other in local communities.[10] Local agnates were seen as the inner layer in an educated man's social world, closely associated with the local community, as in expressions like "He was cordial to his agnates and neighbors." Educated men were expected to offer help and guidance to their agnatic kinsmen. This could mean financial aid, especially to widows, orphans, and those having trouble paying for weddings and funerals. In the *History of the Later Han* men were often praised for using their income to aid their kinsmen or kinsmen and neighbors.[11] Leadership was also supposed to be involved. In times of crisis, educated men were expected to lead their agnates and other local residents to defend themselves or move to safety. Since educated men were supposed to serve as leaders for the entire community, it would be a mistake to infer kinship organization from this sort of leadership. Although historical sources look with favor on groups of local agnates led by educated men, they reveal distrust of groups without educated leaders, for such groups might fall under the sway of a local strongman or bully.[12] These patterns remained common through the Six Dynasties (AD 220–589).[13]

Before the Song, local agnates living in separate households did not often hold property together, not even it would seem the gravesites of their ancestors. Grave lands could be passed down to one son rather than remain the property of all,[14] and nowhere have I found the implication that these graves were a group responsibility or a group resource, rights to be buried there controlled by decision of the group as a whole or its representative. Graves were of great significance, but to individuals much more than to groups. Filial sons spent great sums on building tombs and on moving coffins back to old graveyards; in the Han they often spent the period of mourning for their parents by the side of their tombs.[15] In the Han, sacrifices were offered at graves,[16] and halls (*ci*) might be built there.[17] But the greatest emphasis was on the graves of recent ancestors, so that there is little indication that graves were a focus for distantly related agnates.

In the Han through Tang (618–906) period, men saw their agnates at weddings, funerals, and in some cases the seasonal sacrifices.[18] How wide a group of agnates assembled seems to have depended on how many lived nearby. Some aristocratic families seem to have maintained common graveyards, but others spread their graves over several locations, even when they lived in the same city or county.[19]

So far I have been discussing agnates who lived near each other, especially commoners. During the Six Dynasties and the Tang, some men retained recognition that they shared a common ancestry with people living scattered across the country. This practice, however, was probably restricted to the upper class, since its purpose was to establish and define social status within an aristocratic social system.[20] To characterize this system very briefly, after a "family" (probably more accurately termed a line or set of lines, since ancestors were included) gained national fame, descendants or collaterals who settled elsewhere would still use the place name of the famous "family" as a qualifier to their surname, that is, as a choronym.[21] Thus the Qinghe Cuis were distinct from the Boling Cuis, and each set of Cuis had many members living far from their ancestral area. Some of these aristocratic lines seem to have functioned as kinship groups, but the majority probably did not.[22]

Since the various governments of the Northern and Southern Dynasties (317–589) ranked these "great families" by status and used these ranks in allocating access to political privileges, genealogies were needed to prove membership in a ranked line. In the local context a man was a Hedong Zhang because he was a Zhang living in Hedong, and no one had challenged the presumption of his common origin with the other Zhangs. But if he wanted to claim to be a Hedong Zhang while living in Henei, he needed a genealogy documenting descent from known members of the line. Especially during the Southern Dynasties, the government took the lead in compiling these genealogies, collecting ones for all the leading lines and publishing them together. But private genealogists also flourished along with the aristocratic system, lasting well through the Tang. No Tang or pre-Tang genealogies survive, but from scattered references to their contents, modern scholars have inferred that they were concerned primarily with clarifying lines of descent and offices held by male members. Because lines that did not produce officials were irrelevant for these purposes, they probably were not recorded in any detail.[23]

There is no particular reason to think that these aristocratic practices had any influence on kinship organization at the local commoner level. There is no evidence that commoners kept genealogies or concerned themselves with kinsmen who lived in distant areas.

QINGMING AND WORSHIP AT GRAVES

Almost without exception, the forms of behavior toward agnatic kin that have been described above continued into the Song and later. Men referred to distant agnates as *zuren;* did not marry them; saw them as appropriate recipients of charity and guidance; and would meet with them at weddings, funerals, and other rites. Local groups of agnates without educated men as leaders could be seen as disorderly.[24] Even the practice of labeling "great families" with choronyms unrelated to contemporary residence continued.[25] What changed in the Tang and Song were additions to the repertoire, much more than subtractions. The additions, however, were significant and subtly altered the relationships of the old constants.

Ancestral worship at graves during the Qingming festival was one of the most important of the additions to the basic repertoire of kinship activities. The Qingming festival was held in the spring, 105 days after the winter solstice. In recent times it has been the most significant occasion for ancestral offerings at graves in both North and South China,[26] but this was not always the case. Since the end of the Han, the "Cold Food" (*hanshi*) festival, involving extinguishing fires for three days, had been held at the solar period named "Qingming." However, scholars of folklore have not found references to it as an occasion for visiting graves before the Tang period.[27] Perhaps the earliest reference to this practice is in a Buddhist text dating from the 660s, which refers in passing to a man in the Sui period (581–617) who took food and wine to make a sacrifice (*ji*) at the graves on the day of Cold Food.[28]

By the mid-Tang the association between Cold Food or Qingming and rites at graves was well established. An edict of 732 noted that although the ritual classics had not mentioned visiting graves at the Cold Food festival, it had become customary in recent times. The edict gave approval to the custom: "For gentlemen and commoners who do not get together to make offerings in family altars (*jiamiao*), how else can they exhibit their filial sentiments? They should be allowed to visit the graves and together perform the rituals of bowing and sweeping at the tombs."[29] The edict went on to state that the sacrifice (*ji*) should be made outside the southern gate of the burial ground (*ying*), and that at its conclusion the leftover food should be taken and eaten elsewhere. These rules were to be made a permanent part of the ritual code and are included in the ritual compendium, the *Kaiyuan li.*[30]

From this edict it is clear that by mid-Tang, visiting graves at Qingming was already recognized as *the* occasion for agnates (other than high officials who were allowed family altars)[31] to get together to express reverence for ancestors. Its popularity in this period is confirmed in a letter Liu Zongyuan (773–819) wrote from exile lamenting his forced absence from his ancestors' graves. Whenever the Cold Food festival arrived, he was reminded of "how the country roads are filled with men and women, how slaves, servants, and beggars are all able to visit their parents' graves, and how not one of the ghosts of horse doctors or field laborers is left without care."[32] Late Tang etiquette books even include models of complimentary letters to write on the occasion of visiting graves at Qingming.[33]

During the Song dynasty, there is abundant evidence of the importance of Cold Food/Qingming as an occasion for sacrifices (*ji*). The *Suishi zazhi* of Lü Xizhe (ca. 1050–1120) quoted the statement that "northerners all use this day to sweep and make offerings (*saoji*) at their ancestors' tombs,"[34] implying that southerners did not. During the Southern Song, customs from Kaifeng and elsewhere in the north spread to the capital, Hangzhou, and elsewhere in the south. Zhou Mi (1232–1308) wrote an account of the annual observances of the Qiandao and Chunxi periods (1165–1189) that described grave visits to offer sacrifices as a major activity of residents of Hangzhou, participated in not only by men but also by women leading children.[35] A gazetteer for Fuzhou (Fujian) written in 1182 described a flourishing celebration led by the well-to-do within a set of agnates:

> The people of this prefecture always bow before the graves at the Cold Food spring sacrifice. The rich houses (*fushi*) and great surnames (*daxing*) have land set aside to support the graveyards. When the sacrifice is over they assemble their agnates (*he zu*). The largest groups have several hundred people, the smallest a few dozen. Afterward they have a feast, arranging themselves in order and showing their respect. This is their way to "honor ancestors and encourage warm feelings among agnates" (*zunzu muzu*).[36]

During the Song it also became common to visit graves at other festivals, especially the Buddhist All Souls' Feast (fifteenth of the seventh month) and the Buddhist Stove Lighting festival on the first of the tenth month.[37] The Fuzhou gazetteer records a different set of dates, the second or third of the first month and the winter solstice.[38]

While visiting tombs to make announcements to ancestors was mentioned in the classics, sacrificing (*ji*) to them there was not. According to long established beliefs, individuals had two souls, a *po* that stayed with the body in the grave, and a *hun* that left the body and could be settled in an ancestral tablet. In the classics sacrifices were made to the spirit in the tablet but not the *po* in the grave. In the Song, Confucian ritualists gave the custom of sacrifices to ancestors at their graves qualified acceptance. Cheng Yi (1033–1107) argued that the spirits (*shen*) of the dead did not reside in their graves but in spirit tablets (*shenzhu*), thus meaning that offerings at tombs accomplished nothing. He thought that rulers had taken to making offerings at imperial tombs out of acquiescence to popular customs. He did, however, admit that sacrifices at graves did no great harm to righteous principles.[39] Some other Confucian ritualists accepted the concept of grave rites but wanted to separate their practice from the popular festivals by picking different days by divination, the classical rule for determining the dates for domestic rites.[40] Zhu Xi (1130–1200) gave lukewarm acceptance to grave rites but drew the line at using the fifteenth of the seventh month because of its Buddhist associations.[41]

What is the significance of grave rites to the development of descent group organization? First, it should be stressed that sacrifices at graves developed at the level of local custom. I see no evidence at all that ideological motives led Confucian scholars to promote worship at graves. Rather, those concerned with classical ritual forms tried to find ways to accommodate practices that had become popular. This level of custom appears to have had associations with Buddhism, although the Qingming festival itself was never considered a Buddhist celebration.[42] Yet Buddhist monks had for centuries held ceremonies to pray for the dead, and these seem to have been, at the popular level at least, partially assimilated to the more purely Chinese practice of ancestor worship. As Kenneth Ch'en points out, Buddhists actively promoted the idea that their ways of caring for the dead were the most filial. Buddhist notions of death, souls, and the uses of prayers or offerings to the dead were of course different from classical ones, and these new ideas could have helped encourage worship of distant ancestors. Indeed, the sutra that is the source for making offerings on behalf of ancestors on the All Souls' Feast stated that they should be made for ancestors up to seven generations back, three more than the Confucian classics allowed. The practice of attaching a Buddhist shrine, with monks, to look after a family's graves is a further indication of ties to Buddhism. This practice, often referred to as "merit cloisters," had been common since the mid-Tang.[43] It is perhaps also significant that Fujian – where there were large group rites already in the twelfth century – was a major stronghold of Buddhism in the Song.[44]

For the development of group consciousness among sets of local agnates, two innovations are particularly important: the inclusion of *early ancestors* in rites and the practice of everyone visiting graves on *the same* day. Since at least the Han, men often visited graves to make offerings or announcements, but they could choose any day significant to them, and they would not expect to meet distant kin there. From Tang times on, on Qingming and the summer or fall festivals, people would meet with their local agnates at graveyards in a context that stressed their lines of descent. Whether distant ancestors were regularly included in these rites in the Tang is uncertain from surviving sources. By the Song, however, there is clear evidence that old graves were sites of worship (see below). In such cases the entire group of local agnates would be assembled for the rites for the first ancestor to be buried in that locality, which undoubtedly ties in with the new interest in "first ancestors" that appears in the Song. Rather than all of these people making separate offerings, they might well have come to hold a group ceremony, a step which would certainly increase their group consciousness.[45] In the Fuzhou case a group feast had become part of the Qingming celebrations. Occasionally, as in the Fuzhou case, men may have sought to ensure regular funding for these rites by setting aside land (such estates will be discussed in more detail below).

This process may have had a kind of "snowball" effect. As grave rites became more popular (for religious and social reasons), it would have become more crucial to bury agnates near each other: Some concentration of graves would ensure that as the number of generations increased, old tombs would not be neglected, for many graves could then be visited on a single day. As more generations of graves came to be visited, a larger descent group would have a ritual focus. This focus would provide a principle for deciding who was a member of the descent group (whether or not he was a descendant of the "first ancestor"), excluding later migrants who claimed a common ancestor of an even earlier date. And as the association between grave rites and descent groups came to be recognized, people who wished to promote group cohesiveness among their local agnates could begin by initiating or restoring joint rites to their earliest ancestors. (Some examples of such initiatives will be given below.)

The importance of grave rites and the association of graves and descent groups is made explicit in the writings of a few Song men. Here I will cite evidence from the writings of four men, presenting them in chronological order. The first author is Han Qi (1008–1075), a noted scholar who served as prime minister under three emperors (Renzong, Yingzong, and Shenzong). Han Qi wrote a manual for sacrifices (*Jiyi*), no longer extant, which was quoted in a later source as supporting the practice of grave worship on the Cold Food and first of the tenth month festivals.[46] Another source quoted him as saying, "Being conscientious with the family records and never forgetting the ancestral tombs are the major elements of filial piety."[47] Han Qi also wrote an account of an impressive ceremony he performed on Cold Food at the graves of his parents and grandparents. He followed this ceremony by lecturing to his sons and nephews, urging them to be good and to continue to bury all of their relatives near these two graves where the *hun* and *po* souls of his father and grandfather could give them peace, and warning them definitely not to let the advice of a burial specialist (a geomancer, presumably) lead them to bury elsewhere in the hopes of gaining good fortune.[48] Should anyone act so barbarously, the descent group (*zongzu*) should punish him.[49]

In 1045 Han Qi acted on his own advice and constructed two complex tombs, each with several chambers, each chamber to house a husband and wife or wives plus any children who died young or heirless.[50] In 1051, 1062, and 1071, additional tombs were built for younger relatives, one of these to be used entirely for descendants who died without heirs.[51] Perhaps the best evidence of Han Qi's preoccupation with graves, however, is the extraordinary efforts he took to locate the graves of his great-grandfather and great-great-grandfather, left behind in Hebei when their descendants moved south to Henan. His persistent inquiries went on for over thirty years, as he queried men surnamed Han who came from his ancestors' native place and delegated friends and relatives to pursue leads for him. As he noted, his search was a continuation of his father's attempt to reconstruct the family genealogy by collecting tomb inscriptions.[52]

Han Qi's local descent group in Henan had very little genealogical depth, going back only to his grandfather. Although he refers to it as *zongzu,* the group cannot have been very large. His concern to keep all of the graves together, however, would have provided a clearer focus for later generations (and saved them the sense of dereliction of duty Han Qi felt at never having visited his ancestors' tombs). There are also examples of men who belonged to sizable local descent groups who were concerned to preserve group burial. Chen Liang (1143–1194), a noted political thinker from Jinhua (Zhejiang), wrote that his father was much concerned with the tombs of his ancestors. The grave of Liang's great-great-great-grandfather was still in existence, even though those of his great-great-grandfather and great-grandfather were not, apparently in part because they were not eldest sons and perhaps as such were not given graves intended to be focal points of worship.[53] Chen Liang's father in 1167 wanted to start a new pattern of having all the descendants buried together, not unlike Han Qi's project, but he specified that they should be put in generational (*zhaomu*) order, making the graveyard resemble a genealogical chart (*puxi*).[54]

At the time Chen Liang's father urged this plan, the Chen comprised a recognizable descent group. Chen Liang wrote that in this period the Chen were flourishing and 100 or more people would assemble for the seasonal rites.[55] He also described a great-uncle who because he remained healthy into old age came to be the leader of his descent group (*zhang qi zu*). Chen Liang described this man's activities by remarking that since he had died, within his descent group "Who will care for the young? Who will discipline the wayward? Who will commiserate with the sick? Who will manage affairs for the dead?"[56] Thus Chen Liang would seem to imply that the descent group benefited when someone took on a leadership role, but that this role was not institutionalized, depending instead on a suitable volunteer.

Another aspect of the connection between graves and descent groups is found in the writings of Huang Gan (1152–1221), a resident of Fuzhou (Fujian). Huang Gan was a disciple (and son-in-law) of Zhu Xi, and therefore undoubtedly knew of the ideas of the Neo-Confucian philosophers on "restoring the *zong,*" to be discussed below. However, in his passages on tombs and the descent group organized around them he does not seem to have been acting on ideological principles so much as responding to the needs of an existing group. He had no qualms about worship at graves. In one of his judicial decisions he declared, "People's graves are the place where descendants make sacrifices for a hundred years."[57] He may have felt strongly about this because he and his kinsmen fought encroachment on an old graveyard for over twenty years.

In his last effort to bring this case to court, Huang Gan wrote a detailed charge, giving the history of the graveyard. It was over 300 years old and was located at a Buddhist shrine built by his ancestors. Since its founding, his kinsmen had been getting together every spring and fall to make sacrifices. Unfortunately, Huang Gan's father had lent a female cousin and her husband named Zhao use of the study in this shrine as a place to live, and their sons later came to occupy the whole shrine. As a result the Huangs had to use the monk's quarters when coming or going to make offerings. In the years that followed disputes kept recurring, leading to brawls, vandalism, and lawsuits. Even the so-called "forbidden area" of the tombs was violated.[58] In his final plea Huang Gan argued against a settlement by division of the property:

> In the spring and fall when we bow and sweep the graves, outside of an area to lay out a mat there is hardly room for a person, causing me great sorrow. If the area is divided, how will I be able to face my ancestors in the world below?[59]

Undoubtedly influenced by his family's long struggle over the old grave-yard, in 1221, on the day of the Qingming festival, Huang Gan decided to endow a fund to pay for sacrifices at the graves. He wrote:

> Whenever I think of the importance of the grave mounds I become distressed and grieve that I am already seventy and could die any day without having made a plan to enable my descendants to continue the sacrifices. . . . When graves are close by, one can expect sons and grand-sons to assist each other in maintaining them. Still, the four areas of my ancestors' tombs at the Common Blessings Shrine have been in exist-ence for three hundred years. Although my agnates each spring and fall contribute money to pay for the sacrifices, there are poor ones among them who find this a serious strain. As the generations go by it is easy for people's affections to become remiss. Outside of the sacrifices, few of them visit the graves.[60]

Consequently Huang Gan donated land of more than four *mu*, with an annual income of sixteen piculs, to pay for the sacrifices. (Some details on its management will be discussed later under estates.) Endowments of the sort described in the Fuzhou gazetteer may have provided models for Huang Gan, since he lived in Fuzhou, though little is known of the size or manage-ment of earlier endowments for graves or grave rites.

Finally, let us look at a text, probably dating from the thirteenth century, written by one Zhao Jiming and preserved in a Yuan encyclopedia for popular reference.[61] It is called "A Diagram of Descent Group Burial." The author outlines a plan whereby the first ancestor is placed in the center of the graveyard, facing south. South of him, on the east would be the *zhao* ranks, sons in one row, great-grandsons in the next row further south, and so on. On the west would be the *mu* ranks, first a row of grandsons, then a row of great-great-grandsons, and so on. Descendants were to be buried strictly in order of age, irrespective of who their fathers were; thus the arrangement would match the tablets in an ancestral hall, not a genealogy.

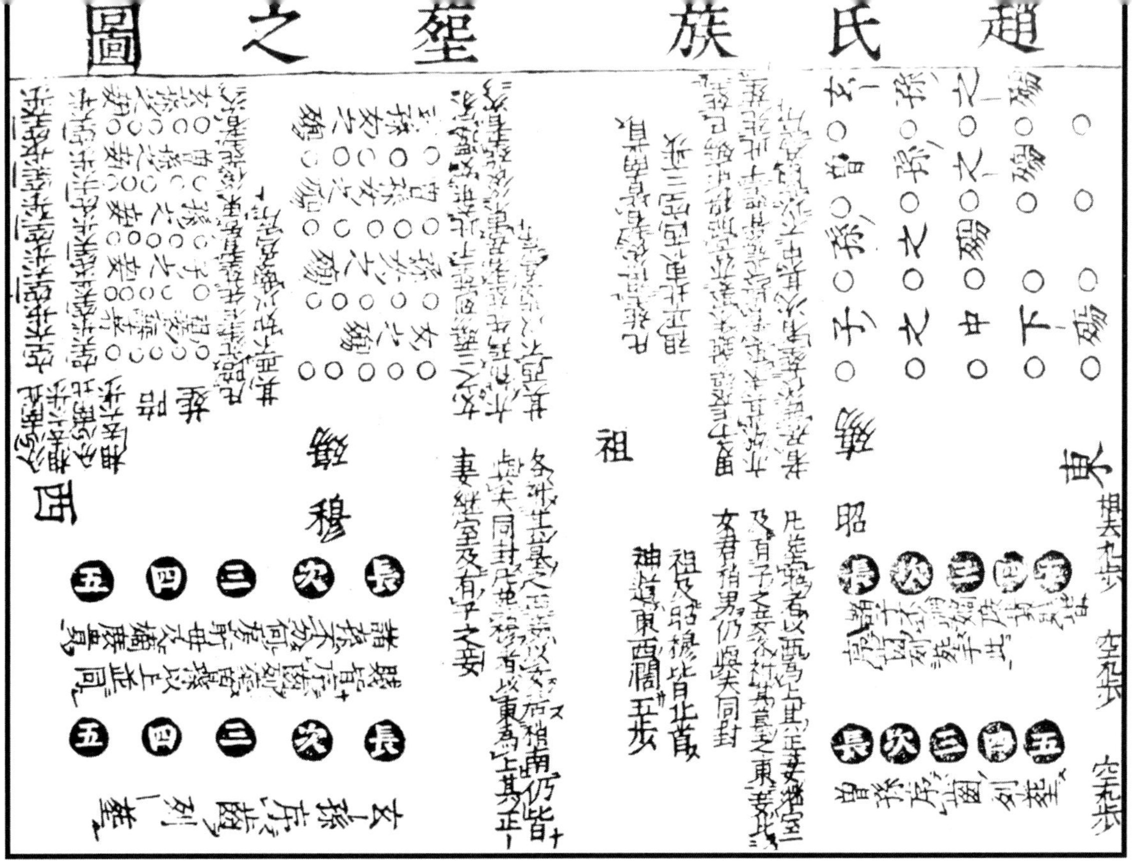

Figure 5.1 Zhao Jiming's diagram of descent group burial. The earliest ancestor is in the center. In front of him are his descendants who lived to marry, lined up by age in alternating generations, left and right. Behind him are descendants who died early, by generation, males on the right, females on the left.

Source: After JJBYSL yi 4.73a–b.

This pattern, by de-emphasizing separate lines of descent, would stress the unity of the group and its common origin. (This point will be elaborated below with regard to name and number systems.) To the north of the founding ancestor would be buried all those born into the family who did not live to marry, arranged by generation, boys on the east and girls on the west. They were members of the group, but not ancestors.

The commentary to this graveyard diagram explicitly justified this practice of rank-ordered burials in terms of convenience for getting together to offer sacrifices. The author also explained that while family rites extend back only to the great-great-grandfather, at the graves they go back to the first ancestor, making graves particularly important. Although it is difficult to evaluate how many people followed this plan, it continued to be cited in reference books, de Groot finding it in manuals in use in Fujian in the late nineteenth century; even in the twentieth century it was practiced in some places.[62]

There are several inferences that can be drawn from the writings of these four men. The first is that graves and descent groups were associated in the authors' minds. The second is that there was an interest in burying people together – overcoming the conflicting imperatives of geomancy if need be – in order to be able to visit more graves at ritual occasions and obtain greater benefits from the spirits of deceased ancestors. Third, there was an interest in arranging burials in patterns that would reflect the descent and seniority principles important in ancestral rites, thereby stressing the unity of the group rather than its separation into lines. Fourth, association with an old graveyard, as in Huang Gan's case, could lead to a group identity as those responsible for it had to protect it from outsiders, in his case affines. Fifth, collecting money to pay for group rites may have been one of the earliest forms of descent group organization. In Huang Gan's case it was first done through annual solicitations (resembling Buddhist clubs in this regard), but later property was set aside to provide a regular income for it. When annual solicitations are made, the group is essentially a voluntary one; once it owns property in common, its nature changes. People no longer have to decide each year whether they wish to contribute and participate; they have a right to participate based on descent from the named ancestor. So long as the property is competently managed (not an easy assumption to make) the rites continue and the group maintains its existence.

It should of course be stressed that not all sets of agnates in the Song had common graveyards or common rites at graves. But then neither did all sets of agnates in later times develop into descent groups. The question is whether there is an association between common grave sites/rites and the development of descent group organization. The Shis described by Richard Davis did not have common burial areas, and as he shows their group identity lasted only about two centuries. By contrast the Wus studied by Keith Hazelton favored a particular burial ground from at least the eleventh century and began compiling genealogies and formulating rules for ritual observances in the mid-thirteenth century.[63]

All considered, I think it can be argued that a key element in the emergence of descent groups in the Song and later was a change in religious ideas and ritual practices related to graves and ancestors, a change that fostered the development of group consciousness among local agnates. This is not to deny that the process would often have been a dynamic one; once the social effects of worshiping at graves came to be understood, people who wished to promote solidarity among their kin probably would urge that rites at the grave of their earliest ancestor be instituted. Yet I would stress the significance of the grave rites in and of themselves.

By putting emphasis on the rituals, I am going counter to the general model of Chinese kinship development that draws largely on the tradition of British social anthropology.[64] Broadly speaking, this school sees economic and political needs leading to the formation of groups, which then adopt rituals to help strengthen the group's solidarity. There are two main reasons why I give primacy to the change in ritual practices in explaining the broader historical change. One is chronology: the changed approach to graves – probably stimulated by the tremendous influence of Buddhism – was well under way in the Tang, considerably before stronger group identity among local agnates becomes evident in the historical sources. The second reason concerns the widespread popularity of sacrifices at graves. The worship of ancestors at their graves, so long as they were located not far from one's home, seems to have become a common practice from Song times on, by no means limited to members of recognizable descent groups. And a sense of group identity, characterized by a consciousness of a focal, apical ancestor, became fairly common, at least in places where migration and settlement patterns led to large numbers of agnates living near each other.[65] Much less common was the leap from group consciousness (which is enough to call the set of people a group in a weak sense) to the solidification of the descent group into a lineage that possessed corporate property and acted as a unit in local politics.[66] Lineages, once they appeared, naturally elaborated their ritual activities to serve group purposes (as in building halls for subbranches). But the needs of members of lineages – a tiny fraction of all sets of local agnates – cannot account for the rituals practiced by the rest; nor would they diminish the consequences such rituals would have had for people's sense of a "we" group.

COMMUNAL FAMILIES

Even if group ritual practices helped foster a greater awareness of descent principles and greater sense of group consciousness among local agnates, these attitudes need not have resulted in a particular type of group organization. During the Tang and Song dynasties, most historical references to organized groups of agnates were to ones of the form called "communal families" and not to descent groups or lineages.

A "communal family" was a domestic unit that had not divided – either property or members – for five, six, or even ten generations. In Chinese terminology this was spoken of as though the unit in question was both a *jia*, a family with common assets, and a *zu*, an organization including distant agnates. In other words, their concept of agnates (*zu*) did not preclude the possibility that they lived together with a common budget. On the contrary, this was seen as the moral and ritual ideal, extremely difficult to attain in practice but much to be admired. These communal families had some resemblance to the kinship system described in the classics (the *zong* system) but do not seem to have been the product of conscious efforts to revive ancient forms; indeed they were as likely to be found among commoners as among the educated. The state celebrated their existence, honoring them with banners and tax and labor service exemptions, but the motivation underlying these state actions does not seem to have been to try to get a higher percentage of commoners to organize themselves as communal families, but rather to promote traditional moral values of family solidarity by honoring extreme examples of their fulfillment. One reason why communal families inspired such awe among Song and Yuan literati is probably that most upper-class families found it difficult to stay together even a few decades after losing a father as a family head.[67]

Communal families can be seen as precursors of lineages in the sense that they were large localized groups that shared in a common estate and were organized on a basis of patrilineal descent. And some may have been protolineages; for lack of an adequate range of concepts, observers may sometimes have labeled as *jia* any patrilineal kinship unit organized around a property base, since to them *zu* implied a much looser grouping without shared property. (This understanding of *zu* would change in time as corporate estates became more common.)

The late Tang and Five Dynasties periods appear to have been a time when families in many parts of the country chose to stay together with a common estate; in all probability they took this course as a way to provide self-protection in a time of endemic disorder. The economic base of these families is almost always unknown, so whether they fared best in specific economic contexts is a matter for speculation.[68] Chapter 456 of the *Song History*, on the filially righteous, describes briefly numerous communal families singled out for their exceptional size. For instance, the Xu family of Jiangzhou (Jiangxi) "maintained a common household of eight generations' depth, with 781 people, young and old." In 982 a special banner honoring them was awarded by the court.[69] The family of Fang Gang in Chizhou (Anhui) had "shared a stove" for eight generations and comprised 700 people in 600 rooms. The history says that they met every morning and ate together. In 1005 they were honored with a banner, and about fifteen years later they had their taxes partially remitted.[70] Six more cases of families with over 700 people are listed, plus another twenty that had remained undivided for eight to ten generations.[71] In the *Draft Continuation of the Comprehensive Mirror*

Figure 5.2 The Chen communal family, whose 700 members ate together, sitting
according to age.
Source: After SYXJ 6.9a.

(Xu zizhi tongjian changbian) and the *Song Collected Documents (Song huiyao)*, there are many more citations of communal families, including some which had one or two thousand members.[72] As Niida points out, these families were found all over the country, with no particular area standing out. There do seem to be some temporal differences, however, as many more were recorded for the first century of the Song than for the next two. (Could it be that this form of organization declined as political stability set in? Or could it be that similar kinship units were later classed as *zu*? Or is this change no more than an historiographical illusion?)

In most of these cases the members of the families seem to have been commoners.[73] A family in Hezhong prefecture (Shanxi) that was noted for its filial piety in the Tang remained undivided into the Song. When they reached ten generations, Emperor Renzong (r. 1023–1063) excused them from labor service. By the end of the eleventh century they had reached thirteen generations. The historian commented:

> The Yao family have been farmers for generations and include no one who studies. The family is not especially rich; it owns several dozen *qing* of land for over a hundred assembled agnates (*juzu*). The junior members do all the farming and sericulture in person, diligently working to provide food and clothing. For over three hundred years no one has separated from the family. Through the wars of the late Tang and Five Dynasties the descendants preserved their graves, and "bone and flesh" did not separate.[74]

All of the cases discussed so far were recorded because of the unusual size and genealogical depth. Among men of literary or political note, one also comes across communal families, but more often ones of four or five generations' depth and perhaps a hundred members. Sima Guang (1019–1086) and Lu Jiushao (b. ca. 1138) both wrote brief instructions on the management of these sorts of families.[75] From the point of view of the development of descent group organization, their writings are illuminating in three ways. First, in these families the only distinctions drawn among members were the traditional kinship ones of age, generation, and sex, and efforts were taken to keep differences in individual wealth from leading to differing standards of living. Second, in each case, rules for management, budgeting, and even everyday courtesies were very much stressed, reflecting undoubtedly the complexities of these organizations. Zhao Ding (1085–1147), a noted scholar and political figure, wrote a similar set of rules for his descendants in the hope that they would never divide their property and thus would in time become a communal family.[76] Thus, despite Fan Zhongyan's invention of the charitable estate in 1049, through the eleventh and twelfth century it was common for educated men to see the ideal descent group (i.e., group of *zuren* or *zongren*) as one organized as a *jia*. Indeed, communal families continued to appear – and be praised – through the Yuan, Ming, and Qing.[77]

The Zheng family of Jinhua, perhaps the most famous communal family, was founded in the eleventh century and attracted much notice in the late Yuan and early Ming; even long after the family's demise it continued to be admired and copied.[78]

The break-up of communal families in some cases led to the formation of descent groups. That is, agnates who were no longer able to keep all of their property together still tried to preserve some group organization and maybe some common assets. For instance, the Wangs of Wuyuan in Huizhou compiled a genealogy in the mid-eleventh century at the seventh generation, and another in 1211 at the tenth, and a third in 1236 at the twelfth generation.[79] Each stressed that the Wangs had earlier been a communal family and that something of this spirit could be revived through genealogical compilation. According to these authors, the family's founder died in 960; he had eleven sons whose names all included the character "Ren," twenty-four grandsons (names, "Wen"), and fifty-one great-grandsons (names, "De"). "From 960 to 1024, some sixty-five years, they lived as a communal family with four generations' depth, comprising 326 people."[80]

> All internal and external affairs, major or minor, were governed by rules, just like a government office, and no one dared violate them. When seniors were sitting in the hall, anyone walking by would scurry deferentially. Everyone was diligent and would not dare make excuses. Not until the twelfth month of each year would people be given clothes, cloth, and floss. Eating was signaled by drumbeat, and if someone failed to show up, no one would eat. Whenever scolded, they would act fearful and submit. They had several hundred *mu* of average fields that they set aside for the expenses of entertaining and paying taxes. There was never the slightest deception in the handling of the family's accounts in money and grain. Whenever an emergency arose, then without exception they would unite to provide aid.[81]

The author of this preface went on to lament the great decline in family behavior that had occurred after the break-up of the communal family. The author of the second preface (1211) noted that the descent group of Wangs currently had officials and wealthy men, but also illiterates and people without an inch of land; it had monks and others who had abandoned the family graveyards to move elsewhere, plus boatmen, peddlers, craftsmen, and government menials. (The last category the author thought was too lowly to record in the genealogy.) Such a diverse group could not form a communal family. But they do seem to have formed a descent group; the repeated updating of their genealogy is evidence of a strong sense of group identity among their educated members and perhaps even of ongoing organization.[82]

As the author of this preface implied, communal families probably survived best when there were no great differences of wealth or social status among their men, for their underlying principle was distribution of income to all members equally according to need, just as though they were members of a small family. Officials' salaries would have to go into a common pool, and the sons of officials would get no benefits the sons of others did not get. Because this went counter to so much of Chinese thinking on the status of literati and officials, it probably seldom worked. Even the famous Zheng family succumbed to the pressure to divide within a few generations after producing officials.[83]

More detail on the transformation of a communal family is given in an account written by Wang Yong. In 1246 he visited the village in Guiji (Zhejiang) that was the home of a communal family named Qiu. This family had been described in the *Song History* and elsewhere as having already stayed together for nineteen generations when they were awarded the banner in 1011, the longest period of joint residence listed for any family in the *Song History*.[84] According to the *Guiji zhi,* a local gazetteer written in 1201, the family head (*zuzhang*) did such things as organize the hundred-odd children under 13 to pick melons.[85] When Wang Yong visited the Qiu in 1246 he found that they were no longer strictly speaking a "communal family," having in recent times separated their family finances. Yet, as he noted, they still retained some central organization, which we might characterize as lineage-like. According to Wang:

> Every generation the Qiu choose one man to be head (*zhang*). Whenever anything needs to be settled, he acts as judge. There is a bamboo rod that is also passed from one generation to the next. The *zuzhang* uses it if he wishes to punish an offender. At the seasonal sacrifices everyone assembles. Up until today they are still exempted from labor service. How many generations beyond nineteen they have now reached, I do not know. I pondered this. The Qius are working farmers, without a scholar-official among them, which is how they have been able to stay together for so long without scattering. If there had been a high-ranking or prominent person among them, then he would have been beyond the control of the *zuzhang*. . . . Although the Qius lack prominent members, their descendants have preserved their patrimony for generations and are a great descent group (*dazu*). How much better this is than sudden upward and downward changes.[86]

Wang Yong seems to have hit upon a crucial point. Officials were regularly transferred and had to go where the government sent them. For a communal family, producing a great many officials would bring not only differences in status but also geographic dispersal. The looser, secondary ties of descent groups might offer advantages in these cases, proving more resilient to the exodus of members and changes in their status.

As a local kinship unit, organized to protect group interest, communal families probably were gradually superseded by lineages. After the idea of corporate estates separate from family property gained widespread recognition (see below), it seems likely that many groups of kinsmen who wished to strengthen their local political and economic power would have set up a lineage estate rather than remain an undivided family. Leaders of a lineage did not have as complete control over its members as the head of a communal family did, but lineages escaped many of the tensions of an undivided family while still providing a means for defense of group interest. The process by which lineages superseded communal families as units in local society, however, does not belong to the early stages of descent group development. During the Song and Yuan periods, local sets of agnates sharing an estate seem more often to have been communal families than lineages.

THE EFFORTS OF INTELLECTUALS TO "REVIVE THE *ZONG*" AND PROMOTE GENEALOGY COMPILATION

At this point I will switch from the signs of organized activity among local kinsmen that can be detected in Song sources to the steps taken by intellectuals in an effort to reform kinship practices among members of their own social class (*shidafu*). Their writings provided the ideological justification for promoting descent group organization for the next several centuries.

In the mid-eleventh century, during the same period when Han Qi was searching for his ancestors' graves and constructing a new graveyard, his acquaintances in the capital, Ouyang Xiu (1007–1072), Fan Zhongyan (989–1052), and Su Xun (1009–1066), and the scholars Zhang Zai (1022–1078) and Cheng Yi (1033–1107) all came to promote reforms in agnatic kinship practices. Fan's establishment of his famous "charitable estate" was formalized in 1049, and in 1051 he compiled a genealogy of the kinsmen to share in this estate. In 1055 both Su Xun and Ouyang Xiu independently compiled genealogies of their kin. The comments by Zhang Zai and Cheng Yi on "reviving the *zong*" are undated, but in all probability they took shape after 1055. These men, each in different ways, wished to reform society. They sensed that something was missing in the family life of most educated, upperclass men, oriented toward the family line and descendants. The family spirit they sought seemed to be more often attained by commoners, long settled in a community, who either maintained communal families or at least got together periodically to make offerings together.

The background of Fan Zhongyan's action has already been fully described by Denis Twitchett, and only a few points need to be highlighted here. First and foremost, there does not seem to have been an active, pre-existing descent group of Suzhou Fan before Fan Zhongyan took the initiative to set up an estate. Second, the group he created did not have much genealogical depth, going back only four generations.[87]

Only a few years after Fan Zhongyan founded his estate and compiled a genealogy through research, Su Xun compiled a genealogy for the descendants of his great-great-grandfather and had it carved on stone and the stele erected at the ancestral graveyard. Su Xun explicitly related his efforts to the classical descent line system, the *zong* system. He described how the ancient *zong* system worked, with its division into the "great *zong*" of the primary line that continues indefinitely and the nesting "lesser *zong*" that break off from it every generation and are composed, respectively, of the descendants of great-great-grandfather, great-grandfather, grandfather, and father, each led in ritual by a "son of the *zong*" (*zongzi*), the representative of the senior line descended from that ancestor. Su Xun noted that only the lesser *zong* was applicable to ordinary educated men in his day. He argued for the social benefits of instituting the *zong* system, for it would lead to improvements both to kin behavior and to the moral climate of local communities. When the *zong* system operated, he said, close agnates mourned each other and informed each other at the event of deaths, burials, or marriages. This was at odds with what he saw around him where relatives became strangers from the time they began to live apart. He noted that although he did not have many agnatic kinsmen (less than a hundred within the circle of mourning obligations), they did not celebrate seasonal sacrifices and festivals together, and "those at all distant do not visit each other."[88] Carving the genealogy of the descendants of his great-great-grandfather on stone and placing it *by the grave of that ancestor* he thought would allow all the descendants to see how closely they were related and remedy this deplorable situation. Clearly Su Xun did not belong to the kind of descent groups Chen Liang or Huang Gan did, but he had hopes of fostering one.

The genealogy Su Xun wrote was a compromise between lesser *zong* principles and filial piety to his direct ancestors, most of whom were younger sons. Thus, he singled out the primary line of descent from each of his own ancestors (that is, his cousins who were responsible for the rites to his grandfather, great-grandfather, and great-great-grandfather). But he gave vital data (age at death, death dates, and wife's surname) only for his own ancestors. In other words, the genealogy was written from Xun's particular point of view, a tack he explicitly defended, but which never became a standard feature of genealogies. The postface to it reads much as a "family account," giving stories of his direct ancestors.[89] Other kinsmen could use the genealogy as a skeleton, which they could then fill in for their own relatives.

Ouyang Xiu's genealogy bears many similarities to Su Xun's. It also covered only the descendants of his great-great-grandfather, and it also was carved on stone and erected at the graves of his ancestors. Its format was different from Su Xun's, providing data on individuals in a commentary after the table proper. Data were very uneven, mostly on offices, with some references to age at death and wife's name. Many men were annotated only as "fact missing," but in a few cases Ouyang Xiu included the man's number within his row (to be discussed below).[90]

In Ouyang Xiu's case, it could be that kinsmen wished to strengthen ties with him rather than the other way around. As Kobayashi points out, Ouyang Xiu did not spend much time in his native place, and compiling this genealogy on the five-generation basis may have been an attempt to restrict the scope of the descent group toward which he had obligations as a wealthy and prominent man.[91] It is of course understandable why Su and Ouyang both had the genealogies erected at the graves: This was the place, and probably the only place, that agnates routinely gathered.

Within much the same intellectual climate, the philosophers Zhang Zai and Cheng Yi called for a more thoroughgoing revival of the *zong* system of antiquity. Zhang Zai wrote an essay on the *zongfa* (system of classical descent groups) in his *Explications of the Classics (Jingxue liku)*. It opens with an often-quoted statement also found in Cheng Yi's sayings:[92]

> In order to control the hearts of the people of the world, to bring together agnates (*zongzu*), and to improve social customs so that people never forget their origins, it is necessary to clarify the genealogical order of descent groups (*zu*) and institute the system of differentiated descent lines (*zongzi fa*).[93]

Zhang Zai then continued:

> When the system of differentiated descent lines is not practiced, people do not know the organization of the lines or the places that they came from. Very few people in ancient times were ignorant of their places of origin. After the system of differentiated descent lines decayed, later generations still honored genealogical writing, so that some of the spirit persisted. Now that genealogical writing has also decayed, people do not know where they come from; there are no hundred year families (*jia*); there is no organization to "bone and flesh kin"; even the closest relatives (*zhiqin*) feel no more than slight obligation to each other. Moreover, without the establishment of the system of differentiated descent lines, the court can have no hereditary officials. For instance, a minister can rise up in a day from a poor and humble position. If he does not set up a *zong* system, once he dies his agnates (*zu*) will scatter and his house (*jia*) will not continue. . . . Nowadays those who accumulate wealth or honor can only plan for thirty or forty years. They may build a residence and occupy it but when they die their sons will divide and separate and soon be bankrupt, so that the house (*jia*) does not survive. If, in this way, they cannot preserve their houses, how can they preserve the state?[94]

Cheng Yi's comments on relations with agnates and the descent group system were not as organized as Zhang Zai's, but if anything they were more influential, being regularly quoted in later genealogies. Particularly noteworthy are his arguments for assembling agnates and compiling genealogies:

Family rules (*jiafa*) should provide that whenever an agnate (*zuren*) comes from a distant place, there should be a meeting of the entire descent group (*zu*). Even when nothing is happening there should be a meeting once a month. One can copy the practice of the Wei family of the past, which had descent group meetings (*zonghui*) under flowering trees. Also at births, deaths, marriages, and the like, agnates (*zuren*) must join in the rituals, so that the idea of "flesh and bone" links are constantly reinforced. The reason that "flesh and bone" relatives every day become more distant is that they do not see each other and are not involved with each other.

When the system of differentiated descent lines is in decay, people do not know where they come from, to the point where they wander off in all directions and then do not recognize each other although they are still within the mourning grades. Now let's have one or two families (*jia*) of great men try to put this system into practice. The procedures should be ones that can be strictly adhered to. As in the Tang system of ancestral altars and halls of fasting, there should be no division of the ancestral property; rather, one man should be given charge of managing it all.

Instituting the system of differentiated descent lines is a Principle of Heaven. It can be compared to a tree: There must be a trunk growing up from the roots, but there also are side branches. Or like a river: There must be a main source, however far away, but there are also streams that divert water away. These are natural tendencies.[95]

Cheng Yi also discussed at some length the forms to be followed for ancestor worship. For ancestors up to great-great-grandfather, he said offerings of fresh food should be made at household altars on the first of each month, with full sacrifices (*ji*) in the second, fifth, eighth, and eleventh months. Besides this there were to be only three other sacrifices. At the winter solstice one could sacrifice to the First Ancestor (*shizu*), defined as the first to have descendants in the line, and thus someone of remote antiquity. On the day of "establishing spring," one could sacrifice to ancestors between the founder and one's great-great-grandfather. Finally, in the last month of fall, there should be sacrifices to ancestors in general.[96] The rites to distant ancestors, while perhaps a concession to popular custom, were not to be done at graves or descent group shrines, but at family altars, and the participants would be the same ones who normally joined in family rites. Despite these qualifications, Zhu Xi, who usually deferred to Cheng Yi's judgment, declared that rites to early ancestors were presumptuous on the part of all but rulers and nobles.[97] Zhu Xi's opinion, however, was largely ignored; in fact, Cheng Yi's approval of *household* offerings to ancient ancestors came to be regularly cited to justify the quite different practice of *descent group* rites to apical ancestors ("first migrant ancestors," *shiqian zu*).

In the generations after Cheng Yi and Zhang Zai, many scholars committed to their philosophy tried to act on their advice. Although I have found no cases of scholars successfully instituting the system of differentiated descent lines, many did try to bring agnates together for group rituals.[98] Others also followed their advice in compiling genealogies (which, of course, had also been recommended by Ouyang Xiu and Su Xun). Often all we know are the steps taken and the goals sought. Whether they led to the creation of an enduring descent group is not clear. In a few cases, however, scholars have left records of their efforts to celebrate or reform pre-existing descent groups. A few of these cases will be discussed in a later section of this essay.

Philosophers' motivation for advocating the strengthening of ties to kinsmen was undoubtedly complex, tied to their goals of bringing order to society at all levels, formulating means of governing the uneducated that were humane and effective, finding ways to maintain some independence from the government for educated men so that they would be free to criticize it, and so on. Leaving these questions of motivation aside, one question should be raised at this point: Were Zhang Zai and Cheng Yi advocating that upper class men (*shidafu*) take steps to develop descent groups organized around rituals and genealogies because of any changes in local kinship organization? Although impossible to prove, I think that they may have written as they did in part because they knew of descent groups that had features (such as group rituals and communal property) that seemed morally preferable to the family or family line orientation typical of the upper class. These descent groups would have included the communal families discussed above but also local descent groups that met for ritual occasions, such as the ones Chen Liang and Huang Gan described. That such families also seemed models of social order, led by the educated, stable over generations, would only have added to their attractiveness.[99]

ENDOWED ESTATES AND LINEAGE FORMATION

In anthropological theories on Chinese kinship organization, attention has been concentrated on lineages, that is, descent groups with substantial corporate properties.[100] Moreover, the estate has been seen as the central feature of these lineages, for they are looked on above all as property-owning organizations. A review of the early stages of descent group organization provides some perspective on this interpretation by showing that from the beginning there was considerable variety in the size of estates, the length of time they survived, the purposes to which they were dedicated, and the ways they were managed. Years ago Hui-chen Wang Liu noted that of 116 nineteenth- and twentieth-century lineages whose genealogies she analyzed, seventy-six had graveyards and fifty-seven had lands set aside to pay the expenses of rituals, but only twelve had charitable estates.[101] This predominance of small estates dedicated to ritual expenses seems to go back to the Song. Moreover, even a small estate did not necessarily provide a permanent base for kinship organization. Shimizu Morimitsu, in his broad survey of lineage estates, found very few estates that lasted more than a couple of centuries.[102] This tendency for estates to succumb to pressures toward division was also evident from the beginning.

The ideal model of the lineage estate was of course that established by Fan Zhongyan (989–1052). His charitable estate (*yitian* or *yizhuang*) was started with a gift of 3,000 *mu* of land, the benefits from which would go to those of his agnatic relatives who lived in Suzhou. As discussed earlier, at the time these relatives were not especially distant, falling within the canonical four generations of the "lesser *zong.*" Benefits were distributed for special expenses (births, marriages, deaths) and on a per capita basis. Financial matters were handled by a manager chosen from among the younger members. The truly poor had a further advantage of getting free lodging in a "charitable hostel." Zhongyan's son made an additional contribution of 1,000 *mu* for *jitian,* "sacrificial lands," to be handled by the monks of an attached Buddhist shrine. He also had the rules modified to subsidize examination candidates and provide the salary for a teacher who would instruct the boys of member families, thus starting a lineage school.[103]

As Denis Twitchett has noted, Fan Zhongyan's decision to set up a permanent estate may have been inspired by Buddhist institutions. Monasteries, with their great landed estates, survived for centuries unaffected by the deaths of individual abbots. Moreover, monasteries sometimes had fields singled out to provide for charitable activities, the so-called "fields of compassion."[104] Since Fan's estate was large enough to subsidize basic living expenses of all the members, it also bore similarities to communal families in which all members had their expenses provided from a common fund. And like communal families, this estate required rules of operation and managers. However, unlike communal families, there were independent households that could hold separate assets, beyond their shares in the estate, and no uniform standard of living was imposed.

Fan Zhongyan's action was much admired, and it continued to be praised for centuries. To some extent, at least, this admiration may have been based on the belief that the charitable estate solved the problem of the upper-class man and his obligations to his kin.[105] Communal families would find it hard to maintain everyone at upper-class status for generations. But a separation of descent group property from household property would make it possible for upper-class families to continue with their higher standard of living, while larger descent groups including many commoners could also continue, without recurrent subsidy from the more wealthy, as ritual and charitable expenses were ensured through the endowment. Just as the well-to-do in a community might get together to endow an estate to pay for all local labor service obligations, saving themselves from repeated annoyance, others might endow a fund to provide for poor orphans and widows among their kin so that they would not have to deal with them individually. Endowing a lineage school, however, probably had a different appeal. It would be especially

義田贍族

Figure 5.3 Fan Zhongyan creating a charitable estate to supply his relatives.
Source: After SYXJ 6.6a.

attractive to the educated members of the lineage who then would not need to worry as much about their descendants losing social status for lack of access to schooling.

The government gave positive encouragement to descent group estates (as it did also to communal families). In 1092 the land law was specifically amended to allow officials and commoners to set aside "land or houses to pay for the expenses of sacrifices to their ancestors." Local government officials were to certify this, changing the tax registration of the property and preventing descendants from ever dividing it. If a surplus resulted, the descent group was permitted to use this for aid to agnates.[106] Nevertheless, the number of wealthy men who imitated Fan Zhongyan seems to have been very small. Shimizu, in a careful study of this subject, found only a dozen references in Song sources to men setting up charitable estates to aid their agnates.[107] Most of these were only for the poor in a lineage, and when the size of the estate is given, it is usually much smaller than the Fan's, a few hundred *mu*. As Lu You (1125–1210) noted in 1207, very few people in the world had been able to copy Fan's example. "Their failure is not due to not considering it righteous, but to lack of means."[108] (Even the estate Lu praised, started with a gift of 700 *mu*, did not last very long. Hu Zhu (fl. 1300–1350) recorded that it had long been out of existence.)[109] Nor were all of the estates established strictly for agnates; some were for agnates and maternal or other "external" relatives.[110] One woman in the Northern Song is recorded to have used her dowry to set up charitable fields to benefit equally relatives through marriage and agnates (presumably this meant the agnates of her husband and son and also the families tied to them by marriage, such as her own natal family and the families her daughters married into).[111]

The relatively small number of references to lineage estates must be compared to the dozens of references to communal families and the hundreds of references to men acting charitably toward their kinsmen (including affines) by supplying them when they were in need from their own income. There are probably even more references to unsuccessful attempts to found estates than to estates that survived for over a century.[112] If anything, Fan's example may have had greater influence in areas outside kinship. Endowments for charitable purposes became extremely common in the Song, but if surviving references are any indication of their prevalence at the time, most were for community-based activities. These included charitable schools, charitable granaries, and estates to defray labor service costs.[113] Sometimes these community services were seen as particularly aiding the donor's agnates, presumably because the community was largely composed of his agnates.[114]

In all probability, estates that provided no more than ritual expenses provided the material base for lineage formation more often than charitable estates did.[115] Most Song references to sacrificial fields refer to very small descent groups. Among Song legal cases there are several references to estates set up to pay for sacrifices, the control of the estate to be rotated among a set of brothers. In one case the estate was based on the dowry of a wife who had died along with her husband and only son. Rather than establish an adoptive heir for the husband, his parents, who had three living sons, had the three rotate management of her dowry land and take charge of the sacrifices.[116]

The advantages of rotation as a means of managing small estates can be seen in a case decided by Liu Kezhuang (1187–1269).[117] A father who was worried about the differing ability of his four sons had divided his property unequally, with the older two getting less and the younger two more. He had also set up a charitable estate to provide for rites at the tombs, complete with rules for its management and allocation. At issue now was the management of the estate attached to the tombs. Each brother wanted the management, claiming "I am the eldest," "I am an official," "I am the most able." There was also an argument that the land should either be divided equally or donated to a temple. But Liu Kezhuang rejected donation because then the "spirit would starve" and provided instead for the sons to rotate management, keeping records that would be open to all of them. He quoted a legal ruling to the effect that if a father feared his sons would be unable to preserve their land, it could be made into an inalienable estate, to be handled in rotation to pay for sacrifices.[118]

Sometimes management of sacrificial lands could call for extensive rules. Huang Gan reports that in 1216 Chen Fudao showed him a three-chapter "Compact for the Sacrificial Fields" for which Huang Gan then wrote a colophon.[119] To deserve such lengthy rules, this estate was probably larger than the one Huang Gan established himself in 1221. Of the management of the latter, Huang Gan wrote that its annual income of sixteen piculs was too slight to allow each household to manage it in turn. Instead, six piculs should be set aside for the sacrifices, and the leaders of the descent group should use the rest for taxes and a contingency fund. Any remaining surplus was to be reinvested to increase the holdings. "After ten years, if the increase is substantial, by rotation, it can be used to supply agnates in need."[120]

Thus, although the Fan example of selecting elders and managers to run the estate may well have been copied by lineages with large estates, the practice of rotation was already well-established in the Song and may well have been the most common form where joint properties were slight.[121]

It has been necessary to discuss estates and their management in some detail because of their importance in the literature on lineages. It should be apparent, however, that I have not found evidence of many lineages with great estates during the early stages of descent group development. Nor do estates always seem to have been the central feature of the lineages that owned them. Even a lineage/descent group strongly identified with an estate might survive its loss. Song Lian (1310–1381) reported that the Lin of Putian in Fujian by the late Song had accumulated 2,000 *mu* of "sacrificial fields," allowing them to conduct more impressive ancestral ceremonies than other descent groups in the area. Yet after this land was lost with the Yuan takeover, the sense of group identity was not extinguished; two generations later the leaders of these Lins erected an ancestral hall as a new focus for descent group activities.[122]

LATER DIRECTIONS IN GENEALOGY WRITING AND ELITE STRATEGIES FOR PROMOTING DESCENT GROUP FORMATION

Although genealogists up to the twentieth century regularly cited the pioneering examples of Ouyang Xiu and Su Xun, within a century after they wrote their genealogies, their model was largely abandoned; the limitation at five generations was ignored and new sorts of information came to be regularly included in genealogies. These new directions appear to be closely related to developments in descent group organization and to a "localist strategy" on the part of officials and other members of the national elite. On the one hand, active descent groups often asked literati (sometimes their own members) to help them compile genealogies, but the kinds of genealogies they wanted were ones that would match their needs, stressing their first (apical) ancestor, any transfers of residence or burial grounds, the name and number patterns they used to distinguish themselves, and the location of all ancestors' graves. But the process could also occur in the opposite order, with politically ambitious men trying to strengthen their local network of allies by compiling a genealogy; this act, they believed, would give group identity to their nearby agnates.[123] As more and more genealogies were written, they came to be increasingly important in establishing pedigree and social status; they became public documents, shown to relatives through marriage who might well write prefaces or postfaces for them. Similarly they could be used to foster alliances between distantly related local descent groups. Thus genealogies came to serve both the internal and external needs of descent groups and compiling them became a major practical and symbolic act of descent groups, handled almost exclusively by the more highly educated of their members. Indeed, as "public" genealogies became a central concern of descent groups with elite members, such descent groups may have progressively diverged from ones composed entirely of commoners of little education.[124]

The information included in a genealogy often provides a good indication of the needs or goals of the group that produced it. The significance of listing the location of graves in genealogies should be obvious from the argument so far; one had to know where graves were to make offerings at them. Concern with "first migrant ancestors" and shifts of residence seems to reflect a concern with specific groupings of people "on the ground," the ones who joined in rites. As mentioned earlier, it was at the grave of the "first migrant ancestor" that an entire local descent group would assemble and it clearly had a special importance in defining the boundaries of the group. Already in the mid-twelfth century (1166) Zeng Feng referred to "first migrant ancestors" (*shiqian zhi zu*) eight generations back to define two branches (*pai*) of Zeng in Linchuan.[125] Thereafter this became very common. From the late Song on, great attention also came to be given to every transfer of residence,[126] a trait of written genealogies that persisted until recent times.[127] This departure from Ouyang Xiu's and Su Xun's model was explicitly justified by Zheng Yu (1298–1358), who said that mourning rules and their limitation at four generations had nothing to do with genealogies, which are concerned with tracing origins.[128]

Naming patterns of various sorts had been followed by high-status families since the Northern and Southern Dynasties.[129] In the fifth and sixth centuries brothers (and less frequently first cousins) were often given patterned names, the pattern either in a common radical of a one-character name, or in a common character in a two-character name. This system continued to be very common through the Tang and was sometimes even extended to second or third cousins, though such cases were rare.[130] The Wangs of Wuyuan, discussed above as a communal family, had generational names from the late Tang.[131]

In genealogies, very often name and number patterns are discussed together. In the preface Ouyang Shoudao (1209–1267+) wrote for a genealogy, he said that the descent group in question could trace back sixteen generations, giving ancestors' names (*ming*), informal names (*zi*), numbers (*di*), rows (*hang*), death dates, and tomb locations.[132] (Rows refer to generations and numbers to a person's seniority by date of birth within a generation.) Dai Biaoyuan (fl. 1260–1290) described a name and number pattern that was consciously put into practice as part of an effort to establish a descent group. He reported that after a man named Sun Yao did extensive research to compile the genealogy of his large descent group (which had included many officials in the previous century), he got together "the worthy and able" and together they assembled their agnates. At this meeting, one generation was selected to be the first row (*hang*) and a naming pattern was designed, using twenty characters in the order of production of the Five Phases; this pattern would be continued indefinitely, returning to the beginning after twenty generations. "Thus for 100 generations the seniority in the *zhaomu* ranks will not become disordered."[133] In other words, the express purpose of this naming system was to make it easy to recognize differences in generations among the members of a large descent group. Some recorded name and number systems follow slightly different principles; for instance one described by Wu Hai (fl. 1350–1370) used the ten celestial stems as generational markers in the numbering system.[134]

Number patterns are less well understood than name patterns. Rather than emphasizing membership in a generation, numbers indicate exact seniority within a generation. Seniority was of course important in Chinese family ethics (the elder brother–younger brother relationship) and this may account in part for the practice. Numbering of people within a family or a small ritual group (e.g., among descendants of a great-grandfather) seems to have been a common practice among the upper class in the Tang; Tang poems and elegies were often dedicated to Wang 11 or Zhang 22. In the Song commoners were often referred to by a name and a number. In legal cases and anecdotes, people of the lowest status were often called Wang 3 or Li 5. Most often one finds low numbers, which could mean only brothers were included within the sequence.

From the earliest stages of descent group development, there seems to have been an association between numbers and descent groups. Ouyang Xiu had recorded some numbers in his genealogy, and in 1098 the Fan estate had required that numbers be recorded for infants.[135] Why did people number sons within a large descent group instead of a family or small ritual group? One possible reason is that the significance of numbers was in ancestor worship (where people and tablets were to be lined up in this order), and the unit involved in ancestor worship in their cases was large. Moreover, as mentioned above in the context of patterned graves, emphasis on seniority within a generation would counter the tendency to divide into separate lines of descent. Genealogies, by their very arrangement, reveal descent lines (referred to as branching, *zhifen paibie*); that is, they place each man under his own father. If each person's birth-order number was also added, something of this emphasis on lines could be countered. Whatever the reason, in the Song it seems to have become common to refer to ancestors by their number and genealogists, by recording these numbers, seem to have adapted the genre of genealogical writing to the requirements of active descent groups.[136]

Song and Yuan genealogies with the features described above seem to have been written by and large for pre-existing descent groups, groups with well-defined needs for recording information. But not all genealogies were of this sort or written for this purpose. Among the upper class at least, genealogies could be used to assert status and establish ties between families. Morita shows how genealogy writing became a more public activity in the late Song and Yuan, as men turned to famous writers to write prefaces and postfaces. Wen Tianxiang (1236–1283), for instance, wrote four prefaces/postfaces, Wu Cheng (1247–1331) wrote thirty-seven, and Song Lian (1310–1381) wrote twenty. In addition, to make genealogies more widely available men began to make multiple copies by printing them.[137]

The importance of genealogies in establishing status was perhaps most acutely developed in Huizhou, where men even published genealogical gazetteers, the first one in 1316.[138] This may well have had something to do with marriage ties. Shu Di (1304–1377) from Huizhou wrote prefaces for the genealogies of the families of his maternal grandfather, his father's sister, and his wife's brother.[139] But the relationship between marriage and genealogy compilation was not limited to Huizhou. Lou Yue (1137–1213) described a man in his native Mingzhou who was thoughtful to all of his relatives, even, for instance, paying his respects to the tombs of his mother's family as well as his own. He also compiled a table of the descent lines and branches of all the families related to his by marriage over the generations.

This then was a genealogy not of a single descent line but of several inter-married ones.[140]

Besides helping in establishing ties to affines, genealogies could also be used to link patrilineally related descent groups and thus to form "higher-order" descent groups. This practice had appeared by the late Song. When Ouyang Shoudao broke the precedent set by his ancestor Ouyang Xiu of compiling a genealogy for only five generations, he justified this by saying he wanted a genealogy that would connect all of the descent groups of Ouyang in Luling. By the Yuan dynasty, writing genealogies explicitly to document the connections between separate descent groups became quite common. Describing a descent group in his home community, Song Lian praised a man who "compiled a genealogy of relatives of the same surname in order to connect their descent groups."[141] In another case, a Zeng wanted to compile a genealogy to record the connections among thirty-five branches (*fang*) under one of the nine segments (*zhi*) of the Zengs of Chalin in Jiangxi. This was difficult because he had to get access to other descent groups' genealogies; many had lost theirs in the wars, and others who had preserved them considered them secret treasures they would not show anyone.[142]

There could be several reasons why men might want to establish links among descent groups. It could be useful to define a set of potential allies, even if no joint endeavor was under consideration at the moment.[143] More-over, prestige was probably also involved. A descent line that had branches throughout the region would seem more glorious than one limited to a single place. Men would like to know that they belonged to such a ramified descent group.

Genealogies could be written not only to create, document, or link descent groups, but also to purify them. This is seen especially in the works of Wu Hai (fl. 1350–1370), a native of Min county in Fujian, who seems to have had an intense distaste for any violation of patrilineal principles. In several prefaces to genealogies he decried the prevalence of nonagnatic adoption, in one place asserting that it confused the family lines of 50 to 60 percent of descent groups.[144] In one genealogy he recorded a rule that anyone who had someone of another surname made heir would be excised from the genea-logy and not recorded. He noted that this policy raised questions in some people's minds:

> Some say, "Although he is of a different surname, he has been a successor to our line for a long time; it would be difficult to exclude him. Couldn't he be recorded in an appendix?" I say, "No. Anyone of another surname who abandoned his ancestors and attached himself to our ancestors, discarding his own surname and hiding under ours, should be labeled unfilial and inhumane!"[145]

In another case, the descent group's "first ancestor" had been an adoptee, and compiling the genealogy was an effort to rectify the error, returning to the original surname. Some of these nonagnatic adoptions were with "external" relatives. As Wu Hai complained in one preface, "Today people do not follow the ritual rules; they take a son-in-law or a daughter's son to be their heir without limit. They are destroying themselves because they cannot go beyond their wives' viewpoint."[146] For Wu Hai, compiling genealogies was a way to overcome this tendency.

Understanding the purposes for compiling genealogies can help us evaluate them as historical sources for the organization or leadership of descent groups. Even from this brief review, it should be evident that not all genealogies correspond in their tables to descent groups. Many Song and Yuan genealogies are explicitly stated to have been products of research in sources such as epitaphs, intended to facilitate formation of descent groups rather than to represent the membership list of an existing one. The genealogies written to link descent groups may well be like the huge compilations done during the last century, which as Freedman noted need not be charters for groups about to embark on joint action; they could simply be history, inspired by "filial piety, hunger for prestige, and scholarly appetite for writing history."[147] Such genealogies should be easily recognized by the statements in the prefaces or the patchy quality of the vital data they contain. A genealogy that includes fairly good vital data for all branches can probably safely be taken as evidence of the existence of a descent group, for a group that got together only once a year for ancestor worship would have records of ancestors and maybe of living members. Yet even a highly detailed genealogy need not indicate that the descent group was a lineage with extensive property unless explicit reference to such property is given. As Johanna Meskill pointed out, lineages barely needed to exist for genealogies to be produced; all that was needed were a few wealthy individuals.[148]

With regard to leadership, genealogies usually portray members of the elite – officials especially – as the active agents in the development of the group. In some cases, this may be the result of recasting what had actually happened into the language of Neo-Confucianism discussed above. In other cases it is probably because the best-educated, especially officials, were the active members of the group and those most concerned with presenting the group to outsiders.[149] And in yet other cases the prominence of educated men in descriptions of descent group activities could be because the only actual descent group activity was the intellectual one of defining themselves as a group through compiling a genealogy.[150]

ANCESTRAL HALLS

The last major addition to the repertoire of agnatic kinship practices made in the Song and Yuan periods was the establishment of ancestral halls as foci for descent groups or "high-order" descent groups.

In Song sources probably 99 percent of the references to halls (*ci*) have nothing to do with descent group organization. Men who had made contributions to a community or to the state were often honored after their deaths by having halls established for them where ritual offerings could be made. Often it was the local county or prefectural government that sponsored the construction of the hall and later looked after upkeep and sacrificial offerings. Not infrequently halls were dedicated to two or three great men. Besides this sort of hall, families of high officials might have *miao* (ancestral altars) in their residences, and Zhu Xi was said to have recommended that families set up halls (*citang*) to the east of their main room.[151] Both of these types of ancestral shrines were for domestic rites, going back only the canonical four generations. During the Yuan period, however, one begins to find references to ancestral halls of the more recent type, permanently focused on an apical ancestor, detached from anyone's residence.[152]

Wu Hai, whose objections to contamination of the patrilineal line were cited above, described an ancestral hall (*citang*) of the Lins of Luotian (Hubei). In this hall were tablets for all the ancestors, going back twenty-one generations, including members of the lineage who had died without descendants. These were all in *zhaomu* order. On the first and fifteenth of each month one of the kinsmen would pay his respects, and on a day chosen by divination in the spring and fall, sacrifices would be performed. In his reformist zeal, Wu Hai wanted this stopped. He said only nobles were allowed to have halls of this sort; commoners were to make offerings in their homes. So he had the Lins bury the tablets (the classical way to dispose of tablets retired from family altars), recording their distant ancestors on a chart instead. On the winter solstice and New Year's Day, this chart could be displayed and all the lineage members could gather to bow before it, all ranked in order, after which they could have a meeting to encourage moral behavior. Consequently Wu Hai had the name of the building changed from hall to "Building for Descent Group Meetings," using a term from Cheng Yi.[153]

Other scholars were not so inhospitable to ancestral halls.[154] Song Lian (1310–1381), a highly respected scholar and teacher, wrote essays on seven he had come across, explicitly justifying their innovative aspects. In one essay he wrote:

The ancients did not have halls at graves, and commoners could only offer sacrifices to their fathers. This was the ritual. In the Han there were halls at graves, and sacrifices went back to great-great-grandfathers. One cannot say that this was contrary to ritual. The Lins of Gaizhu in Pingyang [Zhejiang] have set up a hall at the grave of their first migrant ancestor and make sacrifices there. How can one say this is contrary to ritual?[155]

Song Lian noted that after twelve generations, the descendants of this first ancestor lived scattered in different villages and their ties to each other had become weak. Thus one of their members, an official, wanted to set up a hall at the first ancestor's grave so they would not forget their common origin. His son finished the project, and the whole lineage assembled for the seasonal sacrifices, which were followed by a group feast. In addition, a school was attached to the hall for the education of lineage members. Song Lian ended with strong praise for this institution, saying that a descent group with great depth will have such diverse members (rich and poor, weak and strong) that group rituals will be the only way to overcome their distance.[156]

In another case, in Song Lian's home area of Jinhua, a hall was erected in 1365–66 to unite through ritual three descent groups (*san dazu*) of Zhang who were related ten generations back. The first migrant ancestor and his three sons, the apical ancestors of the three descent groups, were the foci of the hall. Because the elapsed time was so great, the organizers thought that they would not try to offer the seasonal sacrifices at this hall but rather use it to get the entire higher-order descent group together there each New Year festival. On that occasion all recently born sons who had already been named would have their names recorded in the genealogy. Some sacrificial fields were established to pay for these rites, which the three descent groups would handle in rotation.[157]

In another case discussed by Song Lian, a hall was explicitly described as a functional replacement for "sacrificial fields" that had been lost with the Yuan takeover. The hall united the three branches (*fang*) of the Lin of Putian (Fujian) and had five "spirit boards" (*shen ban*), each four feet high, listing all of the ancestors. On each summer solstice the descent group held a joint sacrifice. The essay explicitly noted that "small *zong*" sacrifices to each person's four most recent ancestors would continue to be done separately in homes. The hall, however, would be used for greetings at New Year's and for cappings, weddings, and announcements to ancestors.[158]

Two features are striking about the reports by Wu Hai and Song Lian concerning the descent groups they came across. The first is their high level of organizational complexity. They had great genealogical depth; they conducted ancestor worship as a group ceremony; they did this on a regular schedule; they had records of their ancestors' names written on tablets or boards and arranged in significant ways. The second striking feature is their variability. Some made offerings in the spring and fall, others at New Year's, others at the summer solstice. Whether this reflects regional differences requires further research, but it is possible that many variations co-existed. Indeed, in Song Lian's home county of Jinhua quite different forms and stages of kinship organization existed side by side, for it was the home not only of the "higher-order" Zhang descent group but also of the Zheng communal family and several of its imitators.

Finally I should perhaps note that Song Lian's student, the eminent scholar Fang Xiaoru (1357–1402), wrote a series of essays on descent groups in which he advocated as ideal many of the practices that had appeared over the previous four centuries. In several different essays he stressed joint sacrifices at the tomb of the first migrant ancestor and at halls, followed by banquets, the compilation and regular updating of comprehensive genealogies, and the establishment of estates to provide for rituals, charity, and education.[159] In his writings, the repertoire of descent group activities appears in essentially complete form.

CONCLUSION

In this cursory overview of the development of descent group organization in the Song and Yuan dynasties, I have tried to describe the new practices that appeared, expanding the repertoire of known and accepted ways to interact with local agnatic kinsmen. In 1350 descent groups had a variety of features (halls, sacrificial fields, regularly updated genealogies, and so on) that were not to be found in 1000. Almost all Song and Yuan references to these features are from areas south of the Huai River, the region in which lineages were most highly developed in Qing times. It is true that a few features common in nineteenth- and twentieth-century lineages and descent groups had not yet appeared. Not until mid-Ming were detailed rules of behavior, with sanctions against violation, printed in lineage genealogies or halls erected for all those of one surname in a prefecture or province.[160] Nevertheless, a surprisingly large number of features characteristic of later descent groups and lineages did appear during the eleventh through fourteenth centuries.

My emphasis on innovations should not obscure the larger conservatism of kinship practices. As I mentioned earlier, the repertoire of agnatic kinship practices that existed in the Tang dynasty largely continued into the Song; it also continued into the Ming and Qing. Even after the widespread acceptance of worship at graves, concern with first migrant ancestors, and innovations in genealogy writing, estates, and shrines, there were always men who would have concurred with Su Xun that they seldom saw even their agnates within their mourning circle. Some anthropologists have talked of "lineage atrophy" as a process of social change in areas where well-developed lineages are part of the cultural repertoire.[161] Although some lineages have certainly atrophied, the general trend was just the opposite. As Makino pointed out many years ago, there was a slow but gradual trend toward more organization in the activities of agnates, not less.[162] Nevertheless, most sets of agnates remained at various less-organized levels. Japanese scholars like Uchida found groups of agnates in North China whose only joint activities might be celebration of the Qingming sacrifices, responsibility rotated among households or segments.[163] In this regard, the finding by Evelyn Rawski that a set of wealthy agnates identified as a group by outsiders did not function like a lineage need not be surprising; it was undoubtedly true of many other comparable sets of agnates elsewhere.[164]

By way of conclusion I would like to suggest ways in which a knowledge of the early stages of descent group development adds to our understanding of agnatic kinship in China. In doing so I do not wish to confuse historical and sociological explanation. As I stated in my opening paragraph, features important in the early stages of descent group development need not be the crucial features of fully developed ones, or vice versa. In other words, the fact that in a highly developed lineage a genealogy serves a recognizable function in maintaining the lineage surely cannot be taken as evidence that genealogies were invented or developed to serve those purposes. Nor, if I am correct in stressing the role of innovations in ancestor worship as fostering a broad shift in conceptions of how to deal with agnates, can I then go on to argue that ancestral rites were the catalyst for the formation of particular groups, or even a central feature of all fully developed descent groups.

This caveat aside, I am enough of an historian to think that the historical explanations for a phenomenon provide some insight into its dynamics. Thus I wish to reiterate the central place of ancestral rites in descent group formation. The importance of graves to descent groups has been emphasized throughout this essay. Genealogies and ancestral halls appear to be key features of more developed descent groups, and both had major ritual purposes. Genealogies are in large part lists of ritually relevant information, especially about ancestors. Location of graves, birth and death dates, and seniority within a generation were all ritually significant items of information. This is not to deny that ritual groups could come to play other roles, to act as units in local politics, own property, or dominate communities. But whether or not this happened would have depended on circumstances. I am arguing that there was no internal logic moving all ritual, ancestor-focused descent groups in this direction.

In the early stages of descent group development I have found little sign that membership in a descent group was so basic to social life that it restricted other social activities. It is well known that Chinese literati and officials participated in complex social networks, based on varied ties to friends, teachers, relatives of all sorts, and superiors and subordinates in office. In the Song and Yuan periods at least full and enthusiastic membership in a ritually focused descent group does not seem to have infringed on these other relations. Kinship solidarity would not necessarily take precedence over other solidarities, and communities where several large descent groups resided would not always divide along kin lines.[165]

In stressing the importance of ancestral rites in descent group formation I am also by implication downgrading the part played by corporate estates. Lineages organized around large estates appear to be the functional successors of communal families; like communal families they exerted considerable control over individuals, regulated their access to material benefits, and acted as a social and political unit in the larger society. Thus lineages should not be looked on as the most fully developed descent groups, but as a certain special type of descent group. The more usual type of descent group could flourish without an income-producing estate; to enhance and strengthen its central purpose, its leaders would find ways to finance ancestral halls, genealogies, and schools; estates could be a means to this end, but they were not an essential one.

6   Cremation in Song China*

Disposing of the dead arouses feelings of love, dread, anxiety, and pain. Despite these common human responses, different peoples learn to give form to their emotions in widely divergent ways and thus are often repelled by what others do. The Chinese abhorred some customs of their neighbors and ethnic minorities, such as the Tibetan practice of exposing corpses and the Muslim practice of burying without a coffin. They would surely have been just as horrified by the medieval European practice of dividing bodies. Europeans in China were often made uncomfortable by the northern Chinese practice of keeping encoffined bodies in the courtyard for decades or the southeastern Chinese practice of exhuming bodies after a few years to clean the bones and place them in urns.

These culturally constructed emotional responses to the handling of the dead body do not change easily. In the summer of 1988, the Chinese press carried articles showing that the government had not yet succeeded in its forty-year campaign to replace burial with cremation. For instance, the five children of a deputy chairman of a county party committee had within two days of his death buried him in a hillside grave that took up 90 square meters. They did this although party leaders had tried to keep them from removing the body from the hospital and had then visited their home to insist on cremation. After five weeks of pressure from many party and government officials, the family relented, and the water-logged coffin was exhumed as several hundred villagers watched.[1]

In this essay, I examine a counter-example in the history of Chinese mortuary practice, a case in which customs did change. Beginning in the tenth century, many people willingly gave up the long-established custom of burying bodies in coffins to follow the practice introduced by Buddhist monks of cremating bodies and either scattering the ashes over water, storing them in urns aboveground, or burying the urn in a small grave. Throughout the native Song (960–1279) dynasty and its successor, the alien Yuan (1215–1368) dynasty founded by the Mongol conquerors, cremation flourished

* This article was first published in *American Historical Review* 95 (1990: 406–28). Reproduced with permission of the publisher.

despite strong objections on the part of the state and the Confucian-educated elite.[2] Historians of the West have shown that changes in mortuary customs are an excellent lens for viewing changing religious ideas and social organization.[3] Changes in such practices in China similarly reveal the complex interaction of popular religion, the ideas of the highly articulate, and the state's efforts to regulate behavior.

The spread of cremation marked a fundamental change in the treatment of the dead body because, until the Song period, the dominant Chinese preference had been to dispose of the dead in ways that would delay decay.[4] The Chinese not only used very thick wooden coffins, packed tightly with clothes and shrouds, they also built tomb chambers of wood, stone, or brick and took other measures they thought would preserve the body, such as placing jade objects in the coffins or even, in a famous example, dressing the body in jade. The *Record of Ritual*, a Confucian classic put in final form by the first century BC, repeatedly mentioned the need to settle an ancestor's body, to make it comfortable. The earthly soul (*po*), the soul capable of becoming a harmful ghost, was thought to stay near the body. It could be kept happy if supplied with food, drink, and utensils. Given ancient beliefs about the powers of ancestors, survivors stood to benefit from their ancestors' pleasure. From early times, there was also a strong sense that bodies should be buried intact; part of one's obligation to ancestors was to protect one's body for eventual burial. The Confucian school in particular was identified with pious funeral preparations and reverent sacrifices to ancestral spirits for generations afterward.[5]

In ancient times, some critics opposed the expense incurred by elaborate burial practices, yet they questioned the utility of grave goods and chambers, not underground burial in coffins. The fifth-century BC critic of Confucius, Mozi, advocated economical burial but still wanted coffins 3 inches thick. He described as heartless the customs of the Yichu tribe west of China who cremated their dead in the belief that their souls would ascend with the smoke.[6] Even though many early thinkers argued that the dead were without feelings or consciousness, it was extremely uncommon for them to draw the conclusion that the treatment of the dead therefore did not matter.[7] Chinese ideas about souls, ancestors, and the afterlife began to change even before the introduction of Buddhism,[8] yet new ideas did not undermine the preference for underground burial in sturdy coffins.[9] Even ideas of immortality – especially those associated with the Daoist immortality cult – were corporeal.[10] Moreover, knowledge of cremation as a practice of neighboring peoples did not lead to its acceptance.

At first glance, the history of cremation in China would appear to be a straightforward example of the gradual penetration of Buddhism into Chinese culture and the reassertion of Confucianism in the Song dynasty and later. Given the implications of this model for our understanding of the role of philosophical and religious ideas in the evolution of Chinese culture, it should not be accepted without close scrutiny. Buddhism was introduced by the second century AD, but the process of adaptation to Chinese society was a slow one. Buddhism was not fully incorporated into the common people's social and religious life until the Tang dynasty (618–906).[11] If it could be shown that Buddhism led to changes in the ways ordinary people handled the dead, the magnitude of its impact on Chinese culture would be confirmed. Likewise, evidence that the reassertion of Confucianism was responsible for the decline of cremation after the fourteenth century would demonstrate that intellectual and political changes at the top of the social and political hierarchy changed the everyday lives of ordinary people.

To scrutinize the role of Buddhist and Confucian ideas in these changes in mortuary practices, in this essay I attempt to disentangle different levels of ideas and practices. I distinguish Buddhist ideas from the services provided by Buddhist temples and monasteries, and among Buddhist ideas, I distinguish ones derived from Buddhist scriptures from Buddhist cultic practices and from folk Buddhist traditions not canonical in origin. In a similar way, I distinguish Neo-Confucian ideas from state actions.[12] Neo-Confucian objections to cremation were based on sectarian opposition to Buddhism, on belief in the transformative powers of adherence to ancient ritual protocols, and on deeply felt ideas about respect for ancestors. The Song, Yuan, and Ming (1368–1644) governments sporadically took stands against cremation, issuing laws, urging enforcement of them, and providing alternatives. It is necessary to ask, therefore, whether cremation declined because it came to be thought of as un-Confucian, because it was suppressed, or for other reasons.

In both the spread of cremation and its later decline, ideas from outside these two elite traditions were also important. From studies of Chinese folk religion and mortuary practice in modern China, it is evident that the handling of the dead did not simply belong to the realms of Buddhism or Confucianism; it also involved geomancers, diviners, shamans, and notions of souls and the afterlife better labeled folk, indigenous, or Daoist than either Buddhist or Neo-Confucian.[13] Throughout the Tang (618–907) and Song periods, indigenous religious life was strong and vital and not always readily reformed by the efforts of elites, whether Buddhist or Confucian. New cults, such as those of Mazu, Wenchang, and city gods, were spreading over wide areas of China. Archaeological and literary evidence suggests significant changes in mortuary practice besides the spread of cremation, especially a decline in the use of grave goods, increased delays in burials, and expansion of the cult of the grave. Thus the history of cremation has a context that includes folk religious ideas about bodies, souls, and graves.

This essay pursues the social, religious, and political context of the history of cremation by examining in turn how common cremation became in Song times, why people turned to its practice, how and why authorities attempted to suppress it, and when it declined. The sources, though not adequate to answer these questions as conclusively as one would like, do show that these changes in customs were considerably more complex historical phenomena than the simple Buddhism / Neo-Confucianism model would suggest. Expediency seems to have motivated the choice of cremation as much as belief in its superiority; the ideas that facilitated its acceptance seem to have come as much from the folk level as from Buddhist doctrine; and political efforts to suppress cremation owed as much to anti-foreign sentiments as to anti-Buddhist ones.

THE PREVALENCE OF CREMATION IN SONG TIMES

The incidence of creation can be judged from both literary and archaeological evidence. Beginning in 962, when cremation was first outlawed, sources contain repeated references to cremation as a widespread practice in China proper.[14] In the early eleventh century, Jia Tong (ca. 1020) wrote that cremation had already become the custom among common people and was gradually contaminating the practices of the educated.[15] In the mid-eleventh century, Han Qi (1008–1075) found that, in central northern China, "customs are confused with those of the Qiang and Hu [barbarians]. When people die they are cremated and afterwards buried, though the poor deposit the bones in Buddhist shrines, where they accumulate for years in untold numbers."[16] In 1157, Fan Tong wrote in a memorial,

> Today the people have the custom of "transformation by fire." While their parents are alive they worry only that they cannot provide everything they need, but when they die they roast them and throw them away . . . Some go so far as to toss the remains in water after burning them . . . Nowadays the cruelty of cremation increases every day.[17]

In approximately the same period, Hong Mai (1123–1202) wrote:

> Once the Buddhist theory of transformation by fire arose, everywhere there have been people who burn the corpse on death. When the weather is hot, out of dread of the foul secretions, they invariably lay out [the body] before the day is over and burn it before the flesh is cold.[18]

In 1261, Huang Zhen (1213–1280) described a crematorium outside the large city of Suzhou:

> There is a temple called "Aid for All" one *li* to the southwest of the city. For a long time this temple has had about ten hollow structures for cremating people which it operates to make a profit. All the ignorant people of the city are attracted to it; as soon as their parents die, they cart them off and consign them to the flames. The ashes that are not consumed are collected and thrown in a deep pool.[19]

Not long afterward, Marco Polo spent seventeen years in China (1275–1292). He recorded the use of cremation alongside other Chinese funerary practices – wearing hemp clothes, keeping coffins in the house for long periods, setting food each day in front of them.[20] He referred to cremation as the common Chinese way of dealing with the dead and explicitly mentioned its practice in thirteen of the cities he visited, especially ones in coastal provinces.[21]

Although critics of cremation often used hyperbolic language, stating that "everyone," or "all the poor," or "even filial" sons and grandsons, practiced cremation, it does seem likely that, within a given area, the poor more frequently chose cremation than did the educated, especially the urban poor. Rong Yi, a central government official writing in 1158, mentioned the difficulty the poor had in finding land for burial in the immediate environs of cities.

> Your subject has heard that in Wu and Yue [the southeast] the custom is for burial expenses to be so great that one must save up before proceeding. Poor, lower class families have to make every effort to keep funeral preparations economical. For these reasons for some time many of them have found cremation convenient. Through practice it has become the custom, which is thus difficult to change. Furthermore, as the local authorities have been lax for so long, and the population increases daily, great expanses of land would be needed [to bury them all]. As it is difficult for the officials to acquire land near the cities, some have not set any aside [for graveyards].[22]

A scholar in the late thirteenth century argued that banning cremation was impractical. Every day in the capital, hundreds of people died, and there was not enough space to bury them all.[23]

Yet cremation was not strictly a custom of the poor or of city dwellers. Many of the cremation graves unearthed by archaeologists contain evidence that their occupants were well-to-do. "The rich" were said to practice cremation routinely in "watery" parts of Zhejiang, presumably because burial was difficult there; even "upper households" were said to cremate in some areas of north China.[24] Both Jia Tong and Sima Guang (1019–1086) reported that educated families were especially prone to practice cremation when their members died away from home, Sima Guang noting that sons and grandsons of officials preferred to burn their parents' bodies in order for the ashes to be returned home rather than allow them to be buried far away.[25]

A somewhat different impression of the incidence of cremation – at least for the upper and middle class in central and southeastern China in the twelfth century – can be found in the tales of the uncanny and marvelous in Hong Mai's *Yijian zhi*. Cremation, followed by scattering or burying the ashes, is referred to in a matter-of-fact manner in many tales, confirming the frequent complaint that people were so accustomed to it that they no longer considered it unusual. Nevertheless, there is no sense that cremation was the dominant or preferred practice among those of middling means or better, or even as common as depositing a coffin in a temple indefinitely. To judge from these tales, those who died away from home and those who had no descendants were more likely to be cremated than fathers or mothers who died at home. Cremation appears to have been particularly likely when both conditions were present, when a child, servant, or concubine, for instance, died away from home.

The incidence of cremation also varied from place to place. Literary evidence of the practice of cremation comes from many parts of China. It was found in north and northwest China,[26] in central China,[27] in the lower Yangtze region (east central China),[28] and along the southeast coast.[29] There are references to its practice in major cities such as Luoyang in the Northern Song, Hangzhou in the Southern Song, and Beijing at the beginning of the Yuan.[30]

Archaeological evidence is particularly good for evaluating the geographical spread of cremation but is naturally limited to cremations that resulted in the burial of urns or boxes of ashes. Moreover, because of variations in climate and soil conditions, not all graves that were dug in Song times had an equal chance of surviving to be discovered by modern archaeologists. Nevertheless, archaeologists have found Song period graves with cremated remains in every region of China, including the northern provinces of Shanxi, Henan, Liaoning, Inner Mongolia, Hebei, the central provinces of Sichuan, Hunan, Jiangsu, and the southern coastal provinces of Fujian and Guangdong.[31] There could well have been particular places where no one practiced cremation, but it does not seem to be the case that cremation was practiced only in one or two areas with special conditions.

The size and shape of excavated cremation graves, like graves for full body burial, varied from place to place and from one century to another. A tomb in Luoyang, in the heartland of North China, dating from about 1100, had a square brick chamber 2.2 meters on each side, with a vaulted roof and an arched door connecting it to the sloped path out. The interior was made to resemble the interior of a house, with doors, windows, eaves, and brackets all fashioned out of bricks. This tomb contained the remains of eight people, seven of whom had been cremated and one who had been first buried elsewhere and the bones later reinterred there. Six of the seven cremated remains were in earthenware urns, the seventh in a wooden coffin 2 meters long.[32] Since Song tombs most often had only two coffins, for a husband and a wife, it is possible that the two coffins were for a couple (one moved from elsewhere) and the remains in urns close relatives such as children who died young.

More cremation burial sites have been found in Sichuan than anywhere else, perhaps reflecting the mixing of Han Chinese and minority (non-Han) cultures in this western part of China proper near Tibet. In the area around

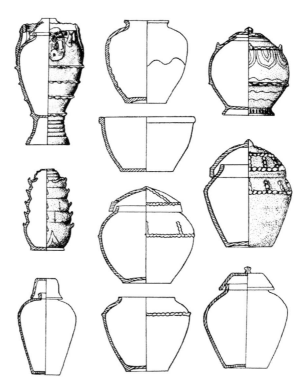

Figure 6.1 Urns holding cremated remains unearthed from Song-period tombs in
        Foshan City, Guangdong province.
Source: After Guangdongsheng wenwu guanli weiyuan hui 1965: 285.

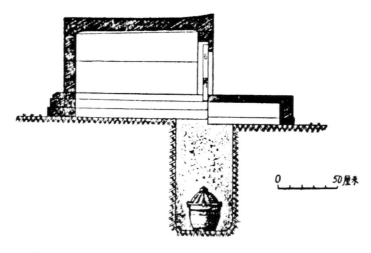

Figure 6.2 Diagram of a tomb dated 1266, with an urn with cremated remains buried
        in a small pit below an above-ground structure.
Source: After Guangzhoushi wenwu guanli weiyuan hui 1957: 70.

the city of Chengdu, 80 percent of 100 or so Southern Song (1127–1279) graves excavated in the 1950s contained cremated remains. These were brick tombs, vaulted, usually about 2.5 meters long, 1 meter wide, and 1.1 meters high, although from the late twelfth century on, there were also some smaller ones, only 1 meter long and 0.5 meters wide. These graves commonly included small cups, urns, coins, and mock deeds of ownership; occasionally, they also had figurines, bowls, incense burners, wine bottles, bronze mirrors, epitaphs inscribed on stone, and Daoist incantations.[33] A few of these small graves were almost totally occupied by large, well-made ceramic figures of soldiers, servants, officials, and animals.[34] In this area, cremation must have been the preferred practice, not a tolerated but inferior choice.

A tentative estimate, based on both literary and archaeological evidence, would be that 10 to 30 percent of the people in Song times were cremated, with the proportion varying by region, period, and circumstances.[35]

THE ROLE OF BUDDHISM

Buddhism clearly had much to do with the spread of cremation. Cremation had been the standard method of disposing of the dead in India, and Buddhist monks practiced it in China.[36] Often, the burnt remnants or "ashes" of eminent monks were preserved through burial at the base of a monument (a stupa), a practice that had already gained popularity in India much earlier.[37] These burnt bone fragments were treated as relics, replicating the devout handling of the Buddha's bones as relics of enormous religious potency.[38] By Tang times, the cult of relics drew on a folk Buddhist belief that the bones of Bodhisattvas (Buddhas-to-be), unlike those of ordinary people, were linked in a chain or miraculously mixed with jewels. After the body was burned, the bones could be inspected and the deceased's status as a Bodhisattva confirmed.[39] Perhaps because of the desire to examine and preserve these bones, it seems to have been common in China for cremation to leave pieces of bone large enough to be held (and, when scattered, to fill up ponds).[40] Even when the person cremated was a commoner, people searched for relics. According to one tale, when the maid in an official family was cremated and her ashes returned home, people nearby smelled the fragrance of lotus flowers and came to search for relics among her burnt bones. In another case, when jewels were found among the remnants of a young wife's cremation, her father-in-law paid for a lavish temple to house them.[41] Thus Buddhist cultic practice placed cremation in a spiritually positive context.

Buddhism provided institutions that undoubtedly played a role in the spread of cremation. All recorded crematoria were run by Buddhist temples, although it was also possible for people to cremate their own dead by constructing a pyre on open ground. Some Buddhist temples provided storage for the burnt remnants, and others had pools of water where they could be scattered. On the other hand, Buddhist faith did not require cremation.

Cremation was not considered a crucial ritual act in Buddhist theology; there are no sutras or commentaries arguing that a person's fate after death depends on burial or cremation, or indeed has anything to do with how the corpse is handled.[42] Buddhist missionaries, in trying to convert the Chinese populace, told people to give up sacrifices of meat but did not tell them to stop burying their dead. In the early centuries of Buddhist growth in China, Buddhist clergy were not known for their assistance with funerals. Even in the Song period, when they had taken on this role, Buddhist monks did not refuse to participate in funerals involving full body burial. Not even all monks were cremated. Chinese critics of cremation generally saw it simply as a foreign custom that had accompanied Buddhism. As one wrote, "The Buddha originally was a barbarian [*huren*]; cremation was the custom of his country."[43] Even within the Buddhist community, cremation was often referred to as the "method of the Western regions."[44]

Despite the lack of concern with cremation in Buddhist doctrine, acceptance of basic Buddhist ideas – especially karma and transmigration of the soul – must have changed the way many people thought of the dead body. These Buddhist ideas provided no support for the ancient idea that the dead could be comfortable or uncomfortable. The dead person was to be reborn into another body: there was no need for the old body to be preserved or its decay delayed. Buddhism taught non-attachment to material things; neither the dead nor the living had reason to be attached to the body after death.

One puzzle in the linkage between Buddhism and cremation is that Song and Yuan period cremation burials rarely contain evidence of visual or textual links to Buddhism.[45] Perhaps those motivated primarily by Buddhist faith had their ashes scattered, leaving no remains. But monks are unlikely to have opposed the burial of burnt bones, as their fellow monks were regularly buried in stupas and even thought of as relics. The explanation probably is that the popularity of cremation owed as much to non-Buddhist as to Buddhist ideas.

Ghosts and bones

In Song tales, the ghosts of the dead often come back in dreams to tell of problems they are having. These ghosts use popular Buddhist terminology to discuss their situations, speaking of rebirth, hell, and various services, but do not complain that they would be having an easier time if they had been cremated instead of buried. Buddhist services might speed their rebirth, but cremation would not. Ghosts do, however, complain about their bodies being left above ground in coffins at temples and ask to be cremated as an alternative. Consider the following case:

> Ruan Yue, a vice director in the ministry of revenue, came from Jiangzhou (Jiangxi). At the end of the Xuanhe period (1119–1125), he was prefect of Zhenzhou (Hunan). While there, his daughter-in-law died

of illness, and her coffin was temporarily left at Heavenly Peace Temple. When Ruan was about to be replaced, he said to his son, "I am old and glad to be able to give up the seal of office and return. But old people are very superstitious, so I will not take the time to bring your wife's body back east for burial. Please ask the monks at the temple to look after it. Some other time you may come to get it." The son did not dare object. That evening, Ruan dreamt that his daughter-in-law came to him, bowed, and said in tears, "I have been left in a coffin in a temple. This makes me a guest-ghost, under the control of the guardian god of the temple. Although at times I get to go back, every morning and evening a bell rings and I must quickly go to hear his orders. This is very bitter for me. Unless I now get to go home with you, I will never have a way to escape. If you are worried about being burdened by the wood of the coffin, I beg to be burned and to go as bones. So long as I am speedily interred in the hills, I will have no more regrets." Ruan woke up and, moved by the dream, told his son to precede him and take the coffin back for burial in Jiangzhou. That night he dreamt that his daughter-in-law came to thank him.[46]

In another, rather similar case, concerning a nursemaid rather than a daughter-in-law, after the dream the coffin was located and burned, then the ashes returned home and buried.[47] Anecdotes of this sort seem to indicate a widely held belief that the dead suffered much more from their bones being left to rest in the wrong place than from the method through which they were reduced to bones. If cremation made it easier for a family to take care of the bones, cremation had much to recommend it. What the dead did not like was the all-too-common fate of being left in a coffin unburied. Because, in early times, slow decay had been seen as more comfortable for the dead, this emphasis on bones rather than complete bodies marks a shift in popular attitudes that helped make cremation more acceptable.

The historical origins of this emphasis on bones are not easy to uncover. Perhaps it was fostered by the Buddhist cult of relics. Or it may have originated in regional cultures of the south, where in later centuries bodies were often exhumed to clean and preserve the bones.[48] Whatever its roots, in Song times it was found in northern as well as southern China. In order to bury their relatives together, people would sometimes move the bones of those who had been dead for generations.[49] Jia Yong, from northeast China (Shandong), recognized that his contemporaries would not want to bury their relatives far from home, so he proposed an alternative to cremation. When a death occurred far from home, he wrote, "Buy land and bury the body. Set up a shelter and stay there to care for the grave. Wait for a long time to pass, then pack up the bones and return with them."[50] Jia considered it unfilial purposely to injure the body of one's parent by cremation but did not object to handling the bones if the body were reduced to bones by natural processes.

But the significance of ideas about bones can be pushed only so far. The modern Chinese notion that bones are the pure, enduring, patrilineal part of the dead and the flesh the dangerous, unclean, polluting part is difficult to find in Song sources.[51] Nor did most people in Song times choose to rid the body quickly of its flesh. Indeed, one of the many puzzles concerning the popularity of cremation in Song times is the simultaneous popularity of a practice almost diametrically opposed to it: retaining coffins for years, decades, or even generations without burying them underground. The motivations for this practice are undoubtedly as complex as for cremation. The two practices were alike in that they could be used as a way to transfer to others the bother of handling the dead: bodies could be quickly brought to temples for encoffining and then abandoned there. But the bodies of parents and grandparents could also be left at temples precisely because the place they were to be buried was so important that descendants needed time to grow up, collect resources, or find an auspicious spot.

The ghost story translated above shows not only that bones were the key material substance of the dead but that their burial in the earth was crucial. This idea had ties to the geomancy of graves, the pseudoscience of locating graves in places where the forces of the earth would lead to the comfort of the dead and the worldly prosperity of their descendants. Although the underlying presuppositions of geomancy rely on the ancient idea that the living benefit when their ancestors are comfortable, its tenets were greatly elaborated over time, drawing on several strains of cosmological thought and divinatory traditions. Belief in the geomancy of graves pervaded all levels of Song society. The few surviving geomantic texts of the Song or Yuan eras refer most often not to bodies or corpses but to bones. The *Da Han yuanling mizang jing* refers to "planting" bones.[52] Another burial classic, the *Zangshu*, edited by Cai Yuanding (1135–1198), refers not to burying parents' bodies but to burying their bones. It also refers to the bones as the essence of what people receive from their fathers and states that proper burial is one method of getting *qi* ("vital force") to re-enter the bones in order to give protection to those descended from them.[53]

Chinese scholars of the classics frequently argued that the dead could be buried wherever convenient; for ancestral rites, the location of the grave did not matter, since the heavenly soul, the *hun*, could be worshiped anywhere.[54] Yet most people in Song times felt strongly that their parents' and grandparents' graves should be close enough to visit. Graves were a major locus of ancestor worship at all social levels. Song literati have left voluminous evidence of their concerns with graves. Some went to great efforts to find old graves, others to preserve graves from encroachment by outsiders, to organize rites to be held there, to erect shrines for these purposes, or to assure the continuance of these rites by endowing them with land.[55] It was common in Song times, and even sanctioned by the government, for officials to set up at their ancestors' graves Buddhist shrines where monks would perform their sacrifices for them.[56]

Graves were so important for settling the soul and providing a place for cultic activity that graves without bodies were sometimes created. When a person drowned at sea or a body could not be found, a grave might be made anyway, with some symbol of the dead person placed in it, to settle the *po* soul and provide a place to present offerings.[57] The significance of graves at every level of Song society undoubtedly explains why considerable sums were often expended to bury cremated remains. When the ashes were scattered, there was no grave. Those who had fully assimilated Buddhist cosmology accepted this and altered their ritual practices accordingly. Jing Tang (1138–1200), a high official from Jiangxi, came from a poor family, and both his father and grandfather had been cremated. Since there was no grave for them, at the Qingming festival Jing offered his sacrifice in an open field.[58] It was also reported that descendants made offerings by the side of the pool into which they had tossed the ashes.[59] Others, however, were distressed by the lack of a grave. In the twelfth century, a man whose mother, a concubine, had been cremated in his youth was so troubled by the lack of a grave that he had a wooden statue of her carved, dressed in grave clothes, and buried in a coffin. He then set aside land to pay for regular sacrifices at the empty grave.[60] During the Yuan period, Fu Shouguang felt anguish when his elder brothers had his father cremated and disposed of the burnt bones in a large body of water. After his brothers left, he took off his clothes and went into the water to collect what bones he could. He stored them in a case and consulted a geomancer to find a place to bury them.[61]

Some of the folk stories in the *Yijian zhi* imply that scattering the ashes could help to weaken the material basis of a ghost. In one, a courtesan had been cremated by her former patron, who kept her ashes in a wooden box. When this box began moving on its own and making noises, he had the ashes scattered over a river. In another tale, a ghost of a woman who had no surviving descendants was causing trouble to some neighbors. They exhumed the coffin and found that the body had not decayed despite the passage of over twenty years and the disintegration of the coffin. To end her interference, they burned the body and threw the ashes into water.[62] Thus scattering ashes was useful when dealing with a resentful ghost rather than a kindly ancestor.

Although these folk ideas show that cremation was a tolerable alternative to burial, especially if the burnt bones were buried, none of them indicate that cremation was the preferred way to dispose of one's own parents. It is difficult to judge how many people chose cremation as the best way to dispose of a body. Many people died away from home (especially because home generally meant where one's ancestors were buried, not where one had lived the last decade or two), and their burials could account for many of the better-furnished cremation graves. The poor who chose cremation may have considered it an inferior way to dispose of their parents, only acceptable because common. Certainly, that is how the educated looked on their actions. The educated did not attribute to the poor an alternative view of the body in

terms of which cremation was superior to burial. Nor do advocates of cremation as a preferred method appear in Song anecdotes and ghost stories.[63]

DATING THE SPREAD OF CREMATION

The timing of the spread of cremation must be taken into account in analyzing
the reasons it gained popularity. By the mid-Tang dynasty, basic Buddhist
ideas were well known in China and cremation a familiar practice of Buddhist
monks. By then, monks performed funeral services at regular intervals after
death, and the Buddhist ghost festival in the seventh month had become a
major occasion for offerings to ancestors.[64] Yet scholars have found almost
no evidence of lay persons being cremated in Tang times.[65] Nor have archaeologists found evidence of lay people's cremation burials in native Chinese
(Han) areas before Song times. If cremation was so convenient, received
support from Buddhist ideas and institutions, limited contact with unpleas-
ant corpses, and preserved the essential material substance of the dead (the
bones), why did it take so long to become common?

One part of the solution to this puzzle may simply be that Buddhism had in
fact more deeply influenced family life by Song times than it had during the
Tang.[66] No reader of the *Yijian zhi* can escape the conclusion that Buddhist
monks, temples, and services were ubiquitous in Hong Mai's twelfth-century
world. Recent scholarly work reveals many other signs of the vitality of
Buddhism in the Song.[67] Although, in Song times, the educated were more
often anti-Buddhist than their counterparts had been in the Tang period,
monks and temples may have been an even more familiar part of the common
people's social landscape than they had been earlier.

A second part of the solution may be that cremation was adopted as
much as an expediency as an act of Buddhist piety. Many of those who chose
cremation did so not because they believed it was better than burial of the
full body but because it was an acceptable second choice. Cremation often
seems to have been associated with special circumstances: death away from
home or the death of someone who had not had children and thus could not
become a focal ancestor. When a man selected cremation as an expediency,
it would not matter what he thought of Buddhist theology, so long as he was
not adamantly opposed to dealing with Buddhist monks. Thus the key contribution of Buddhism may have been to make available Buddhist institutions.
This seems to be the case with another Song funerary practice: depositing
coffins in Buddhist temples until burial could be arranged. There was nothing
in Buddhist doctrine that encouraged delaying burials, the Indian practice
having been very prompt cremation, but Buddhist temples as institutions
facilitated this practice. Even those indifferent to Buddhist religion found it
convenient to take advantage of this service the temples offered.

If expediency was as important as theology, historical circumstances may
have played a major role in the increasing use of cremation. The social and
political conditions of the late ninth and tenth centuries probably provided a

needed stimulus for the expansion of this practice. The period from 880 to 980 was one of constant warfare and extensive migration. In the north, non-Han peoples, especially the Khitan, pushed farther into Chinese territory. Cremation had advantages for those forced to move. They may well have had coffins awaiting burial stored in some nearby temple. Rather than abandon the coffins of close relatives that had never been buried (it was bad enough to abandon the graves of their ancestors), they could have them cremated and carry the ashes in urns. Those fleeing warfare also faced the need to dispose of casualties; cremation was not only quick but allowed them to bring the ashes along and perform the remaining funerary rites en route.[68] The three earliest recorded cases of cremation by lay people were of this sort. In the 880s, a military commander, dying in battle, asked to be cremated and have his remains sent home.[69] In 946, Shi Zhonggui, a non-Han military man who had taken over as ruler of North China from his father, was defeated by the Khitans. He, his mother, and his father's main wife were exiled to the far northeast. When his mother was about to die, she said, "Burn me to make ashes and scatter them to the south so that what survives of my *hun* soul can return to China." Her body was cremated but the ashes saved. In 950, the widow also became ill, and she said, "When I die, burn my bones and send them to the Fanyang Buddhist temple. Do not let me become a ghost in a captive land." She was also cremated, and both sets of ashes were then buried.[70]

Migration placed people in new surroundings where old customs might no longer seem appropriate. Migrants who ended up in large cities may have found disposing of the dead more complicated than it had been for their parents in the countryside; they may then have been quite willing to use Buddhist crematories. Migrants from the north who fled to the Yangtze River Valley or farther south may have been reluctant to bury the bodies of their parents there because soil conditions were so different from what they had known in the north. The heat and humidity of the south led to problems in keeping bodies in coffins for weeks or months before burial. Ants and ground moisture were much greater problems than in the north, requiring elaborate tomb construction if the body were not to decompose rapidly after burial.[71] To newcomers unused to these conditions, the thought of their parents' flesh being quickly consumed by fire may have seemed preferable to slower destruction by ants. In addition, newcomers to any part of the country would not have had ancestral graveyards, making changes in their customary practices somewhat easier.

CONFUCIAN OBJECTIONS

Confucian objections to cremation began to appear almost as early as the practice itself. During the Song period, a succession of eminent scholars and thinkers revitalized Confucianism. They not only developed philosophical theories to provide the metaphysics that ancient Confucianism had lacked, they also set themselves the task of reforming the state and society according to the moral principles found in the classics. The Confucian classics had given great weight to the proper performance of rituals, and Neo-Confucian scholars believed that, to combat the influence of Buddhism, it was necessary to rid life-cycle rituals of contamination by Buddhist practices. They also wanted to purify them of other noncanonical accretions, especially those that could be labeled vulgar, lower-class, or superstitious.[72]

Confucians objected to cremation as cruel, a desecration of the corpse, barbaric, Buddhist, and unfilial. Jia Tong speculated that cremation had been introduced by Buddhist monks who taught "the barbarian customs of the Western regions" and cited the classical rules that "a filial son serves the dead as he serves the living," and "parents give birth to the whole [body], and the child returns the [body] whole, which is filiality," arguing that cremation was mutilation.[73] Neo-Confucian philosopher Cheng Yi (1033–1107) also wanted people to think of cremation as a severe way of hurting a corpse. "Today if a fool or drunkard accidentally hits a person's ancestor's coffin, he will take great offense and want revenge. Yet he may personally drag his parent and toss him into the flames, finding nothing odd in it."[74] Scholar and statesman Sima Guang noted that desecrating a stranger's corpse was a serious legal offense, and yet people were not offended by cremation.[75] Most vehemently criticized were children who cremated the body of a parent or grandparent. Cheng Yi, for instance, portrayed the customs of a certain place as especially evil because "even filial sons and loving grandsons through familiarity are comfortable" with cremation.[76]

The philosopher Zhu Xi (1130–1200) considered cremation much worse than other ritual offenses. His objections were recorded as follows.

Someone asked: "When one's parent dies and in his or her final instructions orders the use of Buddhist or Daoist monks [for the funeral], what should one do?"

[Zhu Xi] answered: "This is a difficult problem."

[The interlocutor] asked: "May one use them or not?"

[Zhu Xi] answered: "There are some things the heart of a son cannot bear to do. This matter requires careful discussion."

[On another occasion] someone asked: "Suppose one's father is still alive when one's mother dies and he wants to follow ordinary custom in mourning garments, to use Buddhist or Daoist monks, and to cremate ["transform through fire"] the body, what should one do? Should one simply disobey?"

[Zhu Xi] answered: "The others are all superficial matters that can be obeyed without harm. But cremation is unacceptable."

[The recorder of this conversation, Hu] Yong said: "This is because cremation destroys the body of the parents."

[Zhu Xi] said: "Discussing this matter [cremation] together with mourning garments and Buddhist [monks], shows an inability to distinguish between the important and the unimportant."[77]

In such conversations, Zhu Xi acknowledged that not everything labeled "Buddhist" or "Daoist" was equally bad, but he classed cremation with those practices so pernicious that a son should oppose them even if doing so brought him into conflict with his father.

Neo-Confucian criticisms of cremation seldom make any reference to karma, rebirth, or any other Buddhist doctrine. Instead, the Buddhist aspect of cremation was condemned primarily on the grounds that both Buddhism and cremation were alien. By the second half of the Song dynasty, when the alien Jurchen had occupied northern China, and later when the Mongols were coming to pose an even greater threat, anti-foreign sentiments seem to have become intense. In 1237, Wang Yue wrote:

> Human beings are different from the birds and beasts; China is different from the barbarians . . . The customs of the Hu and Qiang [northern and western barbarians] are like those of the birds and beasts. The Buddhists, through their doctrines, have turned their backs on human ethical relations and cut themselves off from their kind.[78] Thus it is not surprising that after death they voluntarily take the body that should be valued because Heaven and earth nurtured it, and quickly reduce it to smoke and ashes.[79]

That cremation was alien to Chinese culture could also be argued by historical precedent. To demonstrate that voluntary cremation was not a part of Chinese culture, Huang Zhen provided a long list of examples from Chinese history in which burning a corpse was described as the worst thing one could do to punish the dead or provoke one's enemies.[80]

Neo-Confucian critics of cremation did not emphasize its associations with poverty or try to make the educated feel it would be déclassé to cremate. Nor did they make much of a distinction between cases in which ashes were scattered, leaving no grave, and ones in which they were buried. Neo-Confucians do not seem to have worried that, when ashes were scattered, the soul was inadequately settled or that, without a grave, ancestral offerings might not be offered. In their view, it was enough to label cremation a desecration of the corpse and thus an act of outrageous immorality.

STATE EFFORTS TO SUPPRESS CREMATION

State efforts to suppress cremation were undoubtedly motivated in large part by the sentiments Confucians expressed. The prohibition of 962 was issued on the grounds that cremation was normally harmful. In the Song code, the punishment for cremation was stipulated as strangulation, with exceptions granted for Buddhist monks, foreigners, and those who needed to return remains for burial.[81] Cheng Yi complained that the law itself was not firm enough in its opposition to cremation because it allowed soldiers who died on military campaigns to be cremated and specified that cremations could not be performed less than three *li* (about one mile) away from a city.[82]

The Chinese government, like many others, used the law to define the limits of acceptable behavior, and it often decreed punishments for actions it could hardly expect to monitor. Playing music at funerals, for instance, was declared illegal.[83] Most officials seem to have viewed the ban on cremation as one of these unenforceable statutes. Wang Anshi (1021–1086) complained that, despite the obvious evils of cremation, it was nearly impossible to prohibit a practice so well entrenched.[84]

A few eleventh-century officials, convinced that they could reform society by starting at the local level, tried to eliminate cremation by educating the people and providing them with alternatives. Ouyang Xiu (1007–1072) had argued in his famous essay, "On Fundamentals," that the successful revival of Confucianism required curbing the influence of Buddhism in the common people's ritual activities. "If you shout at people, 'You are forbidden to follow the Buddhists and must perform our rituals and proprieties,' they will object and go away. It would be better to take a gradual approach, attracting them without their noticing."[85] The leading proponent of Neo-Confucianism, Cheng Hao (1032–1085), was reportedly able while magistrate of Jincheng to persuade the local people to give up cremation, but they reverted to the practice when one of his successors had his own mother cremated.[86] Han Qi (1008–1075), later a leading statesman, tried to eradicate cremation by addressing the difficulty the poor had in arranging burials; while serving as a magistrate, he used public funds to buy land for a free graveyard.[87] Fan Chunren (1027–1101) arranged for the burial of three thousand boxes of unclaimed ashes while serving as prefect of Taiyuan (Shanxi).[88] These local initiatives eventually led to new policies at the national level. In 1079, Chen Xiang proposed having all local governments set up charitable graveyards, called "generosity gardens" (*louze yuan*).[89] The court consented and issued detailed regulations on the management of the graveyards and the records to be kept concerning the location and occupant of each grave.[90] Although the response of the local governments was slow, some graveyards were set up in response to these laws.[91] Archaeological evidence shows large-scale burial of the urns of bone remnants left at temples in response to these edicts.[92] Yet, in 1158, an official requested exemption from the prohibition on cremation for any poor person living in an area still lacking a public graveyard, which indicates that such sites were fairly common but not universally available.[93]

Free graveyards were established primarily to solve the problem of the hundreds of coffins left at temples for decades or longer. The original edict ordered the burial of any coffin unclaimed for over twenty years or whose occupant was unknown, as well as bodies or bones found exposed.[94] These graveyards were also to provide a place for beggars and others who could not afford burial. The Buddhist novices who managed the graveyards were to be rewarded with ordination certificates, depending on the length of time served or numbers of people buried.[95] Even when so committed a Neo-Confucian as Zhen Dexiu (1178–1235) set up such graveyards, he had Buddhist and Daoist establishments manage them.[96] Free graveyards, in the end, did not remove all incentives to cremation. In the late eleventh century, one local official reported that better-off families accustomed to cremation did not want to be buried among inferior people in a public graveyard and so did not change their old ways; in the mid-thirteenth century, another local official similarly complained that the local population did not want their bodies lying beside the prisoners and strangers buried in the charitable graveyard.[97]

In the late Song period, Huang Zhen, as magistrate of Wu county (Suzhou), took another approach to eradicating cremation: he focused on the crematoriums, whose reconstruction he wished to forbid.[98] Despite the obvious advantages of his approach, it does not seem to have been widely copied. The Song state regulated the ordination of monks and granted tax exemptions to temples, yet it did not use these regulatory powers to induce monks or temples to stop performing cremations. This failure indicates the limitations of the Song state's commitment to suppressing cremation.

Alternatives to cremation could also be provided by private groups. In many of the areas where cremation was common, such as Zhejiang, Jiangsu, and Fujian, descent groups were also developing in Song times. Many were groups that simply met once or twice a year to make offerings at their common ancestors' graves. By late Song times, the most developed were writing genealogies, erecting halls for their ancestral worship, and setting aside lands to endow ancestral rites.[99] A major avowed purpose of these groups was to tend graves. A secondary but still important purpose was to aid the living members of the group, especially in such ritual responsibilities as the burial of their parents. Whereas charitable graveyards set up by the local government carried a social stigma, assistance from kin was entirely appropriate in the Chinese tradition, especially in funeral matters, which were in theory the responsibility not merely of the deceased's children but of all "mourning relatives," including some as distant as third cousins. In the fourteenth century, Neo-Confucian teacher Wu Hai wrote rules for his descent group that included prohibitions against becoming Buddhist monks or Daoist priests, holding Buddhist funeral services, and practicing the "barbarian ritual" of cremation.[100]

Efforts by officials and private citizens to discourage cremation may have checked its growth, but neither archaeological nor literary evidence suggests that the practice of cremation declined in late Song or Yuan times.[101]

DECLINE IN THE PRACTICE OF CREMATION

During Ming and Qing times, the practice of cremation by Han Chinese did decline. Ming Taizu (Zhu Yuanzhang, 1328–1398, r. 1368–98), the founder of the Ming dynasty, was by no means a narrow Confucian or even an opponent of Buddhism.[102] Nevertheless, he took a strong stand against cremation. According to one account, Zhu stood on the Nanjing city wall during the civil war and was repelled by the odor of cremations taking place. His advisor Tao An (1312?–1368) took advantage of this opportunity to convince him that cremation was inhumane. In ancient times, he argued, people even buried old bones found exposed, but "the current age has been perverted by the customs of the Hu [northern barbarians] so that some burn [the body] and toss the ashes into water. How can a filial son or loving grandson bear this in his heart? Nothing injures reciprocal obligation or destroys customs as much as this." Swayed by these arguments, Taizu ordered that his army begin to bury bodies rather than burn them.[103] Later, in 1370, he issued a general prohibition against cremation. There were not even to be exceptions for officials who died away from home; the local government was required to supply the funds to have their bodies returned home. When the emperor repeated this prohibition in 1372, he complained about the persistence of the customs of the "evil" Yuan dynasty, of which the worst was cremation.[104] And the Ming code, issued in 1397, explicitly stated that, even if, before dying, a family elder had asked to be cremated, the act was illegal and punishable (though ordinary people who died away from home could be cremated). The penalty for cremating a senior relative was decapitation and for cremating a child or grandchild, a beating of eighty strokes.[105] Not only were these laws stricter than Song or Yuan ones, the early Ming government's efforts at social control were more pervasive than those of earlier governments, and therefore these laws were probably more rigorously enforced than were earlier ones.[106]

Archaeological evidence suggests that cremation declined very rapidly in the early Ming.[107] Nevertheless, cremation did not disappear entirely, as complaints of its practice continued to be made from time to time.[108] Unlike complaints voiced in the Song, these Ming and Qing ones rarely suggest that the elite practiced cremation even in special circumstances or that poor people cremated their parents. Instead, cremation seems more and more to have been confined to special situations or the unimportant dead. Zhang Lixiang (1611–1674) reported that, in his home area, cremation was particularly common for children.[109] In the mid-nineteenth century, Justus Doolittle reported that dead lepers were burned, a measure thought to prevent spread of the disease.[110] J. J. M. de Groot, who spent many years in China in the late nineteenth century, wrote that he had never witnessed or even heard rumors of cremation except for Buddhist monks and nuns and soldiers who died away from home.[111]

In what sense, if any, can the decline of cremation be seen as a victory of Neo-Confucianism? Leading Neo-Confucian teachers – Sima Guang, Cheng

Yi, and Zhu Xi – opposed cremation, and their objections became better known in Ming times. Sima Guang's denunciation of cremation was included in Zhu Xi's *Family Rituals* (Jiali), which circulated extensively from the early thirteenth century on.[112] The *Family Rituals* was copied into the *Xingli daquan* (Comprehensive collection on nature and principle), an imperial-sponsored compendium of Neo-Confucian writings published in 1415 and widely read by examination candidates in the Ming. Thus, by Ming times, the disrepute of cremation must have been well known to the educated and probably had an effect on their choices of mortuary practices, even when they had to deal with death away from home and death of servants or other less important people in their households. Their behavior in turn may have influenced the practices of people of lower social standing, especially those aspiring to literati status. Confucian propaganda would have had its greatest impact on how people disposed of their parents, since this act was highly public and commonly used as a gauge of respectability.

Increased awareness of the Neo-Confucian objections to cremation nevertheless does not wholly explain the decline in cremation. In these same books, Sima Guang, Cheng Yi, and Zhu Xi give powerful arguments against the performance of Buddhist services for the dead and against delayed burial, yet there is plenty of evidence that even literati and officials in Ming and Qing times still asked Buddhist monks to perform the ceremony, and delayed burial remained endemic.

Stricter laws against cremation, more vigorously enforced, undoubtedly discouraged its practices, but they were as much a result of Ming Taizu's intense distaste for practices associated with the alien Yuan dynasty as of his acceptance of Neo-Confucian doctrines. The enduring perception that cremation was a foreign or barbarian custom provides the best explanation for why people in the early Ming dynasty were willing to give it up. Other Buddhist practices quickly lost all overtones of foreignness. Burning incense when praying to ancestors, for instance, did not seem in Song or Ming times to be a foreign custom. Nor did services aimed at ensuring a better rebirth. But cremation never ceased to be alien. The handling of dead bodies admittedly arouses stronger emotions than offerings of prayers. Even more important, all through this period, cremation continued to be practiced by non-Han peoples living adjacent to Han-settled areas. The alien character of cremation was underlined in the Song and Yuan law codes, in which cremation was permitted for foreigners. With the massive repudiation of everything associated with the Mongols in the early Ming, cremation was no longer simply a convenient, though inferior, method of disposing of the dead, introduced by Buddhists, but a foreign custom that had flourished under the Mongols.

The alien overtones of cremation probably influenced common people as much as Ming Taizu, who was himself of peasant origin. There is no evidence that cremation was suppressed by force, by large-scale punishment of offenders or destruction of crematoriums. Many poor people, resentful of the Mongols, apparently decided that they would not cremate their parents even though their grandparents had been cremated, because the feelings of revulsion at the thought of treating their bodies in a "barbarian" way outweighed its convenience. Since cremation had never been widely seen as an end in itself, people could turn away from it relatively easily.

CONCLUSIONS

By way of conclusion, I would like to compare the historical processes involved in these two changes in customs, the increase in the use of cremation and its subsequent decline. In each case, ideas of different origins prepared people to change their attitudes toward the dead body. Some of the ideas that promoted cremation came from Buddhist doctrine – such as ideas about rebirth – some from folk Buddhism – such as ideas about relics – and some from indigenous culture with, at best, weak ties to Buddhism – such as ideas about bones and graves. The decline of cremation was influenced by anti-foreign feelings, which greatly enhanced the Confucian view that the old ways of treating the dead were the morally correct ones.

In both cases, centuries passed between the introduction of new ideas and changes in behavior. Customs did not change until new ideas had fostered new institutions and dislocations jarred people out of routines. The most important institutional development in supporting cremation was the entry of Buddhist temples and monasteries into the funeral business: providing funeral services, storing coffins, and above all operating crematoria open to the public. The dislocating events of greatest significance were the rebellions, invasions, dynastic wars, and migrations of the late ninth and tenth centuries. In the case of the decline of cremation, the state provided the most important institutional framework, through both its laws against the practice and its organized social welfare measures. The significant dislocating event was the re-establishment of a native Chinese dynasty and a general repudiation of Mongol ways.

The processes that led to the acceptance of cremation and those that led to its rejection were, however, not entirely alike. Above all, coercion or threats played no part in the increase in cremation. Buddhist lay people were not ordered to cremate or warned of any dire consequences to themselves or their dead loved ones if they failed to cremate. They chose cremation on their own, imitating monks but also finding it convenient, economical, and in some cases, perhaps, emotionally satisfying. The decline of cremation may well have been perceived as voluntary, people losing interest in cremation for a wide range of reasons, from revulsion for the practice to desire to imitate Confucian norms. But the coercive role played by the elite and the state is undeniable. Neo-Confucian scholars labeled as unfilial those who cremated; the state declared them criminals and put mechanisms in place to punish them.

7   Surnames and Han Chinese identity*

Despite enormous geographical diversity and mutually incomprehensible dialects or languages, today more than a billion people consider themselves to be Han Chinese. This situation makes Han Chinese ethnic identity one of the wonders of world history. Whereas Western Europe and the Americas together are home to almost as many people, they divide themselves into several dozen countries and even more ethnic groups. What has made China different? What has made it possible for Han Chinese to imagine such an enormous agglomeration of people as sharing something important, something that makes it possible, even desirable, to live together in a single state? No one would deny that Han Chinese had multiple identities, or that many situations left room for manipulation and negotiation, for choice concerning which identity or identities to assert. But the Han Chinese layer of identity has been and continues to be important in social and political life. In this essay I examine the connection between Chinese surnames and Han Chinese identity.[1] I contend that Chinese understandings of ethnic identity have differed in important ways from ones found elsewhere – ones based on language, race, or place – and that their distinctive features help account for the huge size of the Han ethnic group.

Conventional wisdom has it that the secret to Chinese identity and cohesion was Confucian "culturalism" or universalism, bases for identity fundamentally different from nationalism, racism, and the sort of ethnic identity that sets up boundaries against outsiders. Culturalism was, without question, an important strain of Confucianism. Confucius and his followers over the centuries saw Chinese culture as superior to any other culture; they also saw that culture as something outsiders could acquire. To them the Chinese state and the Chinese family were perfect forms of social organization because they were based on the truest moral principles, universal principles such as loyalty and filial piety; adherence to these forms and principles were what

* This essay was first published in *Negotiating Ethnicities in China and Taiwan*, edited by Melissa Brown (Institute for East Asian Studies, University of California, Berkeley, 1996), pp. 11–36. Copyright © 1996 by The Regents of the University of California. Used by permission of the publisher.

made China Chinese and what made China superior to other places. Confucianism thus offered little grounds for erecting barriers against absorption of outsiders and indeed saw expansion of China through transformation or assimilation of non-Chinese as the natural state of affairs. Because of Confucian universalism, moreover, this openness applied even at the level of rulers. As long as one accepted that virtue and the ability to achieve order were what qualified one to rule as Son of Heaven, even the symbolic center of Chinese society and culture could, in theory at least, be occupied by someone whose first language was not Chinese and whose ancestors were not Chinese so long as he upheld Confucian political principles. Thus, in the late nineteenth century, traditional Chinese ways of thinking about identity differed fundamentally from the sorts of nationalist passions raging in Europe, and modern reformers and revolutionaries tried to awaken in China new notions that would make China more competitive internationally.[2]

This conventional focus on Confucian culturalism encourages us to overlook or underestimate the genuinely ethnic component of Chinese conceptions of a vast "we-group" labeled Xia, Hua, or Han; this is the component that relates to ancestors, to what is primordial; inherited, not acquired. This ethnic dimension of Chinese identity was rooted in the habit of thinking of the largest we-group in terms of patrilineal kinship, that is, imagining the Hua, Xia, or Han, metaphorically at least, as a giant patrilineal descent group made up of intermarrying surname groups (*xing*). If all that mattered to common identity were common customs or a history of common connection to a state, there would be no need to draw attention to common ancestry; indeed, if one truly wished to celebrate the transformation of originally distinct people into Chinese, it would be better to assert that they originally had no kinship connection. But repeatedly in Chinese history, the vocabulary of kinship and surname was adopted. Thus, thinking about the most inclusive we-group drew on and was colored by familiar ways of thinking about patrilineal kinship and its connections to both identity and solidarity.

The Chinese are unusual in world history in their system of family names (*xing*). There are of course many other patrilineal societies, but few if any in which patrilineality was so closely tied to name from so early a period. The Chinese writing system, which allowed the written form of a name to remain the same over centuries, and the Chinese bureaucratic government, which strove to register every one of its subjects, undoubtedly had much to do with the historical development of this distinctive naming system. What is important here, however, is that over time family names became very important for both personal and group identity. A person's family name was much more important than his or her personal name, a situation uncommon elsewhere. These family names were, moreover, central to notions of ancestors and marriage: ancestors shared one's surname; marriage partners did not. By Han times, Chinese had become accustomed to thinking of those with common ancestors generations or even centuries earlier as forming a natural solidarity group. By Tang times, they had even come to think of those with the same surname (and thus presumably a common ancestor several thousand years earlier) as having something important in common. Over time the number of surnames in common use gradually declined. Whereas a study based on historical records found more than 3,000 single-character Chinese surnames, a study based on the 1982 census in China found only 729 Han Chinese surnames. Moreover, surprisingly few surnames account for a very large proportion of the population. Wang, Chen, Li, Zhang, and Liu are used by 32 percent of the population, and half the population have one of only fourteen names.[3] Although Chinese family names often began etymologically as place names, associations with place weakened over time for all the common surnames.[4] Knowing someone is a Li or a Wang does not tell you what province that person comes from or even whether he or she is a northerner or a southerner. And certainly it indicates nothing about culture. The kind of connection provided by surnames thus was a genealogical connection, not a connection based on place, dialect, or local culture.

For evidence of how people conceptualized the connections between surnames and Han Chinese identity, I will concentrate on the Tang (618–906) through Yuan (1215–1368) periods. During this time, Chinese identity needed its symbolic underpinnings shored up. Alien incursions, alien rulers, political division or fragmentation of the country, and large-scale movements of population all were too evident for anyone to think "China" or "the Chinese" were simple, natural products of geography. When the Tang was founded, its rulers may have chosen to hark back to the Han, but they did not hide their connections to the non-Han or partly non-Han ruling groups of the Sui, Northern Zhou, and Northern Wei, reminding all that China was neither continuously unified nor continuously ruled by Chinese and, perhaps most important, that it was often difficult to say for sure who was Chinese or what made a person Chinese. And it was not all that long before similar situations recurred. For five centuries, from the fall of the Tang to the beginning of the Ming, north and south China experienced markedly different fates. The north was at peace and part of a unified China under Chinese rulers for only about a century and a half during the Northern Song (and even then a strip at the northern edge was under the control of the Khitans). North and south evolved along separate paths, so much so that the Mongol rulers classified the Chinese of the north and the south into different ethnic categories and administered them differently. Still, in the imagination, both "China" and "the Chinese" survived the tumult of these centuries.[5]

Confucian culturalism was part of the story of this survival, but not the whole story. There is ample evidence that many people did not fully accept the key premise of Confucian culturalism that others could be transformed into full-fledged Chinese. Perhaps the strongest evidence for their doubts is found in the genealogies compiled in great profusion from the Song period on. In these it is close to unheard of to claim descent from any of the numerous non-Han peoples of south China. The histories tell of many local officials who set up schools or through other means brought Confucian culture to the local, often explicitly non-Han, population.[6] But if genealogies are to be believed, none of these converts ever left much progeny or at least progeny who prospered. Surely some of those who did well enough in Song, Ming, and Qing times to commission genealogies must have had patrilineal ancestors of non-Han origin. But overwhelmingly residents of the area wanted to tell a story of Han Chinese migration, sometimes in the Han but most often in the Tang, Song, or Yuan.[7] Rather than say they became Chinese the Confucian way, by adopting Chinese culture, they wanted to say they were Chinese by patrilineal descent. If Chineseness was actually something one could acquire by learning, why were so few willing to admit that they had learned it?[8] This reluctance was not just an issue of status. Many people were willing to say their ancestors had been peasants or merchants; they did not all claim to be descended from officials. We have to infer they claimed descent from Chinese migrants either because they wanted to believe it (looking down on non-Han themselves) or because it was in their interest to do so (for local politics, social prestige, or whatever).

As best I can tell from sources like the *Tong dian* and *Tong zhi*, Tang and Song observers saw wide variation in naming practices among the indigenous peoples of the south. Zheng Qiao (1104–1162) once commented that ancient China was probably like the Man ("southern barbarians") of his day who had surnames for those of high rank but none for ordinary people.[9] On the other hand, he, like earlier chroniclers, described some but not all local groups as having a handful of *xing*, names that sound like tribal names. Thus the Ba in Sichuan were said to have five *xing*: Ba, Fan, Shen, Xiang, and Zheng; the "Eastern Xie Man" were said to have hereditary chieftains with the name Xie; the "Western Zhao Man" were said similarly to have chieftains with the *xing* Zhao; the "Man beyond the Pine Trees" were said to be divided into several dozen groups and to have several dozen *xing*, of which Zhao, Yang, Li, and Dong were aristocratic ones.[10] In all the cases I have found, these tribal names are transcribed as single characters, making them easy to assimilate to Chinese surnames.[11]

In south China, claiming descent from a Chinese migrant might be hard to prove or disprove. The dynamics of interethnic relations were probably such that groups could, over time, become socially accepted as Chinese.[12] The situation in the north with aliens who were enemies or conquerors was different. As long as they were privileged conquerors, it was to their benefit to have distinctive names, but once they were defeated or ousted, if they had become assimilated such distinctive names labeled them as alien, as non-Chinese, perhaps even hated non-Chinese. Moreover the "northern barbarians" had polysyllabic languages, and their names were usually transcribed as multicharacter names. Among the more educated, at least, people would not be quick to forget that Erzhu, Yuwen, and Dugu were names used by the alien conquerors in the Northern Dynasties, for instance. For those with multicharacter surnames, adopting a single-character surname, preferably

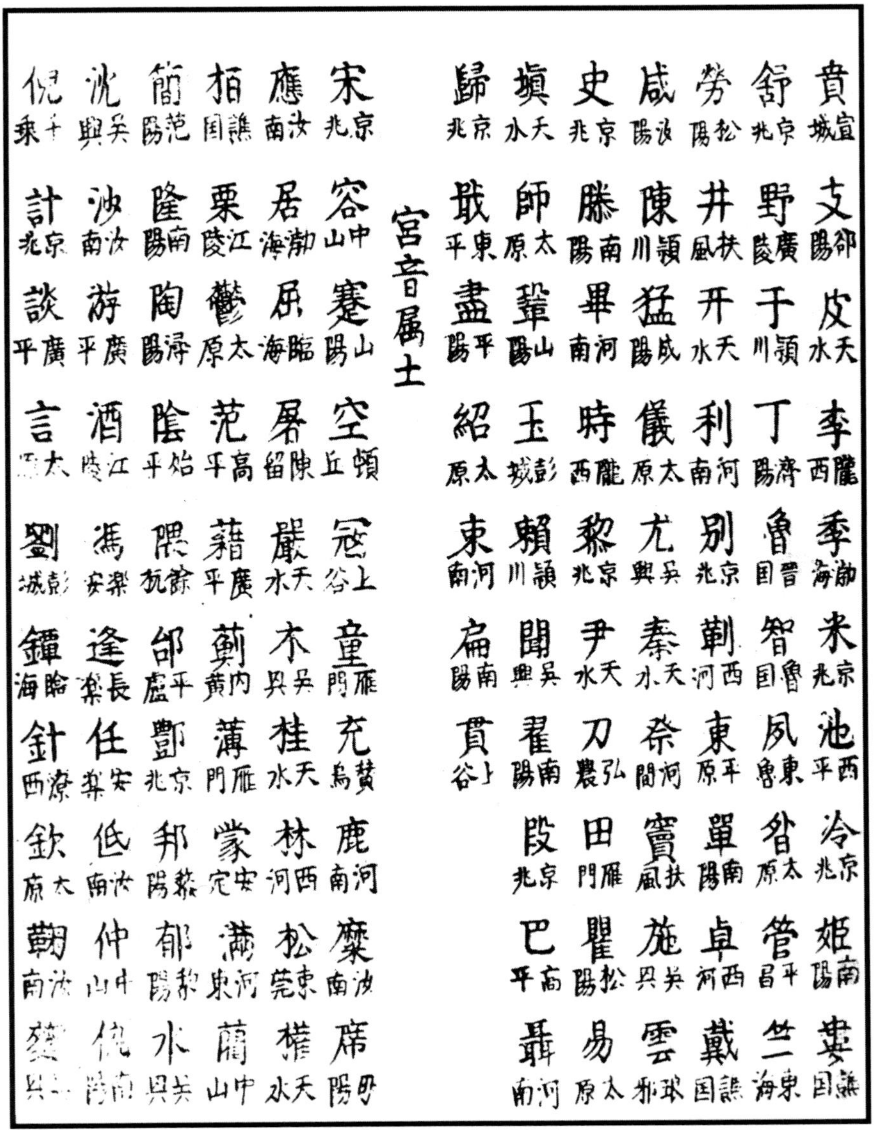

倪 沈 簡 柏 應 宋　　歸 塡 史 咸 勞 舒 賈

計 沙 隆 栗 居 容　宮　戢 師 滕 陳 井 野 支

談 游 陶 鬱 屍 蹇　音　盡 輩 畢 猛 开 于 皮

言 酒 陰 范 屠 空　屬　紹 玉 時 儀 利 丁 李

劉 馮 隈 藉 嚴 冠　土　束 賴 黎 尤 別 魯 季

鍾 逢 邱 薊 木 童　　　扁 聞 尹 秦 靳 智 米

針 任 鄲 薄 桂 充　　　賁 翟 刀 雜 東 夙 池

欽 低 邦 蒙 林 鹿　　　段 田 竇 單 岑 冷

鞠 仲 郁 滿 松 糜　　　巴 瞿 施 卓 管 姬

雍 倪 水 藺 權 席　　　聶 易 雲 戴 竺 婁

Figure 7.1 Page from a late-Song reference work listing surnames with their associated
　　　　place names.
Source: From SLGJ ren 10.1a–b.

one that looked like a Chinese surname, was a potent sign of a desire to
assimilate. In 496 the Xianbei rulers of the Northern Wei ordered the Xianbei
to take Chinese surnames; a few decades later not only was this order rescinded,
but the successor states, the Western Wei and Northern Zhou, gave Xianbei

names to many Chinese.[13] Changing names both ways also occurred during later periods of alien rule, under the Liao, Jin, and Yuan, with or without government permission.[14]

Despite the frequency with which it was done, altering one's family name seemed wrong to many people. When Zhu Yuanzhang founded the Ming dynasty in 1368, he ordered all those who had taken barbarian (*hu*) surnames to cease and desist. Willingness to comply went so far that even people with completely Chinese two-character surnames like Sima, Situ, Gongsun, and Shusun dropped one character, associating two-character names with non-Han origin. But Zhu Yuanzhang's feelings were at least equally aroused by Mongols and other non-Han who took Chinese names. In 1370 he issued an edict that stated,

> Heaven gave birth to this people (*simin*); tribes and clans each have their own origins. The ancient sage kings put particular emphasis on this; they [used surnames to] prohibit marriage and emphasize origins, with positive effects on popular customs. I began as a commoner and after pacifying the various warlords became the ruler of all under heaven. I have already proclaimed that the Mongols and other ethnic groups (*seren*) are all my children, and that if they have abilities I will employ them. But recently I have heard that after they enter service, they often change their surnames and personal names. I am afraid that as the years go by and generations pass, [descendants] will be blind to their origins. This is not the way the former kings were meticulous in matters of descent groups.[15]

On another occasion Zhu Yuanzhang pointed out that it was not so bad when people were given names that were not usual Chinese names, but when they were given or took common names, confusion with Chinese (Huaren) was much too easy. He quoted an official who had complained about Mongols and others taking Han surnames, citing the line from the *Zuo zhuan* that "the thoughts and feelings of those who are not of our descent group are invariably different" (*fei wo zulei, qi xin bi yi*).[16]

The reason Chinese did not feel entirely comfortable with the idea that other people could be transformed into Chinese is probably that the premises of Confucian culturalism ran up against equally strongly held views about ancestors and the connections between ancestors and identity. Those who had been "transformed" wanted to see themselves (or found it useful to present themselves) as Chinese by descent, and those who took themselves as Chinese by descent were neither confident that Chinese culture could or would transform aliens nor comfortable with seeing assimilated descendants of aliens appear to be denying or hiding their actual ancestry. Cross-surname adoption bothered a lot of people, so it is perhaps not surprising that cross-ethnicity transformations would as well.[17]

So far I have been discussing the relationship between surnames and the line between Han and non-Han identity. This is important because to some extent at least Han Chinese identity was a residual category, comprised of all those who were not barbarians. There is a second part to my argument. I contend that within the huge but vaguely defined category of Han Chinese, descent and kinship provided a framework for grasping the whole in a structured way.

What I want to draw attention to is the habit, established by the time of Sima Qian in the Former Han, of tracing ancestry back to the remote mythical past, to the point where all Chinese are descended from the mythical Five Lords, such as Huang Di, usually called the Yellow Emperor. These ideas were still very much in force in Tang and Song times, and the theory behind them can be found many places, such as Du You's *Tong dian* (801) and Zheng Qiao's *Tong zhi* (1149). This theory is that the Chinese are descended from Shen Nong (also called Yan Di) or from his successor, Huang Di, who conferred twelve surnames on fourteen of his twenty-five sons. These were not the only names in existence; even before Shen Nong, there was Fuxi, and he was born to a mother with a clan name. But most names were regularly traced to Shen Nong or Huang Di (though they frequently were changed several times in subsequent history down through the Zhou).

Modern scholars sometimes write as though the idea of tracing the origins of the Chinese to Huang Di began in the twentieth century, with proponents of the *guocui* (national essence) school. Certainly these activists used the concept in a new way in their attempts to heighten emotional identification among Chinese. But the basic metaphor had been around for a long time. I could easily give hundreds of examples of references to Huang Di and comparable remote ancestors in Tang and Song sources. In early Tang they were routinely used in accounts of individual ancestry. Leafing through the funerary inscriptions in the first volume of Mao Hanguang's *Tangdai muzhiming huibian fukao* I found a couple dozen examples. For instance, the 617 inscription for Wei Kuangbo began by stating that he was a descendant of Di Kaoyang (a grandson of Huang Di). The 627 one for Guan Daoai said he was a descendant of Yu (as in Yao, Shun, and Yu). The 632 one of Zhang Rui traced his ancestry from Di Shaohao (a son of Huang Di). The 642 inscription for a Miss Liu mentioned both the remote Di Gao (a great-grandson of Huang Di) and the slightly less remote Yao as her ancestors.[18] Others did not mention which of the figures in remotest antiquity were ancestors but did mention the first to receive the surname in the Zhou period. In some cases, a Han ancestor was the earliest one mentioned, but the omission of earlier ancestors did not necessarily imply that it would have been difficult to trace ancestry earlier: for instance, for Lius the author might merely state which Han emperor was their ancestor.[19] He apparently could assume that readers knew of Liu Bang's descent from Yao.[20]

More important to the issue at hand is the use of remote ancestors to ground group identity in the distant past. All through Tang and Song times, remote ancestors remained the dominant vocabulary where surnames, or groups of people bearing given surnames, were the topic at hand. In other words, giving an apical ancestor was not enough; this apical ancestor had to be linked back to the point where surnames began branching. Such accounts are given by Du You in the *Tong dian* (801), by Lin Bao in *Yuanhe xingzuan* (ca. 810), by Ouyang Xiu and Song Qi in the *Xin Tang shu* genealogical tables (1060), by Deng Mingshi in his *Gujin xingshi shu bianzheng* (ca. 1140), by Zheng Qiao in his *Tong zhi* (1149), by Wang Yinglin in his *Xingshi jijiu bian* (ca. 1280), by Ma Duanlin in the *Wenxian tongkao* (1224), and by Cheng Shangkuan in the *Xin'an mingzuzhi* (1551), the compendium of families in Huizhou. In these works each surname is commonly followed by a statement on its origins, usually including some reference that takes it back to the most remote ancestors.

Two examples should suffice. The *New Tang History* genealogy of the Dou (Dou means "hole") begins as follows:

> The Dou surname (*shi*) branched from the Si surname (*xing*). When Di Xiang [fifth king of Xia] of the Xiahou *shi* lost his state, his consort Youreng *shi* was pregnant. She came out of hiding in a hole and fled back to [her natal family] the Youreng family. She gave birth to Shaokang, who begot two sons, Shu and Long, who stayed with Youreng. Long's sixty-ninth-generation descendant Mingdu served as great officer in the state of Jin and was buried at Changshan. After the six ministers divided Jin, the Dou *shi* lived in Pingyang. Mingdu begot Zhong, who begot Lin, who begot Dan, who begot Yang, who begot Geng, who begot Song, who had two sons, Shi and Yi. Shi begot Ying, who was a chief minister of the Han dynasty and marquis of Weiqi.[21]

The Dou thus were descendants of the Xia kings, the word "Dou" chosen for its meaning. More common were names that began as place names, like Chen:

> The Chen surname (*shi*) branched from the Gui surname (*xing*). [The Chens] are descendants of Shun, the Yu Di. Yu, [first king of] Xia, enfeoffed Shun's son Shangjun at Yucheng. His thirty-second-generation descendant Efu was chief of kilns for the Zhou state, and King Wu gave him his eldest daughter Daji as his wife. She bore Man, who was enfeoffed at Chen and granted the Gui surname with instructions to carry on the sacrifice to Shun. This was Duke Hu. His ninth-generation descendant Duke Ta of Li begot Jingzhong Wan who fled to Qi and took the name of [his former] state as his surname (*xing*). Since he was enfeoffed at Tian he was also considered of the Tian surname (*shi*). His fifteenth-generation descendant, King Jian of Qi, was destroyed by Qin. [King Jian] had three sons, Sheng, Huan, and Zhen. Huan used the Wang ["king"] surname (*shi*). Zhen was chief minister of Chu and enfeoffed as marquis of Yingchuan. On moving there he used the Chen surname (*shi*). He gave birth to Ying, who served as a clerk in Dongyang in the Qin dynasty.[22]

Here three surnames – Chen, Tian, and Wang – are said to be descendants of Shun (and thus of Huang Di). Two of them, Chen and Tian, are described as based on names of fiefs; one, Wang, on a title. All are shown to be almost alternatives, some Chens becoming Tians, some Tians returning to the Chen name, others taking Wang. This sort of easy convertibility largely ended with the Zhou, however. Records of adopting or receiving new surnames in later periods are much rarer.

But let me complicate the situation further. We have already seen that names were used as ethnic markers. Tracing ancestry back to Huang Di offered possibilities for manipulation, for the creation of charters incorporating or excluding groups whose recent histories were known. The practice of specifying the genealogical connections between alien groups and the Chinese was already in use in the Former Han, for Sima Qian gave the basic genealogy of the Xiongnu in a form repeated by all later chroniclers: they were descended from Yu, the founder of the Xia dynasty. In Sima Qian's time there had been great hostility between the Xiongnu and the Chinese state, so offering this genealogy should probably not be taken as an effort to claim brotherhood, but it did put the Xiongnu in the category of people with whom one could marry and with whom one could form peace pacts. As the Chinese were confronted by other northern barbarians over the centuries, they attempted to fit them into comparable schemes. The authors of the *History of the Jin*, finished in the early Tang, did this in their accounts of the founders of the "sixteen kingdoms." The Murong tribe, founders of the state of Yan, were said to be descendants of Youxiongshi (= Huang Di); Yao Yizhong, father of the founder of the Later Qin, was a descendant of the youngest son of Youyushi (= Shun, himself a descendant of Huang Di), who became hereditary chieftain of the Qiang; Lü Guang, a Di who set up the Later Liang in Gansu, was said to be a descendant of a Chinese refugee of the second century BC.[23] Wei Shou in 550 began his history of the Xianbei Northern Wei dynasty by recounting,

> In antiquity Huang Di had twenty-five sons; some were arrayed inside among the many Hua, some were sent out into the wilds. The youngest son of [his son] Changyi received his fief in the northern regions. In his state was Great Xianbei Mountain, and from this [his descendants] took their name.[24]

Such genealogies for the old "northern barbarians" remained common in Tang and Song times.[25] It was much less common for such genealogies to be fashioned for "southern barbarians."[26]

Did positing these sorts of genealogies in some way reduce alienness and thus make those involved more acceptable, as marriage partners if not neighbors? In Song and Yuan times, it is worth noting, there seems to have been no effort to develop such genealogies for the Khitans, Jurchens, or Mongols. Those who stood in a position of enmity could be kept outside the common descent group.[27] Moreover, there were groups that were simply too alien to absorb. Non-Chinese who had no surnames or who did not marry outside their surnames could not very well be brought into the Chinese descent group of intermarrying surnames.[28] And truly alien names could be clearly labeled as alien names, with no efforts made to link them to Chinese descent lines. Deng Mengshi, for instance, annotated some names simply as Japanese, Persian, or Central Asian.[29]

Why does all this matter? Chinese genealogies were discovered, invented, fabricated, or otherwise artfully produced for those who came to be accepted socially as Chinese; from this one could conclude that what matters, in the end, as Confucian culturalism would predict, is acting Chinese, a set of manners and mores. What I want to argue is that the logic of the rationalization does matter, that imagining the linkage among Chinese as a matter of patrilineal kinship differed in interesting ways from other ways of imagining group identities, such as associating the group with biological substance, with a language community, or with a state.

How did the Chinese way of thinking differ from others we know about? Let me start with one of the easiest: how it differs from our use of surnames as ethnic markers. In the United States today we regularly use surnames this way. We casually ask people if their name is Greek or Polish or Italian. They know we are assuming links between surname and ethnic origin and so will offer supplementary information, saying that although their name is Greek, their mother or grandmother was Italian, for instance. In other words, because we do not see ethnicity as strictly or even primarily patrilineal, we therefore realize it does not map perfectly to name.

Another way of thinking about ethnic identity very common among Westerners – linking it to vernacular language – was remarkably absent in China. In Tang and Song sources that describe non-Han groups, spoken language is occasionally mentioned, but it is treated as merely one of many cultural traits, hardly more significant than hairdos or how lapels are crossed. We should remind ourselves how much we are influenced by theories of the branching of language families and their links to genetic connections between ethnic groups. We tend to assume that those who speak Slavic languages somehow share a common origin. By contrast, Chinese could make the Xianbei descendants of Huang Di without any concern with the language they spoke or its connection to the Chinese language. There was, in other words, no conception comparable to the notion of an Indo-European language, no hypothesis that the links between languages and dialects were evidence of remote genetic links between different cultures or peoples.

What about written language as a basis for identity? One of the most influential books on the larger subject of group identities is Benedict Anderson's *Imagined Communities.* In it he groups together traditional China, medieval Christendom, and medieval Islam as forms of cultural unity that preceded modern nationalism. He sees each of the three as a nonterritorial cultural entity built on a sacred center and a sacred language that gave those who mastered it special access to truth, since truth was inherent in that language.[30] These observations are insightful but incomplete. They do not explain the relatively large overlap between territory, polity, and identity in the Chinese case. Nor does Anderson's formulation explain why ethnic identity was never stretched to include the Koreans and Japanese, who in medieval times at least used the same sacred language.

Not that I want to downplay the importance of the written language. After all, the true Chinese surname was a character, not a word (sound and meaning fused). Only barely assimilated barbarians played around with the characters of their names, trying out different ones that sounded the same. And no one thought that those in Guangdong who pronounced their surname "Wong" (using the character for yellow, *huang*) had more affinity to northerners whose families pronounced their name the same way than to northerners who used the same character to write their name. The remarkable powers of the written language influenced Chinese conceptions of kinship just as they did other spheres of Chinese culture.

It is worth noticing that kin-based metaphors of ethnic solidarity like China's do not lend themselves easily to racial categorizing. Patrilineal descent may be biological, but it does not map at all closely to genetic inheritance. In cases of intermarriage, when a Han Chinese man married a local woman, the children of course got genes from both sides and probably even learned ideas and cultural practices from both sides, but identity was very much tied up in the name. Even if we go back only five generations, each person has thirty-two forebears who contributed to his or her genetic endowment, but only one of these thirty-two was the ancestor providing the surname. Going back ten generations, quite commonly done in Chinese reckoning, reduces the average share of biological inheritance from the forebear of one's surname to one part in 1,024. Chinese over the centuries certainly saw patrilineal inheritance as biological inheritance, not thinking in modern genetic terms, but their mental framework made it difficult for them to tie identity to physical traits such as body build, facial features, hair curliness, or skin color, traits inherited from many forebears randomly. The Chinese could be recognized by their surnames but not by their physical appearance. When Chinese in the early twentieth century became interested in Western racial theories of the period, it marked a major departure in their thinking.[31]

By way of conclusion, let me sum up the features of this Han Chinese way of conceiving of themselves in terms of patrilineal kinship and suggest some ways it helps us understand the vast size of the Chinese we-group.

First, like other people's notions of ethnicity, it lends an air of naturalness: it is primordial, tied to sharing ancestors.

Second, it provides a structure for a confusing agglomeration of people, a kind of template for seeing how they all fit together. Benedict Anderson stressed the role of print, especially newspapers, in letting people imagine that others they had never met or ever expected to meet had something in common. But Chinese had long seen people sharing the same surname as having something in common, and this kind of common bond, in weaker form, was also felt by all those who bore names that one's patriline had married with or could plausibly have married with – a group that extended out from the known to the unknown to encompass what was conventionally called the "hundred surnames."

Third, seeing ethnic identity as a kind of kinship makes possible linkages transcending place. Although active kinship groups were rooted locally and people had long labeled families and lineages by their place, people nevertheless recognized kinship ties even centuries after kinsmen had moved away. In a similar way the associations of a surname with a place or region did not limit its capacity to link people in widely dispersed regions. The name Chen was originally the name of a place in Henan, and in modern times the area with the highest proportion of Chens is Fujian,[32] but the inheritance of the Chen surname still has the capacity to link, through images of genealogy and migration, Chens in Shaanxi, Guangxi, Hebei, and beyond China's borders.[33]

Fourth, patrilineal kinship as the key metaphor for connection allows rapid expansion through intermarriage. Chinese were never preoccupied with notions of creoles or half-breeds. One Han Chinese migrant in the Han, Tang, or Song dynasty could be enough to allow thousands or tens of thousands of patrilineal descendants to lay claim to Chinese ancestry and thus Chinese identity (though naturally unless they had absorbed some Chinese culture, they would have had no reason to want to claim such ancestry).

Fifth, seeing identity and connections in terms of genealogy is flexible; it gives room for myth making to adjust to actual circumstances.

And finally, a patrilineal conception of ethnicity coexisted well with Confucian culturalism. The issue was origins, not purity; emphasis was not on keeping others out, but on knowing who you were and how you were connected to others. Those who left written record commonly believed two things, either of which logically would have been enough by itself: (1) what makes people Chinese is acting Chinese, and (2) what makes people Chinese is Chinese ancestry. These two beliefs each provided context for the other and shaped the effects the other had. If we notice only one we do not see the whole story.

8 Rethinking the imperial harem

Why were there so many palace women?*

Chinese emperors, from the First Emperor of Qin (r. 221–206 BC) on, surrounded themselves with attractive young women. Many let the number of palace ladies increase unchecked until it reached several thousand. These women (in Chinese called *shinü, yushi, gongren, gongnü*, or the like) were potential mates, young and unmarried, kept on only as long as they were considered sexually desirable. They formed a huge pool of women available to the emperor, and any he was attracted to could be promoted into the lower ranks of consort if the emperor chose to favor them. Although these women served as palace attendants or servants, they were not recruited, promoted, or retained on the basis of their skill as seamstresses or cooks, but rather for their sexual allure. Despite Confucian criticisms, dating back to the Zhou period, of rulers who let themselves become befuddled by women, no dynastic founder ever proposed refraining from setting up a harem or keeping only two or three women. Even Hong Xiuquan, the nineteenth-century rebel Taiping emperor, who insisted that his followers practice monogamy, ended up with what looked very much like a harem.[1]

Why would an emperor want or need thousands of potential mates? A harem numbering in the thousands incurs all sorts of costs – financial, emotional, managerial, and political – that do not seem obviously balanced by greater benefits. To assure an ample supply of heirs, surely dozens of women would have been sufficient. To demonstrate that the emperor was the most powerful man in the country, a couple of hundred would surely have been plenty, since even the richest subjects did not keep more than a couple of dozen concubines. Another strategy historians often use in looking for explanations – the search for origins – is no more enlightening. The first emperor to keep a really large harem, the First Emperor of Qin, was never held up as a paragon to be emulated by all later emperors who wanted the respect of posterity. To the contrary, those who allowed their harem to grow large in the centuries after Qin Shihuangdi did so

---

* Earlier versions of this essay were presented at Beijing University, Harvard University, Seattle University, and the University of British Columbia. Its present form has benefited from the questions and comments received on those occasions.

despite the general condemnation of his style of governing. To me this is evidence that there were cultural logics, just as "Chinese" as the Confucian protests, that led rulers to let their harems grow to considerable size. In this essay I pursue these logics, looking most closely at the case of the Northern Song (960–1127).

References to the numbers of palace women are not as precise or reliable as one would like. Most of what we have are round numbers used by those criticizing an emperor for extravagance. The First Emperor of Qin, we are told in an early commentary to the *Shiji*, not only built a huge palace complex, but also filled it with women from the harems of the rulers he had conquered, so that his "rear palace" had over 10,000 women.[2] Although the first three Han emperors did not have over 1,000 palace ladies, by about 100 BC, under Wudi, their numbers reached several thousand, and the figure "several thousand" recurs in the Later Han as well.[3] The number "10,000" recurs in the third century AD with the last ruler of Wu in the Three Kingdoms and in the fourth century with Wudi of Jin.[4] This record was surpassed by the early seventh-century Sui emperor, Yangdi, who was said to have had the truly implausible number of 100,000 palace ladies in the secondary palace in Yangzhou.[5] For the Tang emperor best known as a ladies' man, Xuanzong in the mid-eighth century, poets guessed 3,000 or 8,000 palace women but the official history stated 40,000.[6]

Traditionally, there were three main ways of looking on the size of the imperial harem: the voyeuristic, the romantic, and the moralistic. Voyeuristic literature revelled in evocations of the sensual indulgence of the palace. A good example here would be the novels about the second emperor of the Sui, Sui Yangdi, who, as mentioned above, was said to have had 100,000 palace ladies. Westerners have also been fascinated with the erotic possibilities of the imperial harem and written about it in voyeuristic ways. The *Book of Marco Polo* contains a description of the selection process used for Khubilai's harem. Each year the khan had messengers choose 400 or 500 of the most beautiful of the "very handsome and fair-skinned" Ungrat tribe, giving each girl numerical ratings for "the hair, the face, and the eyebrows, the mouth, the lips, and the other limbs." Those rated highest would then be brought before Khubilai. "When they are come to his presence he has them valued again by other judges, and of them all he has thirty or forty who are valued at most carats chosen for his own room." Not only were great efforts invested in selecting the women most likely to please the khan, but efforts were taken to make sure he never grew tired of any of them:

> It is true that every three days and three nights six of these girls are sent to wait on the lord when he goes to rest and when he gets up, both in the room and in the bed and for all that he needs; and the great Khan does with them what he pleases. And at the end of these three days and of three nights come the second six girls in exchange for these, and those depart. And so it goes all the year that every three days and three

Figure 8.1 Illustration from the seventeenth-century novel about Sui Yangdi (*Sui Yangdi yanshi*).
Source: After Hegel 1981: 66.

nights they are changed from six to six girls until the number of those hundred is completed, and then they begin again another turn.[7]

This sort of description can be classed as voyeuristic because it offers male readers the pleasure of observing from afar the sexual lives of the emperors who could have all the women they could possibly want.

The romantic approach to the thousands of palace ladies looks with sympathy at the plight of the women who have to compete with so many other women to win the affections of a single man. The lonely, neglected palace lady became a romantically appealing image. This is seen in the large genre of "palace style" poetry. Poets described anonymous palace ladies as passionate but passive women, women with strong feelings they cannot act on because the object of their passions is a man unavailable to them. Confined spatially in elegant quarters, they spend their time at home with their feelings, often unable to sleep, or silently weeping.[8] There are also stories and plays about particular palace women, such as the famous Wang Zhaojun, the palace lady in the Han who ended up sent to marry a Xiongnu chief because she did not bribe the artist to make her look beautiful so the emperor would not be willing to part with her.[9]

The moralistic approach is found throughout the histories. Confucian moral critics regularly pointed a finger of warning at the examples from history of rulers who came to bad ends because they were too given to indulging their passions for women.[10] Confucian scholars did not worry solely about dissipation, about rulers wasting their time and energy on excessive numbers of women. In their view, even emperors who confined their attentions to a few favorites had to be wary, because the imperial harem was a place that had a pernicious effect on women. Given the level of competition in the harem, and the disparity between those favored and those not, women there were seen as particularly likely to become manipulative and scheming, and emperors therefore had to be on their guard, lest they fall under their influence.

The main reason to keep in mind these traditional ways of viewing palace women is that they create biases in the sources. All of them tend to exaggerate the numbers of women and frame the institution in terms of a sexual relationship between one man and many women, in the process obscuring other aspects of what was going on.

Modern scholarly studies of the "rear palace" have usually concentrated on aspects related to imperial succession and court politics, such as the role of empresses in deciding succession and ruling when the heir was a child, or the selection and promotion of empresses, consorts, and female officials.[11] Many of these studies reflect an early-stage feminist impulse to give women their due as power holders, to show that women, like men, could hold political power and occupy places in complex bureaucratic organizations. Generally they adopt an implicit functionalist framework, which explains the organization of the harem in terms of the importance to the imperial institution of an ample supply of heirs. However, from their work it is evident that the need to staff a female, inner court bureaucracy cannot account for a harem in the thousands. As Priscilla Ching Chung showed, in the Northern Song there were six bureaus in the palace staffed by 279 female officials, including everyone down to the level of clerk.[12] It was not to keep these offices staffed that the numbers of palace women reaches well into the thousands.

Nor can the rate of increase of palace women be explained by linking it to the amorous interests of individual emperors. Northern Song evidence shows that the numbers could increase even when an emperor was a child and an empress dowager ran the palace, or when it is evident that the emperor limited his attentions to no more than a dozen of the women in the palace.

Table 8.1 provides a basic overview of the Northern Song emperors and their consorts and children.[13] Neither of the first two Song emperors, Taizu and Taizong, had large harems. Both came to the throne as married adults (ages 34 and 38), and their habits were set before they lived in the palace. Taizu's first wife had died before he became emperor, and he had his next wife made empress, and when she died, took another empress, but besides these three women he had no other high-ranking consorts. He did take palace women from the harems of the rulers he defeated, and four of his ten

Table 8.1 Northern Song emperors, their consorts and children[a]

Emperor	Age in sui on accession	Years on throne	High-ranking consorts while on throne[b]	High-ranking consorts who had children	Children born while emperor	Children/year on throne after age 18	% of children by lower-rank women
Taizu 960–975	34	16	2		10	.63	40
Taizong 976–997	38	22	11	3	13	.59	38
Zhenzong 998–1022	30	25	11	3	7	.28	57
Renzong 1023–1063	13	41	16	6	16	.44	25
Yingzong 1064–1067	32	4	4	1	0	0	0
Shenzong 1068–1085	20	18	14	9	26	1.44	8
Zhezong 1086–1100	10	15	9	1	5	.71	80
Huizong 1101–1126	19	25	19	13	65	2.6	17

a There are several discrepancies in the number of sons listed for each emperor in the SS and the HSSCGY. Here I have taken the larger number. Also, in the case of the first two emperors, I had to estimate how many of their children were born after taking the throne, and tried to err on the side of counting as many as possible as born after accession.
b This is the cumulative number of empresses and consorts who held high consort titles, as listed in HSSCGY.

children were born to unnamed low-ranking consorts, so it is not as though he was monogamous. Still, the total number of palace women never exceeded 300, and he once dismissed a quarter of the women in his palace, letting anyone go who wanted to go.[14]

His brother Taizong was on the throne longer (twenty-two years) and took a larger number of high-ranking consorts (eleven). Only three of these women, however, bore him children. In addition to the ten children they bore, Taizong had five other children, born to lower-ranking women whose names have not been preserved.

The first emperor reared in the palace, Zhenzong, was on the throne for twenty-five years, from age 30 to 55, but had only seven children. Only three of his eleven high-ranking consorts bore children by him, and they bore only one each; the other four children were by lower-ranking women. In 1008 and 1015 he dismissed 120 and 184 women respectively, but the total nevertheless gradually increased, reaching around 500.

It was under the next emperor, Renzong, that the numbers of palace women soared. Renzong came to the throne at age 13 and lived another 41 years, making his reign the longest in the Northern Song. Although Renzong was generally praised by Confucian scholars and historians, it was not for his handling of the "rear palace." In his early years he was dominated by the Empress Dowager, and once she died in 1032, he promptly ousted the empress she had picked for him when he first took the throne, though to placate the officials, he also had to agree to oust her rival as well.[15]

In the 1040s and until her death in 1054, Renzong was particularly enamored of one consort, named Zhang, who bore him three girls. Nevertheless, during this period, the number of palace women steadily increased. By the Jiayou period (1056–1063), memorials from officials troubled by the expense reported that the number of palace women had reached nearly 10,000.[16] Here the functional explanation of the harem seems to have some validity: one reason for the increase in palace women may have been that despite his many years on the throne Renzong did not beget many sons. Thirteen of his sixteen children were girls, and none of the three boys lived to maturity. As an economy measure, in 1060 the emperor agreed to cut the number of palace women to the level of 1023, but it is unclear how effectively this was carried out.[17] No massive dismissals for 1060 or 1061 are recorded (though 450 had been dismissed in 1059).[18]

Yingzong, Renzong's adopted son, came to the throne as an adult (age 32) and was on it only four years, so his case is too anomalous to be worth considering. All of his eight children were by the woman who was his wife before he took the throne.

Yingzong's son Shenzong came to the throne as a young man of 20. He had been largely raised outside the palace and was already married to a woman who became his empress and would outlive him. In addition to her he had thirteen high-ranking consorts. He had twenty-three children by nine of these fourteen women. Thus, of the emperors discussed so far, he was the

Figure 8.2 Song statues of serving women attending the Jade Emperor, at the Shrine of the Jade Emperor, Jincheng, Shanxi province.
Source: After ZGMSQJ diaosu bian 5.88.

one to take the greatest advantage of the opportunities of the harem: he had children by the largest number of women as well as the most children. However, there are no complaints that the number of palace women increased during his reign.

Shenzong's oldest son Zhezong was only 10 when he came to the throne, and like Renzong was under the domination of an empress dowager, in his case his grandmother. In preparation for Zhezong's eventual marriage, Empress Dowager Gao had over 100 girls from suitable families brought into the palace and eventually selected one named Meng to become the new empress. After Empress Dowager Gao died in 1093 Zhezong seems to have taken out his resentment of his grandmother's domination on the bride she had chosen for him. Not only did Zhezong encourage or at least tolerate his favorite, Consort Liu, to act rudely to his young empress, but on the basis of rumors ordered one of the chief eunuchs to conduct a judicial investigation into alleged conspiracies in the harem. Thirty of the palace women were tortured, some ending up with broken bones or their tongues cut out. After nothing was discovered, Zhezong had Empress Meng deposed and made a Daoist nun. He had her rival Liu installed as empress.[19]

Zhezong was only 25 when he died, but by that time he had five children, only two of whom were by one of his nine high-ranking consorts, the other three by lower-ranking women. His only son died in infancy, so the succession went to his younger brother, then 19 *sui*.

Huizong had spent most of his life in the palace, but had moved out a couple of years before he ascended the throne, and was already married. In his twenty-six years on the throne, he had two empresses and seventeen high-ranking consorts. He copied his father Shenzong in making use of the harem, having children by twelve of his high-ranking consorts (about one for every two years on the throne, just like Shenzong). But he exceeded Shenzong in producing children, averaging 2.6 per year to his father's 1.4, possible because six of his consorts had four or more children.

Most of Huizong's consorts, again like his father's, had entered the palace as ordinary palace ladies. Historical sources describe Huizong as a man who could get very attached to particular consorts. His first favorite, Consort Liu (Mingda), had joined the palace service at age 14 in 1100 and bore her first child three years later at 17. By the time she died at age 27, she had borne six children altogether. Huizong was so distraught that he not only wrote poems in her memory, but also broke precedent to have her posthumously made empress. Even three or four years later, Huizong still missed her a great deal. He even asked Daoist priests to help him communicate with her.[20]

The girl the first Consort Liu had "adopted" then caught his fancy, and the histories report that he let her tend to him from morning to night. This second Miss Liu, we are told, was exceptionally good looking, skilled in applying make-up, and dressed stylishly. Once when Huizong was feasting some of his top officials in the rear garden, he invited them into a hall that had a painted portrait of her, and later let them meet her in person, a rare privilege.[21] After this second Consort Liu died in 1121, Huizong fell into deep grief and would weep with whoever came to console him. One of his consorts, Consort Cui, did not seem to him to be in grief, which annoyed him so much that he had her demoted to commoner, even though she had borne him six children.[22] This seems to be the only time he treated one of the women close to him harshly.

A variety of evidence indicates that by the end of Huizong's reign the number of palace ladies had again reached about 10,000. We know that Huizong periodically released women; from 1108 to 1118 he released 1,819 women, sometimes releasing as few as 68, sometimes as many as 600.[23] Probably these were women who had already served more than five years without attracting any attention or otherwise distinguishing themselves. There was not, however, a simple rotation process of admitting 200 girls a year and after eight years beginning to release 200 or so. For after Huizong abdicated in 1125, 6,000–7,000 palace women were released, and yet there were still several thousand in the palace.[24] This suggests something more like taking in 500 a year and later letting around 200 a year go, so that each year the total increased.

We have further detail on the numbers of women in Huizong's palace because the Jurchens, after seizing the Song capital, Kaifeng, treated these women like booty and made lists of those they seized. When the Jurchen were placing demands on Huizong and his successor Qinzong in the first month of 1127, they were able to demand 2,500 palace women and 1,500 female musicians to distribute among their soldiers.[25] Later, when the authorities made an inventory of the members of the imperial family and palace taken north, they listed 504 palace women, for whom no details were listed, and 143 consorts of Huizong's, who are listed by name, title, and age. The five of highest rank (also referred to as his wives, with ranks of huanghou, guifei, shufei, defei, and xianfei), ranged in age from 34 to 42, and all were mothers of children. The next 31 (also referred to as concubines) held several different titles and ranged in age from 19 to 39. Several of them were also mothers of princes and princesses. The remaining 107, none of whom had borne children, held the lowest titles and ranged in age from 16 to 24.[26] From these figures we can discern a system in which women rise in rank both by bearing children and by getting older, but not in a simple lock-step fashion, as there was a lot of overlap.

We also have a record, something like what Marco Polo reported, of the regular introduction of new girls into Huizong's bedchamber. A man who served as an interpreter for the Jurchen on the journey bringing the palace ladies north was asked about the practices in the palace. He reported that every five to seven days a virgin would be brought to Huizong. The next day she would be given a title, and if he sent for her again, she would get a promotion.[27] This would imply that the 143 women with titles were all ones who had had sexual relations with Huizong. While it is certainly not inconceivable that Huizong took 143 women over 26 years, which would be an average of a new woman every other month, it does seem surprising that he had children by no more than 20. And it is totally implausible that he took a new woman every week for 26 years, which would have meant 1,300 women altogether, and that no more than 20 of them bore children. The Jurchen liked to view their victory as the victory of the vigorous soldiers over decadent courtiers, so the translator may well have told them what he thought they wanted to hear.

Taking all of the Northern Song emperors together, over the course of a century and a half, the size of the palace harem increased many fold, but it did not do it steadily. It grew the most under two emperors, Renzong and Huizong; in each case reaching well into the thousands. These two emperors were both largely reared in the palace and may have been comfortable in this female-dominated world. They also had the two longest reigns. But that is about all they had in common. Renzong had trouble producing male heirs; Huizong had an abundance within a few years of taking the throne. Renzong let Confucian officials like Ouyang Xiu (1007–1072) and Sima Guang (1019–1086) set the tone at court; Huizong went his own way and was more attracted to Daoism than Confucianism.[28]

Evidence that the number of palace women was only loosely linked to individual emperors' love lives is given in Tables 8.2–8.4.[29] Two of these emperors, Renzong and Huizong, had huge numbers of palace women, and even during Shenzong's reign there must have been several thousand, but the differences in the numbers of palace women, or the rate of their increase, seems to have had little to do with their love lives. All three had children by at least seven women, almost all of whom had entered the palace as palace women (not as empresses or as high-ranking consorts). None of the three was a "serial monogamist," interested in only one woman at a time; in at

Table 8.2 Children born to Renzong by two-year period and consort

	Yu	Miao	Zhang1	Zhang2	Dong	Zhou	Other
1037	1	2					
1039	1						
1041			1	1			
1043				2	1		1
1045							
1047							
1049							
1051							
1053				died			
1055							
1057							
1059					2	1	1
1061					died	1	1

Table 8.3 Children born to Shenzong by two-year period and consort

	Xiang	Song	Zhang	Xing	Zhu	Guo	Chen	Wu	Lin	Other
1067	1									
1069		1	1							
1071				1						
1073		1		1						1
1075					2					
1077				2						
1079										
1081					2	1	1	1	2	1
1083		1		1	3					
1085								1	1	

least some period of their lives all were begetting children by several women in a single two-year period. And all of them could lose interest in a particular woman after she had borne him children, although Huizong retained his interest the longest, in several cases for well over a decade; two of the women he remained interested in the longest had their last child at 32. Although Huizong had many more children than his father or great-grandfather, that was due not so much to having sexual relations with many more women, but by retaining his interest in particular women for more years.

On the basis of their sexual habits, then, none of these emperors needed more than a dozen or two palace women at a time, since new young girls were regularly brought into the system and older ones released, ensuring that there would always be some who would be new to the emperor, should his interest flag.

If emperors' sexual appetites do not do much to explain the huge numbers of palace women, is there anything else that does? Two features of Song palace institutions may have played a part. The first is the interests of the consorts of prior emperors. In Song times the consorts of a previous emperor stayed in the palace under his successors. When Yingzong first took the throne in 1063, Sima Guang urged him to release all the palace ladies from his father's time who had never been "favored" or borne a child.[30] All those with higher titles were automatically kept on, even if they had not borne children. When Zhezong came to the throne in 1085, for instance, among the consorts of prior emperors given promotions were six of Renzong's, four of Yingzong's, and nine of Shenzong's consorts. These women were still very much a part of the "rear palace." For instance, in 1190 when Shenzong's widowed consort Lin died, Renzong's widowed consort Feng took to raising Lin's two sons. To put this another way, Zhezong's step great-grandmother took to rearing his half brothers after his step-mother died. Previous emperors' consorts needed palace ladies to attend them, adding to the size of the total establishment. The romantic view of the palace ladies sees them as competing with each other for the emperor's attention,

Table 8.4 Children born to Huizong by two-year period and consort

	Wang	Zheng	Wang2	Liu1	Yang	Qiao1	Wang3	Wei	Cui	Wang4	Qiao2	Han	Liu2	Other
1100	2	2												
1102		1	1	1	1	1	1							
1104		1	2	1		2	1							
1106		1	1	2		1	1	1						
1108	Died	1	1	1		1	1		1					
1110			1	Died	1	1	1		1	1	1			
1112			1			1	2		1	1		1		
1114							1		1	1		1	1	
1116							Died		1				1	3
1118									1				1	2
1120														2
1122													1	4
1124														

but many of the women in the palace were outside that competition, including not only the empress dowager, but also the lower-ranking consorts of previous emperors. There would have been no great reason for these women to oppose the tendency for the numbers of palace ladies to grow, as it made their world larger. Indeed, the palace was something of a women's city. Emperors who grew up in this environment do not seem to have disliked it.

A second institutional feature that could have contributed to the proliferation of palace ladies is the success of the Song at limiting the numbers of eunuchs in palace service to no more than a couple hundred.[31] Thus senior women were largely served by junior women, not eunuchs.

Contributing as well would have been the natural tendency of institutions to grow and the effort it takes to shrink them. In that light, it is not surprising that the only emperor who seems to have managed to curtail growth of the harem was Shenzong. It may be of some importance that he did not grow up in the palace and was not dominated by an empress dowager. But probably more important was his strong desire to establish the New Policies, get the budget under control, and build up funds for military purposes.[32]

Although these institutional factors must have contributed to the growth of the imperial harem, I do not see them as the sole explanation for the growth in the numbers of palace ladies, if for no other reason than they have more to do with the specific case of the Northern Song than the whole period from the Qin dynasty on. This brings me back to "cultural logics," widely held ideas and powerful symbols that fostered the practice.

Consider, first, the relationship between palaces and palace ladies. In China, as elsewhere, rulers tried to manifest the splendor of their rule by building opulent palaces. In Europe, where Christianity required that a king have only one consort, an opulent palace like Versailles could please the senses through gardens, elegantly appointed rooms with paintings, tapestries, and sculptures, as well as by the presence of fashionable dressed courtiers. Certainly servants, primarily male servants, were numerous and well-dressed, but they were not a key component of the aesthetic appeal of the palace.

In China, however, a large part of what made palaces beautiful and splendid was the palace ladies who, in a sense, furnished them. For instance, writers sometimes talk of completing a palace by filling it with "beautiful women." Sima Qian reported that after Qin Shihuangdi built his palace in Xianyang, he filled it with the beautiful women and musical instruments he had taken from the feudal lords he had defeated.[33] In a similar vein, the *Han Wu gushi* told the story that when Wudi built the Mingguang palace, he recruited 3,000 beauties from Yan and Zhao to fill it.[34] The rhapsody that Ban Gu wrote about the Western Palace gave the names of the halls in the rear palace, and described their lavish decoration, with "gilt thresholds, jade stairs, vermilion courtyards" but also the "Red-gauzed beauties, sleeves dangling, with silk-braided ribbons, tangled and twisted, their pure radiance gaily glittering, bobbed up and down like goddesses." He also mentioned that these "modest and retiring" "burgeoning blossoms" numbered in the hundreds.[35] Unlike European palaces, however, this form of splendor was a private, concealed splendor, for the emperor to enjoy and other men merely to imagine.

This image of palaces made beautiful by the presence of palace ladies was later absorbed into Daoist visions of paradise. By the end of the Six Dynasties Daoist paradises were pictured as palaces where elegantly dressed "jade maidens" wandered among brightly-painted halls and flower-filled gardens.[36] Daoist images of paradise in turn shaped notions of the perfect palace, and palace ladies could be likened to immortals. To give a Song example, Hong Mai, in his *Yijianzhi*, records an anecdote that begins by describing the splendors of the Genyue garden that Huizong had constructed outside the palace, with all of its halls and palaces as well as stands of bamboo and other natural scenery. The sight of the palace ladies going in and out among them "like immortals" was enough to get Huizong to climb one of the taller buildings so that he could gaze down at them.[37]

The association of palace ladies with immortality is also worth closer examination. From Qin and Han times on, the popular conception of rulership in China owed a great deal to the elaboration of ideas about the Yellow Emperor.[38] In this tradition, the Yellow Emperor is militarily powerful, extremely yang; he is a Daoist Sage of vast powers; he is associated with immortality, knowing the secrets to it, presiding over various paradises. In medical literature, he is the fountainhead of medical knowledge. In the esoteric sexual treatises, he is instructed in the sexual arts by the Plain Maiden, and mastery of these sexual arts can lead to immortality. But full employment of these sexual arts required an unlimited supply of young virgins – the more women whose yin essence is absorbed, the more progress is made toward immortality. Here it is worth noting that the Song imperial house, ever since Zhenzong, traced its descent back to the Yellow Emperor.[39]

It is unlikely that Renzong or Huizong or any of the other Song emperors ever consciously thought that they could either enhance their yang power, their military might, or their chances for immortality by gathering thousands of virgins in the palace. Nevertheless, ideas of kingly majesty and power were so entangled with ideas of the superhuman Yellow Emperor that they did not need to consciously think about such connections. Even if Confucian moralists condemned large harems as wasteful and dangerous, they were fighting against an equally strong tradition that associated the possession of thousands of young beauties with the Yellow Emperor, immortality, pleasure, and imperial majesty.

***

Does rethinking the imperial harem help us understand any aspects of life beyond the palace walls? Although only a tiny portion of the Chinese population ever had any direct experience of the imperial harem, the cultural significance of the harem should not be underestimated. Not only were

Figure 8.3 Illustration from chapter 21 of the novel *Jin Ping Mei*, showing the protagonist with several of his concubines and their maids.

stories of emperors and their favorites staples of Chinese drama and fiction, but even stories of the amorous adventures of other men often borrow imperial imagery. These stories helped form Chinese conceptions of gender and male–female relations; ideas about the attractiveness of the lonely, longing woman, and the impressiveness of the man attended by several beauties owe a great deal to the power of these images of the most powerful man in the country and his essentially unlimited supply of attractive young handmaidens.

I would like to go further here, however, and suggest that the imperial case offers insight into one of the major questions that has engaged the attention of historians of Chinese women in recent years, the question of change over time. Lately, authors of books on women in Chinese history, myself among them, have made every effort to show that women were not outside of history, but just as much enmeshed in it as men were.[40] We all, for instance, tried to point to aspects of economic change that would have shaped women's lives, ranging from changes in the way textiles were produced and marketed, to the impact of increasing commercialization on the market for women. Moreover, we all bring in intellectual and cultural change, particularly developments in Confucian thought and the steady expansion of print culture. If anything, these books probably all err on the side of exaggerating the impact of change, since if you read them together you cannot help but wonder why women in the eighteenth century had so much in common with women in the eleventh, given the pace of change we all claim. For instance, Susan Mann's description of Qing women making cloth sounds a lot like my description of Song women making cloth, even though Franscesca Bray claims that there was a dramatic change in the social organization of textile production between Song and Qing times. Similarly, despite all the developments intellectual historians talk about, Mann's description of Qing women's Buddhist piety does not sound all that different than what I found in Song times. In other words, no matter how hard we look for change, we keep coming up with a lot of recurrent patterns as well.

It is not difficult to think of possible explanations for recurrent formations, from long-acknowledged ones like the persistent hold of basic Confucian family ethics and the basic patrilineal family system, to more nuanced ones such as Franscesca Bray's emphasis on the ways the basic structure of Chinese houses shaped people's experience of the family and sexual segregation. But the persistent tendency for the imperial harem to grow huge suggests that it is important not to dismiss the power of deep cultural codes underlying conceptions of gender. Notions of imperial majesty seem to have been conveyed outside of the voluminous Confucian literature on emperorship, and indeed in opposition to it. The image of the Yellow Emperor as the alpha male undercut the Confucian literature on the responsible emperor, but at a level that no Confucian adviser could directly address since it was never made explicit. I suspect that notions of manliness and femininity in the larger society similarly drew from ideas conveyed through popular religion and popular literature, including ones that undercut or counter-acted ideas and images conveyed at the explicit intellectual level in Confucian writings on family virtues, theoretical analyses of yin and yang, as well as the laws governing descent and transmission of property. This untheorized level of culture is much harder to dislodge, since it is hard to recognize and hard to attack. When features of gender relations persist despite changing economic and cultural opportunities, we need to think about how the persistence of unarticulated assumptions might be implicated.

9 Gender and sinology

Shifting Western interpretations of footbinding, 1300–1890*

Historians of women often draw from travelers' accounts because features of male–female relations that the authors of one country take for granted may seem noteworthy to those from elsewhere. In the case of China, through the nineteenth century the richest outsiders' accounts were written by those from furthest away, from Europe and later the United States.[1] In the sixteenth through the eighteenth centuries European visitors gave detailed descriptions of the practice of female seclusion, the ways finance entered into marriage arrangements, the cut of women's clothing, and the ways women made up their faces. By the nineteenth century, Western visitors, including some who had lived for years in China, brought up a wider range of topics, from women's opportunities for education, to child-rearing practices, the degree of sexual segregation in everyday activities such as eating meals, and regional and class variation in footbinding and women's work.

An historian of European cultural history could use these writings to analyze the ways changing Western social, political, and religious preoccupations found expression in changing attitudes toward distant non-Christian lands and China in particular. After all, travelers' accounts invariably reveal as much about themselves as about those they describe. But Western writings on Chinese women also are worth the scrutiny of historians of China interested in the intellectual foundations of their field. Western authors, while creating interest in the West in the topic of Chinese women, were framing the topic certain ways and focusing attention on some issues to the exclusion or neglect of others. Even today, when Western writing on Chinese women's history is based more on close study of Chinese texts than on travels through China, the vocabulary and concepts established by these earlier generations are still in use.

In this article I trace some of the elements involved in Westerners' creation of knowledge about Chinese women by looking closely at what they

* This article was originally published in *Late Imperial China*, 2(2) (1999–34). Reproduced by permission. Earlier versions of this paper were presented at the University of Illinois, the University of Victoria, and the Conference on Chinese Women's Studies for the 21st Century in Beijing, 1998. I would like to thank JaHyun Haboush, Nancy Abelmann, and Tani Barlow for their comments and suggestions on earlier drafts.

wrote on the highly-charged topic of footbinding. The focus on footbinding allows me to highlight how issues of gender and sexuality – both those of the observers and the observed – entered into the questions people asked and the explanations they offered. Because I am interested in the creation of knowledge, I concentrate on the most authoritative Western writings on China, not the most outrageous, ignorant, or ethnocentric ones. The more reputable authors drew on the best information available to them, gained respect in their time as authorities on China, and had considerable impact on opinion among educated readers of English.[2]

What first drew me to Western writings on footbinding was the continuing controversy about Marco Polo's silence regarding the practice. In 1871, when Colonel Henry Yule (1820–1889) wrote the introduction to his massively annotated translation of *The Book of Ser Marco Polo*, he listed Marco Polo's silence concerning footbinding among his "singular omissions," and since Yule's time accounts of Marco Polo routinely mention his silence on footbinding.[3] Recently Frances Wood has taken these omissions as evidence that Marco Polo gleaned his knowledge of China from others and never reached there himself.[4] It seemed to me wrong to fault Marco Polo for not mentioning footbinding before first assessing his purposes in writing about Chinese women, then comparing his preoccupations to those of later writers who did bring up footbinding. By the time I had gotten deeply into later travel writers and authorities on China, I found Marco Polo's silence on footbinding a less interesting issue than what later writers wrote about it.

In this essay, I take the story of Western discourse on footbinding only to 1890. By that date an active anti-footbinding movement had gained momentum in China and was rapidly changing both the practice of footbinding and the ways both Chinese and Westerners discussed the practice. My interest here is not in Chinese appropriations and refashioning of the Western discourse on footbinding, as interesting as that subject is in its own right.[5] Rather, I examine the Western discourse on footbinding as a way to gain a deeper understanding of sinology.

HISTORICAL SHIFTS AND PERSISTENT QUESTIONS

Even though the ways Western authors wrote about Chinese women changed markedly over the centuries, certain preoccupations proved persistent. Marco Polo, writing at the end of the thirteenth century, generally commented positively on Chinese women. For instance, he volunteered that the women of Fuzhou were "very fair" and those of Hangzhou "very delicate and angelic things."[6] Beyond that, the facets of Chinese and Mongol male–female relations that elicited comment from him were either part of the standard catalogue of marriage practices that other European visitors also discussed, most of which had something to do with canon law on marriage, or ones that he thought had a message to convey to a European audience.[7] Many of his comments on Chinese or Mongol male–female relations can be read as indirect criticisms of European ways. At times he sounds like a frustrated father, wishing his daughters were more like modest Chinese girls, free from such faults as skipping or dancing or looking out windows, who stay in their rooms at their tasks, "rarely show themselves to fathers and brothers and the elders of the house," and "pay no attention to suitors."[8] At other times Marco Polo makes China seem a better place than Europe to be a husband. Not only are Chinese women "very well made in all respects" but men can "take wives enough, because their religion or their usage does not hinder them," whereas "with us one has but one wife, and if she is barren the man will end his life with her and beget no son, and therefore we have not so many people as they."[9]

China as a realm where desires are fulfilled is perhaps clearest in Marco Polo's description of the pleasure quarters. Like many male travelers to Asia in the twentieth century, Marco Polo was impressed by the ample supply of prostitutes who tend to men's every need. In Hangzhou, he reported, the innumerable courtesans were not confined to one district, but lived all over the city.

> And they stay very sumptuously with great perfumes and with many maid-servants, and the houses all decorated. These women are very clever and practiced in knowing how to flatter and coax with ready words and suited to each kind of person, so that the foreigners who have once indulged themselves with them stay as it were in an ecstasy, and are so much taken with their sweetness and charms that they can never forget them.[10]

Whether or not he personally observed footbinding, Marco Polo apparently saw no need to mention it. The first European (probably the first non-Chinese) to mention footbinding was the Franciscan friar Odoric of Pordenone (d. 1331), who visited China in the 1320s. Late in his dictated account of his time in China, Odoric reported that he had once passed by the house of a very rich man who kept fifty "damsels, virgins, who wait on him continually" and sang while they served him food. Recalling this man apparently reminded Odoric of a couple of other oddities he had learned of in China. Among Chinese men, he remarked, the "mark of gentility" was to let their thumb nails grow and "with the women the great beauty is to have little feet; and for this reason mothers are accustomed, as soon as girls are born to them, to swathe their feet tightly so that they can never grow in the least."[11] Odoric did not say he observed either long fingernails or bound feet, and it is possible he simply heard of these practices, perhaps from a guide or interpreter. Whatever his source, he seems to have misunderstood some of what he learned. Footbinding was never started at birth.[12] Some girls may have had their feet bound as early as four, but older ages were more common.

Odoric treated footbinding off-handedly, as a curious custom in a world full of curiosities. His language suggests neither entrancement nor condemnation. By pairing it with long nails, he drew attention both to its bodily aspect and to its gender symbolism. In China, he seemed to be implying, the ways in which the sexes are distinguished are not limited to clothing and hair styles, but extend to the length of their limbs, men focusing on making the ends of their arms longer, women on making the ends of their legs shorter. If he had not noticed this asymmetry, he might not have mentioned either practice. He described both customs as marks of gentility, suggesting that perhaps only a very small proportion of the population practiced them. And by mentioning them immediately after the account of the man with all the damsels, he gave both practices an air of decadence, of carrying the pursuit of distinction and beauty to rather far extremes.

Footbinding and long fingernails remained paired in Western writings for several centuries, largely, it would seem, because Odoric's story of the man with fifty damsels and his comment about footbinding and long nails were plagiarized by John de Mandeville, a writer who had never been to China but whose imaginary travelogue gained a very wide circulation. In his 1366 *Travels*, Mandeville elaborated on the singing damsels, then went on to note: "and the gentry of women there is to have small feet; and therefore as soon as they are born, they bind their feet so straight that they may not wax so great as they should."[13] Once Odoric and Mandeville had made footbinding something to note about China, few European writers on China failed to mention it and visitors to China arrived expecting to see it.

In the centuries after Mandeville, Europeans began visiting China with increasing frequency, and Western writing on China reflects the changing relationships between the two regions, as authors like Donald Lach and Jonathan Spence have abundantly demonstrated.[14] Spanish and Portuguese seaman and missionaries in the sixteenth century were soon followed by Italian and French Jesuit missionaries of the seventeenth and eighteenth centuries, then British merchants, envoys, and missionaries from the late eighteenth century on. Missionaries wrote a large share of the most influential works, but missionaries rarely agreed on the way to approach China. Even in the early centuries before Protestants made any efforts at proselytizing in China, there were conflicts between the Jesuits and Dominicans. By the nineteenth century, not only were there both Catholic and Protestant missionaries from many countries and denominations, but also more books by men in China for commercial, diplomatic, or scientific purposes.

Later in this article I will analyze the most important of the new ideas about footbinding introduced from the fourteenth through the nineteenth century. But to give a sense of the magnitude of the changes over this period, let me take one nineteenth-century author to compare to Odoric. John Francis Davis (1795–1890), who published *The Chinese* in 1836, was a member of the early foreign community in China. His father was director of the East India Company in Canton from 1810 to his death in 1819, and John Davis joined the company himself at the age of eighteen in 1813. Linguistically talented, he was chosen to accompany Lord Amherst on his unsuccessful mission to Beijing in 1816, and in the 1820s he published two translations from Chinese literature.[15] He was thus both a genuine sinologist and a man deeply tied to the imperialist project of expanding British interests in China. In *The Chinese* he brought up footbinding after discussing the physical appearance of Chinese men and women. He noted that European stereotypes were baseless, that "among those who are not exposed to the climate, the complexion is fully as fair as that of Spaniards and Portuguese" and that people are usually good-looking to the age of 20 before the "roundness of youth wears off." He then pointed to the "very opposite characters of figure admired in the two sexes. A woman should be extremely slender and fragile in appearance; a man very stout, – not in those proportions that denote muscular strength, and what we call *condition*, – but corpulent, obese, alderman-like."[16] After discussing the custom of men letting their nails grow to "inordinate length, until they assume an appearance very like the claws of a bradypus," he took up the topic of footbinding:

> But the most unaccountable species of taste is that mutilation of the women's feet, for which the Chinese are so remarkable. Of the origin of this custom there is no very distinct account, except that it took place about the close of the Tâng dynasty, or the end of the ninth century of our era. The Tartars have had the good sense not to adopt this artificial deformity, and their ladies wear a shoe like that of the men, except that it has a white sole of still greater thickness. As it would seem next to impossible to refer to any notions of physical beauty, however arbitrary, such shocking mutilation as that produced by the cramping of the foot in early childhood, it may partly be ascribed to the principle which dictates the fashion of long nails. The idea conveyed by these is *exemption from labour*; and, as the small feet make cripples of the women, it is fair to conclude that the idea of gentility which they convey arises from a similar association. That appearance of helplessness which is induced by the mutilation they admire extremely, notwithstanding its very usual concomitant of sickliness; and the tottering gait of the poor women, as they hobble along upon the heel of the foot, they compare to the waving of a willow agitated by the breeze. We may add that this odious custom extends lower down in the scale of society than might have been expected from its disabling effect upon those who have to labour for their subsistence. If the custom was first imposed by the tyranny of the men, the women are fully revenged in the diminution of their charms and domestic usefulness.[17]

Davis then went on compare the "folly and childishness" of the way Chinese "have departed from the standard of nature, and sought distinction even in

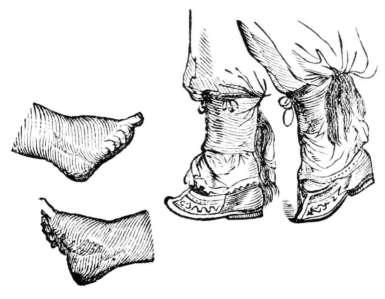

Figure 9.1 Illustration captioned "The small foot of a Chinese lady".
Source: Davis 1836: 255.

deformity" to the practices of other cultures, including European, Malay, South Pacific, and Eskimo.

Davis's take on footbinding was poles apart from Odoric's. Where Odoric was detached, Davis was engaged. Where Odoric was curious, Davis was repelled and used negative terms like odious, mutilation, deformity, and cripples. Like Odoric, Davis related footbinding to both the arbitrariness of taste and the desire to assert high social standing, but he brought in other issues as well, such as its origins, the extent of its practice, and its links to "the tyranny of the men." He made it clear that he did not find bound feet attractive, and to let readers draw their own conclusion, included sketches of bound feet both bare and in shoes (see Figure 9.1).

It would be easy to make the story of the shift from Odoric to Davis simply a story of cultural imperialism or colonialist discourse. Since the publication of Edward Said's *Orientalism* in 1979, few can pretend ignorance of the ways representing another culture is an act of exerting power over it, or the ways Westerners writing about Asia have been implicated in the larger imperialist project of controlling and benefiting from Asia.[18] Certainly, as the power relations between the West and China shifted, so too did the way Westerners wrote about features of Chinese culture they did not find to their taste. Davis, although a serious student of Chinese language and literature like the Jesuits of two centuries earlier, was not uncomfortable identifying features of Chinese culture that he considered ripe for reform. Moreover, from his citations, it is clear that he read and expected to be read by the growing group of missionaries who were in China to transform it. From the sixteenth century on, it was common for missionaries in particular to posit that women's status could never be as high in a heathen country as a Christian one. They presented non-Christian forms of marriage, especially polygamy and concubinage, as demeaning to women. In the nineteenth century, missionary authors – who wrote a substantial share of the English-language books on China from 1840 to 1890 – almost always argued that the status of women in China would improve if Christianity were spread.[19]

Co-existing with these religious views were views rooted in the Enlightenment about historical progress. China came to be looked on as an example of a less advanced form of civilization best labeled "oriental despotism." One of the authors Davis cited regularly was John Barrow, a member of the Macartney embassy of the 1790s. In his *Travels in China*, Barrow argued that the status of women told one something important about another society: "It may, perhaps, be laid down as an invariable maxim, that the condition of the female part of society in any nation will furnish a tolerable just criterion of the degree of civilization to which that nation has arrived."[20] In Barrow's view, in "the despotic governments of Asiatic nations" a woman's "personal accomplishments, so far from being of use to the owner, serve only to deprive her of liberty, and the society of her friends; to render her a degraded victim, subservient to the sensual gratification, the caprice, and the jealousy of tyrant men."[21] By the time Davis wrote in the 1830s, such ideas about social and political progress were commonplace in Britain and the U.S.

Most readers of this article, I assume, do not need me to point out the political bases for the sense of cultural superiority that pervades nineteenth-century Western writings like these. However, I will not similarly assume readers see how gender entered into the mix. Barrow's views are premised not only on assumptions about the differences between countries and civilizations, but also on assumptions about male–female relations. Until the late nineteenth century, Western writing was based overwhelmingly on the observations or research of men who reacted to what they saw or heard as men. Until the eighteenth century most also wrote for a primarily male audience. Thus, the gender system of their own culture limited what they found noteworthy in China and the sense they made of it. At the same time, China's gender system limited how far they could go in pursuing questions that interested them. Most Chinese women did not want to be observed by strange men, much less talk to them, and Chinese men, even if willing to talk to foreign men, would have considered many issues relating to women inappropriate topics of conversation.

Of course, assumptions about gender and sexuality did not exist in a cultural vacuum; they too could be complexly tied to political relations. Consider, for instance, the persistence of the urge to address the very male-centered question of how attractive the women of China were. Nearly all the authors I cite here, from Marco Polo to missionaries in the late nineteenth century, either state that Chinese women are beautiful or offer a more qualified evaluation of their looks. When discussing men, many details concerning their trades, crafts, means of warfare, transportation, or government are of interest, but the first question about women is usually their looks. To some extent the focus on women's beauty may simply reflect the fact that the authors were men, writing for men, and assumed that their readers wanted to share vicariously in the pleasure of looking at beautiful women. But that is evidently not all that was involved, because there is a curious correlation between approving of women's appearance and approving of Chinese culture and institutions. Those who largely had good things to say about China, like Marco Polo and the Jesuits, tended to describe Chinese women as good-looking; those who were more neutral about China tended also to be neutral about Chinese women's appearance; those who thought many features of Chinese culture and institutions should be reformed tended to see ways Chinese women could be made more attractive by dropping customs like face paint and loose clothes; and those repelled by China tended to describe Chinese women as ugly.

A couple of examples should suffice to illustrate this tendency. The physician C. Toogood Downing is typical of those who advocated reforming many features of Chinese culture and institutions and who also thought Chinese women would be prettier if only they presented themselves somewhat differently. From his year among the foreign community in Canton and Macao in the 1830s he spoke positively of Chinese women's looks, their complexions ("resembling that of the Spanish donzellas"), their "beautiful tresses of jet-black hair." But he admitted being repelled by "the practice of painting the face both white and red, so frequently adopted by those who did not seem to need anything of the kind."[22]

The author who best epitomizes hating all things Chinese and finding its women ugly is the British barrister Henry Charles Sirr. In his 1849 *China and the Chinese*, he did not hide the distaste for many things Chinese. When it came to Chinese women, he described their faces as "totally devoid of expression or intelligence."[23] Their figures were "fleshless" and "without those graceful undulations, which we English consider as essential to female beauty." Moreover, they had

> dingy yellow complexion (overplastered with white cosmetic), high cheek bones, small piggish-looking eyes, with penciled eyebrows meeting over the nose, low brow, oblong ears, coarse black hair, which is invariably anointed with stinking pork fat, until it stands on end.[24]

Most likely some visitors, turned off by China, found themselves turned off by Chinese women as well. But changing political relations also gave writers the license to drop the manner of the polite guest. When Western governments no longer felt the need to deal politely with the Chinese government,

Western writers often no longer felt the need to write as though they had been well-treated guests who should only say nice things about their hosts (and the hosts' wives and daughters).

DOMINANT WAYS OF FRAMING FOOTBINDING

Western authors found it natural and easy to write about Chinese women's hair, clothes, and makeup, but footbinding was a difficult subject. Over the centuries, Western authors kept struggling to find adequate ways to present and explain footbinding, in the process shifting the discourse rather markedly. Although new ways of interpreting footbinding were periodically introduced, old ones were rarely discarded altogether. Like Davis already cited, many authors would offer a variety of explanations of the origins or functions of footbinding. Some offered no judgment, leaving to their readers the task of evaluating the different arguments.

Nevertheless, a rough chronology can be discerned among the six most dominant ways of framing footbinding: fashion, seclusion, perversity, deformity, child abuse, and cultural immobility. The first of these constructions is mildly negative, the next mildly positive, and the subsequent ones all distinctly negative. Shifting Western interpretations of footbinding are largely shifts in the weight given to each of these possible ways of thinking about footbinding.

Fashion

All through the period discussed in this article, the Western reading audience was familiar with the idea of fashion as senseless style cultivated by those with wealth in the name of elegance or beauty. Footbinding was interpreted as such a fashion from the start, since Odoric called it a mark of gentility and said it was taken as great beauty. The Portuguese Dominican friar Gaspar da Cruz, who visited Canton in 1556, expanded slightly on these ideas:

> The women commonly, excepting those of the sea coast and of the mountains, are very white and gentlewomen, some having their noses and eyes well proportioned. From their childhood they squeeze their feet in cloths, so that they may remain small, and they do it because the Chinese do hold them for finer gentlewomen that have small noses and feet. This withal is the custom among the well-bred people, and not among the basest.[25]

Nearly two centuries later in 1736 Jean-Baptiste Du Halde, author of a four volume compendium of information on all aspects of Chinese history, culture, and social customs, noted that beauty depends on taste and that Chinese wear large garments, not finding any charm in revealing a person's shape. Later he observed that the gait associated with footbinding was attractive to Chinese but not to Europeans:

> Among the charms of the sex the smallness of their feet is not the least; when a female infant comes into the world, the nurses are very careful to bind their feet very close for fear they should grow too large: The Chinese ladies are subject all their lives to this constraint, which they were accustomed to in their infancy, and their gait is slow, unsteady, and disagreeable to foreigners.[26]

Chinese women, Du Halde asserted, not only undergo the inconvenience of footbinding readily, but "they increase it, and endeavor to make their feet as little as possible, thinking it an extraordinary charm, and always affecting to show them as they walk."[27] The idea that Chinese women showed off their feet is another common error, undoubtedly a result of men like Du Halde drawing inferences from the way they understood fashion to work in the West. Implicit in this fashion interpretation is the idea that women pursue the goal of tiny feet avidly, with no pressure from anyone else. The Abbé Grosier, in the 1780s, noted that a small foot appears to a Chinese woman "so valuable a beauty, that she never thinks she has paid too dear for such an advantage."[28]

A fashion interpretation of footbinding was relativist; comparing footbinding to the inexplicable fashion excesses of his own high society allowed an author to absolve himself of the need to offer any other judgment on the practice. Lord George Macartney, in the diary he kept during his embassy to China in 1793–1794, framed his discussion of footbinding by first expressing a reluctance to "despise or ridicule other nations on the mere account of their differing from us in little points of manners and dress, as we can very nearly match them with similar follies and absurdities of our own." After all, no nation has a monopoly on "dissatisfaction at our natural form." "Boring the ears, painting the face, and dusting and plastering the hair with powder and grease are equally fashionable in London and Otaheite [Tahiti]." Ladies who wore tight shoes in his own society were practicing the same kind of folly as footbinding.[29]

One way to bolster the fashion interpretation was to quote Chinese informants who, when queried about the origin of footbinding, told stories of emperors who had admired it in palace ladies, and the mad rush of others to make themselves equally attractive. Europeans, used to the influence of the court on the fashions of the aristocracy, found this a plausible hypothesis. The Italian priest Matteo Ripa, who lived in Beijing from 1710 to 1723, wrote of an ancient emperor who

> purposely hinted that nothing was more beautiful in a woman than to have the smallest feet possible. This imperial opinion being made public

throughout China, every husband desired that his wife should be in the fashion, and mothers sought to secure to their daughters an imaginary beauty which it was found could be procured by art.[30]

John Bell, a Scottish doctor who visited Beijing when Ripa was there, also placed the beginning of the fashion in court, but had a different story. It all began with a beautiful and virtuous princess whose feet, however, resembled those of birds, and who therefore kept them wrapped up. The ladies of the court followed her example; which, of course soon became general.

No author that I came across paused to consider the differences between court life in China and Europe, or to consider how high-ranking women in China, who did not attend court, would learn of the fashions of princesses and imperial concubines, since even the officials who did attend court did not normally get the chance to see them. Rather they debated which emperor or palace lady began the craze for footbinding, offering dates ranging in date from the Shang dynasty to the Sui to the Five Dynasties. Du Halde offered the theory that it was the last empress of the Shang dynasty (ca. 1000 BC) who adopted the fashion to conceal her club feet, but then was imitated by all the other women.[31] A nineteenth-century English medical missionary, William Lockhart, cited "an intelligent Chinese" as the authority for attributing the custom to the last emperor of the Sui dynasty (ca. 600 AD), who ordered his concubine to bandage her feet in a way that would leave imprints of lotus flowers on the floor where she walked.[32] The English missionary Robert Morrison, in his *View of China* (1817), reported another common Chinese explanation, attributing the practice to a ruler during the tenth century, Li Houzhu, who "ordered his concubine, Yaou, to bind her feet with silk, and cause them to appear small, and in the shape of the new moon. From this, sprung the imitation of every other female."[33]

A relativist interpretation seeks to avoid moral judgment, a stance made explicit by some authors. The French missionary Évariste-Régis Huc in 1855 offered the opinion that Europeans had no right to be severe with the Chinese on the grounds of footbinding, since their own customs could be criticized on comparable grounds:

> What would the Chinese women say, too, if any one should tell them that beauty does not consist in having imperceptible feet, but it does in having an intangible waist, and that, though it is not desirable to have the feet of a goat, it is to have the shape of a wasp? Who knows but that the Chinese and European ladies would end by making mutual concessions, and adopting both fashions at once.[34]

A few years later, the American missionary Justus Doolittle made a similar relativist argument:

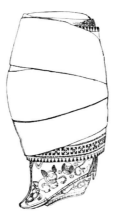

Figure 9.2 Illustration captioned "Appearance of a small shoe on the foot".
Source: Doolittle 1865: 2.199.

While foreign ladies wonder why Chinese ladies should compress the feet of their female children so unnaturally, and perhaps pity them for being the devotees of such a cruel and useless fashion, the latter wonder why the former should wear their dresses in the present expanded style, and are able to solve the problem of the means used to attain such a result only by suggesting that they *wear chicken-coops beneath their dresses*, from the fancied resemblance of crinoline skirts, of which they sometimes get a glimpse, to a common instrument for imprisoning fowls.[35]

Most of these writers strongly implied that there was something about women that made them particularly vulnerable to the pull of fashion, to the point where they would disfigure themselves simply because someone told them a different shape was more beautiful. They thus were tempering any impression that they were criticizing China; indeed they can be read as empathizing with Chinese men who had to put up with women just as foolish as the women of their own country. The missionary John Nevius wrote that footbinding

> probably arose from a strife among women for the pre-eminence of having the smallest feet, fond mothers commencing to bind their daughters' feet before they were grown, and the time for beginning the process being gradually changed to an earlier period.[36]

Some missionaries gave utilitarian reasons for taking a relativistic stance on footbinding. John Nevius's wife Helen Nevius claimed that without tolerating

Figure 9.3 Two illustrations captioned "Feet of Chinese ladies" and "Shape of a
      lady's shoe."
Source: Williams 1849: II.40, 41.

footbinding missionaries would not be able to attract girls from respectable
families to their schools. She reported that their school in Ningbo admitted
girls with bound feet because in that region all respectable women had
bound feet, and the few girls whose feet had not been bound were subjected
to insulting remarks as they passed through the streets. Moreover, it was
nearly impossible to make suitable marriages for them, even among young
men educated in the school.[37] Taking a relativistic stance was also justified
by the fact that Chinese made these relativistic arguments themselves, arguing for instance that compressing the waist with corsets does more damage
to vital organs than binding feet.[38]

   The writers discussed so far, in linking footbinding to the pursuit of arbitrary definitions of beauty, imply that in their eyes it does not actually make
the women more beautiful. Others made this explicit. Lockhart admitted
that the "limping, unsteady gait" produced by footbinding was distressing
for foreigners to behold, in no small part because the women cannot walk
far or quickly without appearing to be in pain.[39] The traveler W. Tyrone
Power blamed the pain of bound feet for the "sickly aspect, drawn features,
and nervous irritability, so frequently to be remarked in the Chinese
women."[40] A British businessman who spent twelve years in China, John
Scarth, liked to make sketches as he traveled. He described country women
as capital subjects, but also wrote that "few things look so disagreeable"
as bound feet of city women, which are "swaddled up in a host of dirty
cloths until they appear larger than they would naturally have been," and
which moreover look as if they had been slept in.[41] A woman traveler in the
1880s, Constance F. Gordon-Cumming, described at some length the women
in a home she visited. She wrote that "However ungraceful in our eyes is the
tottering gait of these ladies when attempting to walk, it is certainly not so

Figure 9.4 Illustration captioned "Ladies being carried by their slaves".
Source: Gray 1878: 1.254.

inelegant as the mode of transport which here is the very acme of refined fine-ladyism," then went on to describe how they are carried on the backs of their large-footed servants.[42]

Seclusion

Authors like Huc and Doolittle who argued for a fashion interpretation of footbinding in the eighteenth and nineteenth centuries were often trying to counter an alternative explanation nearly as well entrenched, the instrumentalist view that footbinding had been designed to keep women in their place.[43] A link between footbinding and the seclusion of women had been posited in the sixteenth century and remained a major theme in the seventeenth and eighteenth centuries. Juan Gonzalez de Mendoza, in his 1586 portrait of China based on Spanish and Portuguese visitors' accounts, had stated that "the lameness of their feet" helps keep women virtuously at home, and that footbinding had been invented by men for that purpose.

> They say that the men hath induced them unto this custom, for to bind their feet so hard, that almost they do loose the form of them, and remain half lame, so that their going is very ill, and with great travail: which is the occasion that they go but little abroad, and few times do rise up from their work that they do; and was invented only for the same intent.[44]

Not long afterward, the eminent Jesuit missionary Matteo Ricci (d. 1610) commented after a brief reference to women's "foot bandages" that "Probably one of their sages hit upon this idea to keep them in the house."[45]

Very much the same interpretation was offered in an English language work first published in 1635, Michael Baudier's *History of the Court and the King of China*. The seclusion of women was treated as one of China's strong points. He pointed out that men have the right to sell their wives but rarely do so because "the women of China are so virtuously educated, that they give their husbands more cause to cherish them than to put them out of their families."[46] The reason they are so virtuous is that they are "perpetually kept in and incessantly employed, to the end that idleness, the nurse of vices, may not soften their minds, and precipitate them into disorder."[47] All this he attributed to a wise king who knew that idle women were a great disaster and ordered that they be kept busy with spinning and needlework. Footbinding he saw as just as useful, and just as much an invention of the rulers:

> Another invention of the Kings of China, who loved the chastity of their women, serves not a little to retrench their ramblings and vain gaddings. They enacted, that the mothers should endeavor to straighten the feet of their daughters in the cradle, to the end that they might not grow, persuading their credulous sex that the beauty of a woman consists in having little feet, and in the effect they so believe it, and so violently squeeze them in their tender age, that they are thereby incommodated, and in a sort lamed, which is yet another reason why they so willingly keep in their houses.[48]

The Spanish Dominican friar, Domingo Fernández Navarrete, who arrived in China in 1659, opposed the elitist and accommodationist policies of the Jesuits, but did not disagree with them on footbinding. To the contrary, he went so far as to propose that footbinding would be something other countries would be well advised to adopt: "The custom of swathing women's feet is very good for keeping females at home. It were no small benefit to them and their menfolk if it were also practiced everywhere else too, not only in China."[49] By the time Du Halde was writing about China in the 1730s, the instrumentalist view was well established. Du Halde noted that most Chinese say they do not know for sure how footbinding arose, but

> The far greater number think it to be a political design, in order to keep the women in a constant dependence: It is very certain that they seldom stir out of their apartment, which is in the most inward part of the house, having no communication with any but the women servants.[50]

By the 1780s, French authors were taking a somewhat more critical approach to customs that kept women at home. The Abbé Grosier, after noting that some say footbinding was a political expedient intended to keep women in a state of dependence, added: "In short, a Chinese woman is condemned almost to perpetual imprisonment in her apartment, and to be visible to none but her husband and a few servants."[51]

The interpretation of footbinding as invented in order to keep women chastely at home was the only one to be vigorously refuted by later writers, who were convinced that it had not been imposed from above and were uncomfortable linking it to virtue. As one writer pointed out, small feet hardly indicated chastity since "the small foot attains its greatest perfection" in the ranks of prostitutes.[52]

Deformity

As admiration for the strict segregation of men and women declined in Europe, footbinding was more and more often called a form of imposed deformity. Authors wrote that footbinding crippled women, made them lame, or deformed their feet. Language of this sort is found already in the writings of the Dutch traveler Nieuhof in the seventeenth century and Ripa and Du Halde in the eighteenth century. By the nineteenth century, undoubtedly reflecting the greater weight given to the question of whether the women of China were subjected, footbinding was regularly referred to with these highly pejorative terms. In the 1830s the reverend Charles Gutzlaff, who still thought footbinding was started in infancy and produced by the use of an iron restraint, remarked that "To an unpractised eye, the feet have more the appearance of malformation than anything else."[53]

It became easier to elaborate on footbinding as a form of crippling with the rise of medicine as a respected science. An 1835 *Chinese Repository* article on footbinding devoted most of its space to the report, published in the *Transactions of the Royal Society of London* in 1829, of a Dr. Branshy Blake Cooper, who had done a dissection of a bound foot from the corpse of a woman found drowned in a river in Canton. Dr. Cooper wrote in the detached language of science, using such statements as

> The upper surface of the foot is very convex; but its convexity is irregular and unnatural, presenting a sudden and prominent projection just anterior to the external malleolus, and above the outer extremity of a deep cleft which traverses the sole of the foot.

Williams, who quoted from Cooper at length, included a picture of the skeleton of a bound foot (see Figure 9.5). Dudgeon, also a physician, not only described how the foot was reshaped but also the effect of this on the leg and on walking, noting, for instance, that among bound-foot women, the calves are underdeveloped, and when they walk the knees and ankles do not bend and the body is never straight.[54]

Many of those who described footbinding as a deformity seem to have been responding viscerally to a sight that repelled them. One reason they

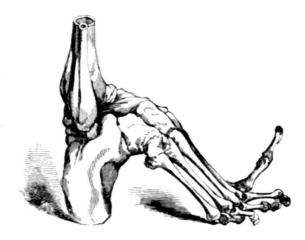

Figure 9.5 Illustration captioned "Appearance of the bones of a foot when compressed".
Source: Williams 1849: 39.

turned to the dispassionate language of physicians to describe footbinding in anatomical terms was to cope with feelings they found too raw for their own comfort.

Perversity

In his diary, Macartney reported that one person suggested to him that footbinding might have arisen from

> oriental jealousy, which had always been ingenious in its contrivances for securing the ladies to their owners; and that certainly a good way of keeping them at home was to make it very troublesome and painful to them to gad abroad.[55]

Once terms like "oriental jealousy" enter the discussion, footbinding begins to move into the realm of sexual perversity. Westerners have a history of attributing sexual depravity to the East.[56] Certainly many of those who wrote about China were fascinated with what was forbidden to them by Christianity, especially concubinage and legal prostitution. When Marco Polo wrote on these topics he sounded more envious than shocked. By the end of the eighteenth century, however, the language of sexual depravity was common in discussions of concubinage. This sort of language occasionally also appeared in discussions of footbinding. For instance, the Italian priest Father Ripa writing in 1720 concluded his strong condemnation of footbinding by declaring "In this particular, indeed, their taste is perverted to such an extraordinary degree, that I know a physician who lived with a woman with whom he had no other intercourse than that of viewing and fondling her feet."[57] Macartney similarly noted that "a reverend apostolic missionary at Pekin assured me that in love affairs the glimpse of a little fairy foot was to a Chinese a most powerful provocative."[58]

In 1869 two medical missionaries in China argued about the implications of the erotic dimensions of footbinding in the pages of the missionary journal, *China Recorder*, one arguing that it made footbinding something missionaries should not mention, the other something that they had to take a stand against. J. Dudgeon, who was affiliated with Peking Hospital, was clearly repulsed by footbinding. He nevertheless thought it was expedient for missionaries to tolerate it rather than insist that Christians unbind their daughters' feet. To strengthen his case, he asserted that footbinding had erotic associations, making it something inappropriate for missionaries to mention. It is because of its eroticism, he said, that

> the small foot is always robed and concealed in pictures, that it is banished from conversation of polite and learned society, that it is rude and immoral to gaze upon it, or seek to examine it, and that having done so, it is made a matter of the confessional in Roman Catholic churches.

Dudgeon went on to refer obliquely to the imputation "of one or two modern French writers" that "some unusual development of certain organs" was "the cause and effect of the practice" but added that he did "not believe that any such results follows from compression of the foot."[59]

The other medical missionary, J. G. Kerr, who wrote from Canton, readily acknowledged the erotic dimensions of footbinding, but declared that they were reason enough for missionaries to take a stand against it. Because the practice originated in lust, it had to be morally wrong and should not be allowed among converts or pupils at Christian schools.[60]

It would be difficult to miss the discomfort nineteenth-century missionaries felt when discussing the erotic side of footbinding. Footbinding had been discussed for so long in Western writings that it was impossible simply to banish the subject, and those who did not see the erotic side of it still found it a potent symbol of women's oppression. Authors who wanted to suggest that Westerners needed to rethink footbinding as an erotic custom found it difficult to put the matter bluntly.

Pain imposed on children

One way to attack footbinding while avoiding its sexual dimensions was to focus on young girls, not grown women. Through the eighteenth century, Western writers did not refer to the pain entailed in the initial binding of a girl's feet. What we might term a child abuse construction of footbinding gradually became more common over the course of the nineteenth century. Barrow, writing at the beginning of the nineteenth century, stressed the

"constant pain and uneasiness that female children must necessarily suffer."[61]
The 1835 *Chinese Repository* article said

> The effects of this process are extremely painful. Children will often tear
> away the bandages in order to gain relief from the torture; but their
> temporary removal, it is said, greatly increases the pain by causing a
> violent revulsion of the blood to the feet.[62]

The American medical missionary Charles Taylor, who spent five years in
China in the 1850s, described the process of footbinding as "exceedingly
painful" and claimed it "produces inflammation and suppuration, resulting
in settled disease and deformity." To make this more vivid he recounted an
incident:

> One day, as Mrs. T. and myself were passing a Chinese dwelling of the
> poorer class, we heard most piteous and imploring screams. On looking
> in at the open door, we saw a mother binding the feet of her little girl,
> who was seated on a high bench. We have seldom seen such a look of
> anguish as marred that fair, young face; and such an expression of cruel
> indifference to the torture of her child as rested on the countenance of
> the mother. We remonstrated and entreated, but in vain.[63]

Slightly less believably, another visitor claimed that "In the early morning
hours the traveler, in moving about a Chinese city, will hear from almost
every house the cries of little girls undergoing their daily torture."[64]

By the time the American missionary Justus Doolittle wrote his *Social Life
of the Chinese* in 1865, as much attention was given to the pain experienced
by girls as to the appearance of the shoes or the effect on the way women
walked. He wrote:

> The operation of bandaging is necessarily very painful. The flesh or skin
> often breaks or cracks in consequence of binding the toes underneath.
> Unless proper care is taken, sores are formed on the foot which it is
> difficult to heal, because it is desirable that the parts should be con-
> stantly and tightly bandaged. If undue haste is endeavored to be made
> by bandaging more tightly than is proper, in order to have the foot
> quickly become small, the pain becomes proportionably greater.[65]

The emphasis on pain and on the victimization of young children undoubtedly
comes from changing European, perhaps especially British, attitudes toward
the unfortunate. The sorts of sentiments that went into the movement to
emancipate slaves, to reform prisons and poor houses, and to temper the
effects of industrialization also made visitors look at Chinese society differently. I suspect that another important element here was the increasing

Figure 9.6 Illustration captioned "Bandaging the feet".
Source: Gray 1878: I.234.

presence of Western women in China. After 1860, with the expansion of missionary activity in the interior, a growing number of missionary wives and female missionaries engaged in "women's work," teaching and proselytizing to Chinese women. Even if they were not yet writing the books that became authoritative, their ideas began to penetrate the larger missionary community.[66]

The first female missionary to write at length on footbinding, Adele Fielde, also included one of the fullest descriptions of the process of binding a girl's feet in her 1887 *Pagoda Shadows*. After describing the first stages of how girls' feet are bound, and the bandages changed each month by soaking and rubbing, she went on to describe in detail how the girls coped with the pain:

> Once a month or oftener, the feet, with the bandages upon them, are put into a bucket of hot water and soaked. Then the bandages are removed, the dead skin is rubbed off, the foot is kneaded more fully into the desired shape, pulverized alum is laid on, and clean bandages quickly applied. If the bandages are long left off, the blood would again circulate in the feet, and the rebinding would be very painful. The pain is least when the feet are so firmly and so constantly bound as to be benumbed by the pressure of the bandages.
>
> It not infrequently happens that the flesh becomes putrescent during the process of binding, and portions slough off from the sole. Sometimes a toe or more drop off. In this case the feet are much smaller than they could else be made, and elegance is secured at the cost of months of suffering. The pain ordinarily continues about a year, then gradually diminishes, till at the end of two years the feet are practically dead and painless.

During this time the victim of fashion sleeps only on her back, lying across the bed, with her feet dangling over the side, so that the edge of the bedstead presses on the nerves behind the knees in such a way as to dull the pain somewhat. There she swings her feet and moans, and even in the coldest weather she cannot wrap herself in a coverlet, because every return of warmth to her limbs increases the aching. The sensation is said to be like that of having the joints punctured with needles.

While the feet are being formed they are useless, and their owner moves about the room to which she is confined, by putting her knees on two stools, so that her feet will not touch the floor, and throwing her weight upon one knee at a time, while she moves the stools alternately forward with her hands.[67]

With the child abuse construct we are moving more toward pity, which of course also assumes a position of superiority as it empathizes with those viewed as victims. It implicitly at least treats Chinese culture not as an undifferentiated set of ideas and practices, to be taken as a whole, but as something more complex, in which men and women, adults and children, can be seen to benefit unequally. Empathizing with the weak and unfortunate within a society is implicitly a criticism of its power structure.

Cultural immobility

In the second half of the nineteenth century, some observers wrote quite lengthy accounts of footbinding that touch on many bases – fashion, class, anatomy, and so on. What they offer in addition is a tone of despair, a lament that although this practice unquestionably should be eliminated, the obstacles to getting people to abandon it are insurmountable, in large part because parents feel their daughters will not be marriageable unless their feet are well bound. Doolittle, in 1865, noted that some Chinese denounced the custom as causing useless suffering to women.[68] Yet "those who admit such to be the real state of the case in regard to the small-footed women, after all, feel obliged to conform, in regard to their own daughters, to the usages of Chinese society," because "families whose girls have small feet marry their sons into families of the same class." Moreover, the poor were not spared this sense of necessity:

Many poor families prefer to struggle along for a precarious living, bringing up their daughters with small feet rather than allow them to grow as large as they would grow, and oblige them to carry burdens and do heavy work, in order to attain a more competent support . . . In the city and suburbs there is a strong tendency to change from the large-footed into the small-footed class. Few or none change from the latter into the former class of society, if living in the city.[69]

The interpretation of footbinding as a deeply embedded custom was in many ways directly opposed to the construction of it as a silly fashion, since fashions are notoriously changeable. Moreover, fashions in the West generally considered silliest – such as men powdering their hair or women binding their waists so tight they could barely breathe – were largely confined to the upper reaches of society, even to court circles. To stress that footbinding was not this sort of custom, many nineteenth-century authors addressed the issue of the incidence of footbinding, pointing out that although there was regional variation, the extent of the practice of footbinding was very widespread. The anonymous author of the 1835 *China Repository* article wrote that the practice was found throughout the empire among the Chinese (but not the Manchus), and that in the largest towns and cities, and in the "most fashionable parts of the country, a majority of the females have their feet compressed," though the rate varied from place to place from 40 or 50 percent up to 70 or 80 percent.[70] In the 1850s the botanist Robert Fortune wrote that

> In the central and eastern provinces of the empire it is almost universal, – the fine ladies who ride in sedan-chairs, and the poorer classes who toil from morning till evening in the fields, are all deformed in the same manner. In the more southern provinces, such as Fokien and Canton, the custom is not so universal; boat-women and field-labourers generally allow their feet to grow to the natural size.[71]

More examples of this line of argument could be given, but perhaps it would suffice to quote one of the most explicit, that written by Adele Fielde.

> The process of binding, the style of shoe worn, and the social condition of the victim, vary considerably in different parts of the empire. The rich bind the feet of their daughters at six or eight years; the poor at thirteen or fourteen.

Yet she stressed that footbinding was not confined to the wealthy:

> It is not a voucher for respectability, for the vilest are often bound-footed. Neither is it a sign of wealth, for in those places where the custom prevails, the poorest follow it. Inferior wives, unless they come as bond-maids into the household, are usually bound-footed women.[72]

Readers of descriptions like these are left to infer that the only way to end footbinding is to bring about a thorough transformation of Chinese culture and society. Unless such deeply entrenched institutions as marriage and class change, there is little hope of getting people to give up binding their daughters' feet.

WHY WAS FOOTBINDING SO DIFFICULT A TOPIC?

Footbinding clearly fascinated Western authorities on China, but progress in understanding the practice was slow. Even reputable authors, with good access to information and a genuine interest in advancing knowledge, repeated old errors such as that footbinding was begun at birth, that only the well-to-do or well-born bound their feet, that Chinese women displayed their small feet in order to attract men, or that men invented footbinding in order to keep women from gadding about.

Gender proprieties were probably the biggest obstacle to more accurate information. So far as I can tell, till the mid-nineteenth century at least, most authors concentrated on consulting other men. They read earlier books written by men, they consulted expatriates living in other parts of the country, and they talked to Chinese men. Virtually none of the male authors admit to talking to Chinese women about the practice, or even asking their wives to talk to Chinese women about it. To some extent, we can interpret this as simply viewing Chinese men as the authorities on China, even on the subject of Chinese women. Yet undoubtedly both Chinese and Western proprieties lie behind this as well. Chinese women were undoubtedly reluctant to talk to foreign men about footbinding – they probably did not readily talk to their fathers or brothers or sons about it either. Some Westerners did find Chinese informants willing to answer their questions, but in many cases these would appear to have been people obligated to talk to them, such as their interpreters, who may have simply told them what he thought they wanted to hear. Others, one suspects, confined their inquiries to foreign residents who had been in China longer than they had.

Looking at unclothed bound feet was of course even more difficult for foreign men. One physician reported that physicians could "by no means" gain a sight of bound feet for examination.[73] The photographer John Thomson said that he had been assured by Chinese men that he would never be able to get a Chinese woman to unbind her feet for him to photograph, and for a long time he was unsuccessful, despite offering financial inducements, until finally, in Amoy, he found an old woman willing to have the young woman in her charge photographed for a handsome fee.[74] The Reverend Ross Houghton, while on a tour of Asia in 1873–1874, claimed that with the help of the preceptress of the mission school for girls in Jiujiang, after a week of skillful diplomacy, "I succeeded in persuading a girl about fifteen years of age to allow me to be present when the gay covering was removed from her feet" and that later, in Shanghai, he got an old woman to remove her bandages for money.[75]

A second obstacle to more accurate information was that sinological expertise was of little use. The most famous sinologists of the nineteenth century have not been cited much here because those most learned in Chinese texts rarely said much about footbinding, and seem, on the whole, to have

Figure 9.7 Illustration of a girl with bound feet, based on a photograph taken by
John Thomson.
Source: Douglas 1882: 127.

preferred to play down footbinding in particular and the oppression of
women in general. For instance, S. Wells Williams (1812–1884) was one of
the most learned of the mid-century missionary authors. In the 1847 preface
to *The Middle Kingdom*, he reported that one of his goals was "to divest the
Chinese people and civilization of that peculiar and almost undefinable impression of ridicule which is so generally given them." Almost every "lineament
of China and her inhabitants," including dress and fashions, social usages,
and even facial features were made objects of laughter by Westerners.
When he got to footbinding, he described it as "more an inconvenient than
a dangerous custom" and argued that it could not cause pain for more than
six weeks since girls with bound feet could be seen playing in the streets.[76]
   Another good example is Herbert Giles (1845–1935), one of the foremost
sinologists of his generation. He was writing about China from the early
1870s, but said very little about women in any of his early works. In his

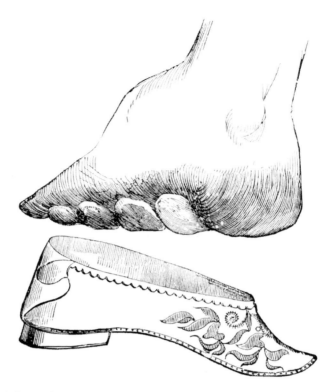

Figure 9.8 Illustration captioned "Chinese Lady's Foot and Slipper".
Source: Houghton 1877: 118.

1902 *China and the Chinese* he makes a point to argue that Westerners have too negative a view of the situation of Chinese women. To him it was important to note that women did not wear veils, could leave the home to pay calls, received educations, got titles and posthumous honors like their husbands. He called footbinding a horrible custom, "which vast numbers of intelligent Chinese would be only too glad to get rid of, if fashion did not stand in the way," but quickly went on to what was to him a much more enjoyable subject, the henpecking of Chinese husbands, the subject of the next several pages.[77]

   In the case of men like Williams and Giles, I suspect that immersion in Chinese books was more of an obstacle to deeper knowledge about footbinding than an aid to it. Footbinding was not a topic Chinese literati would have stressed when tutoring novice foreign scholars, or in any way presented as central to China's moral, philosophical, or cultural values; most tutors probably preferred to plead ignorance if directly questioned about it. To the extent that those who spent years mastering the Chinese literary canon came to identify with the ruling elite, they also tended to downplay footbinding. Sinologists excel where texts are central to the creation and reproduction of a facet of the culture. But no texts were central to the reproduction of footbinding. Mothers did not read how-to manuals before binding their daughters' feet.

Most of us today are relativists on issues of beauty, believing that there are no universal standards. Judged in terms of the advancement of knowledge, however, the relativistic position on footbinding had drawbacks. Writers who wanted to play down anything that made the Chinese seem peculiar rarely probed such issues as how footbinding was performed, or regional or class variation in its practice. To the contrary, they often seemed to truncate what they knew to make forced but comforting comparisons. By contrast, those more comfortable labeling some Chinese practices undesirable or abominable tended to downplay the relativistic fashion construct and lay more stress on perversity, deformity, and pain. Even though those stressing the negative sound offensively arrogant and ethnocentric today, they deserve credit for adding to the store of knowledge by investigating class and regional variations in methods of binding feet, and adding complexity to the analysis by bringing in the perspective of both mothers who saw no choice and daughters who suffered pain.

***

The ways of framing footbinding described in this article are all still with us, though new ones have also been introduced and some old ones turned on their heads. Although the gap is not so large as it once was, Chinese and Western views on footbinding are still rather far apart, though in different ways. The Chinese anti-footbinding activists took up the views of footbinding as arbitrary fashion, as imposed deformity, and as a way to restrain women and keep them docile at home.[78] Women of the generation that abandoned footbinding perceived the process as one of liberation, and this view remains dominant in China.[79] At the same time, Western interpretations of footbinding have gone in other directions. In the 1960s Howard Levy wrote a book on footbinding that drew on the evidence of Ripa, Dudgeon, and others of an erotic dimension to footbinding in a way very different from what they had intended. To Levy, the erotic dimension of footbinding did not make it perverse, but fascinating, an example of human inventiveness in the arts of pleasure, and Levy wrote about the pleasure men took in bound feet with an undertone of envy worthy of Marco Polo.[80] More recently, under the influence of feminism, there have been revisionist attempts to take a more positive view of footbinding, to see what it might have offered women in terms of gaining mastery over their bodies or pride in their beauty.[81] Obviously there is no single correct way to explain footbinding. But there is a history to how we have come to frame it the ways we do.

Notes

1 Women, money, and class: Sima Guang and Song Neo-Confucian views on women

1 That conditions were at their worst in the Qing dynasty was already recognized in the early twentieth century (Lu Hsun 1957: 2.19–20). For more recent studies, see Elvin 1984 and Mann 1987.

2 Chen Dongyuan 1928: 139.

3 Zhu Ruixi 1986: 139. Even Bettine Birge, who tries to put Zhu Xi's views on women into the most positive possible light, states that the Cheng-Zhu school elevated the prohibition against remarriage of widows to a new importance (Birge 1989: 338).

4 Lin Yutang 1939: 165; Levy 1967: 44. Lin cites no sources. Levy cites two sources: Jia Shen 1925: 8b., which in turn cites the oral tradition of the elders of Amoy; and Yao Lingxi 1936: 351, which cites *Lüyun xuan biji*, a source I have not been able to identify by author or century, or locate in any catalog or library.

5 Croll 1980: 14. Cf. the more qualified statements in Gates 1989, esp. 821–23.

6 Yao 1983: 91.

7 Li 1971: 364.

8 Other historians have also noted weaknesses in the charges against Neo-Confucianism. See T'ien Ju-k'ang 1988: 1.

9 On the continuities with regard to family ethics from Han Confucianism to Song Neo-Confucianism, see Kwang-Ching Liu 1990b.

10 For a brief discussion of the evidence on footbinding, see Ebrey 1990b [now see also Ebrey 1993: 37–43].

11 That the context of Cheng Yi's statement has been inadequately understood is made evident by the fact that even the widow of his nephew (Cheng Hao's son) remarried, leaving a child behind. Cheng Yi did not approve the remarriage, but he let her come to see her child and maintained contact with her father and new husband (ECJ *waishu* 11.413).

12 See Ebrey 1991c [reproduced here as Chapter 3].

13 SS 298.9906. Sima Dan's wife may well have been sympathetic. Sima Guang records her friendship with the girl her older brother's wife brought with her as a maid/concubine when she married. This girl had been sold by her stepmother when she was 7 without her father's knowledge. SMCJJ 72.883–84.

14 SSWJL 11.121.

15 LQJ 36.41b. For a case in which the daughter of a magistrate ended up as a maid rather than a concubine, see DXBL 12.90.

16 QSGY 3.35–38 (quote p. 38).

17 OYXQJ 31.217–19.

18 LQJ 39.54b–57a.

19 SSJW 10.184. For slightly different versions of this story, see SSWJL 8.84; SLYY 10.150.
20 SSWJL 8.84.
21 Not all accusations were related to courtesans and concubines. Sun Mian (996–1066) was accused of abducting and raping women under his jurisdiction as an official (SS 288.9689–90; CB 208.5048). Ouyang Xiu was accused of incest with his daughter-in-law (J. Liu 1967: 80–82).
22 CB 153.3715–16; DXBL 4.23–24. Su Shunqin's story was well-known through the Song (e.g. MSYTL 40–41; ZZYL 129.3088–89, 130.3119).
23 MZML 1.1.
24 CB 177.4296–4297.
25 SS 285.9604.
26 SS 285.9605. According to one source, the son planned the murder so that he would have to go into mourning and would not have to take up a provincial post. When the poison administered by the maids failed to kill her, one of them drove a nail into her skull (DDSL 66.2a–b). Zhu Xi told a slightly different version: The son had told his maids that if he were able to go into mourning for his mother, he would arrange good marriages for those who wanted to marry and give money to those who wanted money (ZZYL 130.3119).
27 CB 213.5174.
28 LXABJ 1.4.
29 DDSL 98.4b–5a.
30 CB 211.5121, 213.5173–74, 217.5272–73.
31 CB 219.5325–26.
32 SS 329.10603; SSWJL 12.127.
33 Exactly what sorts of women these are is not clear. Probably Zhou had purchased women who had worked as courtesans or higher-class prostitutes, bringing them into his house as his private harem. At banquets or parties he would presumably have had them serve food, play music, and otherwise entertain guests.
34 LCLZ 4.20. Su Zhe did not consider the official's action admirable as it was based on the chance circumstance that his maid had previously been in Zhou's house. It was, to him, much like charging him with tax evasion instead of murder: the crime for which he was charged happened all the time and very few people were prosecuted for it.
35 SWGWJ 1178–79. The solution was based on the fact that the man's father had once decided to become a monk, and although he had given up his decision almost immediately, the official decided that as a monk he could not have legally taken a wife.
36 CB 212.5143; other versions such as SS 456.13405 say she was sent away while pregnant. XX 6.154 says she was expelled when he was 7 *sui*.
37 SS 456.13405. See also WLCJ 31.174; SWGWJ 3.31; SSWJ 22.643–644.
38 DXBL 10.75; SSWJL 12.148. For a similar story of searching for a birth mother, see MJ 2.29–31. In this case the man waited until his legal mother died to search for his birth mother. When he found her she was the concubine of a rich man, just then marrying out her youngest daughter.
39 HZL *hou lu* 7.174–75.
40 LZYH 1.3.
41 YSHB 510, citing *Huaman lu*.
42 QBBZ 2:160.
43 SMCJJ 23.332. He was also said to disapprove of his wife watching the lantern festival. YSHB 11.514, quoting *Xuanqu lu*.
44 YSHB 5.186–189.
45 SMCJJ 68.840.

46 Judging Sima Guang's originality in this regard is difficult because of the lack of comparable works. Most earlier "Family Instructions" are much shorter than his *Jiafan* and usually concern other subjects besides the family *per se*. The most influential of these was Yan Zhitui's *Yanshi jiaxun*, a book Sima Guang cited quite a few times. On specific points, however, he often took stances different than Yan Zhitui. Sima Guang's thinking also has much in common with the ideas implicit in most collections of exemplary stories, including ones in the dynastic histories, and also with didactic works such as Ban Zhao's *Nüjie*. Sima Guang sprinkles his own observations through his writings on the family frequently enough for me to take it as his own synthesis.

47 On Sima Guang's views on social and political order, see Bol 1992.

48 The way Sima Guang extended these views with regard to the family is made clear in his *Jujia zayi* (SMSSY 4.41–46), in many places in his JF (e.g. 1.463–85), and in his letter to his sons on frugality (SMCJJ 67.839–40).

49 This was indeed the sort of family he came from himself. See Ebrey 1984b: 41–42.

50 JF 8.675–76, based on SuiS 80.1806.

51 Recently Birge (Birge 1989) has stressed Zhu Xi's high respect for competent wives. Mann has similarly pointed to the ways eighteenth-century Confucians "valorized" the role of wife (Mann 1991). It can easily be argued that Sima Guang had similar high regard for what a good wife could accomplish.

52 JF 8.659–60.

53 Cheng Yi expressed rather similar views in his commentary to the *Classic of Changes* [Yijing]. He found implications concerning the correct social roles for men and women in many of the hexagrams. For instance, the hexagram Family had appended to it the judgment that "The female's correct place is in the inside; the male's correct place is on the outside." Cheng Yi explained: "Yang occupies five and resides on the outside; yin occupies two and stays on the inside; thus male and female each attain their correct place. The way of honored and lowly, inner and outer correctly corresponds to the great meaning of Heaven and earth, yin and yang" (ECJ Zhou Yi Cheng shi zhuan 3.884).

54 JF 1.468, 6.591.

55 JF 1.464.

56 SMSSY 4.43.

57 JF 1.467; SMSSY 7.82–83.

58 Zhu Ruixi 1986: 145–48.

59 See his praise for the Liu family in JF 1.479–80.

60 JF 2.488–89.

61 SMSSY 4.33.

62 SMSSY 4.33.

63 SMSSY 3.29.

64 Cf. Ebrey 1984b: 101–120.

65 SMSSY 4.42: cf. Legge 1967: I.458.

66 Cf. Ebrey 1981b. [Now see also Ebrey 1991c, reproduced here as Chapter 3.]

67 JF 8.659–60. Purity would include cleanliness as well as chastity. Sima Guang provided no comparable list for men, but would presumably have included the major Confucian virtues of benevolence, moral duty, loyalty, integrity, trustworthiness, and so on.

68 JF 9.679.

69 JF 3.513–16.

70 SMCJJ 78.968–69.

71 JF 8.662.

72 E.g. JF 8.665–68. For an example among his own relatives, see SMCJJ 79.980–81.

73 E.g. JF 8.665–66, 8.671–72, 8.672–73, 8.674–75, 8.676–77.
74 E.g., a woman killed herself because her husband had killed her elder brother (JF 7.648–79), and another one did so in the case of a father–husband conflict (JF 9.698–99).
75 Perhaps the case that seems the most overdone is one of a widow who cut off her arm after a man touched it out of her sense that she had been compromised by his action (JF 8.676–77).
76 JF 6.599, 6.601–2, 6.602–3.
77 Mann found that Song gazetteers similarly gave considerable attention to brave daughters (Mann 1985, esp. 69–70).
78 SMCJJ 78.967–68.
79 SMCJJ 78.966.
80 SMCJJ 72.883–84.
81 JF 6.594–95. Cf. Swann 1932: 84–85.
82 JF 6.595.
83 The *Biographies of Admirable Women* was written in the Han period by Liu Xiang. See O'Hara 1945. The *Admonitions for Women* by Ban Zhao is one of the few books written in premodern China by a woman author. See Swann 1932.
84 SMSSY 4.45.
85 SMSSY 4.45.
86 For his complaints about the laziness of *shidafu* wives, see SMSSY 10.114.
87 SMSSY 4.43–44.
88 SMSSY passim.
89 JF 3.505.
90 JF 7.655.
91 JF 5.575.
92 JF 7.656–57.
93 JF 3.525–26.
94 JF 7.643.
95 JF 10.713–14.
96 JF 10.714–16.
97 XX 6.191–92, 169.
98 ZZYL 90.2295–96, ZWGWJ 86.13a–b.
99 ZWGWJ 25.12a, 33.21b.
100 E.g. ZZYL 89.2271, 2273; 90.2313, 2314, 2317; ZWGWJ 43.5a–b, 63.19a–20a.
101 ZZYL 7.127.
102 On Zhu Xi's *Family Rituals*, see Ebrey 1991a and 1991b.
103 For instance, the XX 6.164 account of two Dou girls throwing themselves off a cliff to avoid being captured by bandits who might rape them is much closer to JF 6.600–1 than to either JTS 193.5147 or XTS 205.5823–24. As Kelleher notes, Zhu Xi worked with Liu Qingzhi (1130–1195) on the XX, and they also drew on the latter's *Jiezi tonglu* (Kelleher 1989: 221). Her list of sources for the "outer chapters" of the XX (p. 240) underestimates the influence of Sima Guang's writings, since quotations from the dynastic histories and perhaps also those from Wang Tong (584–617) and the *Yanshi jiaxun* often seem to have been taken from Sima Guang rather than directly from the original sources. (This is probably also true of citations to the classics in the inner chapters.)
104 For a good overview of Zhu Xi's views on women, see Birge 1989. Zhu Xi's treatment of women is discussed by Chan Wing-tsit 1989: 548–58.
105 Sima Guang explicitly rejected the argument of advocates of the *zong* that younger brothers living apart from elder brothers could not perform sacrifices. In his view each household should be a political, economic, and ritual unit, with the family head presiding at such rites as weddings. See Ebrey 1984a.

106 See Ebrey 1989 [now see also Ebrey 1991b].
107 XX 5.117.
108 E.g. ZWGWJ 91.14a. Zhu Xi's failure to probe further reconciling women's property and the *zong* may reflect his personal experiences. In all likelihood his wife brought him a handsome dowry. After his father died he, his mother, and sisters turned to a wealthy friend of his father's for support, and this family later gave him one of their daughters to be his wife. See Ebrey 1991b: 113.
109 MZJ 33.31a–b.
110 MZJ 33.34b–37a.
111 See Holmgren 1985: 13:1–27.
112 For an example, see GXZZ xu B.167–68.
113 See Ebrey 1986a, esp. pp. 11–12, 15–18 [reproduced here as Chapter 2].
114 Ebrey 1984b: 286–88.
115 E.g., MTJ 30.26a.
116 JQJ 1.22a.
117 Ebrey 1984b: 148–51.
118 GXZZ *bie* A.244. The remarriage occurred after Wei Liaoweng's death. See also Tang Daijian 1986.
119 QMJ 5.140, 9.353–56, 10.365–66.
120 See the intriguing case made by Holmgren for the importance of the need for the Mongols to change the law concerning dowries after they abandoned the levirate (Holmgren 1986).

2 Concubines in Song China

1 Cai Xianrong 1979; Liu Dehan 1974. *Qie* could also be referred to by literary and colloquial terms; in the Song period these included *houfang, cishi, biqie, shier, zuoyou ren*, and so on.
2 As in any place where polygamy is illegal, some men broke the law. For historical instances of men who took more than one wife, see Niida 1942: 572–76, and Chen Guyuan 1936: 57. I do not think these cases show a common tolerance of polygyny because often a mistake was involved. For instance, a wife could be captured by invaders and the husband subsequently remarry, only to have the wife return; since both women had been married as wives, neither could be demoted to concubine and the man would live in a state of tolerated polygamy. More troublesome are the household records in Dunhuang that list two wives for some men. Either these records are faulty (one wife was already dead, or married to a different man in the family, and so on) or polygamy was tolerated in this area.
3 On imperial consorts, see P. Chung 1981.
4 Goody 1976: 42. On African polygyny, see Clignet 1970.
5 Goody 1976: 47.
6 E.g., Pasternak 1983: 56–58.
7 This estimate is based on a sample of epitaphs for fifty couples, in which about one-fifth explicitly indicated the presence of concubines by mentioning children born of concubines or saying that the wife was not jealous of the concubines or overlooked their minor faults, etc. One-fifth would be a minimum figure since there was no convention requiring the mention in epitaphs of concubines, even when they bore children. On some of the differences in marriage practices that can be attributed to wealth and class position, see R. Watson 1981.
8 See the size of sibling sets in Davis 1986b. For children born of concubines, see Ebrey 1984b. John Chaffee reports that in two lists of Song men who passed the *jinshi* examinations, the men had an average of three brothers. For the *average* family to have four surviving boys (eight surviving children) there must certainly

have been more than one mother in a large share of the cases (Chaffee, personal communication, January 30, 1984).

9 For an example of a modern author writing in this vein (reflecting the traditional anecdotal sources he used), see Y. Lin 1947: esp. pp. 359–68.

10 C. K. Yang 1959: 54–57.

11 Legge 1885: 2.297–98; YLJZ 3.41.

12 YLJZ 29.4b commentary.

13 SMSSY 4.46.

14 Legge 1885:2.52.

15 Legge 1885:2.137.

16 Ebrey 1989.

17 JLYJ 5; see also ZZYL 90.3712, 3470 for Zhu Xi's comments.

18 QYTFSL 77.548.

19 A son had mourning obligations not merely to his mother (see Mann 1987) but also to her parents and siblings. If his legal mother was alive, the son of a concubine mourned these maternal relatives, but there is nothing that explicitly requires or prohibits also mourning a concubine-mother's relatives. (In practice, this often must have been difficult because these relatives were unknown or distant.)

20 YL 30.6a–7a, 33.7a–8a.

21 ZZJL *fulu* 23a.

22 SBYL 11.168.

23 QYTFSL 77.547.

24 SLGJ (yi B.15a–b).

25 ZZLZ 3.25a–b. Another indication of how confusing mourning for a concubine-mother could be is seen in the case of Li Ding. He was accused of unfiliality for not resigning his post to mourn his concubine-mother. Numerous memorials were written arguing different sides of the case (SS 329.10602).

26 QYTFSL 12.175.

27 SHY *yizhi* 10.8b; SS 170.4085.

28 TLSY 3.1–3; SXT 14.1b–3b.

29 TLSY 4.38; SXT 26.18b–19a.

30 TLSY 2.120; SXT 13.15a.

31 E.g., SS 245.8704, 264.9114.

32 LSL 3.6a–b. For other examples of similar actions, see DXBL 12.980; WGJL 11.82; SS 298.9903; LQJ 36.41b; CGL 5.82–83.

33 SXT 22.4a–15a. For more examples, see Ch'ü 1961: 123–27.

34 TLSY 2.121; SXT 13.15b.

35 Ebrey 1984b: 82, 138–39; HZL hou 7.174–75.

36 Ebrey 1984b: 110–12.

37 HCXS 193.11b.

38 See Ebrey 1981b.

39 Cf. QMJ 7.232–33 (old 328–32).

40 SXT 14.3a, YJZ bing 15.491.

41 None of the cases in QMJ disputing posthumous adoption involved a widowed concubine, and Shiga presents evidence from later periods that explicitly indicates that they had no say in such matters (Shiga 1967: 561–62).

42 See the detailed description in DJMHL 5.30–32.

43 Cf. J. Watson 1980; Gronewold 1982.

44 These anecdotes are of several types: amusing stories of famous men that presumably had a core of truth, embellished in the retelling; "strange" events (ghosts, fox-spirits) that were reported as true; accounts of uncanny coincidences or well-deserved divine retribution. In some cases here I cite an anecdote concerning the arrangement a man made to acquire a concubine who turned out not to be

human. Since he had earlier taken her to be human, I see no reason to dismiss these details as unrealistic.

45 MLL 301–02.
46 JXZL 5.
47 CGL 7.110–11.
48 Ebrey 1984b: 288.
49 SSZ 3.6b–7a.
50 E.g., YJZ ding 11.631–32, bu 8.1624–25.
51 LSL 6.16a. On the market in maids and concubines, see also Kusano 1974.
52 Ebrey 1984b: 299–300.
53 On female infanticide in the Song, see Eichhorn 1976 and Kusano 1974: 72–78.
54 McDermott 1984.
55 Wolf and Huang 1980: 272–301.
56 E.g., YJZ zhixu 9.1122–24.
57 Some of these sentiments can be seen in the following anecdote in which an educated man, visiting in the capital, asked his neighbor why he was weeping so sorrowfully:

> The man looked around, hesitated for a long time, then sobbed and sighed: "I wanted to avoid mentioning it to you, but for a certain reason, I owe the government some money; the clerks are pressing me to pay and threatening punishment. I am too poor to pay them, so I discussed the matter with my wife, and we decided to sell our daughter of marriageable age [literally: "pinned"] to a merchant for 400 thousand cash [= 400 strings]. She must leave us soon and we are dejected at losing her."
> Gong said, "It is fortunate that you have not given her to the merchant yet, for I wish to take her. Merchants are inconstant and without principles. She will follow him, moving from place to place, without ever returning. And it is likely that she will be treated like a lowly maid when she loses her looks and his affection has lessened. I am a scholar from Jiangxi; I read books and understand propriety. If I get her, I will treat her like my own daughter. This is not at all like abandoning her to a merchant. Please think it over carefully."
>
> (YJZ bu 3.1566–67)

58 YJZ jia 13.115. See also YJZ bu 22.1754–55 for a case where a broker was called in to formalize an agreement made by a girl's father.
59 YJZ bing 15.491, ding 11.632, bu 3.1566–67, WJQL 11.82, YJZ bu 22.1754–55. Giving some meaning to these prices is not easy. Most of these prices are from the later half of the eleventh century, a period of some inflation. According to someone writing in the period 1208–1224, prices had increased 100 times since 1069, when mortgage rights to one *mu* of land in Suzhou could be had for one string and could produce about 200 cash (one-fifth of a string) in income a year (Quan 1964: 229–300). Thus by about 1200 a *mu* presumably went for 100 strings. Some of the variation in prices, therefore, could reflect inflation, but they do not seem to be fully accounted for by it, since some of the higher prices are for the late eleventh or early twelfth century.
60 Niida 1937: 445–46.
61 QZQQ 11.755.
62 EZXJ 5.56–57.
63 On *dian* of people, see Niida 1937: 370–90.
64 YDZ 57 *xingbu* 19.8b–9a.
65 Comaroff 1980.
66 On divorce of wives, see Tai 1978.

67 E.g., YJZ 999.
68 E.g., YJZ 375–76.
69 YJZ 435–36.
70 YJZ 1620–21.
71 Ebrey 1984b: 298.
72 See YJZ zhiding 4.996 regarding a mother who went to court because her daughter, contracted out at age 5 for seven years to a house of prostitution, had not been returned after nine years.
73 Elvin 1973: 69–83, 253–67; McDermott 1981.
74 J. Watson 1980.
75 For examples, see Kusano 1974.
76 YLJZ 21.10b.
77 E.g., DXBL 12.90.
78 E.g., LSL 4.8a–b.
79 TSJ 16.177.
80 E.g., WJQL 11.82; YJZ 22.
81 YSJ 22.433.
82 E.g., YJZ jia 17.148–50, bu 10.1641.
83 Ebrey 1984b: 287–88.
84 YJZ zhiding 8.1029–30.
85 See YJZ bu 17.1706–07.
86 For examples, see Ebrey 1984c [reproduced here as Chapter 4].
87 SS 312.10245.
88 HCXS 193.11a.
89 AYJ 46.11a–12b.
90 TJJ 8.23b.
91 GXZZ *bieji* 1.249–52.
92 SS 456.13405.
93 MJ 29–30.
94 GXZZ *bieji* 2.272–74.
95 E.g., YJZ yi 19.347, zhiding 2.978–79, sanji 6.1346, bu 22.1753–54.
96 SSHY 6.59a.
97 YJZ sanbu 1807; see also MZML 3.28–29.
98 In a legal case recorded in the Song history a man wrote a will dividing his property in three, one part each for his two sons and one for his concubine. When the sons took this to court, saying concubines had no property rights, the judge pointed out that sons had an obligation to follow their father's wishes. As a compromise they should allow her the use of the property if she stayed on without remarrying; on her death, however, the property would become theirs (SS 412.12381–82).
99 LZYH 2–3; see also LXABJ 6.55 for a comparable example.
100 Topley 1975: 77; Lang 1946: 221; Kulp 1925: 165.
101 Cf. Ebrey 1981a: 236.
102 "A Slave-Mother" in Lau, Hsia, and Lee 1981.
103 Shiga 1967: 554; Uchida 1970: 190.
104 H. Liu 1959b: 90.
105 H. Liu 1959b: 83.
106 Hsu 1971: 256.
107 Dai Yanhui 1966: 243.
108 Shiga 1967: 555–56.
109 See Handlin 1975: 25–29.
110 E.g., Ropp 1976.
111 Ebrey 1981b; Jia 1979.
112 See Mann 1987 and Elvin 1984.

3 Shifts in marriage finance from the sixth to the thirteenth century

1 YLMC 3.98.
2 Steele 1917: 1, 18–23.
3 Cf. Legge 1885: 1:78.
4 TLSY 13.119.
5 See Yang Shuda 1933: 17–19; Dull 1978: 45–48.
6 WX 40.879–81; cf. Johnson 1977b: 9–11.
7 YSJX 1.64; cf. Teng 1968: 20.
8 Comaroff 1980: 40–41.
9 Yan Zhitui had spent his youth in the south but was taken to the north in 554; in his *Family Instructions* he frequently mentioned differences in the customs of north and south. That he mentioned no such difference in regard to bargaining about betrothal gifts may mean this custom was common in both areas.
10 SuiS 76.1733.
11 BQS 42.564.
12 BQS 43.573.
13 See Johnson 1977b: 33–43.
14 SuiS 9.179.
15 ZS 1.11.
16 ZGZY 7.226.
17 ZGZY 7.227.
18 These were specified lines of the Boling and Qinghe Cui, the Zhaojun and Longxi Li, the Fanyang Lu, the Yingyang Zheng, and the Taiyuan Wang. Each family was defined by specifying its focal ancestor, generally two or three centuries earlier, and included several hundred geographically scattered households.
19 THY 83.1528–29.
20 Twitchett 1973; Johnson 1977b; Ebrey 1978.
21 Ebrey 1978: 94–96.
22 Johnson 1977b: 59–60; Ebrey 1978: 94–100.
23 TYL 4.140.
24 Ebrey 1978: 95, 183, 184.
25 XTS 172.5206.
26 JWDS 93.1230. There are also indications that in the Tang betrothal gifts could be substantial even when both families had eminent pedigrees. In a short story by Jiang Fang (early ninth century), a Longxi Li who had recently passed the *jinshi* examination found that his mother had engaged him to a cousin, a Lu of a top-rank family (*jiazu*). The Lu family expected a betrothal gift of one million cash, even though the groom's family was a relative and social equal. As his family was not rich, Li had to borrow from friends and relatives to collect it all (TPGJ 487:4008). If indeed this sum would be returned as dowry, then Li was collecting money for his own wife and children, and the bride's family, by insisting on the sum, was stipulating the money that was to be earmarked for their daughter's conjugal unit.
27 QTW 504.9b.
28 QTW 315.7a.
29 See Chen Guyuan 1936; Ch'ü 1961; Holmgren 1985; Lü Chengzhi 1935; Ma Zhisu 1981; and Tao Xisheng 1966.
30 Cf. Fang Jianxin 1986.
31 CB 14.305.
32 SWJ 108.1439.
33 SMSSY 3.33.
34 Ebrey 1984b: 266.
35 SWJ 61.852–53.

36 PZKT 1.16.
37 SS 317.10338–39. In fact, when his first wife died, Feng Jing married another of Fu Bi's daughters (SuiS 6.90). Feng Jing may even have lived with Fu Bi, as Shao Bowen (SSWJL 9.94) says Fu's two daughters and their husbands and children all lived in his house.
38 BSXJ 13.4a; 13b–14a.
39 Ebrey 1984b: 223.
40 The contrast between these two approaches is reminiscent of differences between England and continental Europe in early modern times as described by Macfarlane (1986: 251–62). In Europe marriages were much more strictly confined to status equals. In England, there was a more flexible process of negotiation in which yeomen's daughters might marry younger sons of gentry, with wealth as much a factor in decisions as "blood."
41 Some forms for Tang engagement letters (*hunshu*) survive in Dunhuang. See Ebrey 1985.
42 MLL 20.304.
43 Such engagement letters are often found in Song literati's collected works (e.g., CLJ 18.247; GKJ 68.916–19; LDLWJ 2.38–40; PZWJ 64.8b–15b).
44 QZQQ 489–90; SLGJ 41 (yi B.4b); XBHL 1; HMDQ *jia* 5.2a–4b.
45 HMDQ i 18.6b. A distinction between land accompanying a bride in marriage and trousseau items was also made by Huang Gan (1152–1221), who argued that land became the property of the husband's family, while a widow could take her trousseau with her on remarriage (MZJ 33.31a–b). Other writers, however, seem to have been quite willing to lump together land and hairpins.
46 SDRJ 8.86–87. I have not seen the term *diyin* elsewhere. Perhaps the 11,000 is money or goods that will remain under the control of the wife and the 5,000 money or goods that will go to the husband or to his larger family. The Song imperial family similarly seems to have divided marriage payments into two categories, though the terms used are not the same (SS 115.2732).
47 Ebrey 1986a: 6 [reproduced here as Chapter 2].
48 This legal protection did not last into the Qing period and thus contrasts with the situation described in Ocko 1991. Some of the forces leading toward weakening of women's property rights after the Song are discussed at the end of this chapter.
49 SXT 12.12b.
50 QMJ 8.290–91; HCXS 193.7a,14a.
51 This change had already taken place by the time the *Song xing tong* was issued in 963. See SXT 12.14a–b.
52 E.g., QMJ 8.280–82.
53 QMJ 8.266–67; HCXS 193.11a. On all of these revisions, see Burns 1973: 259–81.
54 QMJ 7.215.
55 QMJ 8.280–82.
56 HCXS 193.10a–17b.
57 E.g., QMJ 5.141–42, 7:230–32, 238–39.
58 This generalization is based on reading forty-two epitaphs by nine authors in QTW, an exercise that did not uncover any references to their dowries.
59 This is based on a study of 161 Song epitaphs for women, of which twenty-three (about 15 percent) referred to their dowries.
60 GSJ 53.646.
61 NJJYG 22.459.
62 ZWGWJ 91.14a.
63 QZQQ 12.254–55.
64 YSJ14.263.

65 LJJ 28.14a.
66 I do not have space here to analyze the legal status of married women's control over their dowry. Suffice it to say that many Confucians – particularly those I have identified as holding a "descent line" (*zong*) orientation (Ebrey 1984a) – seem to have opposed women's treating their dowries as their private property, though their arguments reveal that such an attitude was common. [Now see also Ebrey 1993: 107–09.]
67 MTJ 34.25a–b.
68 Ebrey 1984b: 266.
69 Twitchett 1960: 9.
70 LDLWJ 10.243.
71 SHY *shihuo* 60.1a–b. One story even suggests that the bride's dowry should correspond to her husband's family property, not to the betrothal gifts he sent. In "The Honest Clerk," an official confides to a matchmaker: "My family has property worth 100,000 strings of cash. For a mate I need someone who will bring a dowry of 100,000 strings" (JBTSXS 13.44; cf. Yang and Yang 1957: 29). This story is set in the Song, but its exact date is unknown and may be early Ming.
72 E.g., SHY *xingfa* 2.154–55.
73 JYYL 117.1889.
74 ECJ *wenji* 4.504.
75 SS 344.10927.
76 ZWGWJ 100.4a–5b.
77 JLB 2.52.
78 YJZ *sanbu bu* 3 1807.
79 YJZ *bu* 3.1574–75.
80 A few other items of evidence are worth mentioning. Bai Juyi (772–846) wrote some model legal decisions for marriage disputes. Several make mention of the return of betrothal gifts when an engagement was broken (e.g., QTW 672.14b; 673.1b–2a, 18b–19a), but none refers to return of dowry or disputes over dowry, even in cases of divorce (e.g., QTW 672.17a; 673.6a–b, 11a–b). A Tang guide to marriage ceremonies preserved in Dunhuang gives elaborate details for the ceremony of delivering the betrothal gifts, but no ceremony is outlined for delivering the dowry (Zhao Shouyan 1963: 185–86). Yet in Song times delivering the dowry was seen as an occasion for colorful display (SMSSY 3.33). Moreover, three studies of marriage in the Tang (Zhang Xiurong 1976; Wong 1979; and Niu Zhiping 1987) uncovered no evidence that provision of dowry was a major expense for girls' families.
81 Goody 1973; 1976.
82 See also McCreery 1976 and C. Chen 1985.
83 Freedman 1979: 258; see also Ahern 1974 and R. Watson 1981.
84 Goody 1976: 99–114.
85 R. Watson 1981; Gallin and Gallin 1985.
86 Mauss 1925.
87 Harrell and Dickey 1985.
88 Harrell and Dickey 1985.
89 Herlihy 1985: 14–23; see also Saller 1984 and Dixon 1985 on the period to AD 200.
90 Hughes 1978: 265–69, 272–73.
91 Hughes 1978: 276, 288.
92 Hughes 1978: 288.
93 Hughes 1978: 287–88.
94 Goody 1983: 257–59.
95 Cohen 1976: 164–91; R. Watson 1984; C. Chen 1985.

96 There recently has been considerable debate on how "open" the Song elite was (Hartwell 1982; Chaffee 1985; Lee 1985; Davis 1986; Hymes 1986b). My own understanding of the situation is shaped especially by Chaffee's statistics on the rapid growth in the educated class (as measured by participation in the examination system); by Hymes's demonstration (from a study of one prefecture) that those who entered the national elite were usually already members of the local elite, and his evidence that the local elite of this particular prefecture was almost entirely new in the Song, having virtually no descent ties to Tang officials; and by Davis's demonstration of how a relatively minor family, once it gained prominence in the national government, could smooth the way for dozens of descendants. See also Ebrey 1988.

97 See Chaffee 1985: 101–05; Umehara 1985: 423–500; Zhang Bangwei 1986.

98 CB 132.3124–26.

99 SHY *xuanju* 16.13a–b.

100 Niida 1942: 287–302 and Zhang Bangwei 1986.

101 CLSXS *shiwen* 251; see also Matsui 1968.

102 Hartwell 1982: 423.

103 Hymes 1986b.

104 QMJ 5.140; MZJ 33.31a–b, 33.34b–37a; Ebrey 1984b: 101–20.

105 Song writers did not necessarily indicate whether someone of nonofficial background was of merchant background because merchants did not share the esteem of officials or educated landlords. But some references to marriages between families otherwise quite unequal raise one's suspicions. For instance, the epitaph for a woman, née Chen, whose father and grandfather had not been officials remarks that her father was too fond of her to marry her to someone in his own town, so he moved to the capital to choose a husband for her (WLCJ 99.629–30). The one he chose was Cheng Lin (988–1056), whose father, brothers, uncles, great-uncles, and so on had all been officials (OYXQJ 21.151–54). One can well imagine that the Chens were merchants and offered a handsome dowry to facilitate this marriage into an official family.

106 For instance, Zhao Li, a rich magistrate, in about 1030 met a young man who had passed the examinations three years earlier at age seventeen. This man's family seems to have been undistinguished: it had moved to its current location about a century earlier during the Five Dynasties and none of his three direct ancestors had been officials. Zhao Li gave him his daughter as well as a handsome dowry (GSJ 53.64b; PCJ 37.489).

107 SMSSY 3.29.

108 No Song source I know makes this argument in full, but there are anecdotes of people thinking along these lines. For instance, the epitaph for a woman from the Li family in Puyang descended from the aristocratic Zhaojun Li family of the Tang described her natal family as one that had produced officials for generations and had accumulated a great fortune. While she and her sisters were young, their dowries were prepared and set aside. When the woman in question reached marriageable age, the estate had declined somewhat because her brother Li Di (971–1047) had repeatedly failed the *jinshi* examination. At this point the girl emptied out her dowry chests to give everything to her brother. The brother accepted the property, then out of a sense of obligation to her secretly selected "a scholar of integrity" to be her husband, presumably because she could no longer marry someone rich. Li Di made a good choice, however, for his sister's husband also passed the examination the same year he did (HNXS 4.3b–4a). In this case, then, property set aside for dowry was diverted to educational expenses, but the great success of the brother in his career made this in retrospect a wise choice and one that they could plausibly claim did not hurt the sister.

109 Ebrey 1981b: 124.
110 Ebrey 1984b: 224.
111 The lingering interests of a natal family in the disposition of dowry can be seen in legal cases in which the woman died without heirs. A woman's family was explicitly excluded as heirs to her dowry in the Song code (SXT 12.12b). If an heir was posthumously set up for the woman and her husband, he would be the appropriate recipient of the dowry, but the wife's family could object if the husband's family tried to keep the dowry without establishing an heir. In a case recorded in *Qingming ji*, a woman, née Chen, had brought a dowry of land worth 120 *zhong* when she married into the Yu family. She and her husband both died without children. Her husband's father, an official, did not want to set up an heir (apparently wanting to keep all the property for a young son he had had by a concubine). Chen's father, also an official, sued, and Yu was forced to select an heir who would inherit the dowry fields and continue the sacrifices for the couple (QMJ 8.248–49). There are also several other cases in which the existence of dowry property underlies the continuing involvement of a woman's natal family in the affairs of her husband's family (e.g., QMJ 6.191–92).
112 Ebrey 1986a [reproduced here as Chapter 2] and R. Watson 1991.
113 Goody 1976.
114 Ebrey 1986b [reproduced here as Chapter 5]
115 Ebrey 1984a; 1986b [the latter reproduced here as Chapter 5].
116 YDZ *hubu, hunyin* 816–17; Tai 1978: 105.
117 Holmgren 1986.

4 The women in Liu Kezhuang's family

1 M. Wolf 1972.
2 For example, Macfarlane 1970; Stone 1977.
3 Sung 1981.
4 Unless otherwise indicated, all references in this article are to HCXS, by Liu Kezhuang.
5 Zhang Yan 1934–1935; Sun Kekuan 1968.
6 On his poetry, see Yoshikawa 1967: 175–81.
7 See HCCJZ for an annotated edition of Kezhuang's songs, which identifies many of the people mentioned in them; see also S. Lin 1978 on the general cultural life of this period.
8 Something of the importance of this correspondence can be seen in a poem (5.16b–17a) in which Liu Kezhuang refers to his joy in receiving a two-line letter from his mother that reported on family finances and asked when he was going to become a successful official.
9 Besides referring to his mother in memorials to the throne requesting permission to resign or refuse posts (Zhang Yan 1934–1935: 14–16), Kezhuang saved two congratulatory letters written for his mother's 77th and 78th birthdays (121.la–b) and a song for her long life written to match a friend's when she was in her mid-eighties (HCCJZ 83–84).
10 153.la–3a, 138.11a–b, 1 lb–12a, 13a, 135.11a–b, 13a–b.
11 148.16a–17b,135.13b,136.5b–7b, 21.9b; HCCJZ 13.
12 See Carlitz 1984.
13 YSJ 16.301–06.
14 PYBS 1.5a–13b.
15 YSJ 20.388–91.
16 151.6b; YSJ 16.305.
17 153.1b.

18 153.1a–b.
19 YSJ 18.351.
20 137.16b.
21 153.1b–2a, 157.3a–b.
22 100.5a–b.
23 157.2b.
24 158.11a.
25 148.16a.
26 163.2a.
27 157.3a.
28 151.7a.
29 153.1b.
30 148.17a.
31 161.l0a.
32 158.11a–12a.
33 160.2b–3a.
34 160.4a–b.
35 153.1b.
36 148.16a–b.
37 Kezhuang's protestations of poverty are, of course, relative to his later prosperity. One sign of his standard of living in his forties and fifties is his account of how he bought neighboring property near his house in order to construct a pond and build a study by its edge. Several years were needed to acquire all of the property. Then in 1236, the purchases completed, he employed 300 workers to dig the pond (100.6a–b).
38 160.4a.
39 160.8b–9a.
40 148.16a.
41 148.16b–17b.
42 148.17b.
43 160.10a.
44 161.l0a–b.
45 135.13a–b.
46 163.2a–8b.
47 153.2b.
48 HCCJZ 64–65.
49 151.4a.
50 151.4b.
51 153.6b.
52 158.11b.
53 153.6a.
54 157.3a–b.
55 153.3a.
56 76.3a–5a.
57 Zhang Yan 1934–1935: 16.
58 153.2a.
59 160.3b.
60 194.17b.
61 165.16b.
62 158.11b–12a.
63 156.5a.
64 156.13b–14a.
65 158.12a.
66 159.4a.

67 Zhang Yan 1934–1935: 25–26.
68 "Asking the Names" (*wenming*) and "Presenting the Gifts" (*nacai*) were two of the six rites in the classical marriage procedure. In Song times they had been collapsed into a single betrothal ceremony. The principle act involved was the exchange of cards that listed the names and offices of the father, grandfather, great-grandfather, and mother of the intended spouse, his or her birthdate, and on the girl's card, the dowry she would bring. See SLGJ 41 (yi B.4a–b).
69 Fu is Fuzhou, where Zhao held office, and Pu is Putian, Liu Kezhuang's home town.
70 140.10b–11a.
71 140.11b, 165.17a.
72 Ebrey 1981b: 125–27. Kezhuang's sister's daughter, a Miss Fang, married a Putian Liu referred to as the son of "*shuangbu*," an official title Kezhuang used to refer to one of his cousins with whom he often wrote poetry (152.1a–b; HCCJZ 121–22). If indeed this was the same person, the couple would have been second or third cousins.
73 This is a term for an engagement arranged by two men whose wives are both pregnant, conditional on one bearing a boy and the other a girl.
74 This would have to be her second marriage. In her father's epitaph (1246) she is said to have married Ting Nanyu (153.6b). He died in 1254 at age 24 *sui* with one son and two adopted joint heirs (156.13b–14b).
75 158.10b–12a.
76 159.4a–b.

5 The early stages in the development of descent group organization

1   Twitchett 1959: 97.
2   For exceptions, see Pasternak 1969 and R. Watson 1982.
3   For objections to this view, see Ebrey 1983 and Sangren 1984.
4   Niida 1942: 103–235; Shimizu 1949; Makino 1939, 1949.
5   Hartwell 1982 and McDermott 1984.
6   See Ebrey 1984a.
7   [In the essay, I follow the definitions for agnate, descent group, lineage, and so on given in Ebrey and Watson 1986: 4–9.]
8   Dull 1978: 29–30.
9   Ch'ü 1972: 18–20.
10 Ebrey 1986c; for later periods see Johnson 1977b: 114–15.
11 E.g. HHS 26.920, 31.1093, 62.2049.
12 Ebrey 1986c. What to call these groups still remains a problem. Elsewhere (Ebrey 1986c) I have called them "clans," using Fried's (instead of J. Watson's 1982a: 610–12) definition of "clan." Fried sees clans as inclusive groups organized for collective security, which therefore easily absorb marginal members ("stipulated descent"), in contrast to the exclusive practices of lineages (1970: 20–33). Very little is known about the internal organization or membership of the groups the historians saw as troublesome sets of local agnates. However, they cannot be called "descent groups" as the term is defined in Ebrey and Watson 1986: 5, since there is no evidence that they joined for ancestral rituals or insisted on demonstrated descent linkages. All that is clear is that they could often dominate a community.
13 Ebrey 1978: 55–58, Johnson 1977a: 18; Tang Zhangru 1959.
14 E.g. WS 57.5b.
15 Yang Shuda 1933: 82–299.
16 SMYL 74 or Ebrey 1974: 187.
17 Ebrey 1980: 336–37.

18 E.g., SMYL 68, 74; BS 33.33; BQS 46.6a.

19 Ebrey 1978: 91–93; D. Johnson 1977a; Twitchett 1973: 52–53.

20 D. Johnson 1977b; Ebrey 1978.

21 D. Johnson 1977b: 29–30.

22 Ebrey 1978: 55–61, 126 nn. 25 and 26, 146 n. 20.

23 D. Johnson 1977b: 33–55, 98–107.

24 All of these assumptions and practices can be found referred to in the *Precepts for Social Life* of Yuan Cai (ca. 1140–ca.1195) (Ebrey 1984b). For an example of a large local group of agnates in the early Song, see Matsui 1968.

25 Hartwell 1982: 406–13.

26 Uchida 1950: 258; Hu 1948: 34–35; Hazelton 1986.

27 Shang Binghe 1941: 440–43.

28 DZJ 53.720.

29 TD 52.1451.

30 KYL 78.6a–7a.

31 According to Tang government regulations, officials of rank five or higher were allowed three altars (*miao*), one each for their deceased father, grandfather, and great-grandfather. The very highest officials could have four altars, and if they had noble titles they could also make offerings to the first ancestor to receive the title. Lower officials and commoners, not allowed altars, were to make offerings in their living quarters (TD 48.1344).

32 QTW 573.3a–6b.

33 E.g. DHBZ 40.72–75.

34 SSGJ 15.155.

35 QCSSJ 14b–15a.

36 SSZ 40.5a.

37 DJMHL 8.218, 9.225; MLL 4.24, 6.45; SSGJ 37.404–05; Gernet 1970: 191–95.

38 SSZ 40.2a, 9a.

39 ECJ yishu 1:6, 18:240.

40 XLDQS 21:29a–306.

41 ZWGWJ 30.29a–30a; XLDQS 19.9b, 21.20a.

42 Qingming or Cold Food is mentioned only a half-dozen times in the Buddhist Canon (at least according to the meticulous forty-odd volume index, *Taisho shinshu daizokyo sakuhin*). Moreover, the only actual discussion of the festival in the Canon concerns whether Buddhist monks should participate in this non-Buddhist custom (*su*). The answer offered was that it would be acceptable to visit the graves of parents but not to join in any partying with relatives (DZJ 54:309).

43 Ch'en 1973: 50–55, 24–25, 139–40.

44 Chikusa 1956.

45 From surviving sources it is not clear whether people held one ceremony for all the ancestors buried in a graveyard, or separate ones for each ancestor. The general rule was that people should make offerings only to their own ancestors. This practice would favor dividing up after a rite for the first ancestor, but some references (such as the 732 edict above and Huang Gan's discussions below) seem to imply one ceremony for all the ancestors by all the descendants.

46 WGJL 160a.

47 ZSZJ 2.29.

48 Grave geomancy has not been fully studied for the Song but it did exist. A Song text on "Combatting Delusions" discussed it, particularly criticizing the way it led to delay in burials (JJBB 2). Hong Mai's *Yijian zhi* also includes some references to geomancers (*fengshui jia*) (e.g. YJZ *sanren* 1.1475). Maurice Freedman discussed the tensions between geomantic burial practices and lineage solidarity in modern times in 1966: 118–43. [See also Ebrey 1997.]

49 AYJ 2.12b–13a.

50 AYJ 46.11a–21a.
51 AYJ 46.20a–33b. Here Han Qi admitted consulting a burial specialist to select the spot within the graveyard for this tomb, AYJ 47.33a.
52 AYJ 46.3a–b, 22.4a.
53 CLJ 27:396. Chen's father is quoted as saying, "My great-great-grandfather's tomb is still extant, but my great-grandfather was a youngest son, so I do not dare *zu* it [treat it as an ancestor?]. Neither my great-grandfather's nor my grandfather's tombs survive, so I am unable to *zu* them" (CLJ 27.396). The implication seems to be that only the primary heirs should *zu* a grave. This would fit in with the *zong* ideology of differentiated descent lines, but I have found no other reference to its applicability to tombs.
54 CLJ 27.396. In strict *zhaomu* order, the odd-numbered generations would be on one side and the even-numbered ones on the other, both sides arranged in order of age, along the pattern specified in the classics for an ancestral shrine. Sometimes, however, the term *zhaomu* order is loosely used to mean in order by generation, and that may be what was meant here.
55 CLJ 22.347.
56 CLJ 22.347.
57 MZJ 33.14a.
58 On the "forbidden area" of graves, eighteen paces long, see QMJ 9.322–24.
59 MZJ 28.31b–34b.
60 MZJ 34.13b–14a.
61 JJBYSL *yi* 4.72a–77b.
62 De Groot 1892–1910: III. 832–34; Gamble 1963: 261–62. For some Yuan cases of people following it, see SXSWJ 30.542–43, 34.606.
63 R. Davis 1986b; Hazelton 1986.
64 For criticisms of this approach, see Sangren 1984 and R. Watson 1985.
65 E.g. M. Yang 1945: 134–42.
66 Cf. J. Watson 1982a: 606–07.
67 Cf. Ebrey 1984b: 92–96.
68 See Satake 1973 for an attempt to explore the economic organization of some of these families. See also Cohen 1976 for a discussion of the economic conditions that could lead to delaying division of a family for a few decades.
69 SS 456.13390.
70 SS 456.13396.
71 SS 456:13390–400.
72 Niida 1937: 550–53.
73 Large communal families were not entirely restricted to commoners. The *Song History* cites the case of a family in Hong prefecture (Jiangxi) with several hundred members. It built a school, collecting 10,000 books and inviting teachers from afar. In 985 it was honored with the banner (SS 456.13390). Another case was of a family in Jiang prefecture (Jiangxi) that was descended from Tang officials. At the beginning of the Song it had seven hundred people, who are said to have met for every meal. The family was excused from labor service by the government and given grants of grain to feed its members, now reaching one thousand. It also ran a school and several of the family managers were made officials (SS 456.13391–92; see also Satake 1973).
74 SS 456.13403.
75 SMSSY 4.41–45; SYXA 57.118–19.
76 JXBL 1–4.
77 See Y. Xu 1980: 33–50; see also the example described in Dennerline 1986.
78 Dardess 1974; Langlois 1981.
79 Morita 1979 restricts his discussion of Song genealogies to the nineteen prefaces found in collected works of Song literati, arguing that ones preserved in later

genealogies are often forged. While ones attributed to famous scholars (and not found in their collected works) may often be later forgeries, that does not mean that all prefaces labeled "Song" are unreliable. Frequently the circumstantial evidence in the genealogies to support the date and authorship of a preface is convincing. In the case of the two prefaces quoted here, the authors are members of the family and their existence is confirmed by the highly detailed *Xin'an mingzu zhi* (XAMZZ 2.89b–90a), which also records the Wangs' earlier status as a communal family. Moreover, the nature of the Song data in the genealogy makes it likely that a table was compiled at the date listed. The first preface is also quoted in later prefaces, even in ones in other descent groups' genealogies.

80 WSZP 1211 preface.
81 WSZP old preface.
82 The Huizhou descent group described in Hazelton 1986 already had some organization in the late Song.
83 Dardess 1974: 33–44.
84 SS 456.13400.
85 GJZ 13.21b.
86 YYYML 5.47–48.
87 Twitchett 1959. The rules Fan Zhongyan established refer constantly to the "various *fang*," here apparently meaning households (*fang* means "room" and refers to collateral divisions within a kinship unit, from nuclear families in a household to branches of a lineage) (FWZGWJ 8.97). The meaning of *fang* in these rules can be seen from the 1051 genealogy. According to the preface Fan Zhongyan wrote to the genealogy, since the time his great-great-grandfather Fan Sui had migrated south with the fall of the Tang, knowledge of their ancestry had become confused. Sui had six sons, but they had scattered to the four directions. The old genealogy had been lost, so Fan had to get his relatives to look among their old family papers to find enough information to reconstruct a genealogy, which he then called a "continued genealogy" (*Xu jia pu*). When the work was done, Fan Zhongyan was able to trace his own ancestry back for four generations, plus detail the currently existing divisions among the younger generation (Makino 1949: 121, FWZGWJ 6.86). Later recensions of the genealogy report that since the Song there had been sixteen *fang* and list the heads of each. These heads were all descendants of Fan Sui, four generations back, and thus during Fan Zhongyan's lifetime all but the youngest were within Fan Zhongyan's mourning circle and the "small *zong*" of his great-great-grandfather. Some were of Fan Zhongyan's generation (brother, first cousin, second cousin), and some of up to three generations younger (great-grandson of a third cousin) (Makino 1949: 123–24). (These *fang* headed by men two or three generations below Fan Zhongyan were probably not in existence in 1049 or 1051 but created later in the Song.)
88 JYJ 13.125–32.
89 JYJ 13.126, 132–34.
90 OYXQJ 21.510–23.
91 Kobayashi 1980.
92 ECJ yishu 6.85.
93 ZZJ 4.258.
94 ZZJ 4:258–59.
95 ECJ yishu 1.7, 15.150, 18.242.
96 ECJ yishu 18.240.
97 ZWGWJ 63.19a–20a; XLDQS 21.25a.
98 E.g LDLWJ 4.67, 10.241–50.
99 Recently some questions have been raised about the significance of the new ideas of the eleventh century – especially the idea of the charitable estate, the

sanctioning of rites to early ancestors, and the renewed interest in writing genealogies. First, J. L. Watson, commenting in part on the notion that the invention of the charitable estate by highly educated men could lead to its adoption by commoners, wrote that "it is difficult for many anthropologists, given their frog in the well view of Chinese society, to accept that lineages and related social forms . . . emerged as a consequence of an ideological transformation among the national elite" (1982a: 618). He also proposed that, from his perspective, the ideological shift from the Tang to the Song seemed to be a shift from alliance to descent as a major organizing principle of society (p. 617). Denis Twitchett responded to this formulation by saying that there really was no new ideology, only a new attitude toward existing ideology that had always stressed descent, and he cautioned against concentrating too much on terms that had only imprecise meanings (1982). David Johnson (1983) came to Watson's defense and argued that words were not used as imprecisely as Twitchett had said, and that written words influence behavior as much as concrete interests and political pressures do (p. 364). Robert Hymes (1986a) argues against opposing alliance and descent, showing that there was no turning away from concern with marriage alliance on the part of the Song elite, even if their interest in organizing along lines of descent grew stronger. Here I have argued that the ideas of Neo-Confucian writers reflected changes in society as much as they helped promote them. That is, grave rituals and associated ideas about ancestors led to an increased group consciousness among local agnates and this "family spirit" attracted intellectuals. Their writings never made anyone start a lineage, but they helped gloss what was going on with a classical vocabulary, something important to the well-educated. I agree that there was no shift from alliance (never provided with much theoretical underpinning) to descent, nor even much of a tension between these principles. But I do see, as I argue elsewhere (Ebrey 1984a), a conceptual tension between the strain of thought centered on the *jia*, the family as a property-owning group, and the *zong* principles of "pure kinship," elaborated by Cheng-Zhu philosophers. In the latter, genealogical linkage greatly outweighed ties based on common interests in property. Generally speaking, glorification of *zong* principles would have favored the development of descent groups by allowing the well-educated to see their efforts to develop such groups as righteous.

100 E.g. Freedman 1966, Baker 1979, J. Watson 1982a.
101 H-C. W. Liu 1959b: 108.
102 Shimizu 1949: 64.
103 Twitchett 1960: 107; Twitchett 1959: 103,110–11.
104 Twitchett 1959: 102–04; Ch'en 1973: 297–300.
105 On this point, see Hymes 1986a.
106 SHY *shihuo* 61.61b.
107 Shimizu 1949: 37–45; cf. Kyo 1976: 303–05.
108 LFWQJ 21.124.
109 CBZLG 19.178.
110 E.g. ZWGWJ 95B.41b, GKJ 89.1221.
111 SXSWJ 42.738.
112 E.g. HCXS 79.10b–12a; ZWGWJ 88.16a.
113 On the latter see McKnight 1971: 157–70.
114 E.g. MSJ 10.22a, 28a.
115 The *Family Rituals* (*Jia li*) circulated under Zhu Xi's name endorsed setting up "sacrificial lands," with separate plots for each ancestor, recommending that 5 percent of a man's land be put aside for this purpose at the time of family division. After the four generations of domestic worship were completed, this land could become "grave fields" (ZZJL 1.3a). Although this type of sacrificial

field system would not lead to an enduring descent group, the association of Zhu Xi's name with sacrificial fields seems to have encouraged their formation. See Dai Yanhui 1936 for a full discussion of sacrificial fields and Ueyama 1982 on Zhu Xi's authorship of the *Jiali* [now see also Ebrey 1991b: 102–44]. See also Hazelton 1986.

116 QMJ 8.248–49. On the relationship of dowry and women's interests to estate formation, see also Dennerline 1986.

117 HCXS 192.10a–11a.

118 Communal families also sometimes started with a dying wish not to see sons divide property (e.g., NJJYG 16.310–11).

119 MZJ 22.10b–11a.

120 MZJ 34.14b.

121 For its use in later periods, see Makino 1949: 135–50, Uchida 1953, F. L. K. Hu 1948: 82–83, Dai Yanhui 1936: 116–22.

122 SXSWJ 24.455–56.

123 See Hymes 1986b.

124 On elite-centered descent groups see Ebrey 1983 and Hazelton 1986.

125 YDJ 17:1b.

126 E.g. WSXSQJ 9:331–32; SXSWJ 6:131; see also Hymes 1986a and Hazelton 1986.

127 Ahern 1976.

128 ShSWJ 1.7a–b.

129 Grafflin 1983.

130 See the genealogical tables in XTS 70–75.

131 For examples of naming patterns used by descent groups in the Song and later, see R. Davis 1986b, Naquin 1986, and Rawski 1986.

132 XZWJ 21.9a.

133 YYJ 10.145–46. Exactly which generation was being designated the first row is unclear. Since one could not rename deceased ancestors, it presumably was the youngest generation then alive or being born. At any rate, since a genealogy had been carefully researched, this was not an attempt to fudge a genealogy by declaring all the adults then alive to be of the same generation.

134 WGZJ 1.2–3.

135 FWZGWJ 8.107 or Twitchett 1960: 14.

136 An additional reason for recording numbers in genealogies may have been the taboo on using a deceased father's *ming*. Officials received posthumous titles by which their descendants could refer to them, but for commoners, finding the appropriate term was not so easy. The practice of calling even commoners after they were dead "so-and-so *gong*" ("lord") had started by the early Song. (Chen Liang says his descent group started to follow the custom [*shisu*] of calling ancestors "*gong*" in about AD 1000, CLJ 27.395.) In some genealogies, the early ancestors' *ming* have been lost and they are known only as "Lord 24" or "Lord Mu 12." The preface to a genealogy written in 1297 gives some insight into how this worked. Hu Yanwu recorded that when he was a very young child a local teacher asked him if he knew his ancestors' row numbers. When he replied that he did not know them all, the teacher taught him six numbers: 4, 6, 2, 10, 7, and 8. Later at five *sui* when he entered school, he learned that his first ancestor was "Lord 4" (perhaps the fourth son in a family) and that *six* generations later there were four branches (*pai*). (Presumably the man who was his own ancestor was called "two," and so on.) (HSZP 1297 preface.)

137 Morita 1979. Robert Hymes describes this trend in Fuzhou, where he relates it to changes in the elite's place in local society (Hymes 1986a).

138 Zurndorfer 1981 and Hazelton 1986.

139 ZSZJ 2.7a–8a, 22b–29a.

140 GKJ 88.1203. Another example of the relation between genealogies and marriage is described by Huang Jin (1277–1357). After he finished making an announcement of posthumous rank at the grave of his grandmother in front of an assembly that included agnates, affinal relatives, and local residents, a relative of his grandmother (a grandson of her first cousin) brought out a copy of their genealogy and asked Huang Jin to fill in the dates and burial place of his grandmother (HWXGJ 7B.300–01). In other words, they were using the genealogy as a means of maintaining contact with a family into which one of their women had married three generations earlier.

141 SXSWJ 69.1099–1100.

142 SXSWJ 40.700.

143 Cf. Hymes 1986a.

144 WGZJ 1.20–21.

145 WGZJ 1.24.

146 WGZJ 1.12. One such case concerned the Ni of Guiqi and the Fu of Jinqi, neighboring areas in Jiangxi. These two lines had intermarried for generations, so when one line among the Ni had no heir, a Fu was adopted. Five generations passed, and one of the descendants asked Wu Hai what he should do. Wu Hai said that there was only one choice, to return to the Fu name. The man replied that a hundred years had passed; reverting would arouse suspicion, and his other agnates did not want to follow him. Wu Hai said he should revert by himself if necessary, compiling a genealogy so that if any of them later wanted to do the right thing, the evidence would be available to them. The man then replied: "The Ni line trusted us to be their heirs. If I revert, will it be all right to cut off their line?" Wu Hai's solution was to set up a Ni as the heir and marry a Fu girl to him (WGZJ 1.13–14).

147 Freedman 1966: 28.

148 Meskill 1970: 141.

149 See Hazelton 1986 and Ebrey 1983.

150 See Hymes 1986a. Hymes argues that what was new in the Southern Song was not the existence of groups or quasigroups of agnatic kinsmen, but "the role of the elite – at even its highest bureaucratic levels – in their promotion, celebration, and, in some cases, creation" and the "new impulse of the elite to define themselves as members of the same groups as (in principle) all their local agnates." Thus he places particular emphasis on the compiling of genealogies in the late Song and Yuan. Taking a longer historical perspective, I evaluate the relative weight of changes in elite strategies and changes in the groups themselves differently. Because historical sources are much thinner before the Song, especially before the Southern Song, we know very little about the local activities of those in the elite who did not rise to high posts in the capital. Presumably many educated men in the Tang and earlier had always followed a localist strategy as the only one available to them; however, they did not develop descent groups or lineages of the sort that appear after Song. There were also long periods (such as the Later Han) when the highest-ranking men sought to be identified with their local community and local agnates; yet lineages were not created. Moreover, many "modern-style" descent groups seem to have emerged without being celebrated or promoted by members of the national elite (although we learn about them in our sources only after this occurred). To me what is new in the Song is not the desire of some men of education, property, and ambition to gain all the local allies they could, but the focus for organization of localized groups of agnates in rites to the first ancestors buried there, the "invention" of the inalienable estate, and the moral value assigned to organizing on patrilineal lines by Song thinkers. Educated men could try to take over, manipulate, or develop for their own purposes the organizations that developed. But when

there was no incipient organization, the efforts of elites to create them – even the compilation of genealogies – may well have resulted in a group of significance to those elite members who tried to promote it, but of little importance to anyone else "defined" as belonging to it. Descent groups were much more likely to have "public" genealogies when they had officials among their members (see Hazelton 1986), but it is not obvious that this sort of genealogy was a necessary feature of all types of descent groups (many Guangdong ones lacked them), though it seems to be typical of what Hazelton calls a "Lower Yangtze" type.

151 ZZJL 1.1a–10b [for a translation, see Ebrey 1991a: 5–20].
152 What might have been a late Song transitional form is found in HCXS 91.13b– 15b. A shrine dedicated to four heroes of one family was later restored by one of the descendants, who arranged to have all his mourning relatives make offerings there.
153 WGZJ 2.41–42.
154 See Dardess 1974: 48–49.
155 SXSWJ 73.1165.
156 SXSWJ 73.1166.
157 SXSWJ 10.183–84.
158 SXSWJ 24.455–56.
159 XZZJ 1.41b–45a; 8.22a; 13.1a–2a.
160 Zuo Yunpeng 1964: 105; Makino 1939: 197–201. Detailed rules had, however, earlier appeared in rules for communal families. See Langlois 1981.
161 Pasternak 1968; E. N. Anderson 1970.
162 Makino 1949: 566–68.
163 Uchida 1953.
164 Rawski 1986. In fact, the only cases reported in Ebrey and Watson 1986 that seem to have had all the standard features of lineages as defined in the introduction are the ones in Huizhou and Wuxi, and Jerry Dennerline 1986 argues that corporate property came relatively late in the development of the Wuxi lineages.
165 The patrilineality of Song and Yuan descent groups does not seem to have been so pronounced that it interfered with relations with affines or with individuals' needs to arrange for heirs from outside the descent group. Of all the authors of Song and Yuan genealogy prefaces and other descent group documents that I have read, Wu Hai was the only one strongly to condemn nonagnatic adoption and uxorilocal marriage. His contemporary Song Lian, a much more highly regarded teacher, had great praise for families that found ways to "continue the sacrifices" through their daughters (SXSWJ 46.809–10). Moreover, many genealogy prefaces, in recording the movements of ancestors, remark that the moves were made to join a wife's parents (usually without change of surname) without implying in any way that this compromised the group (e.g. YYJ 5.75; SXSWJ 10.183–84; see also Dennerline 1986). Indeed, genealogies often seem to have been important among upper class groups precisely to help them arrange good marriages. After all, they document ancestry, proving family standing, something much involved in establishing marriage ties.

6 Cremation in Song China

1 Wan and Huang 1988a, 1988b. See also Whyte 1988.
2 Overviews of the history of cremation in China are provided by de Groot 1892–1910: 3.1391–1417, Naba 1921, Xu Pingfang 1956, Miyazaki 1976, Makio 1968, Seidel 1974: 6.573–85, Yang and Chen 1983, Sun Boquan *et al.* 1987. Chinese scholars writing since 1949 have generally felt obliged to provide a positive historical background for cremation, to show that it had been practiced by Chinese (including "national minorities") in the past and that it was not simply

done out of poverty. Japanese scholars have often been interested in cremation in China because of the different history of cremation in Japan, where it never declined after its early introduction by Buddhist monks.

3 See, for instance, Ariès 1981, P. Brown 1981, E. Brown 1981, and Laquer 1983.

4 Here when I refer to "Chinese," I mean the dominant Han Chinese. Cremation was practiced from early times by some of the non-Han peoples now within the political borders of China, most notably the Qiang (proto-Tibetan). For the non-Han practice of cremation, see Sun Boquan 1987 and Yang and Chen 1983.

5 On Chinese funerary customs in general, see Liu Shiji 1957. De Groot 1892–1910 also provides extensive discussion of the history of various practices.

6 MZJG 6.113, 116. Compare B. Watson 1967, pp. 72, 76. Mo Zi's point in mentioning the aberrant practices of several foreign tribes was that each group considers its own practices moral and foreigners' immoral.

7 See De Groot 1892–1910: 1.659–98.

8 See Y.-S. Yu 1987; Loewe 1982, esp. 25–37; Seidel 1987.

9 Some Daoist ideas seem conducive to cremation, but it is difficult to assess whether these are truly indigenous or inspired by Buddhism. The *Liezi*, a text late enough to incorporate stories influenced by Buddhism, quotes a sage declaring that he was indifferent to the fate of his body after death: it could be burned, thrown into the water, buried with or without a coffin (Graham 1960: 143). Makio 1968 suggested that Huang-Lao Daoism had since the Han favored quick decay but offers only a few examples to support this idea. After the introduction of cremation, however, Daoism may have indirectly facilitated the spread of Buddhism. Medieval Daoists talked about "deliverance from the corpse" (*shi jie*) (Robinet 1979). Although this term was used metaphorically to refer to the state achieved in meditation, less educated followers may have taken it literally and thought that being released from one's corpse as rapidly as possible after death had benefits.

10 See Kaltenmark 1969: 117–21 and Overmyer 1974: 198–225.

11 For surveys of the history of Buddhism in China, see Ch'en 1973.

12 Studies of mortuary practices and ancestral rites in modern times include De Groot 1892–1910, Ahern 1973, and Watson and Rawski 1988. Studies in folk religion are very numerous. Good places to begin are Wolf 1974, Jordan 1972, and Gates and Weller 1987.

13 On folk religion after the introduction of Buddhism through the Song period, see the articles in Welch and Seidel 1979 (especially Stein 1979) and Strickman 1983, 1985. See also Johnson 1985, Teiser 1988, and Hansen 1989. The literature on Neo-Confucianism is very large. A good sense of the range of current scholarship can be found in Chan 1986. On Ming–Qing orthodoxy, see the essays in K.-C. Liu 1990a, especially Liu 1990b.

14 In Chinese sources, cremation is referred to variously as *huohua* (transformation by fire), *huozang* (fire burial), *shaoshen* (burning the body), *fenren* (burning people), *fenshi* (burning corpses), and related terms. Sometimes, a transliteration of the Sanskrit term *dhyapayati* is also used, such as *shepi*, *shewei*, and *toupi* (for these Buddhist terms, see Seidel 1974).

15 GJSWLJ 56.14a.

16 HWGJ 13.202.

17 SS 125.2918–19.

18 RZSB xu 13.374.

19 HSRC 70.14b.

20 Yule 1929: 1.204–05; 2.191.

21 Moule 1957: 44–45.

22 SS 125.2919.

23 CJL 4.126.

24 QBZZ 12.50; SZZL lb.

25 GJSWLJ qian 56.13a–14b; SMSSY 7.76. For an example of a Song official cremated when he died away from home, see YHTC 2.4a–b. Unfortunately, epitaphs cannot be used to judge how common cremation was in such cases, because sometimes when a tomb inscription survives for a burial of cremated remains, it does not mention the cremation. For an example, see Wang Hongtao 1975: 77–78.

26 Han Qi (1008–1075) found cremation prevalent in Pingzhou (Shanxi) (HWGJ 13.202); Fan Chunren (1027–1101) in Taiyuan (Shanxi) (SS 314.10289); Cheng Hao (1032–1085) in Jincheng (Shanxi) (ECJ wenji 11.633); and Bi Zhongyou (1047–1121) in Hedong (Shanxi) (SZZL la–2a).

27 Pan Zhi (1126–1189) found it in Jinghubei (Hubei) (ZWGWJ 94.3b).

28 Rong Yi (ca. 1150s) reported it as prevalent in the entire Wu-Yue area (roughly Jiangsu, Zhejiang, and Fujian) (SS 125.2919); Wang Yue (1237) in Qinchuan (Jiangsu) (QCZ 1.24a–28a); and Huang Zhen (1213–1280) in Wu county (Suzhou, Jiangsu) (HSRC 70.14b). There is also a reference to a crematorium in a temple outside a small city in Zhejiang (XCGYZ 15a).

29 Zhen Dexiu (1178–1235) found it in Quanzhou (Fujian) (XSWJ 40.24b).

30 LQJ 38.31a; MLL 18.294; YDZ 30.8a (p. 1273).

31 Yang and Chen 1983 and Xu Pingfang 1984: 600.

32 Chen Jiaxiang 1956.

33 Hong Jianmin 1959.

34 Liu and Jian 1955: 9.92–98. The archaeological evidence shows that cremation was not only common in the Song, for which there are good documentary sources, but also in the Liao and Jin (neighboring non-Han states that held substantial amounts of previously Chinese territory in the north until defeated by the Mongols). Interesting excavations of Liao, Jin, and Yuan cremation graves include Shanxi sheng wenwu guanli weiyuanhui 1955; Guangzhoushi wenwu guanli weiyuan hui 1957; and Yi Qingan 1956. The last of these reports describes an unusual burial. An urn of ashes was placed in a carefully fitted stone outer coffin shaped like a typical funerary inscription and cover, with an inscription on two sides of the round hole reporting that the deceased, the wife of an official, died at the age of 53 and was buried in 1096. This stone case was then placed in a brick tomb a little over 1 meter square.

35 This estimate must be tentative because of the lack of evidence about children. Presumably, about a third of those who died in Song times died as children and would seem to have been good candidates for cremation. But I have found very little evidence about the disposal of the bodies of infants or young children.

36 Nishiwaki 1979: 130–53 notes that biographies of monks in the Tang seldom mention that they have been cremated, only that they were buried under a stupa, whereas Song ones often mention cremation. Some Tang monks may have been cremated and their ashes buried under the stupa, but it does appear to be the case that Buddhist monks were not always cremated. Bai Juyi, for instance, explicitly states in some epitaphs that a monk's "whole body" (*quanshen*) had been buried (QTW 678:20b, 25a).

37 See Schopen 1987.

38 Cremation was not the only means of obtaining relics. Sometimes, the whole body of a priest would be preserved, perhaps even lacquered and treated as an image for worship.

39 In one anecdote, a pious Buddhist teacher over 90 years old announced that he would die that day and insisted on cremation. His "chain bones" showed he was a Bodhisattva and motivated his neighbors to collect money to build a stupa where his bones could be buried (TPGJ 101.680, 682). An epitaph for a

twelfth-century monk recorded that, after he died, he was cremated and shining relics were found among the burnt bones his disciples collected and buried in a stupa (LFWQJ 40.249).

40 Zhou Hui (1126–ca.1198) reported that, at Buddhist temples, the bones of men and women would mingle in pools until the monks cleared them out to make room for more (QBZZ 12.109).

41 YJZ zhijing 7.936–37; sanzhi 7.1357–58. Lotus flowers were a common symbol of sanctity.

42 I found only one critic of cremation who said that monks linked it to salvation. Che Ruoshui (thirteenth century) reported that monks claimed it would lead to entry to Heaven (JQJ 2.14b).

43 QCZ 1.25b.

44 Nine such references are found in the *Song gaoseng zhuan*, conveniently indexed in Makita 1978: 7:978, 1168, and 1205.

45 One exception is a burial with an inscription dated 1107 found in an area then occupied by the (non-Han) Khitan state of Liao. The inscription on the stone casket referred to karma, and another stone slab had a Buddhist invocation carved on it (Datongshi wenwu chenlie guan 1963). Other nearby cremation graves reported in the same article, however, have walls painted with typical scenes, none distinctively Buddhist (though Buddhist murals were well established for temples), and mock deeds that employ typical geomantic language. In general, visual or textual links to Buddhism in cremation burials were about as rare as they were in other burials.

46 YJZ bing 15.495–96.

47 YJZ bing 11.456.

48 Robert Hertz (1960: 43) has noted that there is a fundamental similarity between cremation and two-stage mortuary rituals that involve allowing the flesh to decay and then reburying the bones: both allow for the destruction of the impure flesh and the "drying" of the bones.

49 For example, in 1041, Shi Jie arranged the burial of all those who had not yet been buried over the past five generations in his family, altogether seventy sets of remains. His family had originally come from Hebei but had moved to Shandong about a century earlier (CLSXS 168–69, 188, 234–35). Anthropologists have found that such relocated bones were not uncommon in North China burials.

50 GJSWLJ qian 56.14a. This is similar to the practice of double burial common in Fujian, Guangdong, and Taiwan in recent times. There is no evidence, however, of any group practicing double burial as its preferred custom in Song times, and none of the numerous complaints about vulgar customs and departures from the Confucian ritual classics mention excavating coffins merely to clean the bones and rebury them in the same general locale.

51 For these ideas in modern southern China, see J. L. Watson 1982b. The closest I have come to such sentiments in a Song source is from a Buddhist advocate of cremation in the early twelfth century who argued that cremation was preferable to burial because it "stops the foulness of smelly decay, avoids consumption by ants, and allows the *po* spirit to escape, the soul to become pure and ascend" (MFLHJJ 47.337d). Song scholars did report, however, that their contemporaries had a variety of fears about mourning activities (RZSB 9.123; ZZJ 301; SMSSY 6.63, 67–68; CJL 124).

52 This text is found in chapter 8199 of YLDD. On this text, see Xu Pingfang 1963.

53 LJDZS lb–5a, 6b. Although geomancy, through its emphasis on bones, can be seen as compatible with cremation, it also can be seen as in tension with it. Wang Yue, in the mid-thirteenth century, claimed that people chose cremation

because they were so confused by the theories of geomancers and afraid of the bad consequences of burying in the wrong place that they simply wanted to get rid of the body quickly by throwing it in a fire (QCZ 1.25b–26a). Luo Dajing, also mid-thirteenth century, cited as evidence against the validity of geomancy the case of a highly successful official whose parents and grandparents had been cremated and their ashes buried (HLYL ping 6:345).

54 Sima Guang, in SMSSY 7.76, wrote, "When Yanling Jizi went to Qi, his son died and he buried him in the region of Ying and Bo, saying it is fate for the bones and flesh to return to the earth, while the soul goes everywhere. Confucius considered that this conformed to ritual. When one definitely cannot return a body for burial, it is acceptable to bury it in the local place. Isn't this better than burning it?" (The allusion is LJ, "Tan Gong" 10: 18b, translated in Legge 1967: 1.192–93. See also ECJ yishu 2b.58.)

55 See Ebrey 1986b: 20–29 [reproduced here as Chapter 5].

56 Chikusa 1982: 111–45.

57 For some Song examples, see YJZ sanxin 3.1407–08. See also SMCJJ 18.276–77, for Confucian objection to this custom.

58 HLYL ping 6.344–45.

59 QBZZ 12.109.

60 MLL 15.260–61.

61 SXSWJ 62.1005.

62 YJZ zhijing 9.948; sansi 9.1375–76.

63 It is possible, of course, that such views existed among the illiterate, who have left no sources. One set of ideas that could have contributed to a positive view of cremation concerns the transformative powers of fire. Fire had strong associations with the world of spirits, especially with transferring material objects into forms that could reach that world. Burning prayers was standard procedure both in Daoist rituals and in communications with ancestors. Burning incense had become a common way of showing respect to spirits of all sorts, including ancestors. Burning mock paper money was the most common way to transmit offerings to spirits. At funerals in Song times, it was a popular custom to burn paper replicas of objects, thereby sending them to the deceased. Why not also send off the dead by burning them? Throughout the Tang period, monks occasionally immolated themselves as a pious sacrifice in imitation of the Bodhisattva described in the *Lotus Sutra*, attracting huge crowds of observers (see Gernet 1960 and Jan 1965). Just as the monks who set themselves on fire were seen as offering their bodies, so perhaps in folk thinking there may have been some sense that the bodies of those who died naturally could be "offered" through cremation. This idea was apparently a part of Hindu thinking about cremation (Parry 1982: 74–110). The possible connections between cremation and other uses of fire to communicate with spirits are intriguing, but I have found no sign that any of the educated in Song times attributed such ideas to those who chose cremation.

64 Teiser 1988.

65 For one reference to cremation of a lay person in the Tang, see Miyazaki 1976: 67. To this could be added the evidence that some societies of lay Buddhists in Dunhuang in the ninth or tenth centuries may have practiced cremation: when a member died, a circular notice would be sent to the others asking for contributions of firewood in addition to grain, oil, and cloth. Whether this wood was used for cooking or for a funerary pyre is unclear; see Naba 1974: 530, 532 and Nagasawa 1980. It should be conceded that an absence of references to cremation is not strong evidence of its absence or rarity. However, one would expect cremation to have at least attracted the attention of scholars who opposed Buddhism and criticized other Buddhist practices.

66 Makio 1968: 56 makes this suggestion.

67 See Chikusa 1982, Huang Minzhi 1988, Foulk 1987, and Levering 1978.
68 One might challenge my emphasis on disorder, warfare, and migration by point-
    ing to similar conditions in the fourth century that did not lead to the spread
    of cremation. The difference between these two periods lies very much in the
    underdevelopment of Buddhist establishments in the earlier period. It was not
    until the Tang dynasty that Buddhist establishments came to play much of a
    role in serving lay people's ritual needs.
69 TPGJ 158.1135.
70 XWDS 17.179–80.
71 ZZYL 89.2286–87.
72 On these efforts, see Ebrey 1989, which deals especially with weddings and ances-
    tral rites. [Now see also Ebrey 1991b.]
73 GJSWLJ 56.13a.
74 ECJ yishu 3.85.
75 SMSSY 7.76.
76 ECJ wenji 11, p. 633. Compare SCSSLY 413.
77 ZZYL 89.2281.
78 This is a reference to Buddhist monks "leaving the family" and not marrying.
79 QCZ 1.26a–b.
80 HSRC 70.15a–17b. RZSB xu 13.374.
81 CB 3.65; SXT 18.9a.
82 ECJ yishu 3.58. One can point to other inconsistencies as well. The government
    periodically instructed local governments to see to the burying of abandoned
    coffins. Sometimes, the local officials had bodies cremated or allowed cremation
    as an alternative to burial (GJZ 13.38b–39a; YJZ jia 11.96). Sometimes, even
    members of the imperial family were cremated, at least if they died as infants or
    concubines (LQJ 38.30a–34b; Wang Hongtao 1975).
83 SXT 1.11a.
84 WLCJ 70.441.
85 OYXQJ 17.123.
86 ECJ wenji 11.633.
87 HWGJ 13.202.
88 SS 314.10289.
89 QSB 3.207–08.
90 SHY shihuo 60.3a.
91 BQSMZ 14.7b, 16.11a, 18.11b, 20.7a, 21.10a; GJZ 13.36b–37a; JLXZ 2.1990;
    JKZ 43.44a–49b.
92 See Sichuansheng wenwu guanli weiyuanhui 1956: 37, for a description of the dis-
    covery of many urns with bricks marked with inscriptions like "Bones deposited
    at Yanbao temple in the fifth month of Xining (1075), of unknown name, buried
    on the seventh day of the twelfth month of Chunning (1104), number 38." See
    also He Zhenghuang 1966, Anon. 1966, and Song and Song 1986.
93 SS 125.2918–19.
94 GJZ 13.36b.
95 SHY shihuo 60.3a, 7b–8a, 9b.
96 JLXZ 12: 71b.
97 SZZL 1b; QCZ 1.24a–28a.
98 HSRC 70.14b–18a.
99 Ebrey 1986b [reproduced here as Chapter 5].
100 WGZJ 1.1–3.
101 Compare the views of James Watson, who argues that the state played a major
    role in achieving a high level of uniformity in Chinese funerary rites but largely
    ignored rites of disposal (burial, cremation, exhuming bodies for reburial of the
    bones, and so on) (J. Watson 1988).

102 Langlois and Sun 1983. See also Dardess 1983 for Zhu Yuanzhang's relationships with Confucian advisors.
103 SHSC 1.12.
104 MSL Taizu, 53.10b–11a; MS 60.1492.
105 DMLJJFL 12.25a (p. 989).
106 See Farmer 1990. On the severity of the first Ming emperor's enforcement of laws, see also Dardess 1983: 183–253.
107 In areas inhabited predominantly by Han Chinese, over 90 percent of the excavated cremation burials date from the tenth through fourteenth centuries (Xu Pingfang, personal communication). In non-Han areas, or in non-Han graves in mixed areas, cremation burials persisted for several more centuries.
108 Wu Kuan (1436–1504) complained that, because of the population density in Suzhou, the lower classes (*xiaomin*) burned the bodies of their parents. In 1497, the prefect banned the practice, and three years later he established a charitable graveyard to help those who as a consequence had left bodies unburied. Still, near the end of the Ming, another scholar observed that, in this same city, while the educated performed proper funerals, "brokers in the markets and government servants all use cremation" (WXZ 41.28a). Zhang Xuan (1558–1641) quoted a proclamation issued by Deng Huaichang, prefect of Wenzhou on the coast of Zhejiang, decrying the prevalence of cremation among the poor in spite of the first Ming emperor's prohibition of it. Poverty was no excuse for cremation, he insisted, as there was a charitable graveyard in the area. Any further cremations, he declared, would be punished according to the law (XYWJL 4.39b–40a). In the early Qing, Zhang Lixiang (1611–1674), from Tongxiang (Zhejiang), complained of the persistence of cremation in his home area, comparing the Yue region (roughly Fujian), where burial was universal, to his area, where cremation flourished (SJZS 5a–b). Zhang Cichen mentioned the case of a poor man in Hangzhou who paid the modest sum of fifty cash to have his mother cremated (JLBD 7.52b). Gu Yanwu (1615–1682) mentioned that cremation had flourished in the Jiangnan area (roughly Zhejiang and Jiangsu) since the Song dynasty, quoting in full two Song memorials against the practice but no later evidence. Commenting on this passage over a century later, Huang Rucheng (1799–1837) noted that cremation was still practiced in Hangzhou in his day (though apparently not throughout the whole area) (RZL 15.366–68).
109 SJZS 5a–b. See similar comments in JLBD 7.53a–b.
110 Doolittle 1865: 2.257.
111 De Groot 1892–1910: 3.1415. For the use of cremation by Buddhist monks and nuns in late nineteenth and early twentieth-century China, see Yetts 1911.
112 On this text, see Ebrey 1989 [now see also Ebrey 1991a and 1991b].

7 Surnames and Han Chinese identity

1 Throughout this essay I use the term "Han identity" in its modern sense. In premodern times, the vocabulary used to refer to what is now labeled "Han" ethnicity was much more complicated, with other terms (especially "Hua" and "Xia") more common in many periods, and no term at all needed in many contexts. For a good discussion of the historical evolution of the use of "Han" as an ethnic term, see Chen Shu 1986.
2 For some recent critical discussions of Confucian culturalism, see Bol 1987, Langlois 1980, Crossley 1990, and Duara 1993.
3 Zhongguo shehui kexue yuan 1990: 1.43. To continue the calculations, 25 names account for about 60 percent, 114 names for 90 percent, and 365 names for 99 percent. Besides the decline in the number of surnames in common use, there has been an even more noticeable decline in the proportion of the people with multicharacter surnames.

4 See the differential distribution of names shown in Zhongguo shehui kexue yuan 1990: 43–67. All of the most common surnames are found in each region, though the percentage of the population with a given name can vary significantly.

5 Concentrating on the Tang-to-Yuan period also allows me to set aside questions of the origins of the Chinese systems of surnames and descent paradigms and concentrate on the mature forms. Very little of what I say about the use of surnames would extend much before the Han period. How something came into being is interesting but may not be good evidence of how it later operated, and here I will not consider origins.

6 Miyakawa 1960; Schafer 1967: 33–61.

7 Eberhard 1962: 199; Faure 1989.

8 See Ramsey 1987: 234–35, for the case of the Zhuang in modern times.

9 TZ 25.439A.

10 TZ 197.3158a–b, 3161c, 3162a, 3162b.

11 On the languages of the southern non-Han ethnic groups, see Ramsey 1987: 230–91.

12 Fan Chengda (1120–1193), for instance, distinguished between "true" Man, who paid no taxes and were a source of trouble for the local officials, and those Man who had become settled, law-abiding citizens (GHYHZ *manzhi* 3a). On the other hand, Du You (735–812) did not accept the claim of one group of Man to be descended from Han settlers (TD 187.1003).

13 Dien 1977.

14 Wittfogel and Feng 1949: 8, 220, 471, 607n; J.-S. Tao 1976: 98; Endicott-West 1989: 81–84.

15 MSL 51.5a–b (pp. 999–1000).

16 RZL 413.16–17; the allusion is to Duke Cheng, year 4; cf. Legge 1961: 5.355.

17 On the notions that led to discomfort with cross-surname adoption, see Waltner 1990: 13–81.

18 Mao 1984: 25, 57, 163, 351.

19 E.g., Mao 1984: 65, 355.

20 Such references to remote ancestors are not so common in late Tang or Song funerary inscriptions, but they do not disappear altogether. For some examples, see SWGWJ 57.868, 872; 58.889.

21 XTS 71B.2288.

22 XTS 71B.2288.

23 JS 108.2803; 116.2959; 122.3053. There were exceptions: the ancestors of Fu Jian, founder of Zhao, were said to be descendants of Youyishi, mentioned in *Book of Documents* as an enemy of the second Xia emperor (JS 112.2867); and Li Te, the founder of Cheng Han, a Ba, has a genealogy that clearly seems to reflect the Bas' own myths of their origins and does not link him to ancient Chinese history (JS 120.3021).

24 WS 1.1. For modern scholarly rejection of such genealogies, see Yao Weiyuan 1962.

25 By Song times slightly more skepticism is occasionally shown. In the genealogical tables in the *New Tang History*, compiled in the Song but probably based on Tang materials, there are two versions offered for the origins of the Yuwen surname. The first is that they are descendants of the Shanyu of the Southern Xiongnu and that Yuwen meant "son of heaven" in the Xiongnu language. The second took them back much further, saying that when Huang Di destroyed the family of Shen Nong, his descendants went to the northern regions, where they were associated with the production of grass, and grass, in the Xianbei language, was called *yuwen* (XTS 71B:2403). Zheng Qiao similarly sometimes mentioned the existence of more than one theory. Still, his chapter on the northern nationalities (*beiguo*) begins by declaring that their ancestors all descended from Huang

Di. Because they lived in the desolate northern regions, they were tough and liked to fight, making them generation after generation the enemies of China (*Zhongguo*) (TZ 199.3179A).

26 See HHS 86.2829 for a story of descent from a daughter of Gaoxin (a great-grandson of Huang Di). See also MSJZ.

27 Deng Mingshi, for instance, after giving a lengthy account of the Xiao surname added at the end the prominent Khitan Xiao family, making it clear that they were in no way related to the Chinese Xiao and not attempting to give them links to Huang Di or other ancient figures (GJXS 10.1a–4b).

28 The *xing* recorded for many of the southern Man were basically clan or tribe names and did not necessarily mark off intermarrying groups. See, e.g., TD 187.1003.

29 GJXS 12.56, 7a, 9a.

30 B. Anderson 1991.

31 See Dikötter 1992. Dikötter does suggest that the Chinese in premodern times had some ideas of outsiders as biologically different from them, pointing mainly to the use of animal metaphors when defaming alien enemies, comparing them to birds and beasts and thus implying a biological difference between Chinese and barbarians. Too much should not be made of this, however, as Chinese, too, could be compared to birds and beasts if one were outraged enough at them. Unfilial behavior, for instance, could be described this way. Thus, animals represent those creatures that have sense and appetites but are not restrained by moral principles, making the comparison primarily a culturalist distinction.

32 Zhongguo shehui kexue yuan 1990: 43.

33 A good example of the influence of this mode of thinking can be found in Li 1928. Li Chi tried to analyze physical differences among Chinese in different parts of China in his day in terms of the migration of peoples from different places, as judged by the changing geographical distribution of surnames in historical sources. Apparently it never occurred to this well-educated scholar that those in the south with names first documented in the north might inherit very little of their physical make-up from a northern ancestor, much less that they might have acquired their name by some means other than inheritance.

8 Rethinking the imperial harem: Why were there so many palace women?

1 See Spence 1996: 150–51, 250–51.

2 SJ 6.239–40, plus commentary.

3 HS 72.3069–71; HHS 66.2161, 78.2529.

4 Chen Peng 1990: 689–90.

5 SuiS 24.672.

6 RZSB 5 bi 3.835–36.

7 Moule and Pelliot 1938: 205–06.

8 See Birrell 1985; Workman 1976.

9 Eoyang 1982.

10 Guisso 1981 provides early examples.

11 For the Song period, there is one such work in English (Chung 1981) and quite a few in Chinese and Japanese (Chiba 1976, 1978, 1981; Liu Jingzhen 1988; Shinno 1993; Zhang Bangwei 1993; Wei Zhijiang 1994; Yang Guanghua 1994; Zhu Ruixi 1994; Huang Jinjun 1997).

12 Chung 1981: 10–18.

13 The main primary sources on the imperial harem in Song times are SS, HSSCGY, and SHY houfei section.

14 ZGJ 10.174; cf. CB 189.4567–68; SSJW 1.19; LPJ 1.23a.

15 Cf. Chung 1981: 62–63.

16 Zhu Ruixi 1994: 62.
17 SHY zhiguan 57.38a.
18 Huang Jinjun 1997: 85.
19 SS 243.8632–34, 8638.
20 SS 243.8644; Hennesey 1981: 35.
21 HZL yuhua 1.277–78.
22 SS 243.8645.
23 Chung 1981: 36; Huang Jinjun 1997: 202–10.
24 JKBS 5.177; JLB 3.107, JKYL 8.155.
25 JKBS 136.
26 JKBS 104–111; 254–61. The ages given in these sources for the women and the evidence in other historical sources does not always match.
27 JKBS 177.
28 On Huizong's Daoism, see Ebrey 2000.
29 The data on which these tables is based is exact on the birth dates of sons, but for daughters gives only the date of their first title. In ordinary cases, the grant of a title could be delayed for a year or more. Moreover, it seems that in some cases titles may have been delayed even longer, especially perhaps posthumous titles. In the case of Renzong's children shown below, all of the six listed from 1059 on were girls. It seems possible that in some of these cases they had been born more than a year before getting their titles.
30 SMCJJ 29.402–03.
31 On eunuchs in the Song period, see Zhang Bangwei 1993: 263–303; Wang Mingsun 1981; Umehara 1985: 163–65.
32 On Shenzong and the New Policies, see Smith 1993.
33 SJ 6.239.
34 Chen Peng 1990: 690.
35 Knechtges 1982: 123–25.
36 Munakata 1991: 130–31.
37 YJZ bing 13.478–79.
38 On the myths of the Yellow Emperor/Yellow Thearch, see LeBlanc 1985–1986, Lewis 1990: 174–93, Robinet 1997.
39 Cahill 1980.
40 Ko 1994; Bray 1997; Mann 1997; Ebrey 1993.

9 Gender and sinology: Shifting Western interpretations of footbinding, 1300–1890

1 Naturally there were many more visitors from Korea, Japan, Vietnam, and Persia, but they did not see the need to comment as fully on women and male–female relations. This can be seen in a comparison of the fifteenth-century diaries of a Korean and a Persian with the accounts written by Europeans in the thirteenth and fourteenth centuries. See Meskill 1965 and Maitra 1970 on the Korean and Persian diaries, respectively, and Yule 1915, C. Dawson 1955, and Olschki 1960 on the Western travelers' accounts.
2 The primary way I have identified authorities has been to look at citations. For instance, John Francis Davis in his 1836 *The Chinese: A General Description of the Empire of China and Its Inhabitants* cited men who participated in the Macartney mission of 1793–1794 (John Barrow and George Staunton, especially), the French works which summed up the writings of the seventeenth- and eighteenth-century Jesuit missionaries (especially Du Halde's 1736 *History* and Amiot *et al.*'s multivolume *Mémoires* of 1776–1814), as well as the work of contemporary missionaries he may well have known in Canton, including Morrison, Gutzlaff, and those writing in the recently started periodical, *Chinese Repository*. Several decades later, Henry Yule, the scholarly translator of Marco Polo, cited not only

Davis and his sources, but also earlier authorities (such as Juan Gonzalez de Mendoza's 1583 synthetic portrait of China based on Spanish and Portuguese visitors' accounts and John Nieuhoff's 1669 account of a Dutch mission to Beijing) and major works published after Davis, including those by the French missionary Évariste-Régis Huc (1855) and the British botanist Robert Fortune (1857), both of whom had spent many years in China.

3 See Yule 1929: I.110–11 The first edition of this book appeared in 1871. See also Yule 1915: II.256. The first edition of this work was issued in 1866. More recently, Raymond Dawson (1967: 11) noted that Marco Polo's reputation as the most magnificent observer of the Middle Ages suffers "when one notices that he failed to observe, or at least to report, many of the fascinating novelties of Chinese civilization," among them footbinding. Nigel Cameron (1970: 88) noted that "there is not a word, among [Marco Polo's] many appreciations of women, about the bound feet which were an essential feature of every Chinese beauty." Other scholars who note this omission are Morris Rossabi (1988: 148) and Colin Mackerras (1989: 19).

4 Wood 1995, especially pp. 72–75. It is widely accepted that Marco Polo did not visit every place he described, but scholars vary considerably in their judgments of the likely extent of his journeys. Haeger (1978) suggested that Marco Polo may never have traveled far from Beijing, picking up knowledge of places further south during a long stay there.

5 Western writing on footbinding had an impact on the Chinese antifootbinding movement, but analyzing the connections between what Westerners wrote and what Chinese drew from it is a very complex subject. The intelligentsia of colonized societies have never been simply passive recipients of Western constructions of their culture. Frequently they have resisted, appropriated, modified, and inverted ideas to suit their purposes, in the process creating a modernity suited to their own goals. In other words, when they have revised laws or instituted schools in ways that show clear Western influence, they need not be looked on as the victims of the onslaught of the rise of the West, but can be seen as doing what elites have always done, creatively adapting ideas and institutions to meet new challenges. In the case of footbinding, the derogatory way Westerners wrote about it certainly had a role in arousing the Chinese reformist elite to take action against it, in no small part because they hated seeing China an object of ridicule. At the same time, Chinese reformers like Kang Youwei and Liang Qichao who criticized footbinding often subtly altered the meaning given various constructions of footbinding. For instance, although they adopted the language of deformity, calling footbinding a way of crippling Chinese women, they placed this in a distinctly nationalist context: it was to make the Chinese nation more physically fit that Chinese had to rid themselves of the practice of footbinding. On the movement against footbinding in the late nineteenth and early twentieth century, see Chau 1966, Levy 1967, Drucker 1991, Tao 1994, Gao 1995, and Hong 1997.

6 Moule and Pelliot 1938: 346, 330.

7 Two European Catholic clerics sent to the Mongols before Marco Polo wrote about Mongol women and marriage practices. These were the Italian Franciscan friar John de Plano Carpini (d. 1252), who was sent by the pope in 1245–1247, and the Flemish Franciscan friar William of Rubruck, who was sent by King Louis IX of France in 1253–1254. On their writings, see Yule 1915, C. Dawson 1955, P. Jackson 1990, Olschki 1960.

8 Moule and Pelliot 1938: 304.

9 Moule and Pelliot 1938: 180–81, 244.

10 Moule and Pelliot 1938: 329.

11 Yule 1915: II.254–56. On Odoric, see also Moule 1930: 241–48; Cameron 1970: 107–20.

12 I suspect that binding an infant's feet would interfere with her learning to walk, which probably explains why it was never practiced.
13 Letts 1953: 220. In this and other quotations from pre-nineteenth century books, I have modernized spelling and punctuation but left word choice as in the original. On Mandeville, see also Campbell 1988: 122–61.
14 Lach 1965; Spence 1998. See also Cameron 1970, R. Dawson 1967, Mackerras 1989.
15 On Davis, see Stephen and Lee 1917: 543–44.
16 J. F. Davis 1836: 254.
17 Davis 1836: 255–56.
18 Said 1979. For an interesting reading of Said, see Clifford 1988.
19 See Dudgeon 1869: 131, Gutzlaff 1834: 175, Abeel 1834: 129–30, Williams 1849: II.54.
20 Barrow 1806: 138.
21 Barrow 1806: 139. The official account of the embassy, prepared by George Staunton, was if anything bleaker in its depiction of Chinese women as subjected. "Women, especially in the lower walks of life, are bred with little other principle than that of implicit obedience to their fathers or their husbands." Even though the wives of the peasantry work very hard at domestic tasks, and do all the weaving in the country, they are treated badly:

> Not withstanding all the merit of these helpmates to their husbands, the latter arrogate an extraordinary dominion over them, and hold them at such distance, as not always to allow them to sit at table, behind which, in such case, they attend as handmaids.
>
> (Staunton 1798: II.109)

22 Downing 1838: II.189–90.
23 Sirr 1849: 314–17.
24 Sirr 1849: I.61–62.
25 Boxer 1953: 149. The attention to skin color and facial paint that was typical in this period remained common in later centuries as well. See, for instance, Nieuhoff 1669: 208, Anderson 1795: 107–08. On comments about skin color and facial features, see also Ko 1997a; Lach 1965: 827, 834. As Lach points out, the Iberians tended to divide the peoples of the world into black, brown, and white, and classed the Chinese as white, which to them also implied superiority.
26 Du Halde 1736: 139.
27 Du Halde 1736: 139. See also Amiot *et al.*, 1776–1814: II.405–07.
28 Grosier 1788: II.299–300.
29 Cranmer-Byng 1962: 229.
30 Ripa 1846: 70.
31 Du Halde 1736: 139. See also Doolittle 1865: 197, Dudgeon 1869: 93.
32 Lockhart 1861: 339.
33 Morrison 1817: 28.
34 Huc 1855: II.405.
35 Doolittle 1865: II.203.
36 J. L. Nevius 1882: 243; cf. Houghton 1877: 116. Ko 1997a, reading a similar set of sources as I have here, makes a different argument about fashion. As she reads it, Westerners saw fashion as good because it entails change, and change leads to progress, and thought the relative unimportance of fashion in China a sign of its inferiority. Most of those I read seemed, if anything, to take the contrary position. When they commented on the relative durability of clothing styles in China, they seemed to be criticizing the West, not China.
37 H. S. C. Nevius 1868: 114–16. A Russian visitor in the 1870s reported that in Hankou he visited Italian nuns who bound the feet of the girls in their asylum,

"not venturing to dispense with this ancient and barbarous habit." (Piassetsky 1884: 192.)
38 H. Nevius 1868: 116–17.
39 Lockhart 1861: 336.
40 Power 1853: 298.
41 Scarth 1860: 41.
42 Gordon-Cumming 1888: 48–49.
43 For example, Huc 1855: II.402–03.
44 Mendoza 1853 [1583]: 31–32. Mendoza's admiration for the seclusion of Chinese women is made clear in other passages, where he notes that:

> You shall not see at any time a woman at her window nor at her doors. And if her husband do invite any person to dinner, she is never seen nor eateth not at the table, except the guest be a kinsman or a very friend. When they go abroad to visit their father, mother, or any other kinsfolk, they are carried in a little chair by four men, the which is made close, and with lattices round about made of gold wire and with silver, and curtains of silk; that although they do see them that be in the street, yet they cannot be seen.
>
> (Mendoza 1583 [1853]: 31–32)

45 Gallagher 1953: 77.
46 Baudier 1682: 19.
47 Baudier 1682: 20–21.
48 Baudier 1682: 21–22.
49 Navarrete 1960: I.162.
50 Du Halde 1736: 139.
51 Grosier 1788: II.300.
52 Cooper 1871: 47–48.
53 Gutzlaff 1838: 480.
54 Dudgeon 1869: 96.
55 Cranmer-Byng 1962: 228.
56 See Mabro 1991.
57 Ripa 1846: 70. The erotic overtones of bound feet are borne out by Chinese literary conventions. Although Chinese pornographic fiction often includes scenes in which bound feet play a role in love-making, bound feet are rarely mentioned in less erotically charged writings such as descriptions of leading courtesans. See McMahon 1995: 127–33; Ko 1997b: 96–99.
58 Cranmer-Byng 1962: 228.
59 Dudgeon 1869: 93–94. The theory to which Dudgeon is obliquely referring is undoubtedly the one described much more directly in Levy 1967: 34. The idea is that footbinding changes the shape and physiology of a woman's sexual organs in a way that makes sexual intercourse more pleasurable for the man.
60 Kerr 1869: 169–70.
61 Barrow 1806: 72–73.
62 Anon. 1835: 538.
63 Taylor 1860: 110–11.
64 Houghton 1877: 120.
65 Doolittle 1865: II.199–200.
66 On Western women missionaries to China, see Hyatt 1976, Hunter 1984, Croll 1989.
67 Fielde 1887: 27–29.
68 Even earlier a Dr. Macgowan, in a report to a medical missionary society, had recounted Yuan Mei's criticisms of footbinding. See Lockhart 1861: 341–42. For Yuan Mei's criticisms, see Ropp 1976: 13–14, Levy 1967: 199.

69 Doolittle 1865: II.201–02.
70 Anon. 1835: 538.
71 Fortune 1857: 248–49.
72 Fielde 1887: 31.
73 Dudgeon 1869: 94.
74 Thomson 1982 [1873–1874]: II. plate XIV, no. 39.
75 Houghton 1877: 116–17.
76 Williams 1849: II.40.
77 Giles 1902: 196–205 (quote p. 202).
78 See sources in note 5.
79 For example Gao 1995. See also F. Hong 1997, written in English.
80 Levy 1967.
81 Blake 1994; Ko 1994: 147–51; B. Jackson 1997.

References

Abbreviations

CSJC   *Congshu jicheng* 叢書集成. Shanghai: Commercial Press, 1935–1937.
GXJBCS *Guoxue jiben congshu* 國學基本叢書. Shanghai: Commercial Press, 1929–1941.
SBCK   *Sibu congkan* 四部叢刊. Shanghai: Commercial Press, 1919–1936.
SKQS   *Siku quanshu* 四庫全書. Taibei: Commercial Press, 1983.
SYDFZCS *Song Yuan difang zhi congshu* 宋元地方志叢書. Taibei: Guotai wenhua shiye, 1980.
ZHSJ   Beijing: Zhonghua shuju.

PRIMARY SOURCES

AYJ *Anyang ji* 安陽集, by Han Qi 韓琦 (1008–1075). SKQS ed.

BQS *BeiQi shu* 北齊書, by Li Delin 李德林 (530–590) and Li Boyao 李百藥 (565–648). ZHSJ ed.

BQSMZ *[Baoqing] Siming zhi* 寶慶四明志, ed. Luo Jun 羅濬 *et al.* SYDFZCS ed.

BS *Bei shi* 北史, by Li Yanshou 李延壽. ZHSJ ed.

BSXJ *Beishan xiaoji* 北山小集, by Cheng Ju 程俱 (1078–1144). SBCK ed.

CB *Xu zizhi tongjian changbian* 續資治通鑒長編, by Li Tao 李燾 (1115–1184). ZHSJ, 1985.

CBZLG *Chunbai zhai leigao* 純白齋類稿, by Hu Zhu 胡助. CSJC ed.

CGL *Chuogeng lu* 輟耕錄, by Tao Zongyi 陶宗儀 (fl. 1360–1368). CSJC ed.

CJL *Chuijian lu* 吹劍錄, by Yu Wenbao 俞文豹 (fl. 1240), in *Songren daji ba zhong* 宋人劄記八種. Taipei, Shijie shuju ed.

CLJ *Chen Liang ji* 陳亮集, by Chen Liang 陳亮 (1143–1194). ZHSJ, 1974.

CLSXS *Culai Shi xiansheng wenji* 徂徠石先生文集, by Shi Jie 石介 (1005–1045). ZHSJ, 1984.

DDSL *Dongdu shilue* 東都事略, by Wang Cheng 王偁 (twelfth century). Songshi ziliao cuibian ed. Taibei: Wenhai, 1967.

DHBZ *Dunhuang baozang* 敦煌寶藏, ed. Huang Yongwu 黃永戊 Taibei: Xinwenfeng, 1981.

DJMHL *Dongjing menghua lu* 東京夢華錄 (1147), attrib. to Meng Yuanlao 孟元老 (fl. 1126–1147). In *Dongjing menghua lu wai si zhong* 東京夢華錄外四種. Shanghai: ZHSJ, 1962.

DMLJJFL *Da Ming lü jijie fuli* 大明律集解附例. Mingdai shiji huikan ed.

DXBL *Dongxuan bilu* 東軒筆錄, by Wei Tai 魏泰 (ca. 1050–1110). CSJC ed.

DZJ *Da zang jing* 大藏經. Taipei: Xinwenfeng reprint of Taisho ed., 1974.

ECJ *Er Cheng ji* 二程集, by Cheng Hao 程顥 (1032–1085) and Cheng Yi 程頤 (1033–1107). ZHSJ, 1981.

EZXJ *Ezhou xiaoji* 鄂州小集, by Luo Yuan 羅願 (1136–1184). CSJC ed.

FWZGWJ *Fan Wenzheng gong wenji* 范文正公文集, by Fan Zhongyan 范仲淹 (989–1052). CSJC ed.

GHYHZ *Guihai Yuheng zhi* 桂海虞衡志, by Fan Chengda 范成大 (1120–1193). In *Shuofu sanzhong* 説郛三種. Shanghai: Shanghai guji chubanshe, 1988.

GJSWLJ *Gujin shiwen leiju* 古今事文類聚, by Zhu Mu 祝穆 (d. 1246+). SKQS ed.

GJXS *Gujin xingshishu bianzheng* 古今姓氏書辯證, by Deng Mingshi 鄧名世 (j.s. 1134). SKQS ed.

GJZ *Guiji zhi* (*Jiatai*) 會稽志 (嘉泰) (1201), by Shi Su 施宿 (d. 1213). SYDFZCS ed.

GKJ *Gongkui ji* 玫瑰集, by Lou Yue 樓鑰 (1137–1213). CSJC ed.

GSJ *Gongshi ji* 公是集, by Liu Chang 劉敞 (1019–1068). CSJC ed.

GXZZ *Guixin zazhi* 癸辛雜識, by Zhou Mi 周密 (1232–1308). ZHSJ, 1988.

HCCJZ *Houcun ci jianzhu* 後村詞箋注, by Liu Kezhuang 劉克莊 (1187–1269), ed. Qian Zhonglian. Shanghai: Shanghai guji chubanshe, 1980.

HCXS *Houcun xiansheng daquanji* 後村先生大全集, by Liu Kezhuang 劉克莊 (1187–1269). SBCK ed.

HHS *Hou Han shu* 後漢書, by Fan Ye 范曄 (398–445). ZHSJ, 1963.

HLYL *Helin yulu* 鶴林玉露, by Luo Dajing 羅大經 (?–1248+). ZHSJ, 1983.

HMDQ *Shiwen leiju hanmo daquan* 事文類聚翰墨大全, by Liu Yingli 劉應李. 1307 ed.

HNXS *Henan xiansheng wenji* 河南先生文集, by Yin Zhu 尹洙 (1001–1046). SBCK ed.

HS *Hanshu* 漢書, by Ban Gu 班固. Beijing: Zhonghua shuju, 1962.

HSJ *Heshan ji* 鶴山集, by Wei Liaoweng 魏了翁 (1178–1237). SKQS ed.

HSRC *Huangshi richao* 黃氏日鈔, by Huang Zhen 黃震 (1213–1280). SKQS ed.

HSSCGY *Huang Song shichao gangyao* 皇宋十朝綱要, by Li Zhi 李摯 (1161–1238). Taipei: Songshi ziliao cuibian ed.

HSZP *Guixi Hushi zupu* 貴溪胡氏族譜, by Hu Zili 胡自立. 1468 ed.

HWGJ *Han Weigong ji* 韓魏公集, by Han Qi 韓琦 (1008–1075). CSJC ed.

HWXGJ *Huang Wenxian gong ji* 黃文獻公集, by Huang Jin 黃溍 (1277–1351). CSJC ed.

HZL *Huizhu lu* 揮麈錄, by Wang Mingqing 王明清 (1127–1214+). ZHSJ, 1961.

JBTSXS *Jingben tongsu xiaoshuo* 京本通俗小説 (anon.). Shanghai: Zongguo gudian wenxue Chubanshe, 1954.

JF *Jiafan* 家範, by Sima Guang 司馬光 (1019–1086). Zhongguo zixue mingzhu jicheng ed.

JJBB *Jujia bibei* 居家必備 (anon.). Ming ed.

JJBYSL *Jujia biyong shilei* 居家必用事類 (anon.). Kyoto: Chumon 1979 fascimile of Japanese 1673 ed.

JKBS *Jingkang baishi jianzheng* 靖康稗史箋証, compiled by Cui An 確庵 and Nai An 耐庵, ed. Cui Wenyin 崔文印. ZHSJ, 1988.

JKYL *Jingkang yaolu* 靖康要錄 (anon.). CSJC ed.

JKZ *Jiankang zhi* (*Jingding*) 建康志 (景定) (1261), ed. Zhou Yinghe 周應合 (1213–1280). SYDFZCS ed.

JL *Zhuzi jiali* 朱子家禮, by Zhu Xi 朱熹 (1130–1200). SKQS ed.

JLB *Ji le bian* 雞肋編, by Zhuang Chuo 莊綽 (twelfth century). ZHSJ ed.

JLBD *Jiali bianding* 家禮辨定, by Wang Fuli 王復禮. 1707 ed.

JLYJ *Jiali yijie* 家禮儀節, by Qiu Jun 丘濬 (1419–1495). Bancan baochi lou ed.

JLXZ *Jinling xinzhi* (*Zhizheng*) 金陵新志 (至正), by Zhang Xuan 張鉉 (fourteenth century). SYDFZCS ed.

JQJ *Jiaoqi ji* 腳氣集, by Che Ruoshui 車若水 (thirteenth century). Baibu congshu jicheng ed.

JS *Jinshu* 晉書, by Fang Xuanling 房玄齡 (578–648). ZHSJ, 1974.

JTS *Jiu Tang shu* 舊唐書 (945), by Liu Xu 劉煦 (887–946) *et al.* ZHSJ, 1975.

JWDS *Jiu Wudai shi* 舊五代史, by Xue Juzheng 薛居正 (912–981) *et al.* ZHSJ, 1976.

JXBL *Jiaxun bilu* 家訓筆錄, by Zhao Ding 趙鼎 (1084–1147). CSJC ed.

JXZL *Jiangxing zalu* 江行雜錄, by Liao Yingzhong 廖瑩中 (thirteenth century). CSJC ed.

JYYL *Jianyan yilai xinian yaolu* 建炎以來繫年要錄, by Li Xinchuan 李心傳 (1166–1243). CSJC ed.

JYJ *Jiayou ji* 嘉祐集, by Su Xun 蘇洵 (1009–1066). GXJBCS ed.

JZJ *Jiezhai ji* 絜齋集, by Yuan Xie 袁燮 (1144–1224). CSJC ed.

KYL *Kaiyuan li* 開元禮 (732), ed. Xiao Song 蕭嵩 *et al.* SKQS ed.

LCLZ *Longchuan luezhi* 龍川略志, by Su Zhe 蘇轍 (1039–1112). ZHSJ, 1982.

LDLWJ *Lü Donglai wenji* 呂東萊文集, by Lü Zuqian 呂祖謙 (1137–1181). CSJC ed.

LFWQJ *Lu Fangweng quanji* 陸放翁全集, by Lu You 陸游 (1125–1210). Hong Kong: Guangzhi shuju punctuated ed., n.d.

LJ *Li ji* 禮記. Shisan jing zhushu ed.

LJDZS *Liu Jiangdong jiacang shanben zangshu* 劉江東家藏善本葬書, by Guo Pu 郭璞 (276–324). Baibu congshu jicheng ed.

LJJ *Lejing ji* 樂靜集, by Li Zhaoji 李昭玘 (d. ca. 1126). SKQS ed.

LPJ *Longping ji* 隆平集, by Zeng Gong 曾鞏 (1019–1083). Taibei: Wenhai chubanshe, Songshi ziliao cuibian ed.

LQJ *Lequan ji* 樂全集, by Zhang Fangping 張方平 (1007–1091). SKQS ed.

LSL *Le shanlu* 樂善錄, by Li Changling 李昌齡 (fl. 1233). Taibei: Sibu shanben congkan, 1971 reprint of Sung ed.

LXABJ *Laoxuean biji* 老學庵筆記, by Lu You 陸游 (1125–1210). CSJC ed.

LZYH *Lengzhai yehua* 冷齋夜話, by (monk) Huihong 慧洪齋 (1071–1128). CSJC ed.

MFLHJJ *Miaofa lianhua jingjie* 妙法蓮花經解, by Jie Huan 戒環 (Song). In *Wan xuzang jing* 卍續藏經. Xin wenfeng ed.

MJ *Mo ji* 默記, by Wang Zhi 王銍 (d. ca. 1154). ZHSJ, 1981.

MLL *Mengliang lu* 夢粱錄, by Wu Zimu 吳自牧 (ca. 1256–1334+). In *Dongjing Menghua lu wai sizhong* 東京夢華錄外四種. Shanghai: ZHSJ, 1962.

MS *Ming shi* 明史, ed. Zhang Tingyu 張廷玉 *et al.*, ed. ZHSJ, 1974.

MSJ *Mingshui ji* 洺水集, by Cheng Bi 程珌 (1164–1242). SKQS ed.

MSJZ *Manshu jiaozhu* 蠻書校注, by Fan Chuo 樊綽 (Tang), ed. Xiang Da 向達. ZHSJ, 1962.

MSL *Ming shilu* 明實錄, by Yao Guangxiao 姚廣孝 *et al.* (Ming). Nangang: Institute of History and Philology, Academia Sinica.

MSYTL *Mianshui yantan lu* 澠水燕談錄, by Wang Pizhi 王闢之 (cs. 1067). ZHSJ, 1981.

MTJ *Mantang ji* 漫塘集, by Liu Zai 劉宰 (1166–1239). SKQS ed.

MZJ *Mianzhai ji* 勉齋集, by Huang Gan 黃榦 (1152–1221). SKQS ed.

MZJG *Mozi jiangu* 墨子閒詁, ed. Sun Yirang 孫詒讓 (1848–1908). Shijie shuju reprint.

MZML *Mozhuang manlu* 墨莊漫錄, by Zhang Bangji 張邦基 (Song). CSJC ed.
NJJYG *Nanjian jiayi gao* 南澗甲乙稿, by Han Yuanji 韓元吉 (1118–1187). CSJC ed.
OYXQJ *Ouyang Xiu quanji* 歐陽修全集, by Ouyang Xiu 歐陽修 (1007–1072). Taibei: Shijie shuju, 1961.
PCJ *Pengcheng ji* 彭城集, by Liu Bin 劉邠 (1022–1088). CSJC ed.
PYBS *Puyang bishi* 莆陽比事, ed. Li Junfu 李俊甫 (Song). Wanwei biecang photo reprint of Wanli ed.
PZKT *Pingzhou ketan* 萍州可談, by Zhu Yu 朱彧 (Song). CSJC ed.
PZWJ *Panzhou wenji* 盤州文集, by Hong Gua 洪适 (1117–1184). SBCK ed.
QBBZ *Qingbo biezhi* 清波別誌, by Zhou Hui 周輝 (1127–1198+). CSJC ed.
QBZZ *Qingbo zazhi* 清波雜誌, by Zhou Hui 周輝 (1127–1198+). ZHSJ, 1994.
QCSSJ *Qianchun suishi ji* 乾淳歲時記, by Zhou Mi 周密 (1232–1308). Taibei: Suishi xisu ziliao huibian ed., Yiwen yinshu guan.
QCZ *Qinchuan zhi* 琴川志, by Bao Lian 鮑廉 (Song) and Lu Zhen 盧鎮 (Yuan). SYDFZCS ed.
QMJ *Minggong shupan qingming ji* 名公書判清明集 (anon.). ZHSJ, 1987.
QSB *Quesao bian* 卻掃編, by Xu Du 徐度 (d. 1156). CSJC ed.
QSGY *Qingsuo gaoyi* 青瑣高議, by Liu Fu 劉斧 (ca. 1040–1113+). Shanghai: Shanghai guji chubanshe, 1983.
QTW *Quan Tang wen* 全唐文, ed. Dong Gao 董誥 (1740–1818) *et al.* Tainan, Taiwan: Jingwei shuju 1965 reprint of 1814 ed.
QYTFSL *Qingyuan tiaofa shilei* 慶元條法事類, by Xie Shenfu 謝深甫 (twelfth century). Taibei: Xinwenfeng reprint of Seikadō manuscript copy, 1976.
QZQQ *Xinbian shiwen leiyao qizha qingqian* 新編事文類要啟劄青錢 (Yuan). Tokyo: Koten kenkyūkai facsimile reprint of 1324 ed., 1963.
RZL *Rizhilu* 日知錄, by Gu Yanwu 顧炎武 (1613–1682). CSJC ed.
RZSB *Rongzhai suibi* 容齋隨筆, by Hong Mai 洪邁 (1123–1202). Shanghai: Shanghai guji chubanshe, 1978.
SBYL *Songben yili Zheng zhu* 宋本儀禮鄭註, ed. Zheng Xuan 鄭玄 (127–200). Taibei: Dingwen, 1972.
SCSSLY *Songchao shishi leiyuan* 宋朝事實類苑 (1145), by Jiang Shaoyu 江少虞 (j.s. ca. 1115–d. 1145+). Shanghai: Shanghai guji chubanshe, 1981.
SDPJ *Su Dongpo ji* 蘇東坡集, by Su Shi 蘇軾 (1036–1101). Taibei: GXJBCS ed.
SDRJ *Shuidong riji* 水東日記, by Ye Sheng 葉盛 (1420–1474). ZHSJ ed.
SHSC *Shuanghuai suichao* 雙槐歲鈔, by Huang Yu 黃瑜 (1425–1497). CSJC ed.
ShSWJ *Shishan wenji* 師山文集, by Zheng Yu 鄭玉 (1298–1358). SKQS ed.
SHY *Song huiyao jigao* 宋會要輯稿, ed. Xu Song 徐松 (1781–1848) *et al.* ZHSJ, 1957.
SJ *Shiji* 史記, by Sima Qian 司馬遷 (145?–86? BC). ZHSJ, 1962.
SJZS *Sangji zashuo* 喪祭雜說, by Zhang Lüxiang 張履祥 (1611–1674). In *Duli congchao* 讀禮叢鈔, ed. Li Fuyao 李輔耀. 1891 ed.
SLGJ *Shilin guangji* 事林廣記, ed. Chen Yuanjing 陳元靚 (ca. 1200–1266). ZHSJ reprint, 1999.
SLYY *Shilin yanyu* 石林燕語, by Ye Mengde 葉夢得 (1077–1148). ZHSJ, 1984.
SMCJJ *Sima Wenzheng gong chuanjia ji* 司馬文正公傳家集 (1741), by Sima Guang 司馬光 (1019–1086). Taibei: GXJBCS ed.
SMSSY *Sima shi shuyi* 司馬氏書儀, by Sima Guang 司馬光 (1019–1086). CSJC ed.
SMYL *Simin yueling* 四民月令, by Cui Shi 崔寔 (d. ca. 170). In *Simin yueling jiaozhu* 四民月令較注, by Shi Shenghan. ZHSJ, 1965.

SS *Song shi* 宋史, ed. Tuo Tuo 脱脱 (1313–1355) *et al.* ZHSJ, 1977.

SSGJ *Suishi guangji* 歲時廣記, by Chen Yuanjing 陳元靚 (ca. 1200–1266). CSJC ed.

SSHY *Shushi huiyao* 書史會要, by Tao Zongyi 陶宗儀 (fl. 1360–1368). SKQS ed.

SSJW *Sushui jiwen* 涑水記聞, by Sima Guang 司馬光 (1019–1086). ZHSJ, 1989.

SSWJ *Sushi wenji* 蘇軾文集, by Su Shi 蘇軾 (1036–1101). ZHSJ, 1986.

SSWJL *Shaoshi wenjian lu* 邵氏聞見錄, by Shao Bowen 邵伯溫 (1056–1134). ZHSJ, 1983.

SSZ *Sanshan zhi* 三山志, by Liang Kejia 梁克家 (1128–1187). SYDFZCS ed.

SuiS *Sui shu* 隋書, by Wei Zheng 魏徵 (580–643). ZHSJ, 1973.

SWGWJ *Su Weigong wenji* 蘇魏公文集, by Su Song 蘇頌 (1020–1101). ZHSJ, 1988.

SWJ *Song wenjian* 宋文鑑, by Lü Zuqian 呂祖謙 (1137–1181). Taibei: GXJBCS ed.

SXSWJ *Song Xueshi wenji* 宋學士文集, by Song Lian 宋濂 (1310–1381). Wanyou wenku ed.

SXT *Song xingtong* 宋刑統, by Dou Yi 竇儀 (914–966) *et al.* Taibei: Wenhai, 1974 reprint of 1918 ed.

SYXA *Songyuan xuean* 宋元學案, by Huang Zongxi 黃宗羲 (1610–1695) *et al.* Shanghai: Commercial Press, 1928.

SYXJ *Shengyu xiangjie* 聖諭像解, ed. Liang Yannian 梁延年 (1673–1681). 1903 ed.

SZZL *Sangzang zalu* 喪葬雜錄, by Zhang Lüxiang 張履祥 (1611–1674). In *Duli congchao* 讀禮叢鈔, ed. Li Fuyao 李輔耀. Guoji jiyao ed.

TD *Tongdian* 通典, by Du You 杜佑 (735–812). ZHSJ ed.

THY *Tang huiyao* 唐會要, by Wang Pu 王溥 (922–982). CSJC ed.

TJJ *Tongjiang ji* 桐江集, by Fang Hui 方回 (1227–1307). Wanwei biecang ed. Shanghai: Commercial Press, 1935.

TLSY *Tanglü shuyi* 唐律疏議, by Zhangsun Wuji 長孫無忌 (d. 659) *et al.* GXJBCS ed.

TPGJ *Taiping guangji* 太平廣記, by Li Fang 李昉 (925–996) *et al.* ZHSJ, 1961.

TSJ *Taoshan ji* 陶山集, by Lu Dian 陸佃 (1042–1102). CSJC ed.

TYL *Tang yülin* 唐語林, by Wang Dang 王讜 (fl. 1100–1110). GXJBCS ed.

TZ *Tongzhi* 通志, by Zheng Qiao 鄭樵 (1104–1162). Kyoto: Chūmon, 1978 reprint of Shitong ed.

WGJL *Wengong jiali* 文公家禮, by Zhu Xi 朱熹 (1300–1200). Cuiqing tang 1589 ed.

WGZJ *Wu Chaozong xiansheng wenguozhai ji* 吳朝宗先生聞過齋集, by Wu Hai 吳海 (fourteenth century). CSJC ed.

WJQL *Henan Shaoshi wenjian qianlu* 河南邵氏聞見前錄 (1151), by Shao Bowen 邵伯溫 (1057–1134). CSJC ed.

WLCJ *Wang Linchuan ji* 王臨川集, by Wang Anshi 王安石 (1021–1086). Taibei: Shijie shuju, 1966.

WS *Wei shu* 魏書, by Wei Shou 魏收 (506–572). ZHSJ, 1974.

WSXSQJ *Wenshan xiansheng quanji* 文山先生全集, by Wen Tianxiang 文天祥 (1236–1282). GXJBCS ed.

WSZP *Wangshi zupu* 王氏族譜, by Wang Renyuan 王仁元. 1625 ed.

WX *Wenxuan* 文選, ed. Xiao Tong 蕭統 (501–531). GXJBCS ed.

WXZ *Wuxian zhi* 吳縣志. Zhongguo fangzhi congshu reprint of 1933 ed.

XAMZZ *Xin'an mingzu zhi* 新安名族志. Peiping National Library Rare Books Microfilm, roll 916.

XBHL *Xinbian hunli beiyong yuelao xinshu* 新編婚禮備用月老新書. Taibei: National Central Library microfilm of Song edition.

XCGYZ *Xianchuang guayi zhi* 閑窗括異志, by Lu Yinglong 魯應龍 (Song). Baibu congshu jicheng ed.

XLDQS *Xingli daquan shu* 性理大全書. SKQS ed.

XSWJ *Xishan wenji* 西山文集, by Zhen Dexiu 真德秀 (1178–1235). SKQS ed.

XTS *Xin Tang shu* 新唐書, by Ouyang Xiu 歐陽修 (1007–1072) and Song Qi 宋祁 (998–1061). ZHSJ, 1975.

XWDS *Xin wudai shii* 新五代史, by Ouyang Xiu 歐陽修 (1007–1072). ZHSJ, 1974.

XX *Xiaoxue* 小學, by Zhu Xi 朱熹 (1130–1200). In *Xiaoxue jijie* 集解, by Zhang Boxing 張伯行 (1651–1725). CSJC ed.

XYWJL *Xiyuan wenjian lu* 西園聞見錄, by Zhang Xuan 張萱 (1558–1641). Zhonghua wenshi congshu reprint.

XZWJ *Xunzhai wenji* 巽齋文集, by Ouyang Shoudao 歐陽守道 (1209–1267+). SKQS ed.

XZZJ *Xunzhi zhaiji* 遜志齋集, by Fang Xiaoru 方孝儒 (1357–1402). SBCK ed.

YDJ *Yuandu ji* 緣督集, by Zeng Feng 曾丰 (j.s. 1169). SKQS ed.

YDZ *Da Yuan shengzheng guochao dianzhang* 大元聖政國朝典章. Taibei: National Palace Museum 1973 reprint of Yuan ed.

YHTC *Youhui tancong* 友會談叢, by Shangguan Rong 上官融 (995–1043). Baibu congshu jicheng ed.

YJZ *Yijian zhi* 夷堅志, by Hong Mai 洪邁 (1123–1202). ZHSJ, 1981.

YL *Yili zhushu* 儀禮注疏. Shisan jing zhushu ed.

YLDD *Yongle dadian* 永樂大典 (1408), ed. Yao Guangxiao 姚廣孝 *et al.* ZHSJ, 1960.

YLJZ *Yili jingzhuan tongjie* 儀禮經傳通解, by Zhu Xi 朱熹 (1130–1200). SKQS ed.

YLMC *Yunlu manchao* 雲麓漫鈔, by Zhao Yanwei 趙彥衛 (?–1206+). CSJC ed.

YSHB *Songren yishi huibian* 宋人軼事彙編, ed. Ding Chuanjing 丁傳靖. Taibei: Commercial Press, 1935.

YSJ *Ye Shi ji* 葉適集, by Ye Shi 葉適 (1150–1223). ZHSJ, 1961.

YSJX *Yanshi jiaxun jijie* 顏氏家訓集解, by Yan Zhitui 顏之推 (531–591). Taibei: Wenming shuju, 1982.

YYJ *Yanyuan ji* 琰源集, by Dai Biaoyuan 戴表元 (1244–1310). CSJC ed.

YYYML *Yanyi yimou lu* 燕翼詒謀錄, by Wang Yong 王栐 (?–1227+). ZHSJ, 1981.

ZGJ *Zeng Gong ji* 曾鞏集, by Zeng Gong 曾鞏 (1019–1083). Beijing: Zhonghua shuju, 1984.

ZGMSQJ *Zhongguo meishu quanji* 中國美術全集. Bejing: Wenwu, 1983–.

ZGZY *Zhenguan zhengyao* 真觀政要, by Wu Jing 吳競 (670–749). Shanghai: Gujin Chubanshe ed., 1978.

ZS *Zhongshuo* 中說, by Wang Tong 王通 (584?–617). CSJC ed.

ZSZJ *Zhensuzhai ji* 真齋齋集, by Shu Di 舒頔 (1304–1377). SKQS ed.

ZWGWJ *Zhu Wengong wenji* 朱文公文集, by Zhu Xi 朱熹 (1130–1200). SBCK ed.

ZZJ *Zhang Zai ji* 張載集, by Zhang Zai 張載 (1020–1077). ZHSJ, 1978.

ZZJL *Zhuzi jiali* 朱子家禮, by Zhu Xi 朱熹 (1130–1200). Baogao tang Qing ed.

ZZLZ *Zhuzi lizuan* 朱子禮纂, by Li Guangdi 李光地 (1642–1718). SKQS ed.

ZZYL *Zhu Zi yulei* 朱子語類, by Zhu Xi 朱熹 (1130–1200). ZHSJ, 1986.

SECONDARY SOURCES

Abeel, David. 1834. *Journal of a Residence in China and the Neighboring Countries from 1829 to 1832*. New York: Levitt, Lord, and Co.

Ahern, Emily M. 1973. *The Cult of the Dead in a Chinese Village.* Stanford, Calif.: Stanford University Press.

——. 1974. "Affines and the Rituals of Kinship," in *Religion and Ritual in Chinese Society,* ed. Arthur P. Wolf. Stanford, Calif.: Stanford University Press.

——. 1976. "Segmentation in Chinese Lineages: A View from Written Genealogies." *American Ethnologist* 3:1–16.

Amiot, Joseph-Marie. 1776–1814. *Mémoires concernant l'histoire, les sciences, les arts, les moeurs, les usages, etc. des Chinois, par les Missionnaires de Pékin.* 17 vols. Paris.

Anderson, Aeneas. 1795. *A Narrative of the British Embassy to China in the Years 1792, 1793, and 1794.* London: J. Debrett.

Anderson, Benedict. 1991. *Imagined Communities: Reflections on the Origin and Spread of Nationalism.* Rev. ed. New York: Verso.

Anderson, E. N., Jr. 1970. "Lineage Atrophy in Chinese Society." *American Anthropologist* 72:363–65.

Anon. 1835. "Small feet of the Chinese females: remarks on the origin of the custom of compressing the feet; the extent and effects of the practice; with an anatomical description of a small foot." *Chinese Repository* 3:537–42.

Anon. 1966 "Henan nanyang faxian Songmu 河南南陽發現宋墓." *Kaogu* 1:54.

Ariès, Philippe. 1981. *The Hour of Our Death.* Helen Weaver, trans. New York: Knopf.

Baker, Hugh D. R. 1979. *Chinese Family and Kinship.* New York: Columbia University Press.

Barrow, John. 1806. *Travels in China.* 2nd ed. London: Cadell and Davies.

Baudier, Michael. 1682 [1635]. *The History of the Court of the King of China.* London [British Library copy].

Birge, Bettine. 1989. "Chu Hsi and women's education," in *Neo-Confucian Education: The Formative Stage,* ed. Wm. Theodore de Bary and John W. Chaffee. Berkeley: University of California Press.

Birrell, Anne M. 1985. "The Dusty Mirror: Courtly Portraits of Woman in Southern Dynasties Love Poetry," in *Expressions of Self in Chinese Literature,* ed. Robert E. Hegel and Richard C. Hessney. New York: Columbia University Press.

Blake, C. Fred. 1994. "Foot-binding in Neo-Confucian China and the Appropriation of Female Labor." *Signs* 19.3:676–712.

Bol, Peter K. 1987. "Seeking Common Ground: Han Literati Under Jurchen Rule." *Harvard Journal of Asiatic Studies* 47.2:461–538.

——. 1992. *This Culture of Ours: Intellectual Traditions in T'ang and Sung China.* Stanford, Calif.: Stanford University Press.

Boxer, C. R., ed. 1953. *South China in the Sixteenth Century, Being the Narratives of Galeote Pereira, Fr. Gaspar da Cruz, O.P., Fr. Martin de Rada, O. E. S. A. (1550–1575).* London: Hakluyt Society, ser. 2, vol. 106.

Bray, Francesca. 1997. *Technology and Gender: Fabrics of Power in Late Imperial China.* Berkeley: University of California Press.

Brown, Elizabeth A. R. 1981. "Death and the Human Body in the Later Middle Ages: The Legislation of Boniface VIII on the Division of the Corpse." *Viator: Medieval and Renaissance Studies* 12:221–70.

Brown, Peter. 1981. *The Cult of the Saints: Its Rise and Function in Latin Christianity.* Chicago: University of Chicago Press.

Burns, Ian Robert. 1973. "Private Law in Traditional China (Sung Dynasty)." Ph.D. dissertation, Oxford University.

Cahill, Suzanne. 1980. "Taoism at the Sung Court: The Heavenly Text Affair of 1008." *Bulletin of Sung and Yüan Studies* 16:23–44.

Cai Xianrong 蔡獻容. 1979. "Zhongguo duoqi zhidu de qiyuan" 中國多妻制度的起源, in *Zhongguo funü shi lunji* 中國婦女史論集, ed. Bao Jialin 鮑家麟. Taibei: Mutong.

Cameron, Nigel. 1970. *Barbarians and Mandarins: Thirteen Centuries of Western Travelers in China.* New York: Weatherhill.

Campbell, Mary B. 1988. *The Witness and the Other World: Exotic European Travel Writing, 400–1600.* Ithaca: Cornell University Press.

Carlitz, Katherine N. 1984. "Family, Society, and Tradition in *Jin Ping Mei*." *Modern China* 10.4:387–413.

Chaffee, John W. 1985. *The Thorny Gates of Learning: A Social History of Examinations.* Cambridge: Cambridge University Press.

Chan, Wing-tsit. 1986. *Chu Hsi and Neo-Confucianism*: Honolulu: University of Hawaii Press.

——. 1989. *Chu Hsi: New Studies.* Honolulu: University of Hawaii Press.

Chau, Virginia Chui-tin. 1966. "The Anti-footbinding Movement in China (1850–1912)." MA Essay, Columbia University, Faculty of Political Science.

Chen, Chung-min. 1985. "Dowry and Inheritance," in *The Chinese Family and Its Ritual Behavior*, ed. Hsieh Jih-chang and Chuang Ying-chang. Taibei: Academia Sinica, Institute of Ethnology.

Chen Dongyuan 陳東原. 1928 [1980]. *Zhongguo funü shenghuo shi* 中國婦女生活史. Taibei: Commercial Press.

Chen Guyuan 陳雇遠. 1936 [1978]. *Zhongguo hunyin shi* 中國婚姻史. Taibei: Commercial Press.

Chen Jiaxiang 陳嘉祥. 1956. "Luoyang Manglujie qinglile yizuo Songmu" 洛陽邙麓街清理了一座宋墓. *Wenwu cankao ziliao* 11:75–77.

Chen Peng 陳鵬. 1990. *Zhongguo hunyin shigao* 中國婚姻史稿. Beijing: Zhonghua shuju.

Chen Shu 陳述. 1986. "Haner Hanzi shuo" 漢兒漢子說. *Shehui kexue zhanxian* 1:90–97.

Ch'en, Kenneth K. S. 1973. *The Chinese Transformation of Buddhism.* Princeton, N.J.: Princeton University Press.

Chiba Hiroshi 千葉. 1976. "Eisō Senjin seiretsu kōgō Gōshi" 英宗宣仁聖烈皇后高氏, in *Kimura Masao sensei taikan kinen Tōyōshi ronshū* 木村正雄先生退官記念東洋史論集. Tokyo: Kyūko Shoin.

——. 1978. "Mō kōgō no koto" 孟皇后のこと," in *Namae Yoshio Sensei kanreki kinen: Rekishi ronshū* 生江義男先生還曆記念—歷史論集. Tokyo: Kyūko Shoin.

——. 1981. "Kisō no kōhi tachi" 徽宗の后妃たち, in *Nakajima Satoshi sensei koki kinen ronshū* 中島敏先生古稀紀年論集. Tokyo: Kyūko Shoin.

Chikusa Masaaki 竺沙雅章. 1956. "Sōdai Fukken no shakai to jiin" 宋代福建の社會と寺院. *Tōyōshi kenkyū* 15:170–96.

——. 1982. *Chūgoku bukkyō shakai shi kenkyū* 中國佛教社會史研究. Kyoto: Dōhōsha.

Chung, Priscilla Ching. 1981. *Palace Women in the Northern Sung.* T'oung Pao Monographie, 12. Leiden: E. J. Brill.

Ch'ü T'ung-tsu. 1961. *Law and Society in Traditional China.* Paris: Mouton.

———. 1972. *Han Social Structure*, ed. Jack L. Dull. Seattle: University of Washington Press.

Clifford, James. 1988. *The Predicament of Culture: Twentieth-Century Ethnography, Literature, and Art.* Cambridge, Mass.: Harvard University Press.

Clignet, Remi. 1970. *Many Wives, Many Powers: Authority and Power in Polygynous Families.* Evanston, Ill.: Northwestern University Press.

Cohen, Myron L. 1976. *House United, House Divided: The Chinese Family in Taiwan.* New York: Columbia University Press.

Comaroff, J. L. 1980. "Introduction," in *The Meaning of Marriage Payments*, ed. J. L. Comaroff. New York: Academic Press.

Cooper, T. T. 1871. *Travels of a Pioneer of Commerce.* London: John Murray.

Cranmer-Byng, J. L., ed. 1962. *An Embassy to China: Being the Journal Kept by Lord Macartney during his Embassy to the Emperor Ch'ien-lung 1793–94.* London: Longmans, Green and Co.

Croll, Elisabeth. 1980. *Feminism and Socialism in China.* New York: Schocken Books.

———. 1989. *Wise Daughters from Foreign Lands: European Women Writers in China.* London: Pandora.

Crossley, Pamela Kyle. 1990. "Thinking About Ethnicity in Early Modern China." *Late Imperial China* 11.1:1–35.

Dai Yanhui 戴炎輝 [see also Tai, Yen-hui]. 1936. "Saiden mata wa saishi kōgyō 祭田又は祭祀公業," *Hōgaku kyōkai zasshi* 54.10:93–122; 54.11:99–113.

———. 1966. *Zhongguo fazhi shi* 中國法制史. Taibei: Sanmin.

Dardess, John W. 1974. "The Cheng Communal Family: Social Organization and Neo-Confucianism in Yuan and Early Ming China." *Harvard Journal of Asiatic Studies* 34:7–52.

———. 1983. *Confucianism and Autocracy.* Berkeley: University of California Press.

Datongshi wenwu chenlie guan 大同市文物陳列官. 1963. "Shanxi Datong Wohuwan sizuo Liaodai bihua mu" 山西大同臥虎灣四座遼代壁畫墓. *Kaogu* 8:432–36.

Davis, John Francis. 1836. *The Chinese: A General Description of the Empire of China and its Inhabitants.* New York: Harper and Brothers.

Davis, Richard L. 1986a. *Court and Family in Sung China, 960–1279: Bureaucratic Success and Kinship Fortunes for the Shih of Ming-chou.* Durham, N.C.: Duke University Press.

———. 1986b. "Political Success and the Growth of Descent Groups: the Shih of Mingchou During the Sung," in *Kinship Organization in Late Imperial China, 1000–1940*, ed. Patricia Buckley Ebrey and James L. Watson. Berkeley: University of California Press.

Dawson, Christopher. 1955. *The Mongol Mission: Narratives and Letters of the Franciscan Missionaries in Mongolia and China in the Thirteenth and Fourteenth Centuries.* London: Sheed and Ward.

Dawson, Raymond. 1967. *The Chinese Chameleon: An Analysis of European Conceptions of Chinese Civilization.* London: Oxford University Press.

De Groot, J. J. M. 1892–1910. *The Religious System of China.* 6 vols. Taibei: Chengwen reprint, 1972.

Dennerline, Jerry. 1986. "Marriage, Adoption, and Charity in the Development of Lineages in Wu-hsi from Sung to Ch'ing," in *Kinship Organization in Late Imperial China, 1000–1940*, ed. Patricia Buckley Ebrey and James L. Watson. Berkeley: University of California Press.

Dien, Albert E. 1977. "The Bestowal of Surnames Under the Western Wei-Northern Chou: A Case of Counter Acculturation." *T'oung Pao* 63.2–3:137–77.

Dikötter, Frank. 1992. *The Discourse of Race in Modern China*. Stanford, Calif.: Stanford University Press.

Dixon, Suzanne. 1985. "The Marriage Alliance in the Roman Elite." *Journal of Family History* 10.4:353–78.

Doolittle, Justus. 1865. *Social Life of the Chinese with Some Account of Their Religious, Governmental, Educational, and Business Customs and Opinions, with Special but not Exclusive Reference to Fuhchau*. 2 vols. New York: Harper and Brothers.

Downing, C. Toogood. 1972 [1838]. *The Fan-Qui in China in 1836–7*. Shannon: Irish University Press reprint of London: H. Colburn.

Drucker, Allison. 1991. "The Influence of Western Women on the Anti-footbinding Movement 1840–1911," in *Women in China: Current Directions in Historical Scholarship*, ed. Richard W. Guisso and Stanley Johannesen. Youngstown, N.Y.: Philo Press.

Du Halde, Jean-Baptiste. 1736. *The General History of China*. London: J. Watts.

Duara, Prasenjit. 1993. "Deconstructing the Chinese Nation." *The Australian Journal of Chinese Affairs* 30:1–28.

Dudgeon, J. 1869. "The Small Feet of Chinese Women." *Chinese Recorder and Missionary Journal* 2.4:93–96; 2.5:130–33.

Dull, Jack L. 1978. "Marriage and Divorce in Han China: A Glimpse at 'Pre-Confucian' Society," in *Chinese Family Law and Social Change in Historical and Comparative Perspective*, ed. David C. Buxbaum. Seattle: University of Washington Press.

Eberhard, Wolfram. 1962. *Social Mobility in Traditional China*. Leiden: E. J. Brill.

Ebrey, Patricia Buckley. 1974. "Estate and Family Management in the Later Han as Seen in the *Monthly Instructions for the Four Classes of People*." *Journal of the Economic and Social History of the Orient* 17:173–205.

——. 1978. *The Aristocratic Families of Early Imperial China: A Case Study of the Po-ling Ts'ui Family*. Cambridge: Cambridge University Press.

——. 1980. "Later Han Stone Inscriptions." *Harvard Journal of Asiatic Studies* 49:325–53.

——. 1981a. *Chinese Civilization and Society: A Sourcebook*. New York: The Free Press.

——. 1981b. "Women in the Kinship System of the Southern Song Upper Class," in *Women in China*, ed. Richard W. Guisso and Stanley Johannesen. Youngstown, N.Y.: Philo.

——. 1983. "Types of Lineages in Ch'ing China: A Re-examination of the Changs of T'ung-ch'eng." *Ch'ing shih wen-t'i* 4:1–20.

——. 1984a. "Conceptions of the Family in the Song Dynasty." *Journal of Asian Studies* 43.2:219–45.

——. 1984b. *Family and Property in Sung China: Yüan Ts'ai's Precepts for Social Life*. Princeton, N.J.: Princeton University Press.

——. 1984c. "The Women in Liu Kezhuang's Family." *Modern China* 10:415–40 [reproduced here as Chapter 4].

——. 1985. "T'ang Guides to Verbal Etiquette." *Harvard Journal of Asiatic Studies* 45:581–613.

——. 1986a. "Concubines in Sung China." *Journal of Family History* 11:1–24 [reproduced here as Chapter 2].

——. 1986b. "The Early Stages in the Development of Descent Group Organization," in *Kinship Organization in Late Imperial China, 1000–1940*, ed. Patricia Buckley Ebrey and James L. Watson. Berkeley: University of California Press [reproduced here as Chapter 5].

——. 1986c. "Economic and Social History of the Later Han," in *Cambridge History of China*, I. ed. Michael Loewe and Denis Twitchett. Cambridge: Cambridge University Press, pp. 608–48.

——. 1988. "The Dynamics of Elite Domination in Sung China." *Harvard Journal of Asiatic Studies* 48:493–519.

——. 1989. "Education through Ritual: Efforts to Formulate Family Rituals in the Sung Period," in *Neo-Confucian Education: The Formative Stage*, ed. John W. Chaffee and Wm. Theodore de Bary. Berkeley: University of California Press.

——. 1990a. "Cremation in Sung China." *American Historical Review* 95:406–28 [reproduced here as Chapter 6].

——. 1990b. "Women, Marriage, and the Family in Chinese History," in *The Heritage of China*, ed. Paul Ropp. Berkeley: University of California Press.

——. 1991a. *Chu Hsi's Family Rituals: A Twelfth Century Chinese Manual for the Performance of Cappings, Weddings, Funerals, and Ancestral Rites*. Princeton, N.J.: Princeton University Press.

——. 1991b. *Confucianism and Family Rituals in Imperial China: A Social History of Writing About Rites*. Princeton, N.J.: Princeton University Press.

——. 1991c. "Shifts in Marriage Finance, from the Sixth to Thirteenth Centuries," in *Marriage and Inequality in Chinese Society*, ed. Rubie S. Watson and Patricia Buckley Ebrey. Berkeley: University of California Press [reproduced here as Chapter 3].

——. 1992. "Women, Money, and Class: Ssu-ma Kuang and Sung Neo-Confucian Views on Women," in *Zhongguo jinshi shehui wenhua shilun wenji*. Taibei: Institute of History and Philology, Academia Sinica [reproduced here as Chapter 1].

——. 1993. *The Inner Quarters: Marriage and the Lives of Chinese Women in the Sung Period*. Berkeley: University of California Press.

——. 1996. "Surnames and Han Chinese Identity," in *Negotiating Ethnicities in China and Taiwan*, ed. Melissa Brown. Institute for East Asian Studies, University of California, Berkeley [reproduced here as Chapter 7].

——. 1997. "Sung Neo-Confucian Views on Geomancy," in *Meeting of Minds*, ed. Irene Bloom and Joshua A. Fogel. New York: Columbia University Press, pp. 75–107.

——. 1999. "Gender and Sinology: Shifts in Western Interpretations of Footbinding, 1300–1890." *Late Imperial China* 20:2. 1–34 [reproduced here as Chapter 9].

——. 2000. "Taoism and Art at the Court of Song Huizong," in *Taoism and the Arts of China*, ed. Stephen Little. Berkeley: University of California Press, pp. 94–111.

Ebrey, Patricia Buckley and James L. Watson, eds. 1986. *Kinship Organization in Late Imperial China, 1000–1940*. Berkeley: University of California Press.

Eichhorn, Werner. 1976. "Some Notes on Population Control During the Sung Dynasty," in *D'Études d'histoire et de litérature chinoises offertes au Professeur Jaroslav Prusek*. Paris: Bibliothèque de l'Institut des Hautes Études chinoises.

Elvin, Mark. 1973. *The Pattern of the Chinese Past*. Stanford, Calif.: Stanford University Press.

——. 1984. "Female Virtue and the State in China." *Past and Present* 104:111–52.

Endicott-West, Elizabeth. 1989. *Mongolian Rule in China: Local Administration in the Yuan Dynasty*. Cambridge, Mass.: Council on East Asian Studies, Harvard University.

Eoyang, Eugene. 1982. "The Wang Chao-chün Legend: Configurations of the Classic." *Chinese Literature: Essays, Articles, Reviews* 4.1:3–22.

Fang Jianxin 方建新. 1986. "Songdai hunyin luncai" 宋代婚姻論財. *Lishi yanjiu* 3:178–90.

Farmer, Edward L. 1990. "Social Regulations of the First Ming Emperor: Orthodoxy as a Function of Authority," in *Orthodoxy in Later Imperial China*, ed. Kwang-ching Liu. Berkeley: University of California Press.

Faure, David. 1989. "The Lineage as Cultural Invention: The Case of the Pearl River Delta." *Modern China* 15.1:4–36.

Fielde, Adele M. 1887. *Pagoda Shadows: Studies from Life in China*. London: T. Ogilvie Smith.

Fortune, Robert. 1857. *A Residence Among the Chinese: Inland, on the Coast, and at Sea. Being a Narrative of Scenes and Adventures During a Third Visit to China, from 1853 to 1856*. London: John Murray.

Foulk, Griffith. 1987. "The 'Ch'an School' and its Place in the Buddhist Monastic Tradition." Ph.D. dissertation, University of Michigan.

Freedman, Maurice. 1966. *Chinese Lineage and Society: Fukien and Kwangtung*. London: Athlone Press.

———. 1979. "Rites and Duties, or Chinese Marriage," in his *The Study of Chinese Society*, ed. G. William Skinner. Stanford, Calif.: Stanford University Press.

Fried, Morton. 1970. "Clans and Lineages: How to Tell Them Apart and Why–With Special Reference to Chinese Society." *Bulletin of the Institute of Ethnology, Academia Sinica* 29:11–36.

Gallagher, Louis J., trans. 1953. *China in the Sixteenth Century: The Journals of Matthew Ricci: 1583–1610*. New York: Random House.

Gallin, Bernard, and Rita S. Gallin. 1985. "Matrilateral and Affinal Relationships in Changing Chinese Society," in *The Chinese Family and Its Ritual Behavior*, ed. Hsieh Jih-chang and Chuang Ying-chang. Taibei: Academia Sinica, Institute of Ethnology.

Gamble, Sidney D. 1963. *North China Villages: Social, Political, and Economic Activities before 1933*. Berkeley: University of California Press.

Gao Hongxing 高洪興. 1995. *Chanzu shi* 纏足史. Shanghai: Wenyi chubanshe.

Gates, Hill. 1989. "The Commoditization of Chinese women." *Signs: Journal of Women in Culture and Society* 14:4.799–832.

Gates, Hill and Robert P. Weller, eds. 1987. "Symposium on Hegemony and Chinese Folk Ideologies." *Modern China* 13.

Gernet, Jacques. 1960. "Les Suicides par le feu chez les Bouddhistes chinois du Ve au Xe siècle." *Mélanges publiés par l'Institut des Hautes Études Chinoises* 2:527–58.

———. 1970. *Daily Life in China on the Eve of the Mongol Invasion, 1250–1276*. H. M. Wright, trans. Stanford, Calif.: Stanford University Press.

Giles, Herbert. 1902. *China and the Chinese*. New York: Columbia University Press.

Goody, Jack. 1973. "Bridewealth and Dowry in Africa and Eurasia," in *Bridewealth and Dowry*, by Jack Goody and S. J. Tambiah. Cambridge: Cambridge University Press.

———. 1976. *Production and Reproduction: A Comparative Study of the Domestic Domain*. Cambridge: Cambridge University Press.

———. 1983. *The Development of the Family and Marriage in Europe.* Cambridge: Cambridge University Press.

Gordon-Cumming, D. F. 1888. *Wanderings in China.* Edinburgh and London: William Blackword and Sons.

Grafflin, Dennis. 1983. "The Onomastics of Medieval South China: Patterned Naming in the Lang-yeh and T'ai-yuan Wang." *Journal of the American Oriental Society* 103:383–98.

Graham, A. C. 1960. *The Book of Lieh-tzu.* London: Murray.

Gray, John Henry. 1878. *China: A History of the Laws, Manners, and Customs of the People.* London: Macmillan.

Gronewold, Sue. 1982. "Beautiful Merchandise: Prostitution in China, 1860–1936." *Women and History* 1:1–114.

Grosier, Abbé Jean-Baptiste. 1788. *A General Description of China.* 2 vols. London: G. G. J. and J. Robinson.

Guangdongsheng wenwu guanli weiyuan hui 廣東省文物管理委員會. 1965. "Guangdong Foshan shijiao Lanshi Tang zhi Ming mu fajue ji" 廣東佛山市郊瀾石唐至明墓發掘記. *Kaogu* 6:284–86.

Guangzhoushi wenwu guanli weiyuan hui 廣州市文物管理委員會. 1957. "Guangzhou Henan Jianjiagang SongYuan mu fajue jianbao" 廣州河南簡家岡宋元墓發掘簡報. *Wenwu cankao ziliao* 6:70–73.

Guisso, R. W. L. 1981. "Thunder Over the Late: The Five Classics and the Perception of Woman in Early China," in *Women in China,* ed. Richard W. Guisso and Stanley Johannesen. Youngstown, N.Y.: Philo Press.

Gutzlaff, Charles. 1834. *Journal of Three Voyages along the Coast of China, in 1831, 1832, and 1833.* London: Frederick Westley and A. H. Davis.

———. 1838. *China Opened: Or, A Display of the Topography, History, Customs, Manners, Arts, Manufactures, Commerce, Literature, Religions, Jurisprudence, Etc. of the Chinese Empire.* 2 vols. London: Smith, Elder and Co.

Haeger, John W. 1978. "Marco Polo in China? Problems with Internal Evidence." *Bulletin of Sung and Yüan Studies* 14:22–30.

Handlin, Joanna F. 1975. "Lü K'un's New Audience: The Influence of Women's Literacy on Sixteenth-Century Thought," in *Women in Chinese Society,* ed. Margery Wolf and Roxane Witke. Stanford, Calif.: Stanford University Press.

Hansen, Valerie. 1989. *Changing Gods in Medieval China, 1127–1276.* Princeton, N.J.: Princeton University Press.

Harrell, Stevan, and Sara A. Dickey. 1985. "Dowry Systems in Complex Societies." *Ethnology* 24:2.105–20.

Hartwell, Robert M. 1982. "Demographic, Political, and Social Transformations of China, 750–1550." *Harvard Journal of Asiatic Studies* 42:365–442.

Hazelton, Keith. 1986. "Patrilines and the Development of Localized Lineages: The Wu of Hsiu-ning City, Hui-chou, to 1528," in *Kinship Organization in Late Imperial China, 1000–1940,* ed. Patricia Buckley Ebrey and James L. Watson. Berkeley: University of California Press.

He Zhenghuang 何正璜. 1966. "Song wuming shi muzhuan" 宋無名氏墓磚. *Wenwu* 1:53–54.

Hegel, Robert E. 1981. *The Novel in Seventeenth-Century China.* New York: Columbia University Press.

Hennessey, William O., trans. 1981. *Proclaiming Harmony.* Ann Arbor: Center for Chinese Studies, University of Michigan.

Herlihy, David. 1985. *Medieval Households.* Cambridge, Mass.: Harvard University Press.

Hertz, Robert. 1960. "A Contribution to the Study of the Collective Representation of Death," *Death and the Right Hand.* Rodney Needham and Claudia Needham, trans. Glencoe, Ill.: Free Press.

Holmgren, Jennifer. 1985. "The Economic Foundations of Virtue: Widow-Remarriage in Early and Modern China." *Australian Journal of Chinese Affairs* 13:1–27.

———. 1986. "Observations on Marriage and Inheritance Practices in Early Mongol and Yuan Society: With Particular Reference to the Levirate." *Journal of Asian History* 20:127–92.

Hong, Fan. 1997. *Footbinding, Feminism and Freedom: The Liberation of Women's Bodies in Modern China.* London Frank Cass.

Hong Jianmin 洪劍民. 1959. "Luetan Chengdu jinjiao Wudai zhi Nan Song de muzang xingzhi" 略談成都近郊五代至南宋的墓葬形制. *Kaogu* 1:36–39, 23, 35.

Houghton, Ross C. 1877. *Women of the Orient: An Account of the Religious, Intellectual, and Social Condition of Women in Japan, China, India, Egypt, Syria, and Turkey.* Cincinnati: Walden and Stowe.

Hsu, Francis L. K. 1948 [1971]. *Under the Ancestor's Shadow.* Stanford: Stanford University Press.

Hu, Hsien Chin. 1948. *The Common Descent Group in China and Its Functions.* New York: Viking Fund.

Huang Jinjun 黃錦君. 1997. *Liang Song houfei shiji biannian* 兩宋后妃事蹟編年. Chengdu: Bashu shushe.

Huang Minzhi 黃敏枝. 1988. *Songdai fojiao shehui jingjishi lunji* 宋代佛教社會經濟史論集. Taipei: Xuesheng shuju.

Huc, Évariste-Régis. 1855. *The Chinese Empire.* 2nd ed. London: Longman, Brown, Green, and Longmans.

Hughes, Diane Owen. 1978. "From Brideprice to Dowry in Mediterranean Europe." *Journal of Family History* 3.3:262–96.

Hunter, Jane. 1984. *The Gospel of Gentility: American Women Missionaries in Turn-of-the-Century China.* New Haven, Conn.: Yale University Press.

Hyatt, Irwin T., Jr. 1976. *Our Ordered Lives Confess: Three Nineteenth-Century American Missionaries in East Shantung.* Cambridge, Mass.: Harvard University Press.

Hymes, Robert P. 1986a. "Marriage, Descent Groups, and the Localist Strategy in Sung and Yuan Fu-chou," in *Kinship Organization in Late Imperial China, 1000–1940,* ed. Patricia Buckley Ebrey and James L. Watson. Berkeley: University of California Press.

———. 1986b. *Statesmen and Gentlemen: The Elite of Fu-Chou, Chiang-Hsi, in Northern and Southern Sung.* Cambridge: Cambridge University Press.

Jackson, Beverly. 1997. *Splendid Slippers: A Thousand Years of an Erotic Tradition.* Berkeley, Calif.: Ten Speed Press.

Jackson, Peter, trans. 1990. *The Mission of Friar William of Rubruck: His Journey to the court of the Great Khan Mönke 1253–1255.* London: The Hakluyt Society, ser. II, vol. 173.

Jan, Yun-hua. 1965. "Buddhist Self-Immolation in Medieval China." *History of Religions* 4:243–68.

Jia Shen 賈申. 1925 [1979]. *Zhonghua funü chanzu kao* 中華婦女纏足考. Beijing: Cuxiang.

Johnson, David G. 1977a. "The Last Years of a Great Clan: The Li Family of Chao Chün in Late Tang and Early Sung." *Harvard Journal of Asiatic Studies* 37:5–102.

——. 1977b. *The Medieval Chinese Oligarchy.* Boulder, Colo.: Westview Press.

——. 1983. "Comment: Chinese Kinship Reconsidered." *China Quarterly* 94:362–65.

——. 1985. "The City God Cults of Tang and Song China." *Harvard Journal of Asiatic Studies* 45:363–457.

Jordan, David K. 1972. *Gods, Ghosts, and Ancestors.* Berkeley: University of California Press.

Kaltenmark, Max. 1969. *Lao Zi and Taoism.* Roger Greaves, trans. Stanford, Calif.: Stanford University Press.

Kelleher, M. Theresa. 1989. "Back to the Basics: Chu Hsi's *Elementary Learning* (*Hsiao-hsüeh*)," in *Neo-Confucian Education: The Formative Stage*, ed. Wm. Theodore de Bary and John W. Chaffee. Berkeley: University of California Press.

Kerr, J. G. 1869. "Small Feet." *The Chinese Recorder and Missionary Journal* 2:169–70.

——. 1870. "Small Feet." *The Chinese Recorder and Missionary Journal* 3:22–23.

Knechtges, David R., trans. 1982. *Wen xuan, or, Selections of Refined Literature.* Princeton, N.J.: Princeton University Press.

Ko, Dorothy. 1994. *Teachers of the Inner Chambers: Women and Culture in Seventeenth-Century China.* Stanford, Calif.: Stanford University Press.

——. 1997a "Bondage in Time: Footbinding and Fashion Theory." *Fashion Theory: The Journal of Dress, Body and Culture* 1.1:3–28.

——. 1997b. "The Written Word and the Bound Foot: A History of the Courtesan's Aura," in *Writing Women in Late Imperial China*, ed. Ellen Widmer and Kang-I Sun Chang. Stanford, Calif.: Stanford University Press.

Kobayashi Yoshiro 小林義廣. 1980. "Oyō Shu ni okeru zokufu hensan no igi" 歐陽修における族譜の意義 *Nagoya daigaku Tōyōshi kenkyū hōkoku* 6:189–216.

Kulp, Daniel Harrison. 1925. *Country Life in South China.* New York: Teachers College Bureau of Publications.

Kusano Yasushi 草野靖. 1974. "Sōdai doboku hisho mondai no ippan." 宋代奴僕婢妾問題の一斑. In *Sōdaishi ronsō* 宋代史論叢. Tokyo: Seishin.

Kyō Heinan 喬炳南. 1976. "Sōdai no gisō seido" 宋代の義莊制度. *Tezukayama daiguku ronshū* 11:74–98.

Lach, Donald F. 1965. *Asia in the Making of Europe* (3 vols). Vol. 1 *The Century of Discovery.* Chicago: University of Chicago Press.

Lang, Olga. 1946. *Chinese Family and Society.* New Haven, Conn.: Yale University Press.

Langlois, John D., Jr. 1980. "Chinese Culturalism and the Yüan Analogy: Seventeenth-Century Perspectives." *Harvard Journal of Asiatic Studies* 40.2:355–98.

——. 1981. "Authority in Family Legislation: The Cheng Family Rules," in *State and Law in East Aria: Festschrift Karl Bunger*, ed. Dieter Eikemeier and Herbert Franke. Wiesbaden: Otto Harrassowitz.

Langlois, John D. Jr. and Sun K'o-k'uan. 1983. "Three Teachings Syncretism and the Thought of Ming T'ai-tsu." *Harvard Journal of Asiatic Studies* 43:97–139.

Laquer, Thomas. 1983 "Bodies, Death, and Pauper Funerals." *Representations* 1: 109–31.

Lau, Joseph S. M., C. T. Hsia, and Leo Ou-fan Lee, eds. 1981. *Modern Chinese Stories and Novellas, 1919–1949.* New York: Columbia University Press.

Le Blanc, Charles. 1985–1986. "A Re-Examination of the Myth of Huang-ti." *Journal of Chinese Religions* 13/14: 45–63.

Lee, Thomas H. C. 1985. *Government Education and Examinations in Sung China.* Hong Kong: Chinese University Press.

Legge, James, trans. 1865–1895 [1961]. *The Chinese Classics.* 5 vols. Hong Kong: Hong Kong University Press.

——. 1885 [1967]. *Li chi: Book of Rites* (Sacred Books of the East). New York: University Books.

Letts, Malcolm. 1953. *Mandeville's Travels.* London: The Hakluyt Society, ser. II, vol. 101.

Levering, Miriam L. 1978. "Ch'an Enlightenment for Laymen: Tahui and the New Religious Culture of the Song." Ph.D. dissertation, Harvard University.

Levy, Howard S. 1967. *Chinese Footbinding: The History of a Curious Erotic Custom.* New York: Bell Publishing Co.

Lewis, Mark Edward. 1990. *Sanctioned Violence in Early China.* Albany: State University of New York Press.

Li, Chi. 1928. *The Formation of the Chinese People.* Cambridge, Mass.: Harvard University Press.

Li, Dun J. 1971. *The Ageless Chinese: A History.* 2nd ed. New York: Scribners.

Lin, Shuen-Fu. 1978. *The Transformation of a Chinese Lyrical Tradition.* Princeton, N.J.: Princeton University Press.

Lin, Yutang. 1939. *My Country and My People.* London: Heinemann.

——. 1947. *The Gay Genius: The Life and Times of Su Tungpo.* New York: John Day.

Lindley, Augustus F. 1866. *Ti-Ping Tien-Kwoh: The History of the Ti-Ping Revolution.* London: Day and Son.

Liu Dehan 劉德漢. 1974. *Dong Zhou funü shenghuo* 東周婦女生活. Taibei: Xuesheng.

Liu, Hui-chen Wang. 1959a. "An Analysis of Chinese Clan Rules: Confucian Theories in Action," in *Confucianism in Action*, ed. David S. Nivison and Arthur R. Wright. Stanford, Calif.: Stanford University Press.

——. 1959b. *The Traditional Chinese Clan Rules.* New York: J. J. Augustin.

Liu, James T. C. [see also Liu Zijian] 1967. *Ou-yang Hsiu: an Eleventh-Century Neo-Confucianist.* Stanford, Calif.: Stanford University Press.

Liu Jingzhen 劉靜貞. 1988. "Cong huanghou ganzheng dao taihou shezheng – Bei Song zhen ren zhi ji nüzhu zhengzhi quanli shitan" 從皇后干政到太后攝政—北宋真宗之際女主權力權利試探. *Guoji Songshi yanjiu taohui lunwen ji.* Taibei: Chinese Culture University.

Liu, Kwang-Ching ed. 1990a. *Orthodoxy in Late Imperial China.* Berkeley: University of California Press.

——. 1990b. "Socioethics as Orthodoxy: A Perspective," in *Orthodoxy in Late Imperial China*, ed. Kwang-Ching Liu. Berkeley: University of California Press.

Liu Shiji 劉仕驥. 1957. *Zhongguo zangsu souqi* 中國葬俗搜奇. Hong Kong: Shanghai shuju.

Liu Zhiyuan 劉志遠 and Jian Shi 堅石. 1955. "Chuanxi de xiaoxing Songmu" 川西的小型宋墓. *Wenwu cankao ziliao* 9:92–98.

Lockhart, William. 1861. *The Medical Missionary in China: A Narrative of Twenty Years' Experience.* London: Hurst and Blackett.

Loewe, Michael. 1982. *Chinese Ideas of Life and Death.* London: Allen and Unwin.

Lü Chengzhi 呂誠之. 1935. *Zhongguo hunyin zhidu xiaoshi* 中國婚姻制度小史. Rev. ed. Shanghai: Lunghu shuju.

Lu Hsun. 1957. "My views on Chastity," in *Lu Hsun: Selected Works*. Yang Xianyi and Gladys Yan, trans. Peking: Foreign Languages Press.

Ma Zhisu 馬之驌. 1981. *Zhongguo de hunsu* 中國的婚俗. Taibei: Jingshi shuju.

Mabro, Judy. 1991. *Veiled Half Truths: Western Travellers' Perceptions of Middle Eastern Women*. New York: I.B. Tauris.

McCreery, John L. 1976. "Women's Property Rights and Dowry in China and South Asia." *Ethnology* 15:163–74.

McDermott, Joseph P. 1981. "Bondservants in the T'ai-hu Basin during the Late Ming: A Case of Mistaken Identities." *Journal of Asian Studies* 40:675–701.

——. 1984. "Charting Blank Spaces and Disputed Regions: The Problems of Sung Land Tenure." *Journal of Asian Studies* 4:13–41.

MacFarlane, A. 1970. *The Family Life of Ralph Josselin*. Cambridge: Cambridge University Press.

——. 1986. *Marriage and Love in England: Modes of Reproduction 1300–1840*. Oxford: Basil Blackwell.

Mackerras, Colin. 1989. *Western Images of China*. Oxford: Oxford University Press.

McKnight, Brian E. 1971. *Village and Bureaucracy in Southern Sung China*. Chicago: University of Chicago Press.

McMahon, Keith. 1995. *Misers, Shrews, and Polygamists: Sexuality and Male–Female Relations in Eighteenth-Century Chinese Fiction*. Durham, N.C.: Duke University Press.

Maitra, K. M., trans. 1970 [1934]. *A Persian Embassy to China, Being an Extract from Zubdatu't Tawarikh of Hafiz Abru*. New York: Paragon (reprint of Lahore 1934 ed).

Makino Tatsumi 牧野巽. 1939. "Sōshi to sono hattatsu" 宗祠と其の發達. *Tōyō gakuhō* 9:173–250.

——. 1949. *Kinsei Chūgoku sōzoku kenkyū* 近世中國宗族研究. Tokyo: Nikkō.

Makio Ryōkai 牧尾良海. 1968. "Sōdai ni okeru kasō shōzoku ni tsuite" 宋代における火葬習俗について. *Chizan gakuhō* 16:47–57.

Makita Tairyō 牧田諦亮. 1978. *Chūgoku kosoden sakuin* 中國高僧傳索引, 7 vols. Kyoto: Heirakuji Shoten.

Mann, Susan. 1985. "Historical Change in Female Biography from Song to Qing Times: The Case of Early Qing Jiangnan (Jiangsu and Anhui Provinces)." *Transactions of the International Conference of Orientalists in Japan* 30:65–77.

——. 1987. "Women in the Kinship, Class, and Community Structures of Qing Dynasty China." *Journal of Asian Studies* 46:37–56.

——. 1991. "Grooming a Daughter for Marriage: Brides and Wives in the Mid-Ch'ing Period," in *Marriage and Inequality in Chinese Society*, ed. Rubie S. Watson and Patricia Buckley Ebrey. Berkeley: University of California Press.

——. 1997. *Precious Records: Women in China's Long Eighteenth Century*. Stanford, Calif.: Stanford University Press.

Mao Hanguang 毛漢光. 1984. *Tangdai muzhiming huibian fukao* 唐代墓誌銘彙編附考. Taibei: Institute of History and Philology, Academia Sinica.

Matsui Shuichi 松井秀一. 1968. "Hoku Sō shoki kanryō no ichi tenkei – Seki Kai to sono keifu o chūshin ni –" 北宋初期官僚の一典型—石介とその系普を中心に—. *Tōyō gakuhō* 51.1:44–92.

Mauss, Marcel. 1925 [1966]. *The Gift: Forms and Functions of Exchange in Archaic Societies*. New York: W.W. Norton.

Mendoza, Juan Gonzalez de. 1583 [1853]. *The History of the Great and Mighty Kingdom of China*. R. Parke trans., ed. George T. Staunton. London: The Hakluyt Society, vols. 5, 14, 15.

Meskill, Johanna M. 1970. "The Chinese Genealogy as a Research Source," in *Family and Kinship in Chinese Society*, ed. Maurice Freedman. Stanford, Calif.: Stanford University Press.

Meskill, John, trans. 1965. *Cho'e Pu's Diary: A Record of Drifting Across the Sea*. Tucson: University of Arizona Press.

Miyakawa, Hisayuki. 1960. "The Confucianization of South China," in *The Confucian Persuasion*, ed. Arthur F. Wright. Stanford, Calif.: Stanford University Press.

Miyazaki Ichisada 宮崎市定. 1976. "Chūgoku kasō kō 中國火葬考," in *Ajiashi ronkō* III. Tokyo: Asahi Shinbunsha, pp. 63–84.

Morita Kenji 森田憲司. 1979. "Sō-Gen jidai ni okeru shūfu" 宋元時代における修普. *Tōyōshi kenkyū* 37:509–35.

Morrison, R. 1817. *View of China for Philological Purposes; Containing a Sketch of Chinese Chronology, Geography, Government, Religion, and Customs*. Macao: P.P. Thoms.

Moule, A. C. 1930. *Christians in China before the Year 1550*. London: Society for Promoting Christian Knowledge.

——. 1957. *Quinsai, With Other Notes on Marco Polo*. Cambridge: Cambridge University Press.

Moule, A. C. and Paul Pelliot. 1938. *Marco Polo: The Description of the World*. London: George Routledge and Sons.

Munakata, Kiyohiko. 1991. *Sacred Mountains in Chinese Art*. Urbana: University of Illinois Press.

Naba Toshisada 那波利貞. 1921. "Kasōhō no Shina ryūdan ni tsuite 火葬法の支那流傳に就いて. *Shina gaku* 1:7.553–58.

——. 1974. *Tōdai shakai bunkashi kenkyū* 唐代社會文化史研究. *Oriental Studies Library* No. 8. Tokyo: Sōbunsha.

Nagasawa Kazutoshi 長澤和俊. 1980. "Tonko no shomin seikatsu" 敦煌の庶民生活, in *Tonko no shakai* 敦煌の社會, ed. Ikeda On 池田温 (*Kyoza Tonko*). Tokyo: Daitō.

Naquin, Susan. 1986. "Two Descent Groups in North China: The Wangs of Yung-p'ing Prefecture, 1500–1800," in *Kinship Organization in Late Imperial China, 1000–1940*, ed. Patricia Buckley Ebrey and James L. Watson. Berkeley: University of California Press.

Navarrete, Friar Domingo Fernández. 1962. *The Travels and Controversies of Friar Domingo Navarrete* (2 vols.), ed. and trans. J. S. Cummings. London: The Hakluyt Society, sec. series, no. 118.

Nevius, Helen S. C. 1868. *Our Life in China*. New York: Robert Carter and Brothers.

Nevius, John L. 1882. *China and the Chinese: A General Description of the Country and its Inhabitants; its Civilization and Form of Government; its Religious and Social Institutions; its Intercourse with other Nations; and its Present Condition and Prospects*. Philadelphia: Presbyterian Board of Publication.

Nieuhoff, John. 1669. *An Embassy from the East-India Company of the United Provinces to the Grand Tartar Cham Emperor of China*. London: John Macock.

Niida Noboru 仁井田陞. 1937. *Tōsō horitsu bunshō no kenkyū* 唐宋法律文書の研究. Tokyo: Daian (1967 reprint).

———. 1942. *Shina mibunhoshii* 支那身分法史. Tokyo: Zayūho kankōkai.

Nishiwaki Tsuneki 西脇常記. 1979. "Tō dai sozoku kenkyū josetsu" 唐代喪俗研究序説 *Tōyō gakushutsu kenkyū* 18:130–53.

Niu Zhiping 牛志平. 1987. "Tangdai hunyin de kaifang fengqi" 唐代婚姻的開放風氣. *Lishi yanjiu* 4:80–88.

Ocko, Jonathan K. 1991. "Women, Property, and Law in the People's Republic of China," in *Marriage and Inequality in Chinese Society*, ed. Rubie S. Watson and Patricia Buckley Ebrey. Berkeley: University of California Press.

O'Hara, Albert Richard. 1945. *The Position of Woman in Early China*. Washington, D.C.: Catholic University.

Olschki, Leonardo. 1960. *Marco Polo's Asia: An Introduction to his "Description of the World" Called "Il Milione,"* trans. John A. Scott. Berkeley: University of California Press.

Overmyer, D. T. 1974. "China," in *Death and Eastern Thought*, ed. Frederick H. Holck. Nashville, Tenn: Abingdon Press.

Parry, Jonathan. 1982. "Sacrificial Death and the Necrophagous Ascetic," in *Death and the Regeneration of Life*, ed. Maurice Bloch and Jonathan Parry. Cambridge: Cambridge University Press.

Pasternak, Burton. 1968. "Agnatic Atrophy in a Formosan Village," *American Anthropologist* 70:93–96.

———. 1969. "The Role of the Frontier in Chinese Lineage Development," *Journal of Asian Studies* 28:551–61.

———. 1983. *Guests in the Dragon: Social Demography of a Chinese District, 1895–1946*. New York: Columbia University Press.

Piassetsky, P. 1884. *Russian Travellers in Mongolia and China*. J. Gordon-Cummings, trans. 2 vols. London: Chapman and Hall.

Power, W. Tyrone. 1853. *Recollections of a Three Years' Residence in China*. London: Richard Bentley.

Quan Hansheng 全漢昇. 1964. "Songmo de tonghuo pengchang ji qi dui yu wujia de yingxiang" 宋末的通貨膨脹及其對於物價的影響. *Songshi yanjiu ji* 2. Taibei: Zhonghua congshu.

Ramsey, S. Robert. 1987. *The Languages of China*. Princeton, N.J.: Princeton University Press.

Rawski, Evelyn S. 1986. "The Ma Landlords of Yang-chia-kou in Late Ch'ing and Republican China," in *Kinship Organization in Late Imperial China, 1000–1940*, ed. Patricia Buckley Ebrey and James L. Watson. Berkeley: University of California Press.

Ripa, Mateo. 1846. *Memoirs of Father Ripa during Thirteen Years' Residence at the Court of Peking in the Service of the Emperor of China*. Fortunato Prandi, trans. New York: Wiley and Putnam.

Robinet, Isabelle. 1979. "Metamorphosis and Deliverance from the Corpse in Taoism." *History of Religions* 19:37–70.

———. 1997. *Taoism: Growth of a Religion*. Phyllis Brooks, trans. Stanford, Calif.: Stanford University Press.

Ropp, Paul S. 1976. "Seeds of Change: Reflections on the Condition of Women in Early and Mid Qing." *Signs* 2.1:5–23.

Rossabi, Maurice. 1988. *Khubilai Khan: His Life and Times.* Berkeley: University of California Press.

Said, Edward W. 1979. *Orientalism.* New York: Vintage Books.

Saller, Richard P. 1984. "Roman Dowry and the Devolution of Property in the Principate." *Classical Quarterly* 34:195–205.

Sangren, P. Steven. 1984. "Traditional Chinese Corporations: Beyond Kinship." *Journal of Asian Studies* 43:391–415.

Satake Yasuhiko 佐竹靖彦. 1973. "Tōsō henkakki ni okeru Kōnan Tōsairo no tochi shoyū to tochi seisaku – gimon no seicho o tegakari ni shiite" 唐宋變革期における江南東西路の土地所有と土地政策―義門の成長を手がかりにしいて. *Tōyōshi kenkyū* 31.4:503–36.

Scarth, John. 1860. *Twelve Years in China: The People, the Rebels, and the Mandarins.* Edinburgh: Thomas Constable.

Schafer, Edward H. 1967. *The Vermilion Bird: T'ang Images of the South.* Berkeley: University of California Press.

Schopen, Gregory. 1987. "Burial 'Ad Sanctos' and the Physical Presence of the Buddha in Early Indian Buddhism." *Religion* 17:193–225.

Seidel, Anna. 1974. "Dabi," *Hōbōgirin: dictionnaire encyclopédique du bouddhisme d'après les sources chinoises et japonaises.* 6:573–85.

——. 1987. "Traces of Han Religion in Funeral Texts Found in Tombs," in *Dōkyō to shūkyō bunka.* Tokyo: Hirakawa.

Shang Binghe 尚秉和. 1941. *Lidai shehui fengsu shiwu kao* 歷代社會風俗事物考. Taibei: Commercial Press reprint.

Shanxi sheng wenwu guanli weiyuanhui 山西省文物管理委員會. 1955. "Shanxi Hongzhao xian fangduicun guyi zhi muqun qingli jianbao" 山西洪趙縣坊堆村古遺址墓群清理簡報. *Wenwu cankao ziliao* 4:46–54.

Shiga Shūzo 滋賀秀三. 1967. *Chūgoku kazokuhō no genri* 中國家族の原理. Tokyo: Sogensha.

——. 1978. "Family Property and the Law of Inheritance in Traditional China," in *Chinese Family Law and Social Change in Historical and Comparative Perspective,* ed. David C. Buxbaum. Seattle: University of Washington Press.

Shimizu Morimitsu 清水盛光. 1949. *Chūgoku zokusan seido kō* 中國族產制度攷. Tokyo: Iwanami.

Shinno Reiko 秦玲子. 1993. "Sōdai no kō to tei shiketsu teiken," 宋代の后と帝嗣決定權, in *Yanagida Setsuko sensei koki kinen: Chūgoku no dentō shakai to kazoku* 柳田節子先生古稀記念：中國の伝統社會と家族. Tokyo: Kyūko Shoin.

Sichuansheng wenwu guanli weiyuanhui 四川省文物管理委員會. 1956. "Sichuan guanjunian TangSongMing mu qingli jianbao" 四川官渠埝唐宋明墓清理簡報. *Kaogu tongxun* 5:31–38.

Sirr, Henry Charles. 1849. *China and the Chinese: Their Religion, Character, Customs, and Manufactures.* London: Orr and Co.

Smith, Paul J. 1993. "State Power and Economic Activism during the New Policies, 1068–1085: The Tea and Horse Trade and the 'Green Sprouts' Loan Policy," in *Ordering the World: Approaches to State and Society in Sung Dynasty China,* ed. Robert P. Hymes and Conrad Schirokauer. Berkeley: University of California Press.

Song Caiyi 宋采義 and Yu Song 予嵩. 1986. "Tan Henan Hua xian faxian Bei Song de louze yuan" 談河南滑縣發現北宋的漏澤園. *Henan daxue xuebao* 4:53–58.

Spence, Jonathan D. 1996. *God's Chinese Son: the Taiping Heavenly Kingdom of Hong Xiuquan.* New York: Norton.

——. 1998. *The Chan's Great Continent: China in Western Minds*. New York: W.W. Norton.

Staunton, George. 1798. *An Authentic Account of an Embassy from the King of Great Britain to the Emperor of China*. Second ed. London: W. Bulmer.

Steele, John, trans. 1917. *The I-li of Book of Etiquette and Ceremonial*. 2 vols. London: Probsthain.

Stein, Rolf A. 1979. "Religious Taoism and Popular Religion from the Second to the Seventh Centuries," in *Facets of Taoism*, ed. Holmes Welch and Anna Seidel. New Haven, Conn.: Yale University Press.

Stephen, Leslie and Sidney Lee, eds. 1917. *Dictionary of National Biography: Supplement*. Oxford: Oxford University Press.

Stone, Lawrence. 1977. *Family, Sex and Marriage in England 1500–1800*. New York: Harper and Row.

Strickman, Michel, ed. 1983, 1985. *Tantric and Taoist Studies in Honour of R. A. Stein*, vols. 2 and 3. Brussels: Institut belge des hautes études chinoises.

Sun Boquan 孫薄泉 *et al.* 1987. "Huozang shi Zhonghua minzu zi gu jiu you de weisheng xiguan" 火葬是中華民族自古就有的衛生習慣. *Zhonghua yishi zazhi* 17:164–67.

Sun Kekuan 孫克寬. 1968. *Yuandai Han wenhua zhi huodong* 元代漢文化之活動. Taibei: Zhonghua Shuju.

Sung, M. H. 1981. "The Chinese Lieh-nü Tradition," in *Women in China*, ed. Richard W. Guisso and Stanley Johannesen. Youngstown, N.Y.: Philo Press.

Swann, Nancy Lee. 1932. *Pan Chao: Foremost Woman Scholar of China*. New York: Century.

Tai, Yen-hui. 1978. "Divorce in Traditional Chinese Law," in *Chinese Family Law and Social Change in Historical and Comparative Perspective*, ed. David C. Buxbaum. Seattle: University of Washington Press.

Tang Daijian 唐代劍. 1986. "Songdai de funü zaijia" 宋代的婦女再嫁. *Nanchong shiyuan xuebao* 3:80–84.

Tang Zhangru 唐長孺. 1959. "Menfa de xingcheng ji qi shuailuo" 門閥的刑成及其衰落. *Wuhan daxue renwenke xuebao* 8:1–24.

Tao, Chia-lien Pao. 1994. "The Anti-footbinding Movement in Late Ch'ing China: Indigenous Development and Western Influence," in *Jindai Zhongguo funüshi yanjiu*. Vol. 2. Taibei: Institute of Modern History, Academia Sinica.

Tao, Jing-shen. 1976. *The Jurchen in Twelfth-Century China: A Study of Sinicization*. Seattle: University of Washington Press.

Tao Xisheng 陶希聖. 1966. *Hunyin yu jiazu* 婚姻與家族. Taibei: Renren wenku ed.

Taylor, Charles. 1860. *Five Years in China*. New York: Derby and Jackson.

Teiser, Stephen F. 1988. *The Ghost Festival in Medieval China*. Princeton, N.J.: Princeton University Press.

Teng, Ssu-yü, trans. 1968. *Family Instructions for the Yen Clan*. Leiden: Brill.

Thomson, John 1982 [1873–1874]. *China and Its People in Early Photographs*: New York Dover reprint of *Illustration of China and its People*.

T'ien, Ju-k'ang. 1988. *Male Anxiety and Female Chastity: A Comparative Study of Chinese Ethical Values in the Ming-Qing Times* (Monographies du T'oung Pao XIV). Leiden: E. J. Brill.

Topley, Marjorie. 1975. "Marriage Resistance in Rural Kwangtung," in *Women in Chinese Society*, ed. Margery Wolf and Roxane Witke. Stanford, Calif.: Stanford University Press.

Twitchett, Denis. 1959. "The Fan Clan's Charitable Estate, 1050–1760," in *Confucianism in Action*, ed. David S. Nivison and Arthur F. Wright. Stanford, Calif.: Stanford University Press.

———. 1960. "Documents on Clan Administration I: The Rules of Administration of the Charitable Estate of the Fan Clan." *Asia Major*, ser. 3, 8:1–35.

———. 1973. "The Composition of the T'ang Ruling Class: New Evidence from Tunhuang," in *Perspectives on the Tang*, ed. Arthur F. Wright and Denis Twitchett. New Haven, Conn.: Yale University Press.

———. 1982. "Comment on J. L. Watson's Article." *China Quarterly* 92:623–27.

Uchida Tomoo 內田智. 1950. "Kahoku nōson kazoku ni okeru sosen saishi no igi" 華北農村家族に於ける祖先祭祀の意義. *Dōshisha hōgaku* 6:1–22.

———. 1953. "Kahoku nōson ni okeru dōzoku no saiso gyōji ni tsuite" 華北農村における同族の祭祖行事について. *Tōyō gakuhō* 22:59–64.

———. 1970. *Chūgoku nōson no kazoku to shinkō* 中國農村の家族と信仰. Tokyo: Shimizu kōbun.

Ueyama Shunpei 上山春平. 1982. "Shushi no 'Karei' to 'Girei kyōden tsūkai'" 朱子の「家禮」と「儀禮經傳通解」. *Tōyō gakuhō* 54:173–256.

Umehara Kaoru 梅原郁. 1985. *Sōdai kanryō seido kenkyū* 宋代官僚制度研究. Kyoto: Dōhōsha.

Waltner, Ann. 1990. *Getting an Heir: Adoption and the Construction of Kinship in Late Imperial China*. Honolulu: University of Hawaii Press.

Wan Runlong 萬潤龍 and Huang Lianyou 黃連友. 1988a. "Yan Ruzhan zinü tuzang qi fu yingxiang elie" 嚴如湛子女土葬其父影響惡劣. *Hangzhou ribao*, August 26, 1988.

———. 1988b. "Yan Ruzhan tuzang yiti zuori huohua" 嚴如湛土葬遺體昨日火化. *Hangzhou ribao*, September 15, 1988.

Wang Hongtao 王洪濤. 1975. "Quanzhou, Nan'an faxian Songdai huozang mu" 泉州，南安發現宋代火葬墓. *Wenwu* 3:77–78.

Wang Mingsun 王明蓀. 1981. "Tan Songdai de huanguan" 談宋代的宦官: *Dongfang zazhi* 15.5:57–60.

Watson, Burton, trans. 1967. *Basic Writings of Mo Tzu, Hsun Tzu, and Han Fei Tzu*. New York: Columbia University Press.

Watson, James L. 1980. "Transactions in People: The Chinese Market in Slaves, Servants, and Heirs," in *Asian and African Systems of Slavery*, ed. J. L. Watson. Berkeley: University of California Press.

———. 1982a. "Chinese Kinship Reconsidered: Anthropological Perspectives on Historical Research." *China Quarterly* 92:589–622.

———. 1982b. "Of Flesh and Bones: The Management of Death Pollution in Cantonese Society," in *Death and the Regeneration of Life*, ed. Maurice Bloch and Jonathan Parry. Cambridge: Cambridge University Press.

———. 1988. "The Structure of Chinese Funerary Rites: Elementary Forms, Ritual Sequence, and the Primacy of Performance," in *Death Ritual in Late Imperial and Modern China*, ed. Watson and Rawski. Berkeley: University of California Press, pp. 15–19.

Watson, James L. and Evelyn S. Rawski, eds. 1988. *Death Ritual in Late Imperial and Modern China*. Berkeley: University of California Press.

Watson, Rubie S. 1981. "Class Differences and Affinal Relations in South China." *Man* 16:593–615.

———. 1982. "The Creation of a Chinese Lineage: The Teng of Ha Tsueh, 1669–1751." *Modern Asian Studies* 16:69–100.

——. 1984. "Women's Property in Republican China: Rights and Practice." *Republican China* l0.1a:1–12.

——. 1985. *Inequality Among Brothers: Class and Kinship in South China*. Cambridge: Cambridge University Press.

——. 1991. "Wives, Concubines, and Maids: Servitude and Kinship in the Hong Kong Region, 1900–1941," in *Marriage and Inequality in Chinese Society*, ed. Rubie S. Watson and Patricia Buckley Ebrey. Berkeley: University of California Press.

Wei Zhijiang 魏志江. 1994. "Songdai houfei lun" 宋代后妃論. *Yangzhou shiyuan xuebao* 3:42–49.

Wei Ziyun 魏子雲 ed. 1987. *Jin Ping Mei yanjiu ziliao huibian* 金瓶梅研究資料彙編. Taibei: Tianyi chubanshe.

Welch, Holmes, and Anna Seidel, eds. 1979. *Facets of Taoism*. New Haven, Conn.: Yale University Press.

Whyte, Martin K. 1988. "Death in the People's Republic of China," in *Death Ritual in Late Imperial and Modern* China, ed. James L. Watson and Evelyn S. Rawski. Berkeley: University of California Press.

Williams, S. Wells. 1849. *The Chinese Empire and its Inhabitants; Being a Survey of the Geography, Government, Education, Social Life, Arts, Religion, &tc. of the Middle Kingdom*. 2nd ed. London: Henry Washbourne.

Wittfogel, Karl A. and Chia-sheng Feng. 1949. *History of Chinese Society: Liao 907–1125*. Philadelphia: American Philosophical Society.

Wolf, Arthur P. ed. 1974. *Religion and Ritual in Chinese Society*. Stanford, Calif.: Stanford University Press.

Wolf, Arthur P. and Chieh-shan Huang. 1980. *Marriage and Adoption in China, 1845–1945*. Stanford, Calif.: Stanford University Press.

Wolf, Margery. 1972. *Women and the Family in Rural Taiwan*. Stanford, Calif.: Stanford University Press.

Wong, Sun-ming. 1979. "Confucian Ideal and Reality: Transformation of the Institution of Marriage in T'ang China (AD 618–907)." Ph.D. dissertation, University of Washington.

Wood, Frances. 1995. *Did Marco Polo Go to China?* Oxford: Oxford University Press.

Workman, Michael E. 1976. "The Bedchamber Topos in the T'zu Songs of Three Medieval Chinese Poets: Wen T'ing-yün, Wei Chuang, and Li Yü," in *Critical Essays on Chinese Literature*, ed. William H. Nienhauser, Jr. Hong Kong: The Chinese University.

Xu Pingfang 徐苹芳. 1956. "Song-Yuan shidai de huozang" 宋元時代的火葬. *Wenwu cankao ziliao* 9:21–26.

——. 1963. "Tang Song muzangzhong de 'Mingqi shensha,' yu 'muyi' zhidu – du 'DaHan yuanling muzang jing' zhaji" 唐宋墓葬中的明器神煞與墓儀制度讀大漢原陵秘葬經札記. *Kaogu* 2:87–106.

——. 1984. "Songcai muzang he jiaocang de fajue" 宋代墓葬和窖藏的發掘, in *Xin Zhongguo de kaogu faxian he yanjiu* 新中國的考古發現和研究. Beijing: Wenwu.

Xu Yangjie. 1980. "The Feudal Clan System Inherited from the Song and Ming Periods." *Chinese Social Science* 3:29–82 (Chinese original in *Zhongguo kexue* 4:99–122).

Yang, C. K. 1959. *The Chinese Family in the Communist Revolution*. Cambridge, Mass.: MIT Press.

Yang Cuntian 楊存田 and Chen Jinsong 陳勁松. 1983. "Woguo gudai de huozang zhidu" 我國古代的火葬制度. *Kaogu yu wenwu* 88–95.

Yang Guanghua 楊光華. 1994. "Songdai houfei, waiqi yuzheng de tedian" 宋代后妃外戚預政的特點. *Xinan shida xuebao* 3:62–67.

Yang, Hsien-yi, and Gladys Yang, trans. 1957. *The Courtesan's Jewel Box: Chinese Stories of the Xth-XVllth Centuries*. Peking: Foreign Languages Press.

Yang, Martin C. 1945. *A Chinese Village: Taitou, Shantung Province*. New York: Columbia University Press.

Yang Shuda 楊樹達. 1933. *Handai hunsang lisu kao* 漢代婚喪禮俗考. Taibei: Huashi chubanshe reprint, 1976.

Yao, Ester S. Lee. 1983. *Chinese Women: Past and Present*. Mesquite, Texas: Ide House.

Yao Lingxi 姚靈犀. 1936. *Caifei lu xubian* 采菲錄續編. Tianjin: Shidai gongsi.

Yao Weiyuan 姚薇元. 1962. *Beichao huxing kao* 北朝胡姓考. Beijing: ZHSJ.

Yetts, W. Percival. 1911. "Notes on the Disposal of Buddhist Dead in China." *Journal of the Royal Asiatic Society*, n.s., 43:699–725.

Yi Qingan 易青安. 1956. "Liaoyangshi Dalin zicun faxian Liao shouchang ernian shiguan" 遼陽市大林子村發現遼壽昌二年石棺. *Wenwu cankao ziliao* 3:79–80.

Yoshikawa, Kojiro. 1967. *An Introduction to Sung Poetry*, trans. Burton Watson. Cambridge, Mass.: Harvard University Press.

Yu, Ying-shih. 1987. "O Soul, Come Back! A Study in the Changing Conceptions of the Soul and Afterlife in Pre-Buddhist China." *Harvard Journal of Asiatic Studies* 47:363–95.

Yule, Henry, trans. and ed. 1915. *Cathay and the Way Thither: Being a Collection of Medieval Notices of China*. Rev. ed., ed. Henri Cordier. London: The Hakluyt Society.

Yule, Henry, trans. 1929. *The Book of Ser Marco Polo the Venetian Concerning the Kingdoms and Marvels to the East*. 3rd ed., ed. Henri Cordier. New York: Dover (1993 reprint of 1929 ed.).

Zhang Bangwei 張邦煒. 1986. "Songdai biqin biji zhidu shuping" 宋代避親避籍制度述評. *Sichuan shida xuebao* 1:16–23.

——. 1993. *Songdai huangqin yu zhengzhi* 宋代皇親與政治. Chengdu: Sichuan renmin chubanshe.

Zhang Xiurong 張修蓉. 1976. *Tangdai wenxue suo biaoxian zhi hunsu yanjiu* 唐代文學所表現之婚俗研究. M.A. thesis, National Zhengzhi University, Taibei.

Zhang Yan 張 1934–1935. "Liu Houcun xiansheng nianpu" 劉後村先生年譜. *Zhixiang xuebao* 1:3.1–26.

Zhao Shouyan 趙守儼. 1963. "Tangdai hunyin lisu kaolue" 唐代婚姻禮俗考略. *Wenshi* 3:185–95.

Zhongguo shehui kexue yuan yuyan wenzi yingyong yanjiusuo Hanzi zhengli yanjiushi 中國社會科學院語言文字應用研究所漢字整理研究室編. 1990. *Xingshi renming yongzi fenxi tongji* 姓氏人名用字分析統計. Beijing: Yuwen chubanshe.

Zhu Ruixi 朱瑞熙. 1986. *Songdai shehui yanjiu* 宋代社會研究. Taipei: Hongwen reset from 1983 Zhengzhou, Zhongzhou shuhuashe original.

——. 1994. "Songdai de gongting zhidu" 宋代的宮廷制度. *Xueshu yuekan* 4:60–66, 26.

Zuo Yunpeng 左云鵬. 1964. "Citang zuzhang zuquan di xingcheng ji qi zuoyong shishuo" 祠堂族長族權的刑成及其作用試說. *Lishi yanjiu* 5–6:97–116.

Zurndorfer, Harriet T. 1981. "The *Hsin-an ta-tsu-chih* and the Development of Chinese Gentry Society, 800–1600." *T'oung Pao* 68:154–215.

Index